Springer Series on Rehabilitation

Myron G. Eisenberg, PhD, Series Editor
Veterans Affairs Medical Center, Hampton, VA
Thomas E. Backer, PhD, Consulting Editor
Human Interaction Research Institute, Los Angeles, CA

2004 **Handbook of Rehabilitation Counseling**
T. F. Riggar, EdD and Dennis R. Maki, PhD, CRC, NCC, Editors

1999 **Medical Aspects of Disability: A Handbook for the Rehabilitation Professional, 2nd ed.**
Myron G. Eisenberg, PhD, Robert L. Glueckauf, PhD, and Herbert H. Zaretsky, PhD

1997 **Rehabilitation Counseling: Profession and Practice**
Dennis Maki, PhD, and T. F. Riggar, EdD

1994 **Personality and Adversity: Psychospiritual Aspects of Rehabilitation**
Carolyn L. Vash, PhD

1991 **Treating Families of Brain-Injury Survivors**
Paul R. Sachs, PhD

1991 **Disability in the United States: A Portrait From National Data**
Susan Thompson-Hoffman, MA, and Inez Fitzgerald Storck, MA, Editors

1988 **Family Interventions Throughout Chronic Illness and Disability,**
P. W. Power, SdD, CRC, NCC, A. E. Dell'Orto, PhD, CRC, and M. B. Gibbons, RN, MS, CPNP

1986 **Applied Rehabilitation Counseling**
T. F. Riggar, EdD, Dennis R. Maki, PhD, and Arnold Wolf, PhD

1985 **Handbook of Private Sector Rehabilitation**
Lewis J. Taylor, PhD, CRC, Marjorie Colter, MS, CRC, Gary Golter, MA, and Thomas E. Backer, PhD, Editors

1984 **Chronic Illness and Disability Through the Life Span: Effects on Self and Family**
Myron G. Eisenberg, PhD, Lafaye C. Sutkin, PhD, and Mary A. Jansen, PhD

1982 **Behavioral Approaches to Rehabilitation**
Elaine Greif, PhD, and Ruth G. Matarazzo, PhD

1982 **Disabled People as Second-Class Citizens**
Myron G. Eisenberg, PhD, et al.

1981 **The Psychology of Disability**
Carolyn L. Vash, PhD

T. F. Riggar, EdD, is a professor, Rehabilitation Institute, Southern Illinois University at Carbondale. Dr. Riggar, recipient of more than a dozen state, regional, and national awards, has published over 80 articles in professional rehabilitation journals. This is Dr. Riggar's fourteenth book.

Dennis R. Maki, PhD, CRC, is a professor, Division of Counselor Education, Graduate Programs in Rehabilitation, at the University of Iowa. Dr. Maki is past president of the American Rehabilitation Counseling Association and recipient of numerous awards, including the National Council on Rehabilitation Education's Rehabilitation Educator of the Year. He has been a consistent contributor to the professional literature and with Dr. Riggar, served as coeditor for special issues for the *Journal of Applied Rehabilitation Counseling* from 1983–1994.

In 1986, Drs. Riggar, Maki, and Wolf coedited the first rehabilitation counseling text in the Springer series, *Applied Rehabilitation Counseling*, with all royalties going to the National Rehabilitation Counseling Association, and, in 1997, Drs. Maki and Riggar coedited, with Springer Publishing, *Rehabilitation Counseling: Profession and Practice*. All royalties for the book went to the American Rehabilitation Counseling Association. For the current book, *Handbook of Rehabilitation Counseling*, all royalties will accrue to the National Council on Rehabilitation Education.

Handbook of Rehabilitation Counseling

T. F. Riggar, EdD
Dennis R. Maki, PhD, CRC, NCC,
Editors

Springer Publishing Company

Springer Publishing Company, Inc.
536 Broadway
New York, NY 10012-3955

Acquisitions Editor: Sheri W. Sussman
Production Editor: Janice Stangel
Cover design by Joanne Honigman

04 05 06 07 08/5 4 3 2 1

Library of Congress Cataloging-in-Publication Data

The handbook of rehabilitation counseling : issues and methods / T. F. Riggar, Dennis R. Maki, editors
p. cm.—(Springer series in rehabilitation)
Includes bibliographical references and index.
ISBN 0-8261-9512-1
1. Rehabilitation counseling I. Riggar, T. F. II. Maki, Dennis R. III. Series.
HD7255.5.H36 2004
362.4'048—dc21 2003045735

Printed in the United States of America by Sheridan Books.

Contents

Contributors

Lyndon J. Aguiar, MS, Psychology, Florida International University. Graduate Assistant (Applied Psychology Bachelor of Science), Department of Applied Psychology, New York University.

Norman L. Berven, PhD, Department of Rehabilitation Psychology and Special Education, University of Wisconsin—Madison.

Chad Betters, MHS, CRC, University of Florida. Doctoral student, Rehabilitation Science Program, University of Florida, Gainesville.

Brenda Cartwright, EdD, Department of Counselor Education, University of Hawaii, Honolulu.

Jack L. Cassell, PhD, Professor, Department of Educational Psychology and Counseling, University of Tennessee, Knoxville.

Fong Chan, PhD, Professor, Rehabilitation Psychology Program Area, Department of Rehabilitation Psychology and Special Education, University of Wisconsin—Madison.

Chih Chin Chou, MS, Rehabilitation Counseling, University of Wisconsin—Stout. Doctoral candidate, Rehabilitation Psychology Program Area, Department of Rehabilitation Psychology and Special Education, University of Wisconsin—Madison.

William Crimando, PhD, CRC, Program Coordinator of Rehabilitation Administration and Services and the Concentrated Rehabilitation Training Program, Rehabilitation Institute, Southern Illinois University at Carbondale.

Michael D'Andrea, EdD, Department of Counselor Education, University of Hawaii, Honolulu.

Dennis D. Gilbride, PhD, Associate Professor and Coordinator, Rehabilitation Counseling Program, Counseling and Human Services, School of Education, Syracuse University.

James T. Herbert, PhD, CRC, Professor-in-Charge, Department of Counselor Education, Counseling Psychology and Rehabilitation Services, Pennsylvania State University.

Marvin D. Kuehn, EdD, Professor, Counselor Education and Rehabilitation Programs, Emporia State University.

Michael J. Leahy, PhD, CRC, Professor and Director, Office of Rehabilitation and Disability Studies, Michigan State University.

Gloria Lee, M. Phil., Occupational Rehabilitation, Hong Kong Polytechnic University. Assistant Professor of rehabilitation counseling, Department of Counseling, School, and Educational Psychology, University at Buffalo State—University of New York.

Donald C. Linkowski, PhD, Professor of Counseling and Director of Doctoral Rehabilitation Counseling Leadership Program, George Washington University, Washington, DC, and Executive Director of the Council on Rehabilitation Education.

William M. Liu, PhD, Counseling Psychology, Division of Psychological and Quantitative Foundations, University of Iowa.

Susan M. Miller, MS, Rehabilitation Counseling, University of Wisconsin—Madison. Doctoral student, Rehabilitation Psychology Program Area, Department of Rehabilitation Psychology and Special Education, University of Wisconsin—Madison.

S. Wayne Mulkey, PhD, Professor, Department of Educational Psychology, University of Tennessee, Knoxville.

David B. Peterson, PhD, CRC, NCC, LP, Associate Professor, The Institute of Psychology, Illinois Institute of Technology.

Steven R. Pruett, MS, Rehabilitation Administration, Rehabilitation Institute, Southern Illinois University at Carbondale. Doctoral candidate, Rehabilitation Psychology Program Area, Department of Rehabilitation Psychology and Special Education, University of Wisconsin—Madison.

Rebecca Rudman, ABD, University of Iowa, MA, University of Iowa, and MA, Northern Illinois University. Rehabilitation consultant, Canada. Former National Director of Rehabilitation Services and Evaluation for the Canadian Paraplegic Association.

Caren Sax, EdD, Associate Professor, Department of Administration, Rehabilitation, and Postsecondary Education, San Diego State University.

Marcia J. Scherer, PhD, MPH, CRC, Director, Institute for Matching Person and Technology, Webster, NY.

Linda R. Shaw, PhD, Associate Professor and Graduate Coordinator, Department of Rehabilitation Counseling, University of Florida, Gainesville.

Julie Smart, PhD, CRC, NCC, LPC, ABDA, CCFC, Professor and Director, Rehabilitation Counselor Education Program, Utah State University.

Robert Stensrud, EdD, Associate Professor, Leadership, Counseling, and Adult Development, Drake University, Des Moines, Iowa.

Vilia M. Tarvydas, PhD, LMHC, CRC, Professor and Program Coordinator, Graduate Programs in Rehabilitation, Division of Counseling, Rehabilitation, and Student Development, University of Iowa.

Rebecca L. Toporek, PhD, Assistant Professor, Department of Counseling, San Francisco State University.

Foreword

The Handbook of Rehabilitation Counseling is much more than a third edition of the authors' previous books by similar titles. It not only updates much of the previous information, but also adds considerably to it. Many new authors are included in this comprehensive volume on the state-of-the art in rehabilitation counseling.

This book is an excellent introduction to the field of rehabilitation counseling but can also help update practicing professionals to new, cutting edge information. I strongly recommend this book as a text to be used in a foundations course. It also can be helpful to someone preparing for certification, licensure, or for a comprehensive examination in rehabilitation counseling. Many issues are presented that can give one an understanding of the basics of the profession. This book can also stimulate thinking that will lead to new research initiatives that may further our knowledge of the profession and the practice of rehabilitation counseling.

The beginning focuses on the profession, including the broad paradigms, societal context, history and systems, and policy and legal bases. It also includes standards of practice and ethics as well as standards that focus on qualified providers of rehabilitation counseling services relating to accreditation of preparation programs and certification of practitioners. The consumer context of the profession is also addressed including individuals and families and the increasing diversity of persons being served as well as those who provide rehabilitation counseling services. Thus the context of the profession is viewed in a holistic and comprehensive manner.

The remainder of the text is more specific and focuses on aspects of professional practice. Both settings (private and public) as well as services are addressed in this section including assessment, job placement, and case management. It also contains other elements of practice including cutting edge uses of technology, and supervision and administration.

The editors assembled an impressive list of contemporary experts who are very well qualified to address the topics selected. The collection of chapters will give the reader an excellent overview of current knowledge and future trends in rehabilitation counseling. This volume is must reading for everyone aspiring to become a rehabilitation counselor or for those who are already in the field. It should be a part of every professional rehabilitation professional's library.

Editors Riggar and Maki have taken on a thankless task, not once, not twice, but with this new version a third time. They have excellent qualifications for the endeavor having many years of experience in the field as well as having authored many outstanding professional publications. I have often said to myself, "never take on positions as an editor or national conference coordinator." There are so many unforeseen glitches that can happen when one has to depend on others and must orchestrate a large collection of papers. I highly commend these two professors for having the courage and the skill to bring this work to fruition. The many hours spent in reminding the writers of the deadlines and reviewing and re-reviewing manuscripts is especially appreciated when one considers that the author-editors have donated all proceeds from this work to the National Council on Rehabilitation Education (NCRE). They are truly dedicated professionals in the full sense of the word and deserve a heartfelt thank you. Appreciation must also be expressed for the generous contributions of the many authors of the chapters. A job well done!

Donald C. Linkowski

This work is dedicated to the Presidents of the National Council on Rehabilitation Education (NCRE), the National Rehabilitation Counseling Association (NRCA), and the American Rehabilitation Counseling Association (ARCA). They continue to fulfill their mission to enhance the lives of persons with disabilities and to advance the professional of rehabilitation. The editors and authors would like to acknowledge these professionals for their leadership and outstanding contributions to the profession over the years.

NCRE Presidents

1955–66	Gregory Miller (early years)
1967–69	Bob Johnson (CRCE officially begins)
1969–70	Robert Wamken
1970–71	Thomas L. Porter
1971–72	Daniel Sinick
1972–73	Bob Johnson
1973–74	Marceline Jaques
1974–75	Joseph A. Szuhay
1975–76	Dan McAlees
1976–77	William H. Graves (CRCE changes name to NCRE)
1977–78	Donald C. Linkowski
1978–79	Glen O. Geist
1979–80	Jack Kite
1980–81	Donald W. Dew
1981–82	William M. Jenkins
1982–83	Martha Lentz Walker
1983–84	Ken Reagles
1984–85	Ann Meyer
1985–86	Joe Afanador
1986–87	Vincent A. Scalia
1987–88	Bobbie J. Atkins
1988–89	Marvin D. Kuehn
1989–90	William G. Emener
1990–91	Jeanne Boland Patterson
1991–92	Bud Stude
1992–93	Sue Gunn
1993–94	Tom Evenson
1994–95	Susanne Bruyere
1995–96	Paul Leung
1996–97	Carolyn Rollins
1997–98	Mike Leahy
1999–00	Donald W. Dew
2000–01	Amos Sales
2001–02	John Benshoff
2002–03	Margaret Glenn
2003–04	Vilia M. Tarvydas

NRCA Presidents

1958–59	David E. Young
	E. J. Buchanan
1959–60	Robert A. Lassiter
1960–61	Harley B. Reger
1961–62	LeRoy C. Larsen
1962–63	I. W. Leggett
1963–64	Richard A. Koebler
1964–65	Gordon D. Smith
1965–66	Charles F. Maine
1966–67	Richard A. Morris
1967–68	Daniel C. McAlees
1968–69	Edwin J. Chorn
1969–70	Alton R. Ray
1970–71	Mary S. Smith
1971–72	Michael A. Oliverio
1972–73	Carl E. Hansen
1973–74	Thomas K. White
1974–75	Betty S. Hedgeman
1975–76	Anne D. Crumpton
1976–77	James E. Gray
1977–78	Philip Chase
1978–79	Arnold Wolf
1979–80	Joyce Pigg
1980–81	Robert Hasbrook
1981–82	Lawrence Warnock
1982–83	Henry C. DeVasher, Jr.
1983–84	Martha S. Wolf
1985	Patricia A. Mundt
1986	Allen Searles
1987	Susan Magruder Pollock
1988	John G. Moline
1989	Ethel D. Briggs
1990	Florence Curnutt
1991	Patricia Nunez
1992	Robert Neuman
1993	Richard Coelho
1994	Madan Kundu
1995	Jack Hacket
1996	Jan La Forge

1997	Joseph Turpin
1998	John Reno
1999	Gregory G. Garske
2000	Win Priest
2001	Lorie McQuade
2002	Chris Reid

ARCA Presidents

1958–59	Salvatore DiMichael
1959–60	William Usdane
1960–61	Abraham Jacobs
1961–62	Lloyd Lofquist
1962–63	C. H. Patterson
1963–64	William Gellman
1964–65	Daniel Sinick
1965–66	John McGowan
1966–67	John Muthard
1967–68	Marceline Jaques
1968–69	Martin Acker
1969–70	Leonard Miller
1970–71	Gregory Miller
1971–72	Richard Thoreson
1972–73	George Ayers
1973–74	Lawrence Feinberg
1974–75	George N. Wright
1975–76	Tom Porter
1976–77	Ray Ehrie
1977–78	Bob Johnson
1978–79	Frank Touchstone
1979–80	Don Linkowski
1980–81	Kenneth Reagles
1981–82	Dan McAlees
1982–83	Stanford Rubin
1983–84	Ken Thomas
1984–85	Paul McCollum
1985–86	Edna Szymanski
1986–87	Randy Parker
1987–88	Brian McMahan
1988–89	John Thompson
1989–90	Ross Lynch

1990–91	Dennis R. Maki
1991–92	Martha Walker
1992–93	Jeanne Patterson
1993–94	John Dolan
1994–95	Linda Shaw
1995–96	Michael Leahy
1996–97	Bill Richardson
1997–98	Vilia Tarvydas
1998–99	Donna Falvo
1999–00	Deborah Ebner
2000–01	Ellen Fabien
2001–02	Susan Bruyere
2002–03	Timothy Janikowski
2003–04	Betty Hedgeman

CHAPTER *1*

Concepts and Paradigms

Dennis R. Maki and T. F. Riggar

Rehabilitation is a robust concept, used in diverse contexts, referring to the restoration of persons, places, or things. In each of these varied contexts, there is an implied connotation of a return to a state of health or useful and constructive activity. As a concept, *rehabilitation counseling* is not as robust, nor is it as generally understood. This concept is, however, used to refer to a profession and to a scope of practice within health care and human service delivery systems. Beginning this discussion with definitions is critical in order to provide a language by which the concepts and paradigms of rehabilitation counseling may be articulated more clearly as both a profession and practice.

Definitions for the following terms are proposed. These terms provide an infrastructure for this and subsequent discussions. Therefore, it is important to first understand each definition independently, then to further consider each definition in relation to the others. There will then be better understanding of the direct, but complex, relationships linking the terms and of the importance of a shared language for the profession.

Rehabilitation is defined as "a holistic and integrated program of medical, physical, psychosocial, and vocational interventions that empower a person with disability to achieve a personally fulfilling, socially meaningful, and functionally effective interaction with the world" (Banja, 1990, p. 615). *Rehabilitation* within the context of the rehabilitation counseling process is "a comprehensive sequence of services, mutually planned by the consumer and rehabilitation counselor, to maximize employability, independence, integration, and participation of persons with disabilities in the workplace and the community" (Jenkins, Patterson, & Szymanski, 1991, p. 2).

Rehabilitation counseling is defined "as a profession that assists persons with disabilities in *adapting* to the environment, assists environments in *accommodating* the needs of the individual, and works toward full participation of persons with disabilities in all aspects of society, especially work" (Szymanski, 1985, p. 3). Rehabilitation counseling, as a *scope of practice*, is defined as

> a systematic process which assists persons with physical, mental, developmental, cognitive, and emotional disabilities to achieve their personal, career, and independent living goals in the most integrated setting possible through the application of the counseling process. The counseling process involves communication, goal setting, and beneficial growth or change through self-advocacy, psychological, vocational, social, and behavioral interventions. The specific techniques and modalities utilized in the rehabilitation counseling process may include, but are not restricted to:
>
> - Assessment and appraisal
> - Diagnosis and treatment planning
> - Career (vocational) planning
> - Individual and group counseling treatment interventions
> - Case management, referral, and service coordination
> - Program evaluation and research
> - Interventions to remove environmental, employment, and attitudinal barriers
> - Consultation services
> - Job analysis, job development, and placement services, including assistance with reasonable accommodations
> - Provision of consultation about and access to rehabilitation technology (Commission on Rehabilitation Counselor Certification, 1994, pp. 1–2)

Definitions of key terms contained in the Scope of Practice Statement are contained in Appendix B of this book.

The field of rehabilitation counseling is thus defined as a specialty within the rehabilitation professions, with counseling at its core, and is differentiated from other related counseling fields. Rehabilitation counseling is a profession, but it is also a practice that has evolved within the context of changing legislative mandates, societal perspectives, and technological and medical advances. Clearly defined terminology, and those concepts and paradigms that operationalize the terms, are critical to developing an understanding of this profession and its practice. Therefore, definitions of terms are provided throughout the text; Appendix A of the book provides a listing of acronyms commonly used in rehabilitation, as a reference to expand a shared language.

An underlying philosophy is embedded within each of the previously listed definitions of fundamental terms. This philosophy is as important to understanding the profession as all the definitions themselves.

REHABILITATION PHILOSOPHY

The philosophy of rehabilitation is premised by a belief in the dignity and worth of all people. It values independence, integration, and the inclusion of people, with and without disabilities, in employment and in their communities. Rehabilitation embodies the philosophy that, whenever possible, persons with a disability will be integrated into the least-restrictive environments. Inherent in this philosophy is a commitment to equalizing the opportunities for persons with disabilities to participate in all rights and privileges available to all people and to providing a sense of equal justice, based on a model of accommodation. In addition, the philosophy contains a commitment to supporting persons with disabilities in advocacy activities, in order to enable them to achieve independence and thus further empower themselves.

Simultaneously, within this philosophy there is a commitment to models of service delivery that emphasize integrated, comprehensive services that are mutually planned by the consumer and the rehabilitation counselor. The philosophy of rehabilitation advocates consumer choice and empowerment. This emphasis serves to define the philosophy of rehabilitation as one that is existential; that is, as people seek to make meaning out of their lives and become more self aware, they take on increased responsibility for, and ownership of, their choices and behaviors, in the face of an uncertain future. Full consideration must be given to the individual's right to success as well as failure, as potential outcomes involved with choice, growth, and risk.

Embedded within this philosophy is the principle of *informed consent.* Informed consent has two central aspects: The first is disclosure and awareness of all pertinent information that the client needs to make a decision; the second aspect is possessing free consent to engage in an activity or intervention, without coercion. Underlying the requirement of informed consent is the view of the client as an autonomous being who is able to direct their own life (Welfel, 2002). The philosophy of rehabilitation embraces a person's right to choose their relationships and goals, both personal and vocational. This philosophy of rehabilitation has been clearly articulated as part of the Underlying Values section of the "Scope of Practice Statement" (Appendix B of this book).

The philosophy of rehabilitation is solution focused and stresses the assets of the person and the resources of their environment. Individuals are conceptualized as interacting within multiple contexts of life, especially within the contexts of their family and culture. The focus is on adaptation and accommodation, from an ecological perspective that is directed toward achieving a meaningful quality of life (QOL) for the person with a disability. Disability and the philosophy of rehabilitation are different in various cultures. Therefore, each of these concepts must be defined and understood within the cultural context.

Levers and Maki (1995) proposed the following definition of *ethnorehabilitation* and suggest the importance of this concept to a rehabilitation philosophy:

> Ethnorehabilitation is an eco-systemic, praxiological construct which acknowledges the comprehensive nature of persons with disabilities through functional relationship to their respective cultures and in person/community-appropriate interaction with their environments. It seeks to establish a holistic prescription for a quality of life that entails consideration of biomedical, psychological, personal-social, educational, and vocational dimensions through spiritual dialectics at the individual, familial, community, and cultural levels. This view simultaneously permits an existential, holistic, and ecological perspective, which is attentive to the spiritual dimensions of the person and reflective of the environmental dialectic. It argues for a culturally specific sensitivity to the individual/environmental confluence. It is embedded in the temporal reality of the person's existence and draws meaning from the multiple dimensions of the person/community interface. The ultimate measure of the attainment of this perspective is the ethical respect paid to the person at the personal, clinical, community, cultural, and metaphysical levels. It results in a philosophy of empowerment considerate of the feelings, beliefs, rights, and behaviors of individuals, their communities, and their environments, and mindful of their interactions. (p. 140)

Cartwright and D'Andrea expand this notion in chapter 9, "Counseling."

Contemporary rehabilitation philosophy is also reflected in several paradigm shifts, which include a movement from an individual problem-solving approach to an ecological solution-focused approach, from institutionalization to community participation, from charity to civil rights, from segregated vocational training models to community-integrated or community-supported employment and independent living models, and from a medical model with an illness and pathology focus to a wellness model focusing on development and life stages. Maki and Murray (1995) provide a more complete discussion of the philosophy of rehabilitation. This reference and its source documents, as well as the discussion found therein, provide an excellent resource for further exploration of this topic.

PERSONS WITH DISABILITIES

The philosophy of rehabilitation begins with a belief in the dignity and worth of all people. The terms and language used in practice must reflect and reinforce this belief, as well. Rehabilitation practitioners use differing terms when referring to those individuals seeking services. Medical professionals refer to their "patients" and educators to their "students"; legal and mental health professionals refer to their "clients." Traditionally, the term *client* has predominated in the rehabilitation counseling profession and its practice. However, the terms *consumer* or *customer* have been advocated as the preference among some persons within disability communities, because these terms are believed to reflect a more empowered status for persons with disabilities in relation to their service delivery systems and professionals. The terminology used may be a sensitive issue for some persons: Asking each person about their preferred terminology is always appropriate. The terms *client* and *consumer* are used respectfully, yet interchangeably, throughout this text, when referring to persons who seek or receive rehabilitation services.

In addition to the terms used in spoken reference to persons with disability, one must be aware of, and to comply with, similar principles concerning written communication. The *Publication Manual of the American Psychological Association* (APA; 2001) provides the standard reference style guidelines for the field. The following discussion, related to nonhandicapping language, is derived from this reference. The guiding principle always is to use language that maintains the integrity and dignity of people as human beings.

When communicating orally or in writing, the APA (2001) guidelines suggest the following rules concerning reference to disabilities:

- Put people first, not their disability. Preferred expressions avoid the implication that the person as a whole is disabled.
- Do not label people by their disability or overextend its severity. Because the person is not the disability, the two concepts should be separate.
- Use emotionally neutral expressions. Terms such as *victim*, *afflicted*, *suffering*, and *confined* are examples of problematic expressions that have excessive, negative overtones and suggest continued helplessness. To this end, language should be avoided that (a) equates persons with their condition (e.g., "the disabled" or "epileptics"), (b) has negative or superfluous overtones (e.g., "AIDS victim"), or (c) is regarded as a slur (e.g., "cripple"). (pp. 75–76)

Consistent with the conceptual framework of practice, use of the term *disability* should occur only to describe an attribute of a person, and *handicap* to describe the source of limitations, such as attitudinal, legal, and architectural barriers. *Disability* and *handicap* are not synonymous. In addition, the terms *challenged* and *special* are often considered euphemistic and should be used only if the people you serve prefer them. The term of the professional's reference, be it *client* or *consumer*, as well as the language used to describe a person involved in rehabilitation services, is a critical consideration.

Some persons with disabilities may choose other language conventions. For example, some members of the deaf community prefer to be referred to collectively as "the deaf" or individually as "a deaf person." This language preference is also found among some members within the blind community. Avoid the use of the term *normal* in any way. As professionals working with persons with and without disabilities, we must communicate clearly and respectfully. An open discussion with the person with whom you are working usually provides a forum for selecting language to be used subsequently with each individual. The language chosen communicates a philosophical and attitudinal orientation at both a personal and professional level.

DEFINITIONS OF DISABILITY

The rehabilitation counselor must be sensitive to the existence of various definitions of disability, their varied uses, and the relationships among them. These definitions are used to define eligibility for programs and services. For example, for a person to be protected by the Americans with Disabilities Act (ADA, 1990), the law specifically defines an individual with a disability as a person who: (1) has a physical or mental impairment that substantially limits one or more of the major life activities of that person, (2) has a record of such an impairment, or (3) is regarded as having such an impairment. Major life activities include caring for oneself, performing manual tasks, walking, seeing, hearing, breathing, learning, and working. This legal definition reflects a perspective that is congruent with that of the medical and rehabilitation conceptualization of adaptation and accommodation. Recent ADA court cases appealed to the U.S. Supreme Court, as well some in litigation as of this writing, may limit the scope of the ADA by defining *major life activity* in a narrower manner than the authors of the legislation intended in the original definition.

The Social Security Administration (SSA) adheres to a different definition of disability. Disability, under Social Security, is based on an individual's inability to work. Income payments are for persons with total, long-term disability only; no benefits are paid to those with partial or short-term disability. Individuals are considered disabled, under Social Security rules, if unable to do the work they did before illness or injury, and if Social Security decides they cannot adjust to other work, given their disabling condition(s). The disability must be expected to last at least 1 year, or to result in death (SSA, 2002). The different definitions of disability, as espoused by the ADA and the SSA, have created some compatibility issues that have not been resolved as of this writing. Persons who have been found to be disabled under Social Security rules have been found unable to do work of any type. Qualified persons with disabilities under the ADA must be capable of doing work, with or without accommodations. The intent of the rules of each program was not to be mutually exclusive, nor to disqualify an individual from accessing either or both programs.

The Rehabilitation Services Administration states that, to be eligible to receive vocational rehabilitation (VR) services through the state–federal partnership programs, an individual must have a disability that causes major problems in getting, preparing for, or keeping a job, and that requires VR services to be able to work. Information is gathered under the authority of the Rehabilitation Act of 1973, as amended (Pub. L. No. 93-112). In addition to eligibility, this information, which must be provided by a medical professional to document disability, is used to determine the category of severity and, if appropriate, to help develop and carry out a plan of services to enable the person to reach a suitable vocational goal, which is indicated in the Individual Plan for Employment (IPE).

Definitions of disability greatly impact which services and programs persons are eligible for. Smart, in chapter 2, provides a description of the three models from which these definitions have emerged. In chapter 3, Peterson and Aquiar describe the history and systems of vocational and independent living rehabilitation programs, including their definitions of eligibility in the United States. Rudman (chapter 4) provides a similar description of the history and systems in Canada, demonstrating the impact of the sociopolitical system on the definition of disability and the nature of those programs established to provide services. Finally, Kuehn, in chapter 5, "Policy and Law," provides an in-depth discussion of the development of, and the issues related to, defining disability from those perspectives. Understanding the definitions of disability from these various points of reference is critical for the rehabilitation counselor, in order to effectively provide for the total rehabilitation of their clients.

PARADIGMS OF REHABILITATION PRACTICE

A conceptual model proposed by Hershenson (1990) provides a rationale for distinguishing rehabilitation counseling from the other helping disciplines involved in rehabilitation, such as medicine or psychology. This system of categories considers rehabilitation from the perspective of primary, secondary, and tertiary prevention of disability:

- *Primary prevention* is characterized by the provision of interventions directed toward preventing the onset of disease or disability. Professionals from such fields as public health and occupational health and safety have traditionally provided primary prevention.
- *Secondary prevention* is characterized by the provision of interventions directed toward preventing or, when that is not possible, limiting the effects of the disease or disability in persons, when primary prevention has failed. Professionals from medicine, psychology,

and similar curative fields have traditionally provided this level of prevention.

- *Tertiary prevention* is characterized by activities directed toward preventing long-term residual conditions from having any greater disabling effects than necessary, once the secondary prevention fields have done all they can do to cure or limit the disease/disabling process. Professionals from rehabilitation counseling and allied fields have traditionally provided tertiary prevention.

Hershenson (1990) described how the attention given to the individual and to the environment differs at each level. Primary prevention, for example, is heavily weighted toward the environment (e.g., drinking-water supply, worksite safety, automobile seat belts) and considers individuals only insofar as that environment affects them. Secondary prevention is heavily weighted toward the individual (e.g., curing or limiting the pathology that exists within the individual) and examines the environment only insofar as it facilitates or impedes the curative process within the individual. Tertiary prevention differs from both of the other categories of prevention, in that it requires an equally balanced focus on both the environment and the individual. This dual focus is necessary, because disability may stem as much from environmental barriers as from individual limitations.

Rehabilitation as a tertiary intervention can be viewed as a process of addressing specific goals with therapeutic interventions. The tripartite model of intervention (Livneh, 1995) builds on Hershenson's earlier work, and identifies three phases or components of rehabilitation intervention. Embedded within the broader model of therapeutic interventions, these three components are 1) disability minimization, as an effort to reduce its impact upon life activities; 2) skill development, as an attempt to compensate for limitations caused by permanent losses; and 3) environmental manipulations to promote physical, psychosocial, and social-attitudinal accessibility.

The paradigms derived from the three categories of prevention provide a basis for understanding and distinguishing the roles of the multiple disciplines that are part of the interdisciplinary rehabilitation process. Each level is represented by a discipline such as public health, medicine/psychology, and rehabilitation counseling. Each discipline and each level is different from the others in its basic science, focus, strategy for intervention, and goals. All disciplines have a unique and important contribution to make in the rehabilitation endeavor.

PARADIGMS FOR REHABILITATION COUNSELING

For intentional, systematic practice to occur, rehabilitation counselors must have a conceptual model or paradigm to guide their work. It has been suggested that rehabilitation counselors have at least three orientations from which to conceptualize their teaching, research, and practice. These paradigms include the *psychomedical model*, the *systems model*, and the *ecological model* (Cottone & Emener, 1990). Each of these orientations has merit and distinguishes itself by the relative emphasis it places on the person, the environment, and the relationship between the two. After a brief discussion of the psychomedical and systems model, a more detailed description of the ecological model is presented.

The Psychomedical Model

The psychomedical model looks within the individual for a diagnosis of the problem, placing the person in a one-down position, relative to the expert, typically a physician or psychiatrist. From this perspective, the person with a disability is considered a patient. The psychomedical model represents a biomedical orientation toward the scientific representation of the person's condition and uses diagnostic categories to administratively classify and subsequently treat the underlying cause of a person's disability. This approach is valuable for understanding the medical and allied health professional's contribution to the rehabilitation team. It underlies the restorative services offered in rehabilitation and is related to the secondary prevention model referred to earlier.

The Systems Model

Cottone and Cottone (1986) provided yet another perspective for conceptualizing rehabilitation counseling practice: the systems approach. This perspective suggests that neither the person nor the environment is the unit of analysis. The unit of analysis is in fact the relationship between the two. This perspective also suggests that focus on either the individual (psychomedical) or the individual–environment transaction (ecological) is inadequate, because the inherent nature of persons is systematic. Disability impacts all persons with a relationship to the person with disability. Focusing on and understanding these relationships with others in those environments in which persons with disabilities live, learn, work, and recreate are critical to this point of view. This perspective argues for the inclusion of family counseling and systems training in the curriculum for the development of competency in the rehabilitation counselor.

The Ecological Model of Rehabilitation Counseling

The Ecological Model of Rehabilitation Counseling proposed herein reflects a tertiary prevention model, with equal consideration being given to the person and to the environment (Fig. 1.1). Cottone and Emener (1990) suggested that such an approach represents an alternative to the psychomedical and systemic models. Historically, the ecological perspective on rehabilitation has emerged from a trait–factor tradition, which measures traits within the individual, as well as factors within the environment. An evaluation is then made to determine the extent of match or congruence between traits and factors. Decisions about the probable success of a person placed in a vocational, independent living, or other environment would then be made, based on this information. This model is based on an existential philosophy. Empowered clients make meaning out of their experiences. They take responsibility and ownership for their decisions, given their increased awareness about their strengths and the demands of the options they are considering.

The Minnesota Theory of Work Adjustment (Dawis, 1996; Lofquist & Dawis, 1969) has provided an empirically valid version of the trait–factor model for VR practice. Maki, McCracken, Pape, and Scofield (1979) suggested that an ecological perspective, with a developmental orientation, transformed a trait–factor approach into a viable theoretical framework for VR. Kosciulek (1993) supported the continuing validity of this approach to contemporary practice. Lofquist and Dawis (2002) agree, describing a person–environment correspondence theory.

Basically, this Ecological Model, in consideration of individual traits and environmental factors, provides a conceptual infrastructure for the profession of rehabilitation counseling and its model of practice. The conceptual discussion that follows is assumed to apply to persons with or without disability. In addition, the model can be applied to tasks and environments other than vocational. The individual traits would, in those

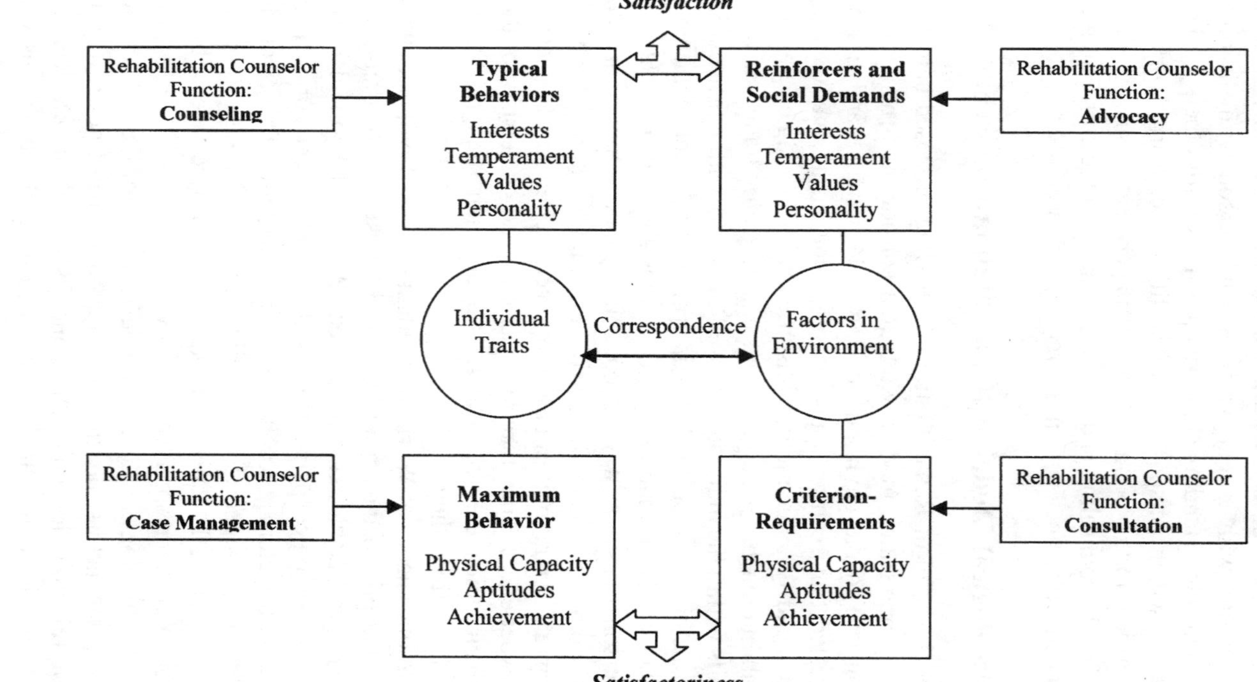

FIGURE 1.1. Ecological Model of Rehabilitation Counseling. A transactional approach seeking correspondence between an individual's maximum and typical behaviors with the criterion-requirements and the reinforcers and demands present in the environment. The rehabilitation counselor's four essential functions are indicated within this model.

instances, be compared to the environmental factors or the task criterion requirements and reinforcers available in environments such as independent living, education, and recreation. Both traits and factors can be measured or assigned numbers, to indicate the extent to which each is present in the individual and the environment. To better understand this Model, this approach is briefly described.

Traits refer to the underlying characteristics that exist in people. Traits account for the observed behavioral consistencies within people and for the stable and enduring differences among people. All people are assumed to possess the same traits, but in differing amounts. Cronbach (1990) has differentiated between those traits that are indicators of *typical performance* and those that are indicators of *maximum performance*. In the process of measuring the traits of an individual, the rehabilitation counselor must infer their presence from samples of behavior, because traits cannot generally be measured directly, other than physical traits such as range of motion. The particular traits that the rehabilitation counselor decides to evaluate will depend on the purpose of the assessment.

Traits indicative of typical performance describe how a person typically behaves in situations. The behavioral consistency principle is applied here, with the assumption being made that past performance is the best indicator of future behavior. These traits include the individual's interests, temperaments, values, and other indicators of personality. The typical behaviors are evaluated through interview, observation, and the occasional use of inventories, in other words, through the use of expressed, manifest, and test strategies. Evaluating these traits, and comparing their correspondence with potential environments, facilitates making more accurate predictions regarding a client's probable satisfaction with the factors present in various environments. The rehabilitation counselor may predict with enhanced accuracy the person's likelihood to remain in a particular environment, by evaluating this satisfaction. The factors against which a person's typical behavior traits are evaluated include environmental reinforcers, such as salary, advancement possibilities, and position prestige, as well as other social and interpersonal factors. Therefore, identifying the client's needs, interests, and personality is critical, as well as the reinforcers and the social/interpersonal factors that are present in environments under consideration. The extent to which factors meet specific needs will provide important data to the client for decision making.

Traits indicative of maximum performance describe a person's capacities and capabilities. These traits include physical capacity, aptitude and achievement, and other indicators of ability. The maximum behaviors are evaluated through test, manifest, and expressed strategies. Evaluating these traits facilitates making more accurate predictions regarding the satisfactoriness of a person's capacity to perform the essential functions and tasks required in education, employment, independent living, and other major life activities. The matching or congruence between the client's performance and the job or task has been described as the "level of satisfactoriness." The factors against which a person's maximum behavior traits are evaluated include the environment's essential and marginal functions, including physical, educational, and skill demands.

In evaluating persons' traits, equal consideration must be made for what they want to do (typical behavior) and what they are capable of doing (maximum behaviors). Therefore, considering the person's interests and the environment's ability to meet these needs is critical, as is their ability to perform essential functions in the environment, in order to enhance their tenure in a given job. Although, in some instances, referral to psychologists and other professionals may be involved in this rehabilitation assessment and information gathering process, rehabilitation counselors themselves may secure this information through interview, observation, and the occasional use of inventories. The question of who secures what information is a matter of each individual professional's scope of practice and of the available resources that define the functions performed by the staff in a particular human service or rehabilitation system.

ECOLOGICAL ADAPTATION MODEL

The Ecological Model of Rehabilitation Counseling provides a framework for counselor practice and client decision making. This trait–factor approach does not address the psychosocial adaptation of persons with their disabilities. The rehabilitation counselor must also have a framework within which to consider the psychosocial impact of disability. The Ecological Adaptation Model (Fig. 1.2) provides such a framework and also, when considered with the Ecological Model of Rehabilitation Counseling, a more robust paradigm for understanding the profession and process of rehabilitation counseling emerges.

The Ecological Adaptation Model is informed by a social learning orientation respectful of the reciprocal nature of both persons and their environments. Scofield, Pape, McCracken, and Maki (1980) described

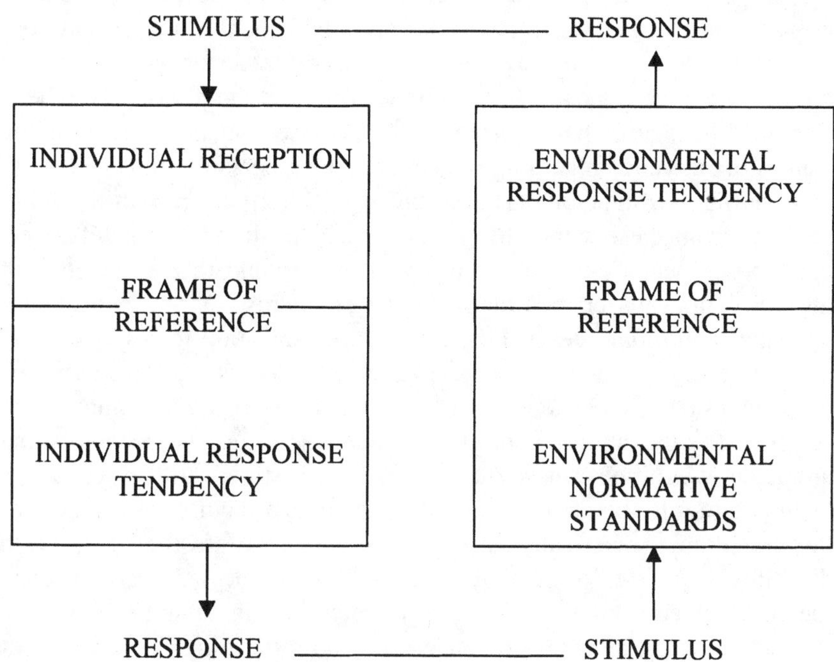

FIGURE 1.2. The Ecological Adaptation Model.

the Ecological Adaptation Model, which conceptualizes this reciprocal relationship, as (1) the nature of the individual with a disability as they interact and to various degrees adapt to various environments, and (2) the simultaneous ability of environments to accommodate persons with disability. This model highlights the importance of not only assessing traits and factors, but also the transactions that dynamically describe the interactive nature of person(s) and their environment(s). *Adaptation*, as a dynamic concept describing the extent to which a person accepts disability as one of their many characteristics, is a concept preferred to *adjustment*, because it infers a more enduring, static, and categorical description, when referring to a person's acceptance of disability.

This Ecological Adaptation Model provides a framework for assessing the normative standards, frames of reference, and response tendencies of environments and persons within these environments, at various levels of intimacy to the person with a disability. The environmental normative standards include cultural values, community moral code, and those policies and laws that set the standards for acceptable behavior in the environment. Persons within the environment develop frames of reference based on the normative standards by which they interpret the behavior of others. The model suggests that environmental response tendencies are based on frames of reference regarding the capacity of a person with disability to meet normative standards. The extent to which a person with disability deviates from these standards, as interpreted in the frame of reference, predisposes persons in that environment to respond to the person with disability in ways compatible with the standards. One such response tendency is *attitude*, defined as learned predisposition to respond in an evaluative manner, which is especially critical to assess, considering its potential impact. This model acknowledges that only verbal or nonverbal responses by the environment, that is, those messages and behaviors that are actually exhibited and observable, serve as stimuli to the person.

In addition to the environment, the model also requires assessment of the individual. Specifically needing to be assessed are the person with disability's capacity to receive overt and covert messages provided by the environment, the person's frame of reference, including self-concept and self-efficacy as a way to understand how meaning is made out of the messages received, and the person's response tendencies, or typical interaction style in response to particular persons, environments, and the messages they send. Disability may interfere with the person's ability to see or hear messages, to cognitively make meaning from the messages, or to establish response tendencies relative to their acceptance, or not, of disability. The manifestation of the response tendency is the actual behavior or message emitted by the person. This then serves as stimuli and sends a message to the environment that will either reinforce the normative standards or act as a catalyst for changing those standards that are inaccurate or inappropriate.

The Ecological Adaptation Model perspective also provides the rehabilitation counselor with a systematic framework for organizing and conceptualizing the complexities of their work with individuals with disabilities, in relation to those significant persons and environments in which they live, learn, work, and recreate. This model can be considered in conjunction with self-efficacy theory, which is concerned with the personal self-judgments that influence the environments that people choose, the activities in which they engage, and the effort and persistence they demonstrate at a task, in the face of obstacles.

The theory provides an overall framework to explain why some clients are successful in rehabilitation efforts and others are not. It also addresses how counselors can most effectively help clients maximize rehabilitation potential. Brodwin and Brodwin (1993) described the usefulness to the field of rehabilitation of Bandura's work (1982) on self-efficacy. They suggest that this growing body of research related to individual response tendencies supports the hypothesis that self-efficacy beliefs are cognitive mediators of assured, purposeful, and persistent behavior. These are behaviors that need to be developed and/or increased in persons with disabilities, if they are to receive maximum benefit from the various rehabilitation systems.

Rehabilitation potential, as defined by those same authors, consists of three characteristics: (1) attaining increased functioning in the direction of maximum physical and emotional growth, (2) having a sense of well-being, and (3) facilitating development of a personally satisfying level of independence. Those authors also note that different rehabilitation systems (e.g., worker's compensation, long-term disability, Social Security, state VR, independent living) define a client's rehabilitation potential within the context of their specific organization's parameters. Crimando and Riggar (1991) stress that counselors need to be aware of the differing requirements of each rehabilitation system providing services.

THE REHABILITATION CONCEPT

Once the rehabilitation counselor has a clear respect for and understanding of the philosophy of rehabilitation, the concept of disability, their own role and scope of practice, and a systematic paradigm to guide that practice, it is possible to revisit and further describe the rehabilitation concept. Maki (1986) operationalized the rehabilitation philosophy, defining the rehabilitation concept in terms of a comprehensive, individualized process, prescriptive in nature and directed toward the development or restoration of functional independence and QOL. Traditionally, VR defines functional independence in terms of economic self-sufficiency; independent living rehabilitation defines it in terms of community integration and autonomous living. Both VR and independent living rehabilitation programs increasingly include QOL indices in their definitions of successful outcome.

The following represent the key elements in understanding the concept of rehabilitation:

- *It is comprehensive in scope and holistic in nature.* The rehabilitation process is an orderly sequence of activities related to the total needs of the individual. Although comprehensive services will differ from client to client, certain basic dimensions are relevant to understanding the total person. The most significant dimensions include the medical, psychological, personal–social, cultural, educational, vocational, and spiritual. To understand the client or to provide services relating to only one dimension of the person's life functioning, without considering the other aspects and their interdependency, would be ineffective and could result in the ultimate failure of the rehabilitation effort. Effective rehabilitation thus often demands the coordinated efforts of a multidisciplinary or interdisciplinary team. The rehabilitation counselor is an integral member of this team.
- *It is an individualized process.* Each person is unique in terms of skills, residual capacities, functional limitations, resources, and personality. The manifestations of disability present themselves differently in each individual, with varying meanings and implications for rehabilitation, depending on the environmental context. Rehabilitation is considered a process based on the needs and assets of each individual client. Rehabilitation counselors must continually be aware of the pitfalls of labeling and stereotyping. Various authors (Feist-Price, 1995; Nathanson, 1979) have noted that counseling professionals are not immune to bias or prejudice regarding disability and must be aware of their own attitudes and expectations.
- *It is prescriptive in nature.* That is to say, a prescriptive course of action is developed with each individual. The type and number of services provided are based on the needs and characteristics of the individual. The services are selected that will remove, reduce, or compensate for the functional and societal limitations of the individual, so that they can achieve the goals established in the individualized plan. Environmental accommodations and modifications must be considered, as well as client development and adaptation.
- *It functions to develop or restore. Habilitation* is the term denoting the development or acquisition of skills and functions previously not attained. This term is used commonly to refer to the service of persons with disabilities who, because of lack of training or experience, are initially developing their functional independence. *Habilitation* refers to an initial learning of skills and roles that allow an individual to function in society. *Rehabilitation* refers to the

restoration or reacquisition of skills and functions lost through injury, disease, or trauma; the term is used here, as well as throughout the text, to describe either process resulting in functional independence.

- *Its goal is functional independence and a QOL. Functional independence* is the capacity of individuals to take care of their affairs to the extent that they are capable. Functional independence is a broad goal: Subsumed under the goal are economic self-sufficiency, as well as personal, social, and community living skills (Morris, 1973). It also reflects the individualized nature of the definition of success and functioning. Functional independence considers the total individual in all their environments.

A QOL perspective on rehabilitation counseling integrates competing program goals, such as client independence or employment, into a higher-order, multidimensional rehabilitation outcome. Counselors committed to a QOL orientation work from a wellness and holistic position, which addresses both the development and adaptation of the individual and the accommodations that environments can achieve, where the person lives, learns, works, and recreates. QOL is directly applicable to the long-standing question of how to define successful outcomes in rehabilitation. Rehabilitation professionals continue to disagree about whether the primary goal of rehabilitation is promoting client independence or vocational placement. QOL offers a higher-order goal that subsumes both independence and employment as legitimate outcomes (Roessler, 1990).

THE REHABILITATION PROCESS AND COUNSELOR FUNCTIONS

Historically, persons with disabilities have received services through a delivery system containing the following ordered components: intake, assessment, services, and outcomes. This generic model accommodates the interdisciplinary nature of rehabilitation. A model presented by Maki et al. (1979) provides a framework for describing this rehabilitation process. This sequence does not represent the delivery of supported employment and disability management services. In addition, these services must be provided ethically by qualified rehabilitation counselors. In chapter 6, Tarvydas discusses the critical issues of providing services ethically and describes the Integrated Model of Ethical Decision Making. Leahy, in chapter 7, discusses the criteria for, and credentialing of, qualified providers.

The client's entry into the rehabilitation service delivery system typically begins with intake. Here, administrative decisions are made regarding the client's eligibility for services, based on predetermined criteria, such as age, qualifying disability, location of primary residence, or financial status. If the client is determined to be ineligible or does not qualify for the program, there is an appeal process available to the client, such as the Client Assistance Program (CAP) in the state–federal VR program. If the client is determined to be eligible, the client begins an individualized assessment. Accurate and effective assessment is a prerequisite to successful rehabilitation planning. Assessment is designed to determine the client's current level of functioning, the goal of rehabilitation, and what services are required to achieve the goal(s). The assessment results in the Individual Written Rehabilitation Plan (IWRP). Berven further discusses client assessment in chapter 11.

The client and rehabilitation counselor work together in assessment and plan development, using the skills of problem solving and resource analysis. Included in the plan are the necessary services to assist the client in attaining the specified outcomes, along with a listing of who will provide these services and a timeline for completion or review. The counselor and client must mutually establish the goals to be accomplished within the parameters of the practice setting, which may occur in a public agency, a nonprofit program, or a private for-profit organization. The practice setting will also affect the range of functions and tasks that are to be performed by the rehabilitation counselor.

The rehabilitation counselor performs four essential functions in the delivery of services to persons with disability: counseling and case management in working with the client, and consultation and advocacy in working with their significant others and environments impacting the person. Technology, as presented by Scherer and Sax in chapter 15, is a strategy for working with both the individual and the environment. Services are selected that will allow the client to achieve their goals, such as acquiring skills and behaviors appropriate for the designed outcomes.

Services provided to the individual by the rehabilitation counselor are generally either in the area of case management or counseling services. *Case management* has been defined by Moxley (1989) as a client-level strategy for promoting the coordination of human services. He refers to a case manager as "a designated person (or team) who organizes, coordinates, and sustains a network of formal and informal supports and activities designed to optimize the well-being and functioning of people with multiple needs" (p. 17). The case manager identifies appropriate providers and facilities, while ensuring that the resources are being used in a timely and cost-effective manner. Mullahy (1995) refers to case management as a collaborative process that assesses, plans, implements, coordinates, monitors, and evaluates the options and services to meet an individual's health needs, using communication and available resources to promote quality, cost-effective outcomes (p. 9).

Two typical areas case-managed by the rehabilitation counselor are education and restoration services. Education is usually a service for clients who lack the skills or knowledge necessary to reach their long- or short-term goal(s) and the objectives outlined in their individual rehabilitation plan. Education may be formal or informal and generally lies outside the scope of practice of the rehabilitation counselor. Restoration services are usually prescribed when the counselor sees that there is a need for enhancing the physical functioning of an individual: Prosthetics, work hardening, or speech therapy are examples of these services. As with education, these services are often coordinated or managed by the rehabilitation counselor, because they lie outside the counselor's scope of practice.

Counseling is a therapeutic or psychoeducational service. This service is provided by the rehabilitation counselor within the relationship and parameters of the agency, organization, or facility in which a particular counselor functions. In the performance of this function, the rehabilitation counselor selects an individual, group, or family counseling theory to guide this aspect of their practice. In chapter 8, Chan et al. discuss the importance of evidenced based best practices, based on research in the provision of effective, accountable counseling services. No matter where or what other functions and responsibilities are engaged in by the rehabilitation counselor, counseling is the central function that is provided continuously throughout the rehabilitation process. G. N. Wright (1980) stated that counseling is

> a nontransferable obligation of the rehabilitation counselor. Consultant and rehabilitation services of other kinds may or should be purchased, but the ultimate professional responsibility for the function of counseling cannot be

> delegated. Professional counseling is indispensable to the proper selection, provision, and utilization of the other rehabilitation services. (p. 55)

Herbert, in chapter 16 discusses the importance of clinical supervision, both in the preservice development of counseling competence and in the maintenance of counseling competency over the course of a rehabilitation counselor's career.

Services provided by the rehabilitation counselor directed toward the environment are consultation and advocacy, when those environments and persons in them are relevant to the success of the client's plan. Moxley (1989) describes both of these functions as environmental interventions and indirect services, because they do not involve direct contact with the client. As such, they involve activities and interventions that are implemented with persons and systems external to the client. These serve as a means to achieve the plan, build the capacities of the systems to respond to the needs of the client, and provide access to resources (Steinberg & Carter, 1983).

Consultation is a function through which the counselor engages in "the process of environmental restructuring and requires consultation with the client's family, employer, and community" (Hershenson, 1990, p. 275). Lynch, Habeck, and Sebastian (1995) discuss the key skills, knowledge, and ethical and professional issues relevant to consultation by rehabilitation counselors. The following discussion of consultation is based on their work. Brown, Pryzwansky, and Schulte (1995) conceptualize consultation as an indirect service provided to a consultee. This service may be formal, with a contract, or more informal in nature. Consultation is frequently interdisciplinary, with the consultant either being internal to the organization or external from it. External consultants are more often readily viewed as experts, but may lack important background information that would be more accessible to an internal consultant.

Consultation may occur as *expert consultation* or *process consultation.* Kurpius and Fuqua (1993) distinguish these two forms of consultation. In expert consultation, the consultant is responsible for the design, implementation, and success of the intervention. In process consultation, the consultant works in active partnership with the consultee, to design and implement change. Here the success of the intervention is shared between the consultant and the consultee.

Consultation may focus on primary, secondary, or tertiary prevention. Each of these foci may be targeted to individuals, groups, organizations, or communities. Primary prevention consultation focuses on such areas as enhanced communication, decision making, and coping. Secondary prevention consultation occurs in areas such as job-enrichment programs or remediation of learning disabilities. Tertiary prevention focuses on reducing the impact of functional limitations (Brown et al., 1995). Shaw and Betters further discuss consultation by rehabilitation counselors in the private sector in chapter 13.

Advocacy, as discussed in chapter 10 by Liu and Toperek, is the action a counselor takes in assisting clients to achieve their goals through participating in their environments. They discuss how advocacy has a role in the other functions (counseling, case management, and consultation). Teaching clients to become self-advocates is another important aspect of this process. In all cases, changing environments for growth and development is the goal. Sosin and Caulum (1983) argue that advocacy involves the use of influence or confrontation to get a third party to make a decision regarding the welfare of the client, who has less power than the decision maker. The rehabilitation counselor, in this way, represents the client to the decision makers.

The final component of the service delivery system is *outcome*. During this stage, placement and follow-up occur. As discussed in chapter 12, "Placement," the rehabilitation counselor may perform these activities, or the client may be referred to a professional who specializes in these functions. In addition to the state–federal VR program's employment criterion of success coded as Status 26 or successfully placed in a job for 90 days, other outcomes related to independent living and QOL are valued criteria of success in contemporary rehabilitation practice.

Counselors are both direct and indirect service providers, and the manner in which they manage their time and activities contributes significantly to the efficiency and effectiveness of the rehabilitation process. As discussed by Cassell and Mulkey in chapter 14, counselors need to develop caseload management practices that result in effective allocation of time and services across all their client and work responsibilities. Finally, Crimando, in chapter 17, describes the role of administration in the service delivery system.

SUMMARY

The purpose of this chapter is to introduce the concepts and paradigms essential to understanding the profession and practice of rehabilitation counseling. Key definitions, as well as the scope of practice, are introduced. In a manner consistent with the holistic nature of rehabilitation counseling, this chapter addresses the philosophy of rehabilitation and its attendant components, the concept and definitions of disability, and various paradigms of both rehabilitation and rehabilitation counseling practice. The Ecological Model of Rehabilitation Counseling and the Ecological Adaptation Model are described, to provide frameworks for effective and intentional practice. The four essential functions of the rehabilitation counselor are presented in this process. These functions are counseling and case management in working with the client, and consultation and advocacy in working with their significant others and with environments impacting the person. Issues related to appropriate and respectful language and terminology are emphasized, along with a discussion of the importance of rehabilitation outcomes, including QOL. This chapter also lays a foundation and introduces the significance of the chapters to follow, in achieving total rehabilitation.

CHAPTER 2

Models of Disability: The Juxtaposition of Biology and Social Construction

Julie Smart

One way to conceptualize the experience of disability is to examine the various models of disability. Smart (2001) defined *models of disability* in this way: "A model is a set of guiding assumptions, concerns, and propositions about the nature of phenomena or human experience. Models have often been defined as human-made tools for understanding and human-made guidelines for action" (p. 33). In addition, models provide definitions of important human constructs and attributional explanations for both causation and solution. In short, models provide a window to our understanding of disability.

This chapter reviews the three major models of disability: the biomedical model, the economic model, and the sociopolitical model. First, the purposes and consequences of these models are presented, then comparisons are offered and conclusions drawn.

PURPOSES OF MODELS OF DISABILITY

Models of Disability Provide Definitions of Disability

If the concept of disability cannot be defined, there can be no discussion about ways to respond to disability. All three models ask the questions, What is a disability? and Who has a disability? Each of the three models answers these questions differently, and each model reduces the concept of disability to a single, narrow quality (Bickenbach, 1993). Therefore, no single model has the capability to completely capture, explain, or describe the disability experience. In addition, no one diagnosis or classification system can represent the complete experience of having a disability. Further, definitions of disability vary with the purposes, values, and needs, and also the intellectual discipline, of the definers. Zola's (1993) article, "Disability Statistics, What We Count and What It Tells Us," provides an excellent introduction to the varying definitions of disability and to the relationship between the values of the definers and the definitions they provide. Models provide definitions, which result in labels (and, often, stereotypes), and these labels have profound power over the individuals who carry these designations. Clinical, legal, administrative, cultural, and personal definitions of disability evolve from these models (Goffman, 1963; Hahn, 1993; Nagi, 1969; Zola, 1989). As you read this chapter, it should become clear that many of the underlying concepts in the definition(s) of disability are only invented human assumptions.

Models of Disability Provide Explanations of Causal Attribution and Responsibility Attributions

In order to begin constructing a model of disability, determining the location of the problem is necessary *Causal attribution* refers to the explanation and understanding of the cause or source of the disability, and *responsibility attribution* refers to the assignment of responsibility for the response to the disability. In other words, attributional theory asks (and attempts to answer) these questions: Who is responsible for the disability? and Who is responsible for the solution? or What, if anything, should be the responsibility of society toward individuals with disabilities? Or, as Yelin (1992) asked, Who benefits? and Who pays? In the biomedical model, for instance, the individual considered to be responsible for the problem is thought to also be held responsible for the solution. Presently, however, there is a trend toward disregarding causal attribution altogether and focusing solely on solution attribution.

Casual attribution (in models of disability) has three inherent difficulties: First, causes of disability are not very well understood; such causes are not easily measured, and they often defy classification (Berkowitz & Hill, 1986). Frequently, the cause of disability is not known, or there are many causes (such as several forms of mental illness), or theories about causation may change (Kiesler, 1999). Second, who is responsible for etiology of disability is often assumed to be a single individual—typically, the individual with the disability—rather than institutional causes, such as poverty, dangerous workplaces, or lack of insurance coverage. Third, determining the cause of a disability asks the question, How? However, often, this is distorted to ask the question, Why did this disability happen? Science and medicine can attempt to answer the "how" question, but these professionals do not and cannot answer the "why" question; indeed, no one, in any field of expertise, can definitively state why a disability occurs. Finally, the rationale underlying causal and responsibility attribution is to gain understanding and explanation and to formulate accountability guidelines. However, casual explanation may be distorted to become fault, blame, and moral accountability placed upon the individual with the disability.

Models of Disability Are Based on (Perceived) Needs

If the presence of needs is established and recognized, then ways in which to meet these needs can be implemented. First, however, these needs must be clearly defined. Each of these three models of disability outlines the needs of people with disabilities in a single, narrow dimension. In the biomedical model, the needs are viewed as medical, and, accordingly, resources are marshaled to meet medical needs; in the economic model, needs are thought to be economic and vocational; and, in the sociopolitical model, the needs of people with disabilities are considered to be full social integration and equal political rights.

Models Guide the Formulation and Implementation of Policy

The history of each of these models can be easily traced, including resulting policies, laws, and public attitudes. Legislation and policy both reflect and affect society's values and perceptions. Because a model defines and describes the needs of people with disabilities, the natural outcome is the formulation of policies into practice. Similarly, if the model used determines the location of the problem, then collective public action will attempt to solve the problem. For example, in general terms, much of workers' compensation law is the result of the medical model of disability; the state–federal vocational rehabilitation (VR) system is the result of the economic model of disability; and the Americans with Disabilities Act (ADA) is based upon principles of the sociopolitical model of disability. As can be seen from the preceding examples of legislation and governmental agencies, there has been no comprehensive and unified disability policy in the United States. This lack of a clear focus can be traced to the use of differing models of disability (Berkowitz, 1987).

Models of Disability Are Not Value Neutral

Because models of disability are human-made representations, these models will reflect the needs and values of those who construct the models. There is no value-neutral language with which to describe disability. Two of these models (the biomedical model and the economic model) have their origins in religious value systems. Further, formalized collective definitions and policies are crystallized in legislation (Wolfensberger, 1972). Those in power construct models, including definitions and diagnoses, then devise and implement policies and laws based on these models (Hahn, 1988). People have had the power and resources to define disability and to determine the types of services (if any) that people with disabilities receive (Albrecht, 1981; Davis, 1997). Powerful people, most often those without disabilities, defined the disability experience and developed the mechanisms with which to respond (Hannah & Midlarsky, 1987). For example, much of the legal disenfranchisement and marginalization of people with disabilities have been legalized and enforced by adherence to and belief in the biomedical model of disability, although the general public often assumes that clinical definitions are neutral. Nonetheless, all three models of disability are neither reality nor objective.

Models of Disability Determine Which Academic Disciplines Study and Learn About People With Disabilities

In the past, disability was thought to be solely a medical and biological phenomena, and therefore only medical schools taught about disabilities. Because disability was not viewed as a social concern or responsibility, few disability issues were taught in the social sciences, such as psychology, sociology, or social work. People with disabilities were (and are) invisible in most college and university courses (Bauman & Drake, 1997). Therefore, professionals graduated unaware, or falsely assuming, that they would not provide services for people with disabilities. As models of disability evolve, the number of people with disabilities increases, and individuals with disabilities develop stronger advocacy systems, the curriculum of professional developments and preparation programs will begin to include information about the disability experience.

Models of Disability Shape the Self-Identity of People With Disabilities

Models provide labels, diagnoses, and theories of causation and responsibility, all based upon (seemingly) authoritative and prestigious sources. These beliefs are widely held, strongly believed, and constantly socially reinforced. Because these beliefs are pervasive and widespread, many individuals with disabilities have adopted these beliefs as self-identifiers (Hannah & Midlarsky, 1987). Simply because they have heard these stereotypes so often, and also because people with disabilities frequently lack role models with disabilities, people with disabilities accept these stereotypes as truth about themselves. Society, therefore, has effectively taught many people with disabilities to feel inferior and dependent.

Models of Disability Can Cause Prejudice and Discrimination

Models of disability are not harmless abstractions or theories (Bickenbach, 1993; Eisenberg, Griggins, & Duval, 1982) (they are abstractions and theories, but they are not harmless). Rather, models of disability guide public attitudes, shape legislation, determine the services provided, and influence the training of professionals, all of which can create prejudice and discrimination. In addition, models of disability have a significant impact on how (or if) people with disabilities are portrayed in the mass media. With a normative emphasis, disability is thought to be inequality or deviance from a valued norm or standard. If a model of disability has a normative element, prejudice, discrimination, marginalization, and reduced opportunity will result. Two of the models of disability (presented in this chapter) consider the absence of disability to be the desired state and, conversely, view the presence of a disability as undesirable deviance. Indeed, the search for the origins of prejudicial attitudes leads back to these models of disability. Further, much of the prejudice and discrimination may not appear (to those without disabilities) to be prejudicial or unwarranted, simply because these models of disability have had long histories, and two of these models have the support, authority, and prestige of the established disciplines of science (biology and economics).

RESULTS OF MODELS

After revising the basic components and functions of models of disability, two issues should become apparent: First, models of disability, although abstractions, result in the daily, lived experience of people of disabilities. The services people with disabilities receive, their social integration—indeed, all aspects of the lives of people with disabilities—are influenced by the model(s) of disability one accepts. Second, both the experience of having a disability and the experience of responding to people with disabilities are not wholly biological in nature, but are also social and cultural constructions (Higgins, 1992).

Examining the ways in which we describe and understand the world around us, including the people in it, is important. Occasionally, our understandings can be flawed or incomplete. Nonetheless, it is essential to be clear about the model of disability in use, including its shortcomings; therefore, we now briefly review the three main models of disability (biomedical, economic, and sociopolitical). Disability scholars have posited other models of disability, but the three presented here are considered to be the most common. Also, these models are occasionally labeled differently; for example, the biomedical model is also termed *the disease model*, the economic model is sometimes referred to as *the functional model*, and occasionally the sociopolitical model is termed the *minority group paradigm*.

THE BIOMEDICAL MODEL OF DISABILITY OR A PERFECT WORLD IS A WORLD WITHOUT DISABILITIES

Of the three models discussed in this chapter, the biomedical model has the longest history: This model has been in use for centuries. Bickenbach (1993) defined the biomedical model of disability:

> The most commonly held belief about (this model of) disablement is that it involves a defect, deficiency, dysfunctional, abnormality, failing or medical "problem" that is located within the individual. We think it is so obvious as to be beyond serious dispute that disablement is a characteristic of a *defective person*, someone who is functionally limited or anatomically abnormal, diseased, pathoanatomical, someone who is neither whole or healthy, fit or flourishing, someone who is biologically inferior or subnormal. The essence of disablement, in this view, is that there is something *wrong* with people with disabilities. (p. 61, emphasis the author's)

There are two important components of this model. First, pathology must be present, and second, the pathology is located within the individual. Disability is not viewed as a valued difference, but as deviance from a desired normality or standard of evaluation. Further, disabilities are treated as objective conditions that exist in and of themselves (Albrecht, 1992). Certainly, the degree of societal stigma toward an individual's type of disability is never considered when clinicians determine the disability's level of severity. According to the biomedical model, people with disabilities, as victims of misfortune, should be grateful for any sympathy, pity, and charity that might be offered. Taken further, their "personal tragedy or flaw" (the disability) relieves society of the responsibility of according full civil rights to people with disabilities. The biomedical model is not considered to be interactional, because the problem of disability exists entirely within the individual. Therefore, society tells people with disabilities, "This is how the world is. Take it or leave it." It is the person with a disability and their aspirations which must be modified.

In order to establish the presence of a disability (or pathology), diagnostic testing and assessment are necessary. In addition, diagnostic classification systems, such as the *International Classification of Impairment and Disabilities and Handicaps* (ICIDH) and *The International Classification of Functioning, Disability, and Health* (ICF) (World Health Organization [WHO], 1980, 2001) and the *Diagnostic and Statistical Manual of Mental Disorders*, fourth edition, text revision (DSM–IV–TR) (American Psychiatric Association, 2000) must be constructed. Therefore, diagnoses and other medical labels are only as good as the diagnostic tools, tests, instruments, and classification systems used (Smart & Smart, 1997). Many scholars argue that these tools and systems are flawed: "Diagnostic categories and classification schemes are acts of the imagination rather than real things in the world. . . . We must not mistake this for reality itself" (Eisenberg, 1996, p. xv). Stone (1984), in a chapter entitled, "Disability as a Clinical Concept," questioned these systems (terming them "false precision") and stated that diagnosis are not the product of "a scientific procedure of unquestionable validity, free from error." Stone also considered diagnoses as "an unattainable quest for neutrality," simply because a physician (who is a person) renders the diagnosis. Therefore, medical diagnoses can be subjective, impressionistic, value-laden judgments of individuals (Kirk & Kutchins, 1992; Smart & Smart, 1997). Medical diagnoses are becoming more standardized, and, also, disability ratings are becoming more numerical in nature. Nonetheless, both still remain subjective and incomplete (Clendinen & Nagourney, 1999). For example, VR counselors are well aware that two individuals with the same medical diagnosis and identical numerical ratings of severity of disability will have very different outcomes.

Clinicians have attempted to include environmental issues in their classification systems. For example, in 1980, the WHO clearly differentiated among impairments, disabilities, and handicaps, and, indeed, the ICIDH is organized around these three concepts. Essentially, *impairments* were defined as purely medical phenomena; *disabilities* were defined as the inability to perform socially valued roles, and *handicaps* were defined as obstacles in the environment. Twenty years later, Peterson (2000) noted changes in the most recent edition of the WHO's ICF. The shortcomings of previous editions of the ICIDH were addressed. Certainly, much clearer and more precise distinctions are made among the individual's disability, level of functioning, and environment. Indeed, Peterson refers to the ICF as "a classification system of human functioning" (p. 1), thus focusing on health and adaptive functioning, rather than on pathology and dysfunction.

In spite of these recent changes to the ICF, it remains a classification system utilized by professionals. Diagnoses of disability also excuse society of the need to value people with disabilities (Davis, 1997). There is a normative foundation to the biomedical model, in that the prevailing picture of normal or typical humankind is of people without disabilities. The conception/definition of normality is often viewed as an exercise in wordplay. However, the concept of normality has guided the development of the built environment. Physical environments are constructed for "normal" people. The absence of accommodations, lack of accessibility, and prejudice and discrimination are not noticed by those who have been designated as normal (Kleinfield, 1979). Even more important, the absence of people with disabilities in society is often not noticed. Not only does the built environment prevent people with disabilities from full participation, but people without disabilities are not aware of this segregation imposed upon people with disabilities (Gleeson, 1999). One disability scholar (Higgins, 1992) has termed this as making people with disabilities "foreigners" in their own country, educating and housing, and employing them in separate (and often inferior) environments.

Every individual with a disability, regardless of their privilege, economic resources, education, or achievements, knows that they belong to a devalued group, and many individuals with disabilities (especially the Deaf) feel there is nothing to be gained by trying to assimilate into society that devalues them. Indeed, the biomedical model considers people with disabilities to be people who have adjustments and adaptations to make. A perfect world, according to the biomedical model, is a world without disabilities. Disabilities are to be prevented. At the extreme, this can be distorted to mean that people who have disabilities should be eliminated. Joanne Wilson, the commissioner of the federal Rehabilitation Services Administration, summarized this concept when she commented, "It's not quite respectable to have a disability."

The biomedical model can be interpreted as *categorical devaluation*. Clinicians and medical practitioners understand that the diagnoses they render describe a condition that an individual experiences and not the individual himself or herself; however, there is a tendency to treat individuals in terms of their diagnoses and categories. Not only are medical diagnoses categories, but they are also devalued and stigmatizing categories. Categorical devaluation allows society to view these individuals as their category, indistinguishable from others in the same category; therefore, categorized people are not viewed as individuals.

> Others respond to devalued persons in terms of their membership in the stigma-laden category. Individual qualities and actions become secondary. . . . Individuals of devalued categories are treated as being . . . substitutable for each other. . . . Stigmatized persons, then are little valued as persons. Classificatory status tends to displace alternative criteria of person worth. . . . Others may claim license—implicitly, if not explicitly—to treat the stigmatized individuals in exploitative and degrading ways. (Schur, 1971, pp. 30–31)

To the general public, the biomedical model is the most familiar and best understood conception of disability. Two factors contribute to this: the long history of the model and the (seemingly) objective and scientific classification and diagnosis systems that render the biomedical model intuitively understandable to most people. A disability scholar, Bickenbach (1993), has proposed a third explanation for the public's facile acceptance of the biomedical model, positing that this model has roots in a religious belief system in which disability was often (and may still be) viewed as a moral defect or the product of sin (of the person with the disability or their parents), and in which biological wholeness is viewed as virtue and righteousness. Therefore, the biomedical model appeared to add scientific confirmation to these religious beliefs. This combination of religion and science can be deep-rooted and powerful.

In the biomedical model of disability, the location of the problem is within the individual, although clinicians would argue that the biomedical model does not involve blame or culpability for which the individual with the disability could be held responsible. Smart (2001) summarized:

> The natural result of holding *someone* responsible for the disability is to hold that same person totally responsible for the treatment and the care of the disability. The rationale is, whoever created the situation, should also deal with it. Therefore the individual and his or her family should manage the disability and not subject others (who are totally blameless) to requests for assistance, accommodations, resources, or rights. (p. 103)

If the problem exists within the individual, then all attention and efforts are focused on fixing or rehabilitating the individual. Neither the physical environment nor the social environment is thought to be part of the solution or part of the problem. The responsibility for both the problem and the solution lie within the individual with the disability. In this model, disability is an individual, personal matter. Further, the assumption that the individual is totally responsible for the etiology of the disability is stigmatizing for the individual with a disability. Blaming the individual for their disability results in prejudice, discrimination, and reduced opportunities for the individual, because it is thought that the individual should have done something to have prevented the disability (Smart, 2001). Explanation of the cause (etiology) of the disability often results in blame. The general public seeks for a cause and ultimately blames the individual. This is an example of how a model of disability can act as a source of prejudice and discrimination.

The biomedical model is "often perceived to be that of experts delivering services to passive recipients who are expected to be compliant and to whom little information and few treatment options are presented" (Smart, 2001, p. 35). Because the high skill levels and the years of training required to enter medical professions, the biomedical model relies on the use of experts. The individual with the disability is not considered to be an active decision maker, simply because they (most often) do not have the education, expertise, or experience required of physicians.

In addition, once people are labeled as being disabled, they are socialized to the role. Everyone, with or without a disability, is socialized to certain roles (and the rules of these roles) within society. This model teaches the general public to consider the disability to be the "master status," or the defining characteristic, of the individual (McCarthy, 1993; B. A. Wright, 1991). However, most individuals with disabilities do not view their disability as their primary identifier. Adherents of the biomedical model have stigmatized people with disabilities as victims with special needs. The Disability Rights movement has termed this as a "socially imposed disability."

Claire Liachowitz (1988), in her book, *Disability as a Social Construct*, asserted that, in spite of these modifications to the ICIDH, the responsibility for dealing with a disability, according to the medical model, is doubly incumbent on the individual who has the disability. The individual is responsible for two types of responses: the medical/physical management of the disability and the emotional/cognitive response:

> In traditional medical views, the long-term or permanent functional limitations produced by physical impairment are called disability. Recent medical textbooks go further and construe disability as a variable dependent upon characteristic of motivation and adaptability as well as upon the limiting residue of disease and injury. However, both sets of medical views consider *personal* dysfunctional a sufficient criterion for disability. (p. 12, emphasis the author's)

By focusing on the individual's motivation and adaptability, looking for solutions in the physical or social environment is not necessary. The individual with a disability is expected to be resilient, courageous, and to demonstrate self-control and optimism. The Disability Rights movement refers to this expectation as the "Try Harder" syndrome, and it is easy to understand that, if the individual is held totally responsible for the management of the disability, the general public is not required to provide accommodations (such as elevators, curb cuts, and Braille text) nor should the general public be required to accord civil rights to Americans with disabilities.

Stone (1984) also regarded as troublesome the WHO's attempt to separate medical, biological, and individual phenomena from the individual's role functioning. She presented compelling arguments about the inaccuracy of medical diagnoses and, further, considered the clinician's judgment of role functioning to be even more impressionistic, subjective, and value laden:

> A third element of the impairment concept, the idea that the purely *medical* judgment of the impairment is separable from the more subjective and value-laden judgment of disability, is crystallized in a set of guidelines created by the American Medical Association to assist physicians in their certifying roles. (p. 110)

Implications of the Biomedical Model

Most public and private disability programs rely on the biomedical model to some extent. Certainly, those who design and administer these programs rely on medical expertise (Tannebaum, 1986, p. 136). Eligibility to receive services is based upon the documentation of the presence of pathology and role limitation. Physicians are regarded as the gatekeepers to disability services, because they both define and subsequently establish the presence of a disability in an individual. The Disability Rights movement has termed this the "medicalization of disability." Legislation in the United States, up until the passage of the ADA, tended to be incremental, simply adding layers of law, regulations, and policy to an underlying foundation based on the medical model (Bickenbach, 1993). In turn, both the medical professions and government agencies have effectively educated the public (including people with disabilities) to believe that a condition is actually disabling.

The biomedical model of disability has its origins in the historical two-outcome paradigm of medicine. In the past, there were two outcomes to medical treatment: total recovery or death. Long-term chronic care is relatively new to the profession of medicine, because medicine's history has been one of providing short-term care for acute needs. Presently, the management of disabilities consists of treating chronic conditions, avoiding secondary disabilities, maintaining a high quality of life, and treating symptoms. Naturally, the practice of medicine has evolved and expanded to include long-term, chronic care, but some vestiges of the two-outcome paradigm are still apparent in insurance policies and disability programs that withdraw treatment and benefits once progress toward full recovery stops. This makes sense, because both the business of insurance and public and private disability programs were originally developed with the biomedical model of disability as a guiding assumption.

The biomedical model of disability is better suited for physical disabilities than it is for cognitive, intellectual, emotional, and psychiatric disabilities. This is understandable, because, for centuries, physical disabilities were the only conditions regarded as disabilities. Yet, the definition of disability continues to expand and evolve; thus, impairments such as learning disabilities, mental illness, and addiction disorders do not lend themselves well to the biomedical model, either for definitional assumptions, for causal and responsibility attribution, or for treatment and policy considerations.

Harlan Hahn (1988, 1993) was a gifted writer and disability activist who criticized the biomedical model of disability, citing its silence on issues of social justice (because disability is thought to be a private, individual matter), its legitimatization of the handicapism of the general population, and its fragmentation of the disability community. We have observed how the prestige and authority of science and medicine allowed the general public to detach itself from the issue of disability.

Perhaps the greatest criticism of this model, according to Hahn (1988), was the resulting division of the disability community. The biomedical model separates individuals into diagnostic categories (the blind, the mentally ill, or the HIV-positive). Professionals and clinicians provide services based on the divisions of these categories, and the general public also subscribes to the categorical identity of people with disabilities. This categorization objectified and dehumanized people with disabilities; often, a person with disability was not thought of as "one of us." Even more important, individuals with disabilities often thought of themselves as these categories. Rather than focusing on the universal problems of people with all types of disabilities, the disability community is divided along diagnostic, clinical categories, competing for both resources and civil rights. Bickenbach (1993) summarized:

> Hahn believes that it has fragmented the disability community by stressing the functional traits that divided them rather than the external obstacles they faced as a common problem. Groups representing the rights of the people with disabilities are invariably organized around diagnostic categories and must compete among themselves for social attention. As a result, few broad attempts are made to form alliances or coalitions that might facilitate the emergence of a broad, social and political movement of citizens with various types of disabilities. (p. 85)

The subordinate, inferior status of people is reinforced by the power differential present in the biomedical model. Because this model relies on the expertise and education of physicians and their diagnostic systems, people with disabilities have been socialized to assume a compliant, passive role. Therefore, the medical model of disability contributed to the fragmentation of the disability community in a second way: It taught individuals with disabilities to be dependent and inferior and certainly not to politically mobilize, demanding rights and accommodations.

Hahn (1988, 1993) concluded his criticism of the biomedical model by terming it a "metahandicap," meaning that the model contributes to prejudice and discrimination, and further, that the model itself is a handicap. Hahn was critical of the model's emphasis on the relationship between causal factors of disability and outcome factors, advocating that these two phenomena are not related and serve only to increase prejudice and discrimination. By focusing attention away from the social and physical environments, the medical model is silent on issues of social justice. Further, powerful professions and policy-making bodies have endowed the medical model with the appearance of science, objectivity, and reality, thus legitimizing the handicapism of the general population.

The biomedical model is one way to choose to view the disability experience. No disability scholar advocates the total abandonment of the medical model. Every disability scholar, however, advocates the total abandonment of the medical model. Indeed, the medical profession itself is moving away from many of the basic assumptions of the medical model.

THE ECONOMIC MODEL OF DISABILITY OR IN A PERFECT WORLD, EVERYONE CONTRIBUTES ECONOMICALLY

Both the biomedical and the economic models of disability have their roots in well-established academic disciplines—biomedicine and economics—resulting in unchallenged positions in the general population, because these conceptions of disability are easily understandable and straightforward. Essentially, the economic model of disability defines disability as the inability to perform socially valued roles, most often work roles (sometimes referred to as "role failure"). Similar to the medical model of disability, the economic model of disability is normative, meaning that the desired condition is the ability to work and that deviance is, therefore, the inability to work. In short, although the biomedical model reduces the definition to the single dimension of biology, the economic model reduces the definition to an economic dimension.

Those who subscribe to the economic model will accord respect, accommodations, and civil rights to people with disabilities, based on their perception of individuals' potential to work and to provide economic resources. In the economic model, social assimilation for anyone is based on their (perceived) cost-effectiveness. Much like the biomedical model, the economic model has origins in value and religious systems. In many religions, the values of personal, moral, and social worth are closely related to the ability and willingness to work, and, further, a great deal of American legislation is based upon these principles. Certainly, the principles of self-reliance and individualism are enshrined in American culture. Also, throughout history, measuring (albeit subconsciously) an individual's worth by their earning or production capacity has been commonplace. Accordingly, this model has the capability to shape the self-identity of people with disabilities, because those who do work and do not require public assistance typically are valued by society. Those individuals who consume scarce public resources, especially without (perceived) repayment, will be devalued. Many individuals with severe and multiple disabilities not only do not work and produce resources, but they also consume resources. An individual with a disability (who does not work) will be in a permanent position of dependence and indebtedness. These individuals are often labeled as "burdens" or "drains." Liachowitz (1988) asserted that the public confers "civil inferiority" on people with disabilities who do not work. Higgins (1992) made a stronger statement: "Utility . . . cheapens people with disabilities. . . . Utility merely 'uses' disabled people [*sic*]. If they and (the policy addressed toward them) cannot produce a 'profit' (i.e., if benefits do not exceed costs), then they have little or no value" (p. 199).

As stated, the conception of normality is the ability to work and produce, and, accordingly, the definitions of the biomedical model and the economic model can conflict. Thus, in this model, not every impairment or disorder (as defined by the medical model) is a disability. For example, the professor in a wheelchair does not have a disability nor does the accountant with diabetes (in the economic model). However, the airline pilot with diabetes, a relatively easily controlled disability that does not carry much societal stigma, does have a disability. Therefore, in the economic model, disability is defined in relation to work requirements. Obviously, a disability for one type of work may not be a disability for another type of work. In the biomedical model, a disability is thought to be an individual trait (or problem) that goes with the person with disability to every setting. Therefore, judging the presence of a disability in the economic model is more difficult and complicated than it is in the biomedical model.

In theory, the economic model is considered to be an interactive model that defines the disability in relation to aspects of the environment as Reno, Mashaw, and Gradison (1997) explained:

> While a chronic health condition or impairment is an important element of disability, work disability occurs only when an impairment, in conjunction with the person's other abilities, the demands of the work, and the broader environment make him or her unable to perform the tasks of work. (p. 3)

In Reno et al.'s definition, work disability is defined in terms of the other abilities and skills the individual may have, the job requirements, and, if we were to broadly interpret the phrase "the broader the environment (which) make him or her unable to perform the tasks of work," prejudice and discrimination can also be considered disabling to the individual, if these prevent the individual from obtaining and maintaining employment. Therefore, it is possible, in the economic model, to take into account the degree of prejudice and discrimination experienced by the individual (however, in reality, societal prejudice is rarely considered). Also, if the location of the problem is shifted, the focus of policy and laws must be shifted. For example, there are laws that make prejudicial hiring biases illegal, thus shifting some of the responsibility to the employer (rather than focusing on only the applicant with a disability).

The history of the policy formulated on the basis of the economic model can be traced. For example, many consider the Vocational Rehabilitation Act of 1920 to be a product of this model, because of "its implication that only people who contributed to the nation's economic welfare were worthy of assimilation. That even those 'worthy' people were viewed as inherently inadequate, however, is evidenced by their frequent restriction to relatively menial work" (Liachowitz, 1988, p. 65).

As would be expected, workers' compensation laws are also based on the economic model of disability, or, what is probably more accurate the VR acts and the various workers' compensation laws have theoretical foundations in two models of disability: the biomedical model and the economic model. In contrast, Social Security Disability Insurance (SSDI) policy seems to be a product of the biomedical model. Berkowitz and Hill (1986) explained:

> The U.S. Congress seems to have been singularly unimpressed by such a construct (the economic model of disability). By emphasizing medical improvement as the criterion for removal of beneficiaries from the SSDI rolls, the legislators have

> seemed to downplay the role of demographic, human-capital, and socioeconomic variables that the economists stress. (p. 26)

The economic model of disability has been criticized on several fronts: First, there are disability activists, especially in the Independent Living movement, who question the definition of work as the only function considered. Activities such as leisure and community services are not discussed. Some have labeled the economic model as "the functional model," but the term *economic model* is more accurate, because work and earning capacity are the only functions considered. Indeed, in large government censuses, work activity is routinely surveyed: In these large censuses, individuals with disabilities who are younger than 16 years and older than 64 years are not asked about their work activity, because they are assumed to be excused from work demands. The criticism of the economic model can be more readily understood from the following description:

> The intellectual foundations of the concept of impairment are to be found in these industrial accident schedules. There are lists of physical or medical conditions, with a percentage of loss attached to each condition. Thus, the early schedules share two assumptions essential to the impairment concept. First, they postulate a correspondence between a concrete bodily condition and a more abstract loss. Some purport to describe loss of "earning capacity," actual "economic loss," or "loss of function." But they all presume a link between bodily condition and some more abstract notion of performance. Second, the schedules all assume that a person (or more properly, a person's ability to function) is a collection of arithmetically manipulable separate entities. Human performance is divided into percentiles, so that disability is conceived in terms of missing parts. Impairments become entities to be subtracted from the presumed wholeness of the individual. (Stone, 1984, p. 110)

Another criticism of the economic model concerns its failure to keep pace with the actual demands of the labor market. As the nature of work changes, the definition of work disability changes. Smart (2001) summarized:

> The shift of the economy of the United States from an economy that depended on physical labor such as farming, mining, and manufacturing to an economy based on service and information processing has influenced the definition of disability. In an economy based on physical labor, many individuals with cognitive disabilities, such as learning disabilities or mild mental retardation, were successful workers. In contrast, in that economy, an individual (especially a man) with a physical disability would have been severely limited. In today's economy, a cognitive disability is much more limiting than a physical disability because service jobs and technology/information-processing jobs require high levels of cognitive functioning. Today, an individual with a physical disability, who has the use of assistive technology, has many employment options. (p. 39)

Many policies and laws have a foundation in the economic model of disability; however, most of these laws also have a foundation in the labor market of the early twentieth century; thus, these laws are not as helpful to people with disabilities as they once were. In addition, these laws have not kept pace with the revolution in assistive/adaptive technology, which allows many individuals with disabilities to work. A generation ago, most assistive technology was mechanical and homemade. Today, in contrast, most assistive technology designed for individuals with disabilities is computerized, highly technological, and capable of being customized to the individual. Such technology changes the definition of work demands (or the individual's capabilities to meet the work demands) (Tannebaum 1986; Thomason, Burton, & Hyatt, 1998).

Changing sociodemographic characteristics and their effect on the labor market can render the laws that define work ability to be inflexible and obsolete. Sobsey (1994), speaking about one disability (that of mental retardation), clearly illustrated this: "Wars and labor shortages have repeatedly redefined who has mental retardation" (p. 132). Hahn (1997) used the term *industrial reserve army* in speaking about people with disabilities, who, when the American economy needs them, are hired and perform well, and, when they are no longer needed, are laid off.

> In World War II, physical exams and other conditions of employment were waived by many corporations to open up jobs for disabled [*sic*] persons, and other members of the industrial reserve, who compiled favorable records of productivity and work performance. During the war, the unemployment rate among disabled [*sic*] adults temporarily declined, only to rise again when these job requirements were reinstated to permit the hiring of returning veterans. (p. 173)

As can be seen, nothing changed in either the individual with the disability or in the disability itself. The labor market (the environment) changed. World War II was a time of great employment opportunities for many groups of disenfranchised peoples, including people with disabilities.

THE SOCIOPOLITICAL MODEL OF DISABILITY OR A PERFECT WORLD IS A WORLD IN WHICH PEOPLE WITH DISABILITIES ARE ACCORDED FULL CIVIL RIGHTS AND ACCOMMODATIONS

The sociopolitical model of disability requires a radical shift in perspective, specifically a shift in the location of the problem of disability, which, as we have seen, determines the response or solution. If the solution shifts, then the policy will also reflect this change. Radical shifts are neither easy nor fast. In the sociopolitical model, the environment is thought to be the problem, and therefore laws and policies will focus on rehabilitating the environment. The history of the model is short: Many scholars trace its genesis to the Independent Living movement and Disability Rights movement, which began in the 1960s.

In the sociopolitical model, disability is defined as a social and civil construction, meaning that there is nothing inherent in a disability or individuals with disabilities that warrants prejudices, stereotypes, and reduced opportunities. Often, proponents of this model distinguish disability and impairment (the biological condition of the individual) from handicap (the social, attitudinal, and institutional barriers that people with disabilities experience). In other words, social structures can exaggerate disability and even construct disability. The behavior and attitudes of others (reduced opportunity and legalized prejudice and discrimination) have nothing to do with a disability. These disadvantages are socially constructed, and therefore they can also be changed or ameliorated without making any changes in the individual with the disability. If disability is socially constructed, it can also be reconstructed or deconstructed.

Tamara Dembo, 20 years ago, asserted that disability is in the eye of the beholder: "Handicapping conditions are *between* people rather than *in* people. . . . Curiously enough, if the handicap is not *in* a person, then there are no handicapped persons. . . . Handicapped people exist only in the eyes of a **viewer**" (Dembo, Leviton, & Wright, 1975, p. 131). Itzak Perlman, the world-famous violinist and a survivor of polio, stated that people with disabilities experience two problems: 1) a physical environment that is not accessible, and 2) the attitudes of people without disabilities toward people with disabilities (Smart, 2001). Perlman's observation clarifies the sociopolitical model of disability: He made the point that disabilities are difficult, but much of the difficulty is not the result of anything about the disability itself or about the individual with the disability. Further, it can be seen that both of these types of difficulties because can be changed.

In many cases, there is a fine line between the designations of *normality* and *disability* (Gleeson, 1999). Occasionally, moreover, these designations may be arbitrary. Regardless of the degree of accuracy or objectivity in the biomedical and economic models, the professional experts drew the line between normality and disability. Thus, professional and differential power gave people the necessary power to define people with disabilities.

Some scholars have termed disability as a civil and social inferiority. Liachowitz (1988) explained (the terms *handicap* and *disability* are used interchangeably here):

> (There are) three ways that legislation conditions the abilities . . . of impaired people to function. (1) Laws disable . . . handicapped [*sic*] people by prescribing their activities. (2) Less directly, and perhaps more effectively, laws also construct disability by promoting particular expectations among the able bodied segment of the population. And, (3) because knowledge of these expectations can shape the personality and behavior of handicapped individuals, laws can lead to ostensibly "self-inflicted" disability. (p. 19)

Reviewing these ideas, it can be seen that (according to Liachowitz) law disables people (and not a biological impairment within the individual). Further, the prestige and authority of law and government teach society to think of some people as having disabilities and to think of other people as not having disabilities. In addition, laws have the power to legalize, institutionalize, and legitimatize prejudice and discrimination toward people with disabilities. Liachowitz's last point asserted that disabilities are also learned social roles, rather than behaviors and attitudes that are a direct result of a disability. In other words, society teaches people with disabilities to believe the meaning of the labels that society (and legislatures) attach to them and also to summit to prejudice, discrimination, and reduced opportunity, with equanimity—to be a good sport. Liachowitz termed this a *self-inflicted* disability.

Laws and policies can have the power (and purpose) of medical classification systems (such as the ICIDI, the ICF, and the DSM–IV–R) because these formalized, collective public actions have become label makers and category makers. Individuals are housed, treated, and educated according to the provisions of these laws. As successive groups of people become objects of government legislation, disabilities experienced by these people become their category, their label, and, to some extent, their self-identity. Therefore, in the sociopolitical model, disability is a politically manipulated category. These manipulated categories affect the daily lives of individuals with disabilities, relieve society of the necessity to value and respect individuals with disabilities, and influence their self-identity.

The sociopolitical model is an interactional model, because it considers both the individual with a disability and their situation. Policy makers, professional service providers, and the general public are part of the problem of disability, or, stated differently, if disability is a collective concern, then the response required is a collective duty. If society does not respond, it can be said to choose to refuse to pay the price to remove barriers and discrimination. Bickenbach (1993) quoted from the Canadian law, the Bill of Human Rights: "All Canadians are responsible for the necessary changes that will give disabled persons the same choices of participation that are enjoyed by those who are not disabled" (p. 161). The concept of collective responsibility is clearly communicated in Canadian law.

In this model, people with disabilities claim the right to define disability—both the experience of having a disability and the ways in which to respond. But, in contrast to biomedical and economic models, the sociopolitical model has no academic/professional field of expertise to provide a theoretical foundation. As we have seen, the appeal to a single field of expertise has four results: First, the professional field defines and describes disability and its treatment; second, a power differential is put into place; third, and perhaps most important, people with disabilities are segmented and stratified by varying classification systems, service providers, and bureaucratic organizations; and fourth, it excuses society from the need to respond, simply because the public thinks that professionals can and do meet all needs of people with disabilities. Stated differently, models that have professional fields of expertise diffuse responsibility for disability among the differing types of service providers.

Individuals who experience disability are beginning to communicate their conception of disability, often in direct contrast to that of professional caregivers. The most clear-cut example of this is the Deaf culture, who define themselves as having a separate culture, rather than as a disability group. Citing the use of sign language (a rich repository of culture, tradition, and mutual understanding) and their group cohesiveness, the Deaf culture refuses to accept the normative role of "the disabled." In doing so, they have freed themselves from what they view as professional tyranny. Another example of this is a former president of the American Association for the Blind, who stated that vision is useful, convenient, and pleasant. Implicit in this notion, by its very absence, is the idea that vision is not a necessity for a satisfying and fulfilling life. If people with disabilities have, to a great extent, constructed the sociopolitical model of disability, then it seems reasonable that this model most closely reflects the lived daily experience of those with disabilities.

Some disability scholars, most notably Hahn, have referred to the sociopolitical model as the minority group model of disability (Hahn, 1988). Using the same foundation as the sociopolitical model, but adding the comparison to racial/ethnic/cultural minority groups, individuals of sexual orientation groups, and women, Hahn pointed out that Americans with disabilities have experienced the same types of prejudice that these other groups of minority Americans have experienced. Furthermore, and perhaps more important, the rationale (or justification) for the institutionalized and legalized prejudice toward racial minority individuals, gays, and women is based on the same principle as prejudice against people with disabilities: All four of these groups are treated unfairly because society has judged them to be biologically inferior or pathological. Presently, there are few people who actually believe that racial minorities, gays, or women are biologically inferior. This change was brought about by these groups defining themselves, advocating for themselves, then demanding their rights as Americans.

Some disability scholars, moreover, have asserted that, as groups, people with disabilities have experienced more prejudice than any other minority group.

> More recent studies suggest that prejudice against impaired persons is more intense than that against other minorities. Bowe (1978) concludes that employer attitudes toward impaired workers are 'less favorable than those . . . toward elderly individuals, minority group members, ex-convicts, and student radicals.

Hahn (1983) finds that handicapped persons are victims of "greater animosity and rejection than many other groups in society." Bowe and Hahn agreed with Yuker (1988) that prejudice increases with the visibility of impairment (Berkowitz & Hill, p. 245). Therefore, people with disabilities are forced to meet their need for personal and political recognition by joining groups comprised of "their own kind."

The Disability Rights movement and the Independent Living movement used many of the methods of the other civil rights movements, resulting in the ADA. However, many disability advocates see flaws in the comparison of persons with disabilities to other disenfranchised groups. These critics point out that people with disabilities, as a group, do not possess intergenerational continuity and history or have a cultural identity that racial/ethic/cultural/linguistic groups experience. Although there is great social, cultural, and economic variability within each racial/ethnic minority group, there is even greater variability among people with disabilities. Indeed, the only source of commonality among people with all types of disabilities is the experience of prejudice and discrimination. Nonetheless, the minority group definition has merit, in that it can build and expand upon the civil rights efforts of these other groups. In addition, the generations required to correct the widespread misconception that some groups of individuals deserve legalized inferior treatment, because of assumed biological pathology or inferiority, has already been accomplished.

Many consider the sociopolitical model to be the most powerful model of disability, because this model, of the three discussed here, is the only model that has mobilized people with disabilities. In contrast, the biomedical and economic models have divided and isolated Americans with disabilities, by their insistence on viewing disability as an individual and biological phenomena. If the value of models of disability is twofold (to explain as accurately and precisely as possible and to develop guidelines to human action), then the sociopolitical model of disability has the greatest accuracy and power.

COMPETING DISCOURSES AND COMPETING FOR RESOURCES

We began our discussion of these models of disability by emphasizing that none is reality itself. Nonetheless, we have seen that the general public had often thought of these models as total reality. We have also learned that no one model completely describes the disability experience, in large part, because of the one-dimensional definition of disability that each model provides. Disability is a complex, multivariate experience that exists in a social environment, and therefore these incomplete definitions distort the representation of the experience.

If the models are incomplete in defining disability, then it follows that each focuses on a single set of problems, which does not and cannot give an accurate and complete picture of the lived experience of a disability. For example, if an individual cannot find and obtain employment, the economic model would best describe their disability experience. But no individual with a disability neatly divides up their life into three models. Among the three models discussed here, the sociopolitical model most accurately and completely describes the daily lived lives of people with disabilities, because most of the difficulties they experience are more social in nature than has previously been acknowledged. However, the sociopolitical model represents a challenge to traditional patterns of thought and action (Albrecht, 1981; Berkowitz, 1987; Reno et al., 1997).

Here is the problem. Disability laws and policies trace their origins to a theoretical foundation in a single model of disability. Indeed, many experts (e.g., Bickenbach, 1993) view the development of disability law and policy as neither comprehensive nor unified. In their view, national legislation (with the exception of the ADA) tends to incorporate incremental change, rather than fundamental and radical change. Liachowitz (1988), for example, viewed the VR Act of 1920 to be based on the biomedical model of disability, and therefore all subsequent VR acts and their amendments (as direct descendants of the VR Act of 1920) bear the disabling and limiting influence of the biomedical model of disability.

TABLE 2.1 Models of Disability

Model	Field of Expertise	Causal Attribution	Solution Responsibility	Normative?	Interactional?	Needs	Policy Formulated	Capability to Mobilize People with Disabilities
Biomedical model of disability	Medicine Biology	Pathology	Individual	Yes	No. Disability exists solely within the individual.	Only medical	SSDI SSI	No
Economic model of disability	Economics	Economic problem Role failure	Individual	Yes	No. Role failure results from the individual's disability.	Only economic and vocational	VR Workers' Comp	Somewhat
Sociopolitical model of disability	None	Irrelevant	Society	No	Yes	Civil Rights Full political and economic participation Accommodation	ADA	Yes

Note: SSDI = Social Security Disability Insurance; SSI = Supplemental Security Income; VR = vocational rehabilitation; ADA = Americans with Disabilities Act.

All models are capable of change, and, indeed, if they are to continue in use, they are required to change. The biomedical model of disability had added the concepts of disability and handicap to the definition of impairment, and the economic model had made, and will continue to make, adaptations, based on changes in the labor market and advances in assistive technology. However, perhaps because of their long history, their appeal to (seemingly) intuitive public understanding, and their roots in religion, medicine, and economics, it seems doubtful if these changes in these two models have been acknowledged or understood by the general public. For instance, Nagi (1980) published his differential classification of impairment, disability, and handicap, in an attempt to render the medical model interactional (attempting to take the broader environment into consideration). This was almost 25 years ago, and yet, today, most people, including professional service providers, consider the three terms to be synonymous and interchangeable. The newer ICF has attempted to heighten clinicians' sensitivity to environment and functioning; thus, it appears that the medical profession itself is moving beyond the medical model of disability. The sociopolitical model, in contrast, has as it primary tenet that disability is created by society, and therefore, if society makes disability, society can also remake disability.

Is this a contest among models? Or, can the history of these models of disability be thought of as in an ascendant trajectory, with the sociopolitical model being the strongest and most accurate? On the one hand, no one advocates the complete abandonment of the medical model (including people with disabilities); on the other hand, no one (including people with disabilities) considers the sociopolitical model to be a complete definition of, and total solution to, the experience of disability. However, most disability scholars question the capability of the biomedical model to incorporate the political demands of people with disabilities.

These three models can be thought of as building upon each other: Certainly, the biomedical model is viewed as a starting point from which to understand disability. However, they can also, in this time of limited resources and rationed services, be thought of as competing discourses, because each model guides policy formulation and implements service provision in very different ways. Obviously, there are not resources available to respond to each of these models. Leslie Milk humorously captured this reality by stating, "Just when it's our turn to get a piece of the pie, people decide that we can no longer afford dessert" (cited in Bowe, 1980, p. xv).

Each model, in addition, provides definitions and underlying assumptions of disability that shape public perception. Some of these definitions are in direct conflict with each other. How is the public to decide on the most accurate definition? How are individuals with disabilities to shape their self-identities?

This discussion on the three models of disability raises more questions than it answers. Is this a contest among models or an ascendant trajectory? The answer is "yes" to both. Disability is a combination of biology and social construction. Nonetheless, at minimum, we now possess some basis to pose these questions.

CHAPTER 3

History and Systems: United States

David B. Peterson and Lyndon J. Aguiar

The history and systems of rehabilitation counseling have been effectively reviewed by a number of texts addressing the development of disability policy (Jaet & McMahon, 1999; Maki & Riggar, 1997; Obermann, 1965; Parker & Szymanski, 1987, 1992, 1998; Rubin & Roessler, 1978, 1987, 1995, 2001; Weed & Hill, 2001; G. N. Wright, 1980). These resources were carefully reviewed and greatly influenced the totality of this chapter. Notwithstanding previous efforts, all, including this writing, highlight how disability policy development addressed the vocational, independent living, social, and educational needs of people with disabilities; the removal of environmental and attitudinal barriers to full inclusion in society; and the establishment of civil rights that prevent discrimination against people with disabilities.

HISTORICAL PERSPECTIVES OF DISABILITY AND SOCIAL SERVICES

Understanding the history and systems associated with rehabilitation counseling is essential to effective functioning in contemporary rehabilitation counseling practice, because it teaches us that inevitable industrial, social, and policy changes require flexibility and innovation. We are not moved by every wind of change, although these changes can be substantial and challenging for our profession. Consider, for example, the impact of the Industrial Revolution, the Civil War and the world wars, or civil rights movements on the provision of disability-related health and social services over the last two centuries.

Rubin and Roessler (2001) suggested that society's treatment of people with disabilities over time has depended upon perceptions related to the cause of disability, medical knowledge, the threat posed to persons without disabilities, economic conditions of the time, and prevailing sociocultural philosophy. Literature reflecting social perceptions of disability dates back to before the Classical period of ancient Greece and Rome, where we begin our historical overview.

Ancient Greece and Rome

Prior to the Classical period of ancient Greece and Rome (450 B.C.), individuals with disabilities, such as epilepsy and mental retardation, were thought to be victims of supernatural forces, perhaps possessed by evil spirits (Hergenhahn, 2001). Practitioners used magic and temple medicine in an attempt to cure these individuals. In ancient Greece, many individuals with disabilities were often mistreated or killed, as were children born with disabilities centuries later in ancient Rome. Infanticide was rationalized on eugenic (improving the human race by controlled selective breeding) and economic bases (Rubin & Roessler, 2001).

In ancient Greece, Pythagoras (ca. 580–500 B.C.) believed that health depended on a harmonious blending of elements in the body. He ultimately influenced Hippocrates (ca. 460–377 B.C.), who believed that all physical and mental disorders were "caused by natural factors such as inherited susceptibility to disease, organic injury, and an imbalance of bodily fluids" (Hergenhahn, 2001, p. 33). This paradigm contributed to more humane (but far from ideal) treatment of individuals with disabilities.

The Greek philosophy of Stoicism, as manifested in the Roman Empire (ca. 27 B.C. to 14 A.D.), held that all events happen for a reason; thus, one should calmly accept all occurrences as divine will or natural order. Individuals with disabilities were expected to accept their condition and not complain or seek assistance. Individuals (with and without disability) who came from higher social classes were treated more humanely than those from lower classes (Rubin & Roessler, 2001). One can only imagine the plight of people with disabilities after 395 A.D., as the Roman Empire split and later succumbed to barbarian invaders and ultimately fell to the Germanic Goths in 476 A.D.

The Middle Ages

In medieval times, between antiquity and the Renaissance (476 A.D. to 1453), the Christian Church held immense power throughout Europe. Church dogma focused on sin and retribution, with disability sometimes viewed as punishment from God or possession by the devil—a throwback reminiscent of preclassical perspectives. Physicians of the day were poorly prepared to affect any change on this perspective. People with mental illness were often treated by clergy, whose techniques ranged from gentle prayer to cruel punishment, to drive out unwanted demons (Rubin & Roessler, 2001). Prior to the 1400s, people with disabilities were treated as troubled souls, with public reactions ranging from cultural oppression to socially sanctioned extermination.

The Renaissance

Between the fourteenth and sixteenth centuries, the transition from medieval to modern times was accompanied by major strides in science, which suggested that the etiology of mental illness and cause of disabilities were biological in nature. People with mental illness and disabilities were sent to asylums for care, such as the Hospital of St. Mary of Bethlehem, infamously known as Bedlam, in fifteenth- and sixteenth-century London. However, "the treatment in these early asylums was often far from therapeutic. . . . It was not unusual for patients to be found chained to the wall in dark cells" (Rubin & Roessler, 2001, p. 4).

During the 1600s, manual communication was developed in Europe for people who were deaf, and was later imported to the United States by Thomas Gallaudet (Obermann, 1965), in his effort to establish instruction for deaf children in this country. Although this advance helped a particular segment of the disability community, the majority of individuals with disabilities continued to struggle to receive humane treatment. Early innovations in rehabilitation in Europe did not spread quickly to colonial America.

Colonial America

Conditions for people with mental illness and disabilities remained poor in the seventeenth and eighteenth centuries, improving only after Dorothea Dix began her now-famous crusade to improve the treatment of persons with mental illness in the middle of the nineteenth century. In early colonial America, immigration policy restricted access for people with physical and mental impairments, because the new territory could be feral and cruel. To make matters worse, many early colonists continued to interpret disability as punishment from God. Similar attitudes continued to prevail in other countries. However, in the mid-eighteenth century, Benjamin Franklin, in partnership with people of the Quaker faith, established the first colonial general hospital in Philadelphia, which laid the foundation for more-contemporary medical care in the nineteenth century (Grob, 1973).

Early Nineteenth Century

The 1800s were characterized by limited government, which was an understandable reaction to the struggle for independence from England in the previous century. Limited resources notwithstanding, several people made a remarkable impact on services for people with disabilities during the first half of the century. Two such people were Thomas Gallaudet and Dorothea Dix. Gallaudet, with the assistance of his colleague from France, Laurent Clerc, in 1817, established the American Asylum in Hartford, Connecticut, to teach individuals with hearing disabilities how to communicate. Gallaudet's influence in the field of rehabilitation of the deaf led to the founding of the first institution of higher education for the deaf, Gallaudet University, established in 1857.

Dorothea Dix, as noted earlier, was directly responsible for exposing the inhumane condition of the treatment of persons with mental illness, which led to humanizing such treatment, between 1841 and 1854. Her work had a great influence on state and federal funding for improvements in mental health facilities. For a detailed review of disability services development in the nineteenth century, specific to people who are blind (e.g., the work of Samuel Gridley Howe), people with developmental disabilities, people with mental illness, and people with physical disabilities, see Rubin and Roessler (2001).

Late Nineteenth Century

From 1861 to 1865, the Civil War in the United States indirectly helped the rehabilitation movement by dramatically increasing the visibility of individuals with physical disabilities. Although medical and surgical practices were very crude and survival rates were poor, the sheer number of injured veterans resulted in a sizable number of survivors with physical disabilities. The latter part of the nineteenth century was also witness to the Industrial Revolution in America. People moved from rural farm communities to urban centers to benefit from the increase of employment in manufacturing.

Between 1880 and 1900, the Social Gospel movement was prevalent, promoting the role of religion in social reform. Washington Gladden led the movement that supported beneficence to the disadvantaged, which resulted in better treatment of people with disabilities; however, several developments in the latter part of the nineteenth century were not beneficial. Contrary to the Social Gospel movement of the day, three other movements were afoot. First, the science of eugenics was promoted by Sir Francis Galton, and was a philosophical regression to the days of ancient Greece and Rome. This movement resulted in state policies on restricted marriage and involuntary sterilization, which lasted well into the twentieth century (e.g., the first law permitting sterilization of people with mental retardation was passed in 1907).

A second movement contrary to the Social Gospel movement was Herbert Spencer's theory of social Darwinism, which embraced the laissez-faire government of the time. "Survival of the fittest" was the theory's maxim. Neither eugenics nor social Darwinism boded well for people with disabilities. The third social dynamic involved the government operating under a laissez-faire policy, by which, apart from establishing compulsory education programs, it discouraged government involvement in all but essential matters of national security. Assistance to people with disabilities was left mostly to their communities, through philanthropy.

The end of the nineteenth century was witness to emerging support for state involvement in the affairs of those with greater needs, and to the development of philanthropic organizations to assist people with disabilities. Unfortunately, many such organizations ascribed to religious dogma suggesting that moral inferiority was to blame for the plight of anyone less fortunate. Regardless of their shortcomings, these charitable ventures helped form the foundation for future vocational rehabilitation (VR) services (Rubin & Roessler, 2001).

DISABILITY POLICY IN THE TWENTIETH CENTURY

Early Twentieth Century

Individuals leading the Populist movement in the 1890s and early 1900s wanted the government to assume responsibility for economic and social service issues, particularly those of the farmers and laborers rather than of the privileged elite, countering the former laissez-faire tradition. Similarly, the Progressive movement, comprised of Republican insurgents, wanted to create a "square deal" for all, countering the trend of the accumulation of wealth and power by a select few. Both movements requested more government involvement in addressing matters of social justice. Today's VR system is most like the Progressive movement, in which government intervenes to help level the playing field for those who have fewer resources. However, increased government involvement came with a price: Most of the funds that paved the way for federally provided rehabilitation services came from income taxes, which were established in 1913.

The first modern rehabilitation facility, the Cleveland Rehabilitation Center, was established in Cleveland, Ohio, in 1899. It served as the model for other centers established in the early twentieth century, by attempting to provide restorative treatment to individuals with disabilities, but almost a half-century passed before a facility existed that was devoted to the science of rehabilitative medicine. In 1948, Howard Rusk founded, at New York University, the first center to utilize the emerging science of rehabilitative medicine in the treatment of individuals with disabilities (Rusk, 1977a, 1977b).

The *Federal Employees' Compensation Act (FECA)* of 1908 was the first workers' compensation (WC) law enacted in the United States. Initially, the law only covered federal employees who were in the most hazardous occupations, such as the Coast Guard (Nordlund, 1991). Unfortunately, the vast majority of workers in the country in 1916 were not federal employees, and FECA did not apply to them.

Increasing numbers of workers in the early twentieth century were employed in manufacturing, as a direct result of the Industrial Revolution. Although the agricultural trades had their share of job-related injuries, the level and scope of job-related injuries in industrial trades were unprecedented, and led to the expansion of WC to all employees. The law was greatly expanded in 1916 and provided all federal employees with wage replacement, VR, and medical benefits for work-related injuries and occupational diseases (U.S. Department of Labor, n.d.).

Although New York was the first state to pass a compulsory WC law in 1910, the law was declared unconstitutional the following year. Wisconsin's WC law passed in 1911 and was allowed to stand in court (Texas Workers' Compensation Commission, n.d.). By 1917, many states had adopted WC laws, following a U.S. Supreme Court decision that allowed states the ability to enforce such laws.

Rehabilitation services were greatly impacted by World War I (WWI), in which, from 1914 to 1918, the United States and the Allies defeated Germany and the Axis powers. As with the Civil War, WWI resulted in a great number of individuals with physical disabilities. Improvements in surgical procedures in the early 1900s assured that greater numbers of injured veterans survived. As a direct result, in 1916, the National Defense Act was established to help returning soldiers prepare for civilian life.

In 1917, the *Smith-Hughes Act* made federal money available, primarily for veterans, to fund vocational education programs (trade and agricultural schools). The services were educative, not restorative. The act also provided for the creation of the Federal Board for Vocational Education.

The *Soldiers Rehabilitation Act* (Smith-Sears Veterans Rehabilitation Act) of 1918 provided the first U.S. federal program for VR of veterans with disabilities. WWI injuries were a major force in the development of this legislation. The Federal Board of Vocational Education was responsible for program development. Opponents to the act believed it to wax too closely to socialism, but, ultimately, it served as the basis for the civilian VR program.

The 1920s

The *Civilian Vocational Rehabilitation Act* (Smith-Fess Act) of 1920 extended services to civilians, with the federal government providing 50% matching funds to the state government contribution. Persons with physical disabilities, age 16 years and older, were provided guidance, education, prosthetics and other restoration, training toward employment, and, ultimately, job placement. Although this act had the potential to serve many individuals who desperately needed services, many states did not enact legislation to utilize the matching funds.

The period of Prohibition began in 1920, when the 18th Amendment to the U.S. Constitution forbade the manufacture and sale of alcoholic beverages. The societal paradox to Prohibition was a notable carefree attitude of the individuals in power during the Roaring Twenties, an era noted for speakeasies, indulgence, and excess; altruism was not the flavor of the day. The public was not very supportive of idealistic crusaders, resulting in very little progress in rehabilitation services.

The 1920s culminated with Black Thursday, the Stock Market Crash of October 24, 1929. Ironically, the subsequent Great Depression, which was marked by decreased business activity, falling prices, and high unemployment, serendipitously highlighted the value of VR services in helping people return to work.

The 1930s

The year Prohibition ended (1933), President Franklin D. Roosevelt proposed a 25% reduction in VR services, but the measure failed. One may argue that

FDR's stoicism in the face of his own disability influenced his intention to reduce services to persons with disabilities. On the other hand, during the 1930s, Americans were facing great economic challenges, and the needs of people with disabilities may have been lost in the enormity of problems at the national level. FDR's New Deal promoted economic recovery and social reform, in order to alleviate the hardships of the time, but without special consideration to people with disabilities.

The *Social Security Act* (SSA) of 1935, the first permanent source of federal funding related to vocational issues, established the VR program as a permanent one, rather than as experimental, and it established a foundation of income as a supplemental retirement fund to assist those who were aging out of the workforce. The SSA also set the groundwork for the Randolph-Shepard Act (1936) and the Wagner-O'Day Act (1938), by requiring the federal government to explore markets for products manufactured by individuals who were blind.

In 1936, the *Randolph-Shepard Act* surveyed potential jobs for people who were blind, to help expand job opportunities away from stereotyped occupations. The most immediate provision of the act allowed people who were blind to operate vending stands on federal property. The *Wagner-O'Day Act* of 1938 established the nonprofit National Industries for the Blind and mandated government purchases of their products.

In 1938, the *Fair Labor and Standards Act was* established a minimum wage, addressed overtime, and prohibited child labor. This act indirectly affected individuals with disabilities, by reducing the potential that they could be exploited economically and otherwise by unscrupulous employers.

The 1940s

World War II was fought from 1939 to 1945, when the United States and Allies defeated Germany, Italy, and Japan. The labor shortage in the United States, which resulted from military demands, proved useful in establishing the competency of the labor force of people with disabilities. Medical advances at that time resulted in procedures and medications that radically changed the mortality rate of some injuries, resulting in a larger population of people with disabilities.

VR Act Amendments of 1943 (*Barden-Lafollette Act*) extended services to people with disabilities beyond the physical, to include people with mental retardation and mental illness. More types of physical restoration were made available, and the conditions for provision of VR were more specifically defined (e.g., services provided were based upon financial need). This act was also the first of its kind to provide rehabilitation program support for people who are blind, resulting in rapid growth of such services in subsequent years (Rubin & Roessler, 2001).

Also in 1943, the *Disabled Veteran's Act* was established, which authorized any necessary services to assist servicemen with disabilities to adjust to the world of work following their honorable discharge. In 1944, the *Servicemen's Readjustment Act* provided training and education assistance to servicemen whose education was interrupted by military service. The *Veteran's Readjustment Assistance Act* of 1952 provided education and training for all Korean War veterans.

The 1950s

The 1950s were considered to be the beginning of the golden era of rehabilitation (Rusalem, 1976). A number of amendments and laws were passed during this era, which greatly increased benefits to, and services for, individuals with disabilities. Funding for rehabilitation continued to increase dramatically from 1954 to 1965, during the presidencies of Dwight Eisenhower, John F. Kennedy, and Lyndon B. Johnson.

The first new legislation established during this period was the *VR Act Amendments of 1954*. Also known as Public Law 565, it provided a disability income allowance (Supplemental Security Income, or SSI) for individuals who were blind, poor, aged, or otherwise disabled. The amendments also increased the federal matching funds ratio from 1:1 to 3:2, expanded services for people with mental retardation and mental illness (see the previously mentioned Barden-Lafollette Act of 1943), and provided major funding for research and demonstration grants. It also led to the creation of graduate programs in rehabilitation counseling and rehabilitation facility development.

SSA Amendments (1956) authorized Social Security disability allowances for persons with permanent disabilities, aged 50 years and over, who were otherwise considered incapable of returning to competitive employment. These amendments were not tied directly to VR, but they provided income replacement to entitlement recipients. The expansion of the SSA in the following decade would change the impetus of the act from dependence on financial maintenance toward VR and independence.

The 1960s

In 1962, the *Public Welfare Amendments* were introduced, marking the beginning of the well-intended, but ill-fated cooperative efforts between VR and departments of public assistance. The intention was to move welfare recipients from dependence on entitlements to gainful employment, using vocational training and social services. Similarly, the 1964 *Economic Opportunities Act* sought to empower the economically disempowered, through self-help and reeducative programs. The idea was to bring people out of welfare dependence and into gainful employment and tax paying status, but both initiatives failed, because of the enormity of the task at hand, insufficient planning, and limited human resources.

The *Civil Rights Act* of 1964 prohibited discrimination against any individual with respect to hiring, terminating, compensating, or any other terms, conditions, or privileges of employment, on the basis of race, color, religion, gender, or national origin (eventually amended to include the Pregnancy Discrimination Act in 1978). The act established the Equal Employment Opportunity Commission (EEOC), a natural outgrowth of the prevailing Civil Rights movement and Ralph Nader's pioneering efforts in consumer protectionism.

The *VR Act Amendments of 1965* increased federal funding from the ratio of 3:2 to 75% matching funds, and increased services to several underserved populations, including people with behavior disorders (diagnosed by a psychologist or psychiatrist), substance abuse issues, public offense records, and people from socially disadvantaged backgrounds. The option of an extended evaluation was introduced to the VR system, in order to provide time and opportunity to adequately assess people with severe disabilities. Economic need was eliminated as a requirement for VR services, but the amount of assistance could still be moderated by need. The amendments also earmarked funds to support planning of service delivery in states and the construction of new rehabilitation centers. The VR Act Amendments were revised in 1968, to change the federal contribution to 80%, add follow-up services to maintain employment and services to family members, and to expand vocational evaluation and work adjustment services.

The National Commission on Architectural Barriers was authorized in 1965 by the amendments of that year. The commission began the process of reviewing the accessibility of public places for individuals with disabilities. Their work led to the formation of the Architectural Barriers Act (ABA) in 1968, which established accessibility standards. The ABA required "handicapped" access to buildings that were built, leased, or altered with federal funding (see Access Board, n.d.). The Architectural and Transportation Barriers Compliance Board (later renamed the Access Board) was created in 1973, to ensure that federal agencies complied with the ABA. However, it was not until 1990 that access for individuals with disabilities was greatly expanded in Titles II and III of the Americans with Disabilities Act (ADA). This is discussed at length later, in our coverage of the 1990s.

The independent living movement was gaining momentum in the 1960s, with the National Rehabilitation Association's efforts to push a congressional bill that would fund independent rehabilitation services to many individuals in vocational programs. The bill was defeated because the Department of Health, Education, and Welfare was concerned that many individuals were still waiting to receive VR services.

Another important policy authorized in 1965 was the SSA Amendments of that year, which included the establishment of Social Security Disability Insurance (SSDI), to pay benefits to people with disabilities who have paid into the federal insurance program. State VR agencies were reimbursed for providing services to recipients of SSDI.

Several important policies were endorsed in 1967, by President Lyndon Johnson. He first signed *Executive Order 11246* that expanded the scope the Civil Rights Act of 1964, requiring affirmative action to ensure equal opportunity in employment for employers holding federal contracts of $100,000 or more. That same year, the *Age Discrimination in Employment Act* (1967) ensured that persons over 40 years old were not discriminated against on the basis of their age. Finally, the VR *Amendments of 1967* established the National Center for Deaf–Blind Youths and Adults, as well as federal funding for pilot projects to serve migrant workers and their families.

The 1970s

The 1970s could be characterized as a dark time for disability policy, particularly under the presidency of Richard M. Nixon (as were the 1980s, under Ronald Reagan). President Nixon intended to eliminate VR services as they existed, but, fortunately, he was unsuccessful. Useful policy for the general workforce was developed in 1970 in the Occupational Safety and Health Act, which established federal standards for safe and healthy work environments. That same year, the Urban Mass Transit Act began the plan and design of transportation for people with mobility impairments.

The *SSA Amendment of 1972* provided health care entitlements through Medicare from federal funding, and states provided funding for health care through Medicaid. In addition to education amendments that forbade discrimination on the basis of gender in all federally assisted programs, the EEOC successfully advocated the Equal Employment Opportunity Act, ensuring that state and local governments, government agencies, and political subdivisions and departments offer equal employment opportunities to all people.

The *Rehabilitation Act of 1973* was also known as the "billion dollar program." The act consisted of six titles (see Table 3.1), which emphasized increased services to persons with the most severe disabilities and greater consumer involvement in the rehabilitation planning process. A seventh title was added in 1978, establishing policy that supported independent living services (reviewed later). All titles are reviewed in Table 3.1.

In 1975, Public Law 94-142, the *Education for All Handicapped Children's Act*, mandated free appropriate public education to children with disabilities, and emphasized education in the most fully integrated and barrier-free environment possible. Mandatory individual education plans (IEPs) were required for each student. In 1990, this act was reauthorized and retitled the Individuals with Disabilities Education Act (IDEA). Following the trend in educational reform, the 1997 amendments to IDEA sought to establish greater educational outcomes for children with disabilities. A major change in these amendments was a reevaluation of assessment practices and the IEP, with a greater emphasis on integrating the needs of children with disabilities into the general education curriculum.

The Late 1970s

Several important pieces of legislation were developed toward the end of the 1970s. The Developmental Disabilities Assistance and Bill of Rights Act (DDA) of 1976 was established to help children with disabilities achieve their maximum potential. In 1978, Targeted Jobs Tax Credit was available for those who hired specific disadvantaged groups who had high levels of unemployment. Employees were generally referrals from VR agencies. The Health Maintenance Organization Act was also established, which encouraged the development of the now-pervasive health maintenance organizations. Also, the Civil Rights Commission's jurisdiction was expanded to include protection against discrimination on the basis of handicap, through the Civil Rights Commission Amendments of 1978. Finally, the EEOC, the U.S. Office of Personnel Management, and the Departments of Labor and Justice created Uniform Guidelines on Employment Selection Procedures. These guidelines addressed testing and selection, hiring, promotion, demotion, memberships (as in labor organizations), referral, retention, licensing and certification, and training or transfer.

Toward the end of the 1970s, the Department of Education Organization Act (1979) established a Department of Education, in which state–federal VR is currently administered by the Office of Special Education and Rehabilitative Services. Before we conclude with our review of the 1970s, we turn next to

TABLE 3.1 The Rehabilitation Act of 1973

Title	Description
Title I	Promoted consumer involvement (writing of the Individual Written Rehabilitation Plan—now the Individual Plan for Employment), provided a forum for applicants to contest ineligibility determination, the Client Assistance Program, and expanded the definition of *handicap* to include behavioral disorders (handicapped individuals defined as "any person who has a physical or mental impairment which limits one or more major life activities and has a record of such impairment"). Also mandated service to persons with severe disabilities. Provided for a 90% matching funds commitment to tribal bodies for Native Americans.
Title II	Established the National Institute on Disability and Rehabilitation Research, to administer research projects, establish research and training centers, and disseminate information.
Title III	Provided training and special projects, including graduate traineeships, supported employment projects, transitional services (from high school to work), reader and interpreter services, and recreational projects.
Title IV	Established the National Council on Disability.
Title V	The "Civil Rights Provisions" include the following sections 501–504: *Section 501*: Nondiscriminatory federal hiring, or Affirmative Action in federal hiring. Agencies were required to produce an affirmative action plan. The intent was to serve as a model program, but the program was not enforced in the public sector. *Section 502*: The Architectural and Transportation Barriers Compliance Board was established to enforce the accessibility standards from the Architectural Barriers Act of 1968, applied to buildings constructed with federal funds. *Section 503*: Affirmative action by federal contract recipients. Prohibits discrimination on the basis of disability, and requires affirmative action to employ and to advance in employment persons with disabilities who, with reasonable accommodation, can perform the essential functions of the job. Organizations receiving more than $25,000 from the federal government were required to comply. The Department of Labor was responsible for enforcing affirmative action. *Section 504*: Equal opportunities in federal programs, prohibited discrimination in allowing participation in any program or activity receiving federal funding, based upon disability status of an otherwise qualified candidate.
Title VI	Established employment opportunities for persons with disabilities, including Projects with Industry, cooperative-training agreements with government-funded supports, small business opportunities, and supported employment. Much of this funding has diminished.
Title VII (1978)	Added in 1978, Title VII authorized grants to provide services for independent living of persons with disabilities. The focus was on nonemployment potential, addressing attendant care, advocacy, skills training, housing and transportation referrals, and community group living. Related amendments were also created in 1992.

one of the most important policy developments of this era, related to independent living services.

Independent Living Services

In addition to those policies just reviewed, in 1978, policy was enacted that supported independent living services, or those services for people with disabilities that were not necessarily tied to a vocational outcome. In addition to Title VII being added to the Rehabilitation Act of 1973, the Rehabilitation, Comprehensive Services, and Developmental Disabilities Act of 1978 mandated comprehensive independent living services, added the *Bill of Rights Act* to Title V, and established the National Council on the Handicapped (now the National Council on Independent Living), and the Interagency Committee on Handicapped Research was developed. Centers for Independent Living became partners with the state–federal VR system in providing comprehensive support services to people with disabilities. Further amendments in 1992 enhanced independent living services, as we see in our review of contemporary disability policy.

Contemporary Disability Policy

As we near the end of the twentieth century in our disability policy review, it seems appropriate to take some time to address how to remain current with disability policy developments. Clearly the review thus far contains a great deal of information. Proposals for new policies are in a constant state of flux, as various stakeholders participate in the democratic process of moving a bill from a proposition to a new law, and disability advocates need to have their voices heard in the process. New laws progress through the regulations development process, in which advocacy work continues to be essential in maintaining the original intent of a new law. Finally, case law develops around litigation that has an impact on future enforcement of policies already established. How can one keep up with all of this activity?

Professional organizations are among the most useful resources for remaining current with disability policy developments. The American Rehabilitation Counseling Association and its parent organization, the American Counseling Association, the National Council on Rehabilitation Education, and the National Rehabilitation Counseling Association and its parent organization, the National Rehabilitation Association, serve their membership by providing Web sites, newsletters, and other forms of communication to coordinate member resources in disability advocacy efforts. Networking with other rehabilitation counseling professionals can also provide tremendous, experience-based assistance in dealing with disability policy. Finally, the Internet is the best resource for remaining current on latest developments. *Thomas: Legislative Information on the Internet* (http://thomas.loc.gov/) provides a service, through the Library of Congress, that provides up-to-the-minute updates on all matters of policy before Congress. Information on technical assistance with the ADA (reviewed later) is available at http://www.adata.org/. The SSA provides a Ticket to Work Program (also reviewed later) Web site at www.ssa.gov/work/Ticket/ticket_inf.html. Many other such resources are on the Internet; one need only type in key words related to specific disability policies to uncover a wealth of information.

We conclude our review of disability policy with a review of the 1980s, the introduction of the ADA, the 1992 amendments to the VR Act, the Workforce Investment Act (WIA), and, finally, the Ticket to Work/Work Incentive Improvement Act (TWWIIA).

The 1980s

The 1980s were marked by decreased government involvement in education, health, VR, and disabilities. A utilitarian perspective was adopted, in which the agenda was "the greatest good for the greatest number." Ronald Reagan was noted for his infamous speech addressing how he was tired of hearing about the needs of special interest groups; he wanted to support the average American who put in a full day's work for the good of their family. President Reagan did not establish a climate that was supportive of disability-related services, including his failure to support proactive intervention at the beginning of the HIV/AIDS epidemic (Shilts, 2000).

The *Job Training Partnership Act* of 1982 was a cooperative effort between government and employers, which prepared youth and unskilled adults to move into the labor force. The act provided job training to economically disadvantaged individuals and to those in need of special training.

In 1984, the Rehabilitation Act Amendments reauthorized 1973 and 1978 legislation. The *Client Assistance Program* was formally established in 1984, serving as an advocate for consumers of VR services in the state–federal VR system. The National Council on the Handicapped moved from the Department of Education to become an independent agency. Also in 1984, in order to assure that Centers for Independent Living employed people with disabilities, a rule was established that 51% of independent living center employees and board of directors must be people with disabilities.

Two important policy developments occurred in 1986. The *Air Carrier Access Act* (1986) prohibited discrimination against any persons with disabilities, by all air carriers, and provided for enforcement by the Department of Transportation. Additionally, the *Rehabilitation Act Amendments* of that year encouraged maximum employment of persons with disabilities, through the addition of rehabilitation engineering and supported employment programs (services provided to individuals with disabilities who require ongoing support in acquiring and maintaining employment), and promoted independence and integration into the community. The primary goal of supported employment was to establish competitive employment, rather than employment in workshop settings.

The Americans with Disabilities Act of 1990

The ADA provides civil rights protection similar to those provided to other minorities, to individuals with disabilities. The twofold purpose of ADA is to bring persons with disabilities into the economic and social mainstream of American life, and to end discrimination against individuals with disabilities. The ADA accomplishes this by extending the civil rights protection afforded in the Rehabilitation Act of 1973, from only federal and state employment to private sector employment, to public accommodations (e.g., hotels, restaurants), to state and local government services, to transportation, and to the establishment of telecommunication relay services for people who are deaf or hard-of-hearing. A review of the major titles of the ADA is presented in Table 3.2.

The ADA served to fill the gap that resulted from a number of laws that were passed from 1968 through 1988, which only partially addressed the issue of discrimination on the basis of disability (National Council on Disability [NCD], n.d.). Laws that addressed discrimination based on disability included the ABA (1968); Sections 501, 503, and 504 of the Rehabilitation Act (1973); DDA (1975); Air Carrier Access Act (1986); Civil Rights Restoration Act (1987); and the Fair Housing Amendments Act (1988).

The ADA brought new clarity to several disability- and employment-related terms. *Disability*, with respect to an individual, for example, is defined by the ADA as a physical or mental impairment that substantially limits one or more of the major life activities of the individual, or a record of such impairment, or an individual being regarded as having such impairment. Major life activities include functions such as self care, manual skills, walking, seeing, hearing, speaking, breathing, learning, and working. *Functions of a job* are considered essential if the job exists to perform the given function, if there are a limited number of employees at a location who can perform the function, or if the function is highly specialized and requires special

TABLE 3.2 Titles of American with Disabilities Act (ADA) of 1990

Title	Description
Title I	*Employment* requires that an employer provides reasonable accommodation to a qualified individual (able to perform the essential functions of a job) with a disability, unless it would result in undue hardship to the employer or a direct threat to others in the operation of a business (covers employers with 15 or more workers).
Title II	*Public Services*, such as state and local government agencies, services, programs, and activities, may not discriminate against persons with disabilities (extended beyond the 1973 recipients of federal funding requirement). Part I covers public bus systems, including accessible buses or other forms of public transportation, or availability of paratransit systems for those who cannot use fixed route services. Part II covers accessibility to public rail systems.
Title III	*Public Accommodations*, for businesses that are privately owned, must provide equal access to all goods, services, facilities, privileges, advantages, and accommodations of any place of public accommodation (restaurants, hotels, professional offices, pharmacies, grocery stores, shopping centers, private schools, spas, senior centers, rehabilitation clinics, funeral parlors, museums, libraries, parks, day care centers, and other similar establishments). Accessibility changes must be readily achievable and accomplished without much difficulty or expense (usually defined in a court of law). Houses of worship are not required to comply with this title.
Title IV	*Telecommunications*, significant for individuals who are deaf or hard-of-hearing, requires that common-carrier phone companies provide telecommunication relay service that will allow persons with hearing impairments, who use TDDs, to communicate with anyone who has a telephone. Rates for this phone service are the same as for regular calls.
Title V	*Miscellaneous provisions*: Addresses the relationship between the ADA and other state and federal laws (e.g., state and local governments are not immune from legal actions in federal court, concerning violations of the ADA, although this has been hotly debated in court); individuals can bring private actions against those in noncompliance with ADA, and may be awarded court fees as the prevailing party.

expertise or ability. In order to determine whether a specific function is essential or not, one can use employer judgment, job descriptions, job analyses, or other expert opinion. *Reasonable accommodations* can include modifications or adjustments to a job or work environment that enable a qualified applicant with a disability to perform the essential functions of a job, or any other modification or adjustment that allows a person with a disability to enjoy opportunity equal to that of people without disabilities. Environmental modifications or job restructuring are two examples. *Undue hardship* is the consequence of an action that requires significant difficulty or expense for the employer.

Clearly, the ADA presents new challenges for business management in navigating the myriad of ADA-specific terminology and developing case law surrounding the legislation. The provisions of the ADA have resulted in unprecedented opportunities for rehabilitation counselors to provide consultation and technical assistance to employers wishing to remain in compliance with the ADA (Jaet & McMahon, 1999).

Related to the ADA, the *Revenue Reconciliation Act* (1990) provides a 50% tax credit for the first $10,000 of eligible costs for ADA compliance. It also provides a tax deduction of up to $15,000 for removal of physical barriers. Employers and individuals with disabilities continue to litigate over the definitions and accommodations afforded by the ADA (NCD, n.d.), with recent Supreme Court decisions disempowering some aspects of the ADA.

1991 Civil Rights Act

The 1991 Civil Rights Act overturned previous Supreme Court decisions that were adverse to the interests of victims of employment discrimination with respect to gender-, religious-, and disability-based biases. The act provides for potential collection of increased damages, as well as for jury trials. The act also required the EEOC to establish the Technical Assistance Training Institute, which provides educational and outreach activities for victims of job bias. The Glass Ceiling Commission was also established to study barriers to advancement of women and minorities.

1992 Amendments to the Rehabilitation Act

President G. H. W. Bush signed the Rehabilitation Act Amendments into law in 1992. Those amendments addressed a number of important issues in the field of rehabilitation, including increased emphasis on independent living services and an underscoring of employment outcomes for persons with disabilities. Philosophically, the most significant contribution of the Rehabilitation Act Amendments of 1992 was the amplification of the client's participation in the planning and implementation of rehabilitation services. The increased emphasis on the client, in terms of the provision of services, was known as "client-centered planning" and "consumer-driven planning" in various states. The specific 1992 amendments to various titles of the Rehabilitation Act are reviewed in Table 3.3.

Workforce Investment Act of 1998

The WIA of 1998 promotes customer choice, through the development of a consumer-responsive job training and employment system. The WIA is designed to give workers the information and training they need, and to give employers the skilled workers they need. The goals of this new system are to improve the quality of the workforce, reduce welfare dependency, and enhance the productivity and competitiveness of the United States in the world marketplace.

WIA brings together various job training programs that provide assistance to people seeking employment, including people with disabilities. Administrative stakeholders include the federal government (Rehabilitation Services Administration, the Department of Labor, other federal agencies), state governments (state workforce investment boards, governors, and state unified plans), and local governments. Workforce investment boards are established at state and local levels (in some cases, the state boards may serve at the local level as well), and are reflective of the system's partners. Board composition is under the authority of the governors; the majority must be comprised of business representatives in upper-management positions, including chairpersons of the board. A *state unified plan* describes the methods used for coordinating partner programs and activities.

Seven Key Principles

In crafting the new policy, the Department of Labor established seven key principles to guide the new Workforce Investment System:

1. streamlined services (one-stop delivery system);
2. empower individuals (individuals will be empowered to make choices about their training and providers);
3. universal access (all can get core-employment related services in the one-stop system);
4. accountability (funding will be linked to performance);
5. strong roles for local boards and the private sector (business-led boards);
6. flexibility (state and local governments can tailor delivery systems to meet their particular community needs); and
7. youth programs (connect learning with the local labor market).

TABLE 3.3 1992 Amendments to Rehabilitation Act of 1973

Title	Description
Title I	1. Rehabilitation agency bears the burden of proof that individuals cannot benefit from services, and existing records can be used to determine eligibility. 2. Increased consumer control over Individual Written Rehabilitation Plans (IWRP: statement of the consumer, describing their involvement in the IWRP development; now the IPE). 3. Values incorporated throughout that reflect equal opportunity, full inclusion and integration, independent living perspective, and promotion of economic and self-sufficiency 4. Emphasize service to minorities, unserved, and underserved populations 5. Input from Client Assistance Project solicited. 6. Transitional services aspire to be smooth from secondary school to work. 7. Increase the use of technology and the use of worksite assessments. 8. State–federal programs are to work more closely with Centers for Independent Living (CILs). 9. The rehabilitation advisory council for each state is to include a majority of persons with disabilities. 10. Scope of services provided include personal assistant services, transition services, and supported employment.
Title II	1. Research via National Institute on Disability and Rehabilitation Research, establishment of relevant research and training centers (e.g., rehabilitation engineering research centers). 2. Establishes a rehabilitation research advisory council.
Title III	1. Establishes training and demonstration projects. 2. Construction authority is replaced with increased personnel training in existing facilities (career advancement, technical expertise, in-service training). 3. Supported employment projects (use of natural supports, serve "low functioning" individuals.
Title IV	Encouraged an increase in the number of people with disabilities to the membership of the National Council on Disability (increase to a majority).
Title V	1. Applied the standards of ADA to sections 501, 503, and 504 of the 1973 act. 2. Established an Access Board within the Architectural and Transportation Barriers Compliance Board, ATBCB, to access electronic media and data.
Title VI	Continued to increase employment opportunities for persons with disabilities through Projects With Industry, establishing Business Advisory Councils, which include members with disabilities, and encouraging the use of supported employment.
Title VII	1. Consumer-controlled CILs. 2. Community-based and cross-disability services. 3. Promote nonresidential housing. 4. Limit CILs to private, not-for-profit organizations. 5. CILs based in local communities, run by individuals with disabilities. 6. Establishment of state-wide independent living councils.
Title VIII	Established special demonstration training projects.

The act itself is organized into five titles, as outlined in Table 3.4.

One-Stop Partners

A one-stop delivery system enables customers (job seekers and employers) to easily access information and a wide array of services for multiple training and employment programs. One-stop partners participate (with approval of local boards) in local operation of the system. The partners provide the core services through the system. The partners required to be involved in the system include:

1. WIA Title I entities: adult, youth, dislocated worker, Native American programs, Job Corps, and migrant worker programs;
2. employment services (established under the Wagner-Peyser Act);
3. Senior Community Service Employment (Title V, Older Americans Act);
4. state unemployment compensation programs;
5. programs under Title I of the Rehabilitation Act;
6. welfare-to-work programs;
7. HUD employment and training activities;
8. Community Services Block Grant employment training activities;
9. adult education and literacy activities;
10. postsecondary vocational education activities (Perkins Act);
11. Trade Adjustment Assistance and NAFTA assistance activities;
12. local veterans employment representatives and Disabled Veterans Outreach programs; and
13. other partners that can be named by the governor.

TABLE 3.4 Workforce Investment Act (WIA) of 1998

Title	Description
Title I	Authorizes new workforce investment systems, establishes state and local workforce investment boards, and a one-stop delivery system
Title II	Adult education and literacy programs
Title III	Amends the Wagner-Peyser Act to include employment service activities as part of the one-stop delivery system
Title IV	Reauthorizes the Rehabilitation Act and links vocational rehabilitation to the workforce investment systems
Title V	State unified plans, incentive grants, transition from the Job Training Partnership Act.

Memorandum of Understanding

A Memorandum of Understanding links all one-stop partners. It is a negotiated document that outlines the partners' agreement to work together within the system. Funding within the one-stop system comes from several sources under WIA. There are limits on spending funds, and performance accountability may affect the amount of funds a state or local areas receives.

The Pyramid of Services

The one-stop service provision is conceptualized as a pyramid of services: the base or core services; the middle or intensive services; and the top or training services. The core services have no eligibility requirements, and many of these services may be self-service: such basic labor exchange services as labor market information for job seekers/employers, information, initial assessment for services, follow-up, outreach or intake, preliminary assessment of skills and support service needs, welfare-to-work or financial aid information, workplace counseling for 12 months, or help with searching for a job or placement.

Intensive services may include comprehensive or specialized assessment, development of an individual employment plan (similar to Individualized Plan for Employment [IPE] of the state–federal system: identify employment goal and objectives, and describe intensive services needed to achieve the goal), counseling/career planning, case management, or short-term prevocational services.

Special services may include training, provided the consumer demonstrates potential for success and is unable to gain other financial means (such as a Pell grant, etc.). Priority is given to recipients of public assistance and to low-income adults, if funds are limited. Individual Training Accounts empower customers to choose their service providers.

1998 Amendments to the Rehabilitation Act

The Rehabilitation Act was integrated into WIA as Title IV of the act, but the state–federal system maintained its autonomy from the one-stop system. In addition to restating some of the priorities noted in prior amendments to the Rehabilitation Act, new or enhanced emphases were proposed, including outreach to underrepresented groups (e.g., racial minorities), increased role for rehabilitation counselors in transition planning from school to work (as integrated in the Individual Education Plan [IEP] required by Pub. L. No.

94-142), increased client control over the IPE (formerly the Individual Written Rehabilitation Plan), better networking between service providers, and service provision by qualified personnel (qualified providers of VR counseling services were defined as professionals able to obtain the Certified Rehabilitation Counselor credential).

1999 Ticket-to-Work/Work Incentive Improvement Act (TWWIIA)

The following overview of the TWWIIA was previously presented by Peterson and Growick (2000). A $500 million effort, and possibly the most important piece of disability legislation since the passage of the ADA of 1990, WIIA has the potential to increase the employability of America's disability community (an estimated 8 million people), in the same way that the ADA has increased their participation and accessibility to public activities. The WIIA provides critical first steps toward the removal of barriers to work for Social Security beneficiaries and toward the ability to bring financial solvency to the SSA trust fund. The WIIA provides an opportunity for beneficiaries to receive return-to-work services and not lose their indemnity and health care benefits entirely. The language of the ADA departed historically from prior disability legislation, in that it was based in a civil rights context, rather than in an entitlement context. The innovation of the WIIA is that it attempts to bridge the two contexts, providing one method of achieving the ultimate purpose of the ADA by combining return-to-work services with sustaining disability benefits.

Cost Benefits of WIIA

The cost of the new program is estimated to be recouped if 70,000 people leave the SSA disability roles and return to work, and, if 210,000 do so (only 10% of the number of people in the disability community who are estimated to be willing to avail themselves of this new opportunity according), the savings would reach $1 billion annually in disability payments. The best-case scenario could ideally yield savings in excess of $10 billion per year to the SSA disability trust fund.

To assist in the implementation of WIIA, the act calls for establishing a Work Incentives Advisory Panel composed of 12 members of different political and constituent backgrounds, which has the responsibility of helping the SSA to devise the rules and regulations for the program. Overall, different parts of the legislation (extension of health care benefits, availability of return-to-work services, etc.) have different phase-in dates. The act in its entirety was to be phased in over a 5-year period from the date of its passage.

The three major provisions of the WIIA that are important to rehabilitation counselors and their consumers are (1) expanded health care coverage, (2) new and improved employment services, and (3) the elimination of certain disincentives to return to work.

Expanded Availability of Health Care Services. WIIA provides the opportunity for SSA beneficiaries to retain their health care when they return to work. For SSI beneficiaries who receive Medicaid, the WIIA removes limits on a buy-in option for workers with disabilities; states will now be allowed to remove the upper income limit, which was 250% of the established poverty level for income (about $21,000 per year). This provision allows individuals to buy into Medicaid when their jobs pay more than low wages, but do not give them the necessary level of health care. The WIIA also gives the states the option to allow people to retain Medicaid when their medical condition improves secondary to medical coverage. Finally, the WIIA also provides $150 million, over the course of 5 years, to states (e.g., state-administered health care infrastructure grantees), to help them administer this new benefit.

For SSDI recipients who receive Medicare, under previous rules, they could maintain medical benefits, through Medicare Parts A and B, for 3½ years postemployment, at the rate of $350 per month. Under the WIIA, people with disabilities who return to work will be able to extend Medicare Part A for an additional 4½ years (reducing the aforementioned cost to about $46 per month during 8 years of gainful employment). Additionally, prescription drug assistance will be available nationwide, even in states that do not elect the Medicaid options.

A $250 million demonstration project is included in the law, which will support the early intervention of medical treatment for those individuals who are working and whose medical condition has not deteriorated enough to prevent employment. Individuals with muscular dystrophy, Parkinson's disease, AIDS, or diabetes can obtain Medicaid coverage, in order to prevent further deterioration and loss of employment.

New and Improved Return-to-Work Services. The portion of WIIA enhances the employment opportunities of SSI and SSDI recipients, by allowing beneficiaries to obtain VR and employment services from their choice of participating public or private service providers. In addition to the state–federal system of VR (historically, the sole provider of services), beneficiaries will be able to select from a registry of private providers, forming an employment network, and responsibility will be to help the beneficiaries return to work. If a beneficiary becomes gainfully employed, providers can be paid a portion of the annual savings to the trust fund, for up to 5 years after employment. Such remuneration will encourage providers to maintain contact with consumers through follow-along services and to subsequently reduce recidivism.

To encourage the utilization of these new services, work-incentives outreach programs have been established to help workers with disabilities to obtain employment services and support. It is hoped that the new service delivery paradigm will result in many more people receiving rehabilitation and training services. To this end, $23 million annually, over 5 years, was appropriated to help consumers understand the new benefits through Work Incentive Planning Assistance Outreach grants.

Elimination of Certain Work Disincentives. The single greatest disincentive to returning to work for individuals with disabilities is the sudden and complete loss of benefits. For people with disabilities who achieve gainful employment, disability cash benefits will be phased out, based upon income. Rather than a sudden cut-off of benefits, a sliding scale will be established, in which benefits would be reduced by $1 for every $2 earned (removing the "cash cliff" disincentive in the SSDI program). This impediment was one of the often-cited disincentives to employment for people with disabilities. Additionally, obtaining employment by beneficiaries will now not trigger a disability review for termination. It simply prohibits the SSA from using work activity as a basis for disability review, as long as the individual has been receiving benefits for at least 24 months. Finally, if a SSA beneficiary does have their benefits terminated for employment reasons, they can have themselves reinstated within a 5-year period from the date of termination, without a judicial review by SSA.

FUTURE POLICY DEVELOPMENT

The landscape of disability policy consists of bills proposing new legislation, policies waiting to be codified, and case law that reflects on future applications of policy. Keeping up with disability policy developments can be overwhelming to the new rehabilitation counseling professional, as well as for the seasoned professional. We can all play a part in lobbying our government in support of new bills, in drafting the rules and regulations that will govern implementation of new policies, and in proposing amendments based upon new developments. We should all make it our responsibility to know who our representatives to Congress are, how to contact them, and what important issues are coming to the floor for discussion. Our professional associations, and the Internet, can serve us well in keeping abreast of contemporary disability policy developments.

CHAPTER 4

History and Systems: Canada

Rebecca Rudman

REHABILITATION PHILOSOPHY IN CANADA

The United Nations' International Year of Disabled Persons (1991) gave impetus and momentum to Canadian rehabilitation systems and disability policy approaches. Canadian stakeholders, representing diverse perspectives, often cite that year as a key turning point in Canadian policies and systems. As part of the United Nations initiative, the World Health Organization developed key terms. Although specific terminology that establishes eligibility criteria for social programs varies from program to program, the World Health Organization's definitions form the basis for social policy and discussions of disablement in Canada (Federal/Provincial, 1997; McKenna, 1998; Torjman, 2001). McKenna (1998) summarizes these terms from the United Nations:

- Impairment: Any loss or abnormality of psychological, physiological, or anatomical structure or function.
- Disability: Any restriction or lack (resulting from an impairment) of ability to perform an activity in the manner or within the range considered normal for a human being.
- Handicap: A disadvantage for a given individual, resulting from an impairment or disability, that limits or prevents the fulfillment of a role that is normal, depending on age, sex, social and cultural factors, for that individual. (p. 163)

Although some critics have argued that these definitions focus on the individual exclusively and do not provide enough focus on social conditions (Crichton & Jongbloed, 1998), these terms have been utilized in emphasizing a philosophical approach consistent with valuing individuals and promoting socio-political models.

Current Canadian approaches to disability policy and the provision of rehabilitation services involve guided socio-political models of participation that focus on the full citizenship and participation of individuals with disabilities. This is in contrast to earlier biomedical models that focused on an individual's deficits and corrective measures, rather than on locus of responsibility within society (McKenna, 1998; Titchkosky, 2001; Torjman, 2001). These values of participation and social responsibility are similarly found in a variety of traditions and approaches to rehabilitation, such as rehabilitation counseling (Canadian Association of Rehabilitation Professionals [CARP], 1999; Commission on Rehabilitation Counseling Certification [CRCC], 1990; Leahy, Chan, & Magrega, 1997), community rehabilitation (Browne et al., 1994), independent living (Boschen & Krane, 1992; Hutchinson, Dunn, Lord, & Pedlar, 1996), consumer advocacy group approaches (Holleman, 1991; Torjman, 2001; Walker, Johnson, Sanders, & Nikias, 1998), and disability studies approaches (CARP, 1999; CRCC, 1990; Leahy et al., 1997).

Strong similarities exist between the overall philosophy of rehabilitation in Canada and those described in chapter 1. Additional similarities and differences in rehabilitation approaches, based on political, medical, and legal systems, are further explored throughout the remainder of this chapter.

POLITICAL, MEDICAL, LEGAL, AND SOCIAL SYSTEMS

Canada's political structure, and consequently its medical, legal, and social policy systems, differ significantly from those in the United States. The Canadian political system is comprised of a federal government, 10 provincial governments, and 3 territorial governments. The structure and the relationship between the federal and provincial governments and their jurisdictions have played a key role in the development of disability-related legislation and policy. These relationships are most evident in legislation establishing the division of responsibilities between federal and provincial governments, legislation establishing national health care, and legislation governing civil rights, and, finally, disability policy. These areas of legislation and policy create the political, medical, and legal contexts in which rehabilitation services are delivered in Canada, as well as the rights and services that are available to individuals with disabilities.

Division of Responsibilities: Federal and Provincial Governments

The structure of the Canadian government and jurisdictional authority was established in the British North America Act of 1867, then further delineated in the Constitution Act in 1982 (Banting, 1987; Choudry, 2000; Crichton & Jongbloed, 1998; Jones, 1994; Torjman, 2001). The British North America Act gave responsibility to the federal government for "peace, order, and the good government of the country." The federal government's responsibility includes areas that affect the well-being of the entire nation, such as the armed forces, international trade, and communications (Banting, 1987; Choudry, 2000; Torjman, 2001). Responsibility for health and welfare issues were granted to the provinces (Choudry, 2000; Torjman, 2001). The act also allows the federal government to provide funding in areas in which it does not have specific authority or responsibility (Torjman, 2001).

A critical pair of decisions by the Supreme Court of Canada and the Privy Council in 1938 established the constitutional basis on which Canada's national health system and social policy systems rest. The Court ruled that jurisdiction over unemployment insurance rests with the provinces. Choudry (2000) explains the implication of the rulings for health and social programs:

> [The ruling] contained broader language that suggests publicly operated insurance schemes which seek to safeguard persons against the risk of illness or poverty lie outside the federal jurisdiction. As a consequence, the conventional wisdom is that direct federal regulation of social policy, including health insurance, is unconstitutional. However, these decisions also stated that it would be entirely constitutional for the federal government to spend monies in the areas of provincial jurisdiction by making transfer payments to provinces, and by attaching conditions to those funds. (pp. 33–34)

The rulings set the stage for the structure for the future of national health care and social policy initiatives in Canada.

National Health Care

Medicare was introduced in 1966, following the recommendation of the 1964 Royal Commission on Health Services. The medicare program created a national system of health care that was actually a collection of provincial health care systems. The medicare program established a 50–50 cost-sharing between the federal government and the provincial governments, if they established insurance programs that adhered to five principles: "universality of eligibility, comprehensiveness of coverage, portability between provinces, accessibility achieved by prepayment of fees through taxation, and public administration on a non-profit basis" (Dickinson & Bolari, 2002, p. 23). The focus of the original medicare program was on funding physician-provided services, either in or out of the hospital. The federal government had no control over the program costs, because they were based on the amount of provincial expenditures. Provinces were dissatisfied with the arrangement, because, when they implemented cost-saving measures, they lost federal funding (Dickinson & Bolari, 2002).

The medicare program was revised with the introduction of the Federal–Provincial Arrangements and Established Programs Financing Act. This legislation increased incentives for community-based care, reduced the federal government's share of program costs to approximately 25%, unlinked federal costs from provincial expenditures, and limited federal funding to the growth of the gross national product. Reforms brought about by this legislation resulted in higher costs, in the form of user fees to individuals, government cost-cutting that resulted in longer waiting lists, mobilization of medical professionals seeking privatization, and crowded emergency waiting rooms (Dickinson & Bolari, 2002).

In 1984, both the provinces and the federal government were seeking to recommit themselves to the principles of coverage outlined in the original medicare system. The Canada Health Act was created to solidify these commitments. In addition, that act explicitly banned user fees, significantly increased federal transfer payments to provinces for funding health care, and allowed for the withholding of funds if the conditions were not followed (Choudry, 2000; Dickinson & Bolari, 2002; Himmelstein & Woolhandler, 1998; Torjman, 2001). The principles outlined in the original medicare program, then revitalized in the Canada Health Act, not only form the basis of health care service delivery in Canada, but they have influenced other social and disability policies. In addition, elements of these principles are embedded within Canadian social and disability policy.

Civil Rights Legislation

The United Nations International Year of Disabled Persons was cited earlier in this chapter as a critical point in Canadian disability policy and law. One of the key reasons is the focus it created on disability rights and issues at a critical point in Canadian history. A Special Committee of the Disabled and Handicapped was formed by the House of Commons to advise Parliament on policy issues (Boschen & Krane, 1992; Crichton & Jongbloed, 1998;

Jones, 1994). This committee brought together diverse organizations that had been working on behalf of individuals with disabilities. Many of these groups had focused solely on providing support to individuals with one disabling condition and had never met collectively (Crichton & Jongbloed, 1998). The group produced a report entitled *Obstacles*, which identified key disability policy objectives for persons with disabilities: adequate income, equal access to public buildings, equal access to employment, housing, transportation, communication, information, and community supports to decrease the need for institutionalization (Crichton & Jongbloed, 1998). These discussions, and the resulting report, played a key role in the inclusion of persons with disabilities in the Charter of Rights and Freedoms (Boschen & Krane, 1992; Crichton & Jongbloed, 1998; Torjman, 2001).

Charter of Rights and Freedoms

The Constitution Act in 1982 supplemented the British North America Act from 1867. The Constitution Act introduced a Charter of Rights and Freedoms, which outlines basic rights for all Canadians. Together with the British North America Act, it forms the supreme law of the land. All jurisdictions must respect and comply with the Charter (Torjman, 2001).

The Charter's basic rights for all Canadians include democratic, mobility, legal, equality, and minority language education rights (Campbell, 2001; Crichton & Jongbloed, 1998; McKenna, 1998; Torjmann, 2001). The most important of these, for persons with disabilities, are mobility rights and equality rights (Crichton & Jongbloed, 1998; Torjman, 2001).

The equality rights are outlined in subsection 15 of the Charter, which states:

> Every individual is equal before and under the law and has the right to equal protection and equal benefit of the law without discrimination and, in particular, without discrimination based on race, national or ethnic origin, colour, religion, sex, age, or physical or mental disability. (Crichton & Jongbloed, 1998, p. 183; Torjman, 2001, p. 155)

The equality rights form the basis for additional federal and provincial legislation protecting and promoting the equality of individuals with disabilities (Crichton & Jongbloed, 1998; Torjman, 2001). In addition, the equality rights establish and justify a federal role in disability policy, when, previously, it was considered primarily a provincial responsibility, because of the jurisdictional authority granted in the British North America Act (Torjman, 2001).

Torjman (2001) also argues that the mobility provisions of the Charter embed the responsibility of the federal government to ensure that all Canadians are treated broadly similarly, regardless of language or residence. Torjman (2001) cites Section 36 of the Charter in describing this right "to provide essential public services of reasonable quality to all Canadians" (p. 156).

The Charter of Rights and Freedoms forms the basis for advancing the citizenship agenda of equal participation in all aspects of Canadian society. Disability groups have recognized that focusing only on advancing health and social spending programs would not allow individuals with disabilities to access equal opportunities to employment, education, transportation, and communications. The citizenship agenda includes a focus on accessing these opportunities, as well as disability-related supports and services (Torjman, 2001). The Charter's primary focus is on regulating government's relation to individuals.

Human Rights Legislation

Private relations between individuals are regulated by a system of provincial human rights legislation or codes (Campbell, 2001). Each province has its own human rights code, designed to protect the rights and freedoms of individuals who are members of disadvantaged groups. This includes individuals with disabilities. The first human rights code was created in 1962 in Ontario (Campbell, 2001). Definitions of disability and the specific rights afforded to individuals, other than those identified in the Charter, vary from province to province. One of the central themes of provincial human rights codes, relating to individuals with disabilities, is the duty to accommodate individuals with disabilities (McKenna, 1998).

Human rights codes have been criticized for failing to create a consistent system of protection for individuals. Enforcement of human rights legislation is dependent upon a complaints-based system, in which individuals must bring a complaint to a human rights tribunal, if they feel their rights have been violated. This results in a legal patchwork of case law that does not create a strong system of legal protections (McKenna, 1998).

Federally, legislation has also been created to promote human rights. The federal Employment Equity Act is one such example. The goals of the act are to increase the participation of disadvantaged groups in the labor force. Similar to the provincial human rights codes, the employment equity legislation has been criticized for not incorporating stronger enforcement mechanisms (McKenna, 1998). Revisions have recently been made to the act, but it is too soon to determine if the revisions will be effective (Torjman, 2001).

Social and Disability Policy Frameworks and Programs

Social and disability policy have a structure similar to health care programs in Canada. Responsibility for social programs is a provincial responsibility. However, some programs have been created through federal–provincial agreements and payment systems.

Policy Frameworks

Two major policy frameworks have been created to develop the process and content for federal agreements. The first of these, the *Social Union*, was formed by provincial premiers in response to unilateral cuts to social programs by the federal government. The federal government had packaged together funding for social, health, and education programs into block funding, while providing more flexibility to provinces in how to spend those funds. In addition, it reduced overall federal spending. In response to these unilateral changes, premiers called for a collaborative strategy. The key features of the *Social Union* agreement are that it outlines the principles and processes by which the federal government and provinces will work together collaboratively on substantive issues affecting social policy. One of the concerns raised by disability groups is that, in taking a more collaborative role, the federal government may water down disability-related issues and concerns (Choudry, 2000; Torjman, 2001).

The second major policy framework is *In Unison: A Canadian Approach to Disability Issues*. This document is a vision paper that outlines how full citizenship can be achieved for individuals with disabilities. It outlines three key elements, or building blocks, of proposed disability policy: disability support, employment, and income. The vision commits to protection of mobility rights, by proposing an uncoupling of disability supports from income and employment programs. The document argues that disability supports should be attached to the individual and contain portability to move with the individual across settings (Torjman, 2001; Federal/Provincial, 1997).

Social and Disability Programs

A myriad of social and disability programs exist to provide income, disability supports, and employment assistance for individuals with disabilities. The responsibility for these programs is split primarily between the federal government, which has responsibility for income programs, and the provincial governments, which have responsibility for welfare, education, health, and social programs.

Federal income programs include the Canada Pension Plan (and its sister program, the Quebec Pension Plan) and Employment Insurance. The Canada Pension Plan provides income support to individuals who have met criteria for having fulfilled a certain number of years in the workforce and payments into the system. To qualify for this program, individuals must demonstrate that they are totally and permanently disabled (Crichton & Jongbloed, 1998; Torjman, 2001). The Canada Pension Plan developed some pilot programs, to remove economic disincentives to work and to authorize the provision of vocational rehabilitation (VR) services. These programs are currently being reviewed (Crichton & Jongbloed, 1998; Torjman, 2001). Employment Insurance is a federal program that provides benefits on a short-term basis for interruptions in work caused by unemployment, illness, or disability (Crichton & Jongbloed, 1998; Torjman, 2001). The federal government also provides indirect income support, through a system of tax credits for disability-related expenses (Torjman, 2001).

In addition to income programs, the federal government also has established binational agreements with First Nations to deliver funds for local Bands to create their own employment programs. A separate health system also exists for some First Nations groups (Torjman, 2001).

In the area of employment, the federal and provincial governments have a shared responsibility. The Employment Assistance for People with Disabilities (EAPD) framework agreement provides funding for employment supports and programs geared toward enhancing the employability of individuals with disabilities. These programs are funded, in part, on a federal basis, and are implemented at a local level. Some provincial programs include employment counseling, but others do not (Torjman, 2001). This program replaces the former Vocational Rehabilitation of Disabled Persons Act (VRDP), which established VR programs within provincial governments, on a cost-share basis. Since the move from VRDP to EAPD, most provincial governments have devolved public rehabilitation services into service delivery agreements with private providers and nongovernmental organizations (Torjman, 2001; Walter et al., 1998).

The remainder of social and disability-related programs that individuals with disabilities can access fall within provincial responsibility. These systems include workers' compensation systems, income assistance through welfare, and disability-related supports, such as home care, technical aids and equipment, and other health programs. These programs vary from province to province (Torjman, 2001).

In contrast to service delivery systems in the United States, the federal programs, and most of the provincial programs, do not prescribe what constitutes a qualified provider of rehabilitation services. In addition, most of the focus is on the provision of the income or disability support component, rather than on its delivery within a rehabilitation counseling framework. Few programs incorporate rehabilitation counseling or VR as a specific program component. Despite the gaps in defining qualified providers or incorporation of rehabilitation services as an entitlement, many systems utilize the expertise of rehabilitation counselors and other providers.

REHABILITATION SERVICE SETTINGS

Many disability-related programs and benefits are accessed through a variety of rehabilitation service settings. These settings include workers' compensation systems, private insurance systems, private rehabilitation centers, nongovernmental organizations, and independent living resource centers.

Workers' compensation systems in Canada were responsible for some of the earliest VR programs in the early 1900s. These systems utilize rehabilitation counseling and case management services, to effectively manage the return-to-work process for workers sustaining workplace injuries (Crichton & Jongbloed, 1998).

Private insurance systems include both auto insurers and long-term disability insurers. Automobile insurers require the provision of rehabilitation services as part of return to quality of life goals for individuals with disabilities. Long-term disability insurers provide rehabilitation services on a voluntary basis, to promote the goal of facilitating a faster return to employment. Private insurers may provide these services through in-house personnel or through contracting private, for-profit rehabilitation companies to provide these services (Crichton & Jongbloed, 1998; Steeves & Smithies, 1998).

Nongovernmental organizations, such as community-based groups, disability organizations, and other organizations, provide rehabilitation services funded by fundraising efforts or through contracts and service agreements with federal and/or provincial governments. The type of services provided through these organizations ranges from broad, comprehensive and holistic services to more project-focused services designed to achieve specific objectives (Crichton & Jongbloed, 1998; Holleman, 1991; Walker et al., 1998).

Another type of setting in which rehabilitation services are provided is through the Independent Living Resource Centres (ILRC). In contrast to other settings, ILRCs utilize a philosophy based on a self-help philosophy that believes individuals with disabilities can best identify their own needs and can have productive lives without the assistance of rehabilitation professionals.

Approaches used by ILRCs are similar to those in the Unites States: self-help, empowerment, advocacy, and the removal of environmental, social, and economic barriers (Boschen & Krane, 1992; Hutchinson, Dunn, Lord, & Pedlar, 1996).

PROVIDERS OF REHABILITATION SERVICES

Although federal legislation in Canada does not define the role and qualifications of rehabilitation service providers, a number of voluntary credentialing programs exist, and some services are provided by other professionals, including the Canadian Certified Rehabilitation Counsellor (CCRC), Certified Vocational Evaluator (CVE), Canadian Certified Counsellor, and the Registered Rehabilitation Professional. Because the field of rehabilitation is diverse within Canada, rehabilitation counseling services are also provided by individuals from allied health fields and psychology, as well as from other backgrounds (Adair, Paivo, & Ritchie, 1996; Leahy et al., 1997).

Canadian Certified Rehabilitation Counsellors

The most relevant of these programs to this text is the CCRC designation. CCRCs and Certified Rehabilitation Counselors (CRCs) share a common core and body of knowledge, including the same scope of practice statement (CRCC, 1990; Leahy et al., 1997). The move toward certification began in the 1980s, when consumers requested that the Accredited Rehabilitation Worker designation, offered through the CARP, move toward a model that provides more accountability to consumers, with respect to the qualifications of the individuals providing services (Leahy et al., 1997). The CARP approached the CRCC, requesting that a certification process be developed for Canada (CRCC, 1990; Leahy et al., 1997; Leahy & Holt, 1993).

A certification process, based on competencies defined in the U.S. certification process, was researched, to determine its applicability to the Canadian context. With the signing of a joint proclamation by CARP and CRCC, the certification process began in 1990 (CRCC, 1990; Leahy et al., 1997). The role and functions of CCRCs were subsequently validated by Leahy et al. (1997), in a replication of the role-and-function studies in Canada.

The role-and-function study confirmed that the two countries shared a common core of knowledge, but the training needs and relative importance of each knowledge domain area were different. The items rated highest in Canada were ethical standards, case management, planning for rehabilitation services, vocational implications of disabilities, medical aspects of disability, and functional capacities of individuals with disabilities. Leahy et al. (1997) noted these were similar to the areas rated by the U.S. counselors, with the exception of group counseling, family counseling, and school-to-work transition.

The standards required to obtain the CCRC include evidencing educational and work experience. These criteria were developed to reflect the Canadian educational system and include a minimum of a bachelor's degree with substantial work experience, ranging to a master's or doctoral degree with less work experience (CRCC, 1990). In addition to meeting the education and work experience criteria, individuals must pass a certification exam that is based on validated knowledge domains of the profession (CRCC, 1990; Leahy et al., 1997; Leahy & Holt, 1993). To maintain certification, individuals must adhere to the CRCC Code of Ethics and complete continuing education as part of a recertification program (CRCC, 1990; Leahy & Holt, 1993).

Certified Vocational Evaluator

For rehabilitation counselors wishing to obtain further specialization, or for rehabilitation professionals wishing to focus in the area of vocational evaluation, the CVE certification is available. The CVE can be obtained by evidencing a minimum of a bachelor's level education and work experience in vocational evaluation and achieving a passing score on a certification examination. The credential includes adherence to a code of ethics and a recertification program that involves obtaining continuing education as part of the process (Commission on Certification of Work Adjustment and Vocational Evaluation Specialists, 1999).

Canadian Certified Counsellors

Another related credential that can be obtained by providers of rehabilitation services is the designation of Canadian Certified Counsellor. This designation was introduced in 1987 by the Canadian Counselling Association, formerly the Canadian Guidance and Counselling Association. The certification is a voluntary certification for individuals who wish to identify themselves as a counselor who has been prepared at the master's degree level and who can evidence coursework to support the broad scope of practice. This credential contains a continuing education component and adherence to a code of ethics (Canadian Counselling Association, 2001; Handelsman & Uhlemann, 1998). The certification program does not require an examination.

Registered Rehabilitation Professionals

The CARP offers the designation of Registered Rehabilitation Professional, for individuals wishing to denote their area of interest and experience in the rehabilitation field, broadly defined. Work experience can be obtained through working with individuals from any "disadvantaged population." This designation can be obtained by evidencing completion of educational criteria, including a bachelor's degree, and providing references. The registration provides for a continuing education process and an adherence to a code of ethics (CARP, 2000). The designation does not require an examination.

SUMMARY

The Canadian perspective on rehabilitation and disability presents an interesting point of comparison for the U.S. system. The profession of rehabilitation counseling within Canada shares a common scope of practice, theoretical foundation, and roles and functions validated through empirical evidence. The Canadian system, however, presents a different context in which these services are provided. Some of the primary differences include the relational context of federal–provincial agreements and collaborations, a differing legislative history, and a differing perspective on the provision of health and social services.

CHAPTER 5

Policy and Law

Marvin D. Kuehn

The practice of rehabilitation counseling has been influenced by numerous professionalism issues, rehabilitation agency priorities, federal legislation, and federal program initiatives. The priorities and mandates of federal disability legislation, and the implementation policies that have been established, have resulted in an implicit, yet significant impact on the professional practice of rehabilitation counseling.

Numerous articles discussing the role and functions (practice) of rehabilitation counselors in various work settings verify the diversity and uniqueness of rehabilitation counseling practice (Kuehn, 1991; Leahy, Szymanski, & Linkowski, 1993; Parker & Syzmanski, 1998; Rubin & Roessler, 2001; Smart, 2001). These articles frequently identify new skill and knowledge competencies or expanding responsibilities for counselors, and generally reflect the functions that counselors perform and the employment settings in which they work. This chapter, however, focuses on the general factors that influence rehabilitation counseling practice, which are related to agency priorities and policies, the problems in defining the term *disability*, professionalization issues, mandated legislation versus roles and functions per se, and challenges for rehabilitation counseling practice in the future.

It is important to understand how changing legislative priorities and political issues have determined the various parameters that impact the scope of rehabilitation services, employment settings, populations to be served, advocacy efforts, and intervention strategies to be utilized. Further, influences on professional practice must be examined from the perspective of the events and decisions that have occurred over time, that is, a series of transitional factors involving change, rather than discrete priorities or laws that suggest simple directions and parameters for rehabilitation counseling practice.

Earlier chapters reviewed the history and philosophies that have formed the foundation of the profession of rehabilitation counseling; however, some important historical influences and service delivery priorities need to be revisited briefly, to understand the issues and limitations that policies and laws have created for service provision. Evidence of these influences on rehabilitation counseling practice can be seen most clearly in the differing interpretations of the term *disability*, the types and purposes of different government agencies and programs, and the emphases identified in federal legislation (E. Berkowitz, 1992; Sales, 2002; Scotch, 2000). These factors have all had an indirect and implied impact on rehabilitation counseling practice, although the broad scope and intent of both public and not-for-profit vocational rehabilitation (VR) services have been clearly articulated and addressed in the professional literature.

IMPLICATIONS OF DISABILITY DEFINITIONS

Evaluating rehabilitation counseling practice and the parameters that have influenced service goals is challenging, because of the inability of professionals, credentialing organizations, and persons with disabilities themselves to agree upon a set of operational concepts for defining the scope of professional practice and rehabilitation counseling programs.

A substantial roadblock to more effective rehabilitation counseling practice lies in the fact that *disability* has different meanings, depending upon the eligibility requirements or purposes of programs. This definition problem continues to influence professional practice and delays the articulation of a strong, rational, national disability policy.

Defining disability is difficult, because it is a complicated multidimensional concept. Attempts have been made to define disability with simple statements, theoretical models, classification schemes, and even through different forms of measurement (Altman, 2001). Identifying the variety of definitions, the implications of each, and understanding the strengths and weaknesses of the meaning of terms used, are crucial to understanding the applications and significance that may be suggested in policy and law.

Lacking a clear understanding of the meaning of disability, the result has often been conflict, contradiction, and confusion. The lack of consistency is most dramatic when a person is defined as disabled in one context and not in another. An individual may receive therapies for a serious impairment, but does not qualify for certain disability-related benefits provided by their employer or by the government. Recognizing the context of the application of the term *disability* is critical and assumes different parameters: Medical or research projects, service eligibility determination, or benefits evaluation are examples of situations in which context and definition must be clearly understood (Altman, 2001).

Disability, if a medical model is used to characterize disability policy, is defined as a chronic pathology or impairment associated with an incapacity to perform physical functions or activities of daily living. The politics implied in this medical model definition will focus on securing resources for services or for benefits, and policy and law will be influenced. Nonmedical models of disability are usually associated with different issues and dynamics. A social model of disability conceptualizes disability as a social construction that is the result of interaction between physical or mental impairment and the social environment (Barnartt, Schriner, & Scotch, 2001).

To illustrate the confusion, Moore and Feist-Price (1999) identified three definitions of disability, which have come from medical, economic, and sociopolitical perspectives. The medical perspective emphasizes functional limitations associated with the disability. The economic perspective suggests that an analysis of disability impact should be based on a limitation of the amount of work an individual can perform. The sociopolitical paradigm promotes the concept that people with disabilities are not labeled as deviant because of their disability, but because of those around them, who perceive them as different. Recently, disability has been perceived as a consequence of the barriers one encounters in the environment and in peoples' attitudes. Since passage of the Rehabilitation Act of 1973, promoters of a coherent disability policy have attempted to transcend the limitations of the definitions of disability by focusing on the civil or human rights of people with disabilities (Bruyere, 2001).

Policy definitions of disability, even though general and unique to individual programs, are also very important, because they often have the impact of law. Legal and governmental definitions tend to be formal and specific, depending on legislative, regulatory, or judicial interpretation. These expanded or restricted definitions add to the complexity of the issues in service delivery. The definition of disability may be based on only one perspective and can create frustration and misunderstanding, as agencies attempt to determine whether a person or a population is disabled (Kuehn, Crystal, & Ursprung,

1988; Smart, 2001). To qualify for payments such as workers' compensation, Social Security Disability Insurance (SSDI), and Supplemental Security Income, an individual's disabling condition must meet certain medical, psychological, or vocational criteria. Laws are made by elected officials who are influenced by lobbyists and the changing public mood; judges who respond to evidence presented by health and social experts, advocates, and the personal condition of the individual, may not interpret these laws in accord with the intent of lawmakers (Hahn, 1993).

Individuals entering the rehabilitation field to become service providers must learn the differences and implications of the definitions of disability used in their respective work settings. In the worker's compensation program and in the courts, *disability* means "the damages that one person collects from another as a result of an insult or injury." In the SSDI program, *disability* refers to "a condition that links ill health and unemployment." In addition, policy analysts have spent a great deal of time puzzling over the distinctions among such terms as *functional limitations, impairment, disability,* and *handicap.* Despite the scholarly efforts to explain the relationships among the terms, different programs use the terms inconsistently or, in some cases, interchangeably (Berkowitz, 1987; Sales, 2002). These definitions or interpretation issues dictate the breadth of rehabilitation counseling practice and the focus on rehabilitation services. Disability is, by most policy definitions, chronic and frequently permanent; however, many impairments are not static (Zola, 1989). Impairments may have progressive and exacerbating characteristics and consequences, both in relation to particular social environments and over the life of the individual. Frequently, accommodations must be tailored to the individual involved and may require periodic alterations, to reflect changes in the individual's impairment or the environment inside and outside of the workplace.

Ultimately, the lack of a consistent disability policy has led to unneeded competition, conflict, a splintering of professional preparation disciplines, program administration inconsistency, and vagueness regarding professional role identity. Many disability programs reflect overlapping priorities and service delivery initiatives, which have, at times, caused duplication of services and uncertainty in purpose and administrative vision and confusion in decision making. Some programs rely on the court system and the private sector, of rehabilitation to award benefits to persons with disabilities; others operate through the tax system and the public sector, to provide needed services. Other programs compensate people who have severe physical limitations, and still others attempt to minimize disability through training and other rehabilitation services (Berkowitz, 1987; Kuehn, 1991; and Meili, 1993).

PARAMETERS INFLUENCING REHABILITATION SERVICES

In establishing rehabilitation service priorities, both state and federal politicians and other decision makers consider a multitude of relevant factors. They examine the available and projected resources, ascertain the needs and aspirations of their constituents, identify other targeted populations, and establish funding levels to accomplish desired outcomes. In addition, several other environmental, assessment, and service delivery trend influences determine the type and quality of rehabilitation services provided.

As the education and training demands of an increasingly information-based economy continue to grow, the social isolation of many people with disabilities may be exacerbated. Yelin (1992, 1997) has linked this trend, along with increases in the prevalence of disability since 1970, to changes in the structure of the economy and the nature of work. Many impairments, in and of themselves, do not prevent people from working; rather, it is the emerging social organization of work in a knowledge-based economy.

Changes in the nature and availability of jobs will continue to accompany economic changes in society and influence rehabilitation counseling services and disability policy. Jobs in the public service sector will tend to be highly technological, labor-intensive, interpersonally interactive, and increasingly complex. Many jobs are projected to be greatly dependent on communication skills, to be knowledge or information-based, and to require new expertise related to technology and computer applications (Roessler & Schriner, 1991; Roth, 1985).

The use of psychological testing as a tool in vocational placement, along with other vocational assessment techniques, has shaped a distinctive approach toward rehabilitation counseling services. In workers' compensation, emphasis has been placed on use of legal criteria and physical-functioning tests to determine the degree of a person's disability. By contrast, in public VR programs, functional assessment techniques and psychological tests have been utilized to determine a person's potential for successful employment.

The availability of sophisticated emergency medical and trauma services, advances in neonatal care, and improvements in medical therapeutics and diagnostics are also having substantial impact on the alternative and intervention services available and on the quality of disability services provided and needed (Pope & Tarlov, 1991; Zola, 1989). These services are frequently technologically expensive, for example, incorporating ventilators for breathing, electric wheelchairs for mobility, and computer systems for communication and life skills management.

AIDS is emerging as a disabling condition for which individuals are accorded rights under the Rehabilitation Act of 1973. Counselors are challenged to provide an array of services to meet the multi-faceted needs of this consumer population. Cohen (1990) has suggested that counselors will face unique and substantial ethical and policy dilemmas about confidentiality and disclosure. With the growing incidence of AIDS, some rehabilitation agencies may be confronted with increased costs for long-term medical benefits.

The importance of transition-to-work programs has become a major issue, which, because of the size of the population to be served, could have significant policy implications related to resource allocation and case-service (time) obligations of counselors. Transition programs are a variant of supported employment, which relies heavily upon the strategies of job coaching, industrial enclaves, and mobile work crews. Successful implementation of transition programs requires multi-disciplinary cooperation of schools, rehabilitation counselors, employers, parent groups, and consumers. Rehabilitation counselors and educators may need to develop new intervention strategies and to relinquish previously held notions about professional roles, in order to provide optimal services (Benshoff, 1990).

Supported work initiatives have also increased the scope of rehabilitation services available, and the continued growth of these programs may have major monetary implications for service delivery. Supported employment programs are characterized by intensive skill training and ongoing support services delivered at the employment site after initial job placement. These functions have significantly expanded the roles of the counselor in ways many professionals believe are not desirable (Thomas, 1991). These factors may have only an indirect influence on day-to-day responsibilities of counselors, but they have a significant impact on the priority and funding available for rehabilitation counseling services that are provided to consumers.

Many agency policies have encouraged or mandated the use of computer technology; however, some studies have found an escalation of visual, neuromuscular, and headache difficulties resulting from prolonged use of keyboards and video display terminals (Kiernan, Sanchez, & Schalock, 1989). These mandated policies suggest that curricula modifications related to assistive and computer technology may be needed in academic programs in rehabilitation counseling. In addition, legislation that has funded the use and application of new technologies, especially ergonomics, has great potential to prevent or reduce job-related injuries.

The development of both medical and vocational model approaches in private sector rehabilitation has pointed out two different philosophical orientations that have created planning and outcome inconsistencies for rehabilitation counselors. The medical model centers on the provision of medical case management, generally provided by a rehabilitation nurse. This model suggests that intensive, efficient medical services will result in a more timely return to work. The vocational model, more closely akin to traditional rehabilitation endeavors, stresses the importance of VR services offered by a rehabilitation counselor, as a complement to medical and other services. This model assumes that the rehabilitation process will be more closely synchronized to the needs of the employer and individual with a disability, resulting in greater mutual satisfaction (Benshoff, 1990).

Perhaps one of the most significant issues that affects disability policy and professional practice is litigation. Issues of economic feasibility, availability of technology, and discrimination have received new attention since passage of the Americans with Disabilities Act (ADA). Because aspects of the process can be time-consuming, litigation frequently delays rehabilitation services (Holmes, Hull, & Karst, 1989). Because of inconsistency and fragmentation of disability policy, the trend toward more litigation is often not adequately addressed in academic training programs nor is it recognized as a problem by many program administrators and members of Congress.

POLICY EVOLUTION AND PROFESSIONALISM

Passage of VR legislation in 1954 was a major event that fostered professional counseling services in the public rehabilitation delivery system. That year, the federal government, through the Rehabilitation Services Administration, authorized grants to public and nonprofit agencies and organizations, including institutions of higher education, to establish master's- and doctoral-level rehabilitation counseling programs. The purpose was to improve the quality of professional practice, which would result in employment of persons with disabilities (Kuehn et al., 1988). This legislation also initiated new types of federal grants to subsidize rehabilitation research and to enable counselors to attend new professional development and education programs at public expense. The impact on professional practice was profound. In essence, rehabilitation counseling was elevated to a profession that had been defined, created, and paid for by the federal government. A significant consequence of the 1954 law has been that the profession grew and expanded as a result of the efforts of professional organizations, which helped develop academic preparation standards for counselors. The result of the emerging status and importance of professional practice is that the professional rehabilitation counselor is now required in most states to have a relevant master's degree.

Cost–benefit analysis (i.e., accommodation to the politics of disability), the creation of a self-sustaining professional culture, and the ability to purchase or deny services from other agencies, have also helped to define the scope of practice for the professional VR counselor. Each of these factors reinforces the natural appeal of the public VR program as a source of hope, rather than as a cause of consumer dependency. However, the result of the interplay of these factors has, in effect, created agency policy that evolved out of self-interest, rather than from a well thought-out, rational plan (Berkowitz, 1987). In the early 1970s, the VR program, like many social welfare programs, reached a time of transition, which was noteworthy, because it fostered negative attitudes about funding rehabilitation programs and the value of counseling services. Failure of the economy to grow as rapidly as it had earlier limited the number of new jobs available and put pressure on the federal budget. The increasing participation of women and members of the baby-boom generation in the labor force exacerbated the problem. Protected entitlement programs, such as Social Security, laid claim to diminishing federal funds. VR, not an open-ended entitlement in the federal or state budgets, was far more vulnerable to financial constraints than were the other disability programs, such as workers' compensation and disability insurance (Berkowitz, 1987). These issues clearly resulted in low morale and the pessimistic attitudes of service providers.

Another trend that emerged in the 1970s involved the manner in which rehabilitation counselors selected their caseloads. Typically, counselors favored consumers with mild impairments, in contrast to consumers with more severe disabilities (Berkowitz, 1987). In 1973, Congress produced a new VR bill that signaled a major change in who should be served in the public program. Emphasis was to be placed on the VR of persons with severe disabilities, rather than on those individuals who could readily be placed in employment. In addition, attention was given to serving individuals with mental retardation and those having other developmental disabilities, as well as persons with severe neurotic and psychotic conditions. The focus on the severely disabled was an attempt to eliminate "creaming" (i.e., the practice by an agency of serving only those individuals from the applicant pool most likely to be employed) and to shift the focus to more difficult cases.

The 1973 Rehabilitation Act also mandated the use of an individualized written rehabilitation plan (IWRP) signed by the counselor and the consumer; this new policy became a significant parameter, which influenced the planning process and collaborative involvement between consumers and counselors. Central to rehabilitation counselors' efforts to promote consumer involvement and advocacy is accurate and timely information. The consumer must have a thorough understanding of their medical condition, personal goals, knowledge of the rehabilitation services available and the implications for vocational decision making, and rights and disability policies. They must make informed decisions, and practitioners must provide information necessary for the consumer to experience success in their personal rehabilitation plan. This effort may shift the evaluation of rehabilitation services to consumer outcomes versus rehabilitation/agency outcomes. The refocus on priorities and awareness of policy and legal implications by the consumer has major implications for the training, continuing education, and credentialing of professional rehabilitation counselors.

Congress also initiated client-assistance projects, which established ombudsmen in the rehabilitation agencies to protect the rights of the consumer; furthermore, these programs were required to be independent of the VR program itself. In this manner, some client assistance projects became a source of legal advice that a disgruntled consumer could use to pursue a grievance through the courts. Legislated priority on employment outcomes and consumer involvement in rehabilitation plan development, in the past few years, has helped to define more clearly the scope and mission of the practice of rehabilitation counseling (Rubin & Roessler, 2001).

To reinforce the emphasis on consumer involvement and rights, Bickenbach (2001) suggested that disability advocacy was the single most important political development in the struggle for equal participation by people with mental and physical disabilities. He identified the human rights approach as the mechanism to promote this advocacy. Historically, four basic categories of rights have been suggested: moral, legal, civil, and human. An understanding of each has implications for services to people with disabilities.

The human rights approach gave rise to the social model of disability, which fostered the belief that disability is a social phenomenon shaped by historical, cultural, political, and economic forces. Models can be complicated and confusing, but it does make sense to insist that one has a basic human right to be treated as an equal (Bickenbach, 2001). The implications of advocacy efforts and disability rights for professional practice became obvious: Training programs for rehabilitation counselors needed to provide, for students, expanded educational opportunities and experiences addressing ethics, advocacy, and disability rights.

Contrary to the intent of the 1973 law, some program administrators became primarily concerned with the number of people successfully served, and individuals with severe limitations noticed their frequent exclusion from the VR program (Coudroglou & Poole, 1984). Consumers argued that they were being screened out and denied services; agencies, on the other hand, called this practice "screening out the undermotivated." Individuals also objected to the way in which counselors consigned them to low-paying or low-status jobs (Percy, 1989; Schriner, 1990). Program goals have seemed at times to be incongruent and often incompatible with the needs of individuals with severe disabilities or those interested in independent living issues. This situation created pressures on counselors, because quantity, in contrast to needed services, seemed to be the goal driving many programs.

The development of the rehabilitation counseling profession was also stimulated by the growing variety of work settings available and by the expanding specialized functions rehabilitation counselors were expected to perform. The varied roles have included case manager, coordinator of services, job developer, consultant/advocate, placement specialist, client assessment specialist, therapeutic counselor/facilitator, and vocational evaluator. With complex, wide-ranging responsibilities, rehabilitation counselors were also given a great deal of power and control over the options available to consumers, the goals of programs, and the services that may be provided.

The influence of certification and accreditation procedures has generally facilitated clarification of professional identity issues for counseling practice (Szymanski, Linkowski, Leahy, Diamond, & Thoreson, 1993). However, Thomas (1991) suggests that, in establishing professional standards for practice and directions for the future, the roles and influence of practitioners, educators, policy makers, and professional organizations have often been controversial and created conflict. The ultimate issue appears to be curriculum control. The fear that special interest groups or new federal priorities will mandate standards that could dictate a change in the roles and functions of counselors has been viewed as the key concern.

Professionalization in public VR, and in the delivery of services, has also become a vital component in agency growth and program evaluation and success. The emergence of the rehabilitation counseling profession, unlike some of the other established human service professions, has been tied to federal legislative mandates, and its development has been closely related to the expansion of the state–federal system of VR (Jenkins, Patterson, & Szymanski, 1992; Rubin & Roessler, 2001; Sales, 2002). Like other factors, concerns about professional services and quality were apparent early in the developmental years of public VR (Berkowitz, 1987; Boschen, 1989; Roessler & Schriner, 1991). Even as state VR program administrators struggled with changing federal initiatives every few years, they strove to adopt an ethical and professional approach to the rehabilitation process. As the profession of rehabilitation counseling has grown and evolved, the importance of expanded and relevant counselor competencies and services, to be provided specific groups of clients/consumers, has strengthened the need for a focused disability policy in America.

Finally, professional practice will always need to respond to the unique work settings and the multi-faceted needs of consumers. Therefore, to promote a concise, simplistic description of disability policy and the future of rehabilitation counseling may not be desirable or realistic. However, vigilance and reassessment of federal legislative intent must be maintained to address the philosophical assumptions that form the framework of rehabilitation counseling practice.

PUBLIC REHABILITATION DELIVERY SYSTEM OBJECTIVES

A major goal of VR agencies is to get individuals with disabilities working at a paying job in an integrated work setting. However, the utilitarian side of rehabilitation services receives more attention, because most industries are in business to make money, and government is accountable to Congress and the voting public. On the other hand, publicly articulated goals of rehabilitation have mostly reflected the values of American society.

Beyond the philosophical assumptions of rehabilitation counseling are additional objectives. Employment is primary, but assisting the individual in improving their self-image, and promoting the importance of respect for and dignity of each person, are also of value in our society. In America, these goals have been approached through a variety of disability policies and programs, many of which have been oriented around the medical care system. Unfortunately, the services and behaviors of some well-meaning professionals are motivated primarily by money. The attainment of appropriate rehabilitation goals, and the pursuit of vocational and psychological adjustment by consumers, are frequently influenced by the economic benefits that accrue to service providers.

As new disability policies are proposed that affect professional practice, their importance and impact must be weighed against the goals that agencies promote. Practice issues must be examined in relation to the need for early intervention programs in the schools, which might assist special educators, high school counselors, and vocational educators (Boschen, 1989). The use of computer technology and its advantages and curses must be rationally evaluated. Finally, the impact of policy decisions on special populations must be continually reviewed (Bowe, 1993).

During the past 20 years, the use of cost–benefit analysis and cost effectiveness evaluations have been widely accepted tools in assessing the goals and values of disability policies and rehabilitation counseling services. Because of the concern about costs and outcomes, rehabilitation efforts must be quantified to validate the use of these assessment tools. A positive, justifiable "numbers game" plays a most important role in making policy and program decisions. The bottom line usually equates to the number of persons served, evaluated, and placed in employment; this criteria greatly influences policies in the rehabilitation delivery system and the day-to-day practice of a counselor.

Currently, public VR programs attempt to restore the productivity of persons with disabilities by job placement and job training. It is by far the least expensive of the major disability programs; SSDI has emerged as the nation's most expensive (Bowe, 1993; Kiernan et al., 1989).

At present, there is little evidence, other than discussions about national health care, that major disability policy reforms are forthcoming. Both state and federal government continue to authorize and fund programs with overlapping objectives and services, without regard to program ramifications and to the discrepant system that is being created (Kuehn, 1991). The passage of new legislation during the last 5 years, on Social Security and Department of Labor initiatives that created a new Office of Disability Programs, raises questions about whether a coherent, comprehensive disability policy will ever be developed. Governmental agencies seem to have differing priorities and use definitions and policy rationale to justify the existence of new, often politically motivated, priorities.

LEGISLATIVE AND POLITICAL INFLUENCES

The formulation and implementation of national policies and the passage of federal and state laws regulating disability programs and needed services are not major public issues when there is satisfaction with the economy. However, declining job opportunities, increasing taxes, and the perceived inequitable allocation of resources are the bases of societal change (Hahn, 1985). When limited financial resources are not sufficient to meet increasing demands, it is imperative to establish policies that are justifiable and critical for addressing discrimination and service delivery issues.

Despite the demonstrated cost-effectiveness of VR, the rise of the independent living movement, and the disability rights revolution of the past three decades, the vast majority of public policy spending still is used to compensate people with disabilities, with a meager ticket out of the workforce and the social mainstream (Berkowitz, 1987).

Berkowitz (1996) has estimated that, in 1996, 49.47% of federal funds spent on disability programs went to health care, and 42.31% was spent on income maintenance and support. Less than 4% of the funds was allocated to education and rehabilitation. The vast majority of our public dollars are being spent on ameliorative programs that ease the burden of individuals' impairments, rather than on corrective programs that seek to enhance the productivity of people with disabilities or to alter the environment in which they function.

Broadly conceived, disability policy is comprised of three general components that affect professional practice in rehabilitation counseling: (1) civil rights laws and regulations, (2) income and in-kind assistance programs (e.g., medical), and (3) skill enhancement programs such as education and VR (Berkowitz, 1987). Unfortunately, these components are not synchronous and often do not reflect current professional beliefs about the role of people with disabilities as productive citizens who desire respect and dignity (Scotch & Berkowitz, 1990).

A significant policy influence, with political overtones, on rehabilitation counseling practice and services is the debilitating effect of new governmental initiatives for special interest groups. Everchanging federal training priorities and guidelines, calling for new program emphases, are often vivid examples of politically motivated priorities. The challenge for academic training programs has been to respond to these changes in a timely manner and to understand the rationale for the changes in priorities; sometimes the responses to these emphases, which are often reflected in grant applications, illustrate a typical political reaction to changing federal priorities, i.e., write what is needed to get funded.

Rapidly increasing disability costs, emphasis on employment outcomes, collaboration efforts, and the resulting political pressures, provided adequate rationale for the reauthorization of the Rehabilitation Act in 1998. However, the reauthorization was included as a part of a larger piece of workforce reform legislation known as the Workforce Investment Act (WIA). Although rehabilitation maintained its original intent, WIA required state VR agencies to collaboratively develop employment programs in one-stop centers, in cooperation with the Department of Labor. It also changed the IWRP to the Individual Plan of Employment, and it permitted rehabilitation counselors to expand informed choice by allowing the consumer to write their own rehabilitation plan (Roessler, 2002). Finally, to improve rehabilitation outcomes, WIA required the implementation of a Comprehensive System of Personnel Development. Its purpose was to provide consumer protection, to ensure that qualified rehabilitation specialists provide services to individuals with disabilities. It required that all staff hired or trained in state rehabilitation agencies attain the level of professional certification required by a state and, if no state certification exists, to meet the national certification requirements for rehabilitation counselors. Sales (2002) stated that 43% of the rehabilitation counselors employed within the state–federal VR program did not meet this standard.

These recent legislative efforts all have influenced the need for, and role of, professionally trained rehabilitation counselors. The legislation and resulting policy changes have placed new emphases on advocacy efforts, empowerment, and informed consumer choice in the practice of rehabilitation counseling. The historical role of paternalism in service delivery was slowly being replaced by new consumer-controlled initiatives and involvement, creating new expectations and challenges for professionals in the field. Collectively, these legislative mandates signaled the beginning of a societal attitude shift, which places increased value on diversity and focuses on capacity rather than disability (Evenson & Holloway, 2002).

Another critical factor relates to the lack of adequate national recognition of the profession of rehabilitation counseling. This illustrates why disability programs have never attracted a political following and, therefore, partially explains why it has been difficult to establish a comprehensive, national disability policy. The contrast with programs such as aid for the elderly is a striking example of this phenomenon. Highly visible congressional committees monitor public policy toward the elderly, but few congressional committees air the grievances and publicize the problems of individuals with severe disabilities (Berkowitz, 1987; DeJong & Batavia, 1990). Until the passage of the ADA in 1990, few leaders of the disabled community had risen to national prominence, nor had people with disabilities received the sustained attention from media as had other special groups.

An illustration of how policies (priorities and services) are influenced by politics (power) can be seen in some disability programs, such as public VR, which formulated policies and procedures for reasons that often had little to do with the people and agencies served (Berkowitz, 1985). People with disabilities have, therefore, tried to gain control over disability policy, to take power away from professional administrators, and to assume both of these for themselves. This effort led to the creation of independent living centers, which are mostly run by persons with disabilities, rather than by professional administrators and people without disabilities.

There have been several recent laws and policies enacted that have emphasized or suggested new priorities for professional practice. Kuehn et al. (1988) suggested that, in the 1970s, when agencies began to serve the consumer with severe physical disabilities, state rehabilitation agency caseload size began declining, because of the complexity of services and the length of time often necessary to meet consumer needs. In addition to the various antidiscrimination laws passed in the 1980s, federal legislation was passed that increased the value and viability of VR programs (i.e., client assistance services). The rehabilitation legislation of 1986 fostered establishment of rehabilitation engineering services that could expand options for individuals, as well as encourage the development of collaborative programs leading to supported employment services. Consumer involvement was given new attention in the 1992 amendments, with the emphasis on informed choice and increased control in development of rehabilitation goals. The provision for annual review of IWRPs, handling of applications and eligibility determination, expeditious provision of expanded transition services, personal assistance services, expanded supported employment services, and expansion of services through renewed commitments to interagency cooperation, were also emphasized (Rubin & Roessler, 2001). All of these new initiatives have forced counselors and agencies to reevaluate priorities and related day-to-day responsibilities.

The passage of the ADA, which reflects a new thrust in American disability policy, emphasizes discrimination issues. The ADA offers an opportunity for both the administration and the Congress to act positively, in the face of the changing needs and aspirations of an increasingly politicized population of persons with disabilities, and to do so at a relatively low cost to the federal government. The political unwillingness to make fundamental changes in our disability assistance programs made the passage of the ADA all the more urgent. Even if the legal requirements of ADA and efforts to eliminate discrimination are enforced vigorously, the law cannot adequately substitute for other policy changes that need to be made (DeJong & Batavia, 1990). Important policy issues that predate the passage of ADA still remain unresolved.

The confusing state of disability policy in this country can be attributed in part to the belief that some of the nation's disability programs were ill-conceived and appeared unreasonable. For example, in the past decade, questions have been raised about the ADA passed in 1990. Conservatives in Congress, academia, and the media have questioned the legitimacy of the ADA's mandates, expressing skepticism over the validity of the claims of those seeking protection under its provisions and the remedies they have sought. To many critics, the ADA was a case of ill-considered legislation in which an overly broad category of supposed victims demanded unreasonable accommodations from society (Scotch, 2000). Policy formulation for disability service programs became confused with disability benefits programs, which added more misunderstanding of the purposes and objectives of disability policy. Benefit programs were often organized around a medical model of disability, in which impairment is automatically associate with incapacity. Within this paradigm, the significance of an impairment is its effect on the individual's ability to work, and the policy objective is to compensate for incapacity through custodial services and income maintenance. If a person can work, then that individual does not have a disability.

Scotch (2000) examines the assumptions of incapacity around which Social Security disability programs are organized—assumptions that require people to be totally and permanently disabled to receive benefits. The implication suggests an all-or-nothing approach that does not take into account the diverse, dynamic, and highly individual effects of disabilities. Disability policy models that focus on services are advocated, which promote individualized approaches, such as the Individuals with Disabilities Education Act and the public VR program, but even these programs have limited resources and enormous caseloads for service providers, which create pressure to routinize services and limit flexibility. The negative effects of large caseloads and limited funds for service delivery result in routinization and boilerplate services, all the while attempting to facilitate informed choice.

To complicate this concept of incapacity, 1999 Supreme Court decisions excluded individuals from the ADA's protection from discrimination, if their impairments can be corrected with medication or devices. Thus, if someone is truly disabled, they are unable to work and are therefore not entitled to benefit from civil rights remedies.

The Ticket to Work and Work Incentives Improvement Act of 1999 (TWWIIA) provides supports and incentives designed to increase the return-to-work rates of Social Security beneficiaries and recipients. This legislation outlines benefits planning and work incentives, such as expedited reinstatement of benefits and extension of Medicare and Medicaid coverage. Whether these initiatives have their intended impact depends on their ability to remove or reduce barriers to employment by experienced people with disabilities. Although significant barriers exist (Marini & Reid, 2001; Marini & Stebnicki, 1999), the primary concern of many people receiving Social Security benefits is the perceived cost of going to work. The success of TWWIIA rests on the ability of people to return to work without losing substantial medical benefit coverage or incurring unacceptably high costs, particularly medical expenses.

Even though discrimination, program priorities, and policy issues persist, the philosophy and changing attitudes regarding the purpose of VR services have had a positive influence on the professional rehabilitation counselor, as well as on federal policy makers. The principles and philosophy supporting disability services are attracting new interest and proponents, as disability programs emerge that focus on benefits and incapacity. The values of ethical, self-enhancing rehabilitation strategies are fostering a renewed commitment to professional rehabilitation counselor practice.

FUTURE OF REHABILITATION COUNSELING PRACTICE

To identify a clear picture for professional practice in the twenty-first century is difficult, at best. No one person has all the necessary expertise to comprehend the diverse legal, economic, and social phenomena encompassed by disability policy and legislation. Few people understand all the parameters, and most do not have sufficient background to view the entire rehabilitation system from a holistic perspective. Legislators, for example, operate by means of subcommittees that are heavily dependent on experts, special interest groups, and others who have learned the specialized language of policy discourse. Rarely does the level of analysis rise above individual programs, to include the larger picture. Schriner (1990) stated that the focus often becomes "justification of program," rather than "development of rational disability policy."

There are strong economic reasons to presume that a disability and rehabilitation delivery system, composed of professionally trained personnel, will not go out of existence. Although disability costs may be becoming a national problem and social policies for rehabilitation are being developed and tested, there are, at the same time, social and political reasons to suggest that disability services will not be eradicated; many businesses and industries ultimately depend on the misfortunes of individuals to justify or guarantee their existence. Disability benefit programs sometimes provide a stable source of income to consumers, which often surpasses the amount one could have earned through employment, creating discouragement for individuals to seek work. Professionally trained counselors are therefore needed to help consumers understand the implications of the disincentives or incentives that are created.

Another way to improve the practice of rehabilitation counseling, and to make it more responsive to consumer needs, might be to introduce innovative approaches to the delivery of rehabilitation services, involving more competition in the marketplace. This could provide the consumer with more options on the types, level, and location of service that one is receiving. Federal government funding of innovative delivery approaches has received considerable support in the 1990s. An open market for rehabilitation counseling services could force both the consumer and the providers of services to dramatically reassess the priorities, needs, and services in the rehabilitation process. This approach could also allow the consumer to be maximally independent in the decision-making process, from the beginning. The implications of successful alternative services could have major ramifications for state and federal policies concerning the use of monies allocated for implementation of programs specified in federal laws.

Consumers with disabilities complain of symbolic compliance to federal laws, in which individualized plans are often little more than predetermined agreements prescribing services that are dependent on established organizational routines and the availability of resources. New forms of accountability, which empower clients and limit professional autonomy, may be required to accommodate the complexity of disability, yet such changes are controversial and difficult to implement.

DeJong and Batavia (1990) suggested that, to facilitate changes in disability policy and to support the improvement of professional practice, several additional alternatives should be considered:

1. Provide greater economic incentives and financial deductions for persons with disabilities to obtain employment. Modify tax policy to offer greater deductibility of, or tax credits for, disability-related expenses.
2. Eliminate any assumption in policy decisions that a person is, or is not, totally disabled. Disability may be a non-static condition.
3. Alter the assumption that a disability necessarily reduces the capability to work. Rely less on medical eligibility criteria and give more consideration to individual functional capacity and to environmental accommodations that a person with a disability may require.
4. Create incentives to work, and separate employment status from program eligibility status. Assistive devices and health care benefits should be available, regardless of employment status.

These ideas are not particularly radical or new. They reflect traditional American values that emphasize individual initiative, self-determination, private responsibility, and community support (Berkowitz, 1987; DeJong & Batavia, 1990). All persons who can contribute productively to our society must be encouraged to do so. The scope of professional practice can easily embrace these values, and practitioners can focus rehabilitation efforts on the dignity, independence, and employment of consumers.

The perception of the importance and value of rehabilitation counseling in America seems to be at a turning point. With recent federal budget deficit concerns, the social policy agenda has basically been placed on hold. Finally, in the midst of economic recession, the threat of unemployment, and an exorbitant cost of living, there has been a strong public outcry for fiscal conservatism and also a political backlash against programs making demands on the public purse. Individuals with disabilities who might benefit from rehabilitation counseling services are not exempt from the outcry and backlash. Because priority changes in the funding of programs often involve unanticipated consequences, the administration and Congress have been unwilling to risk changes that will require additional funds in the short run, even though such changes would be likely to stimulate greater economic productivity in the long run. Prospects for expanding disability programs have also been made worse by a slow-growth economy, the nation's unwillingness to accept new taxes, and the continued rapid growth in health care costs (DeJong & Batavia, 1990).

SUMMARY

The factors that have influenced the practice of rehabilitation counseling have become the parameters that, in some ways, are controlling the development and viability of the profession. The impact of factors such as public policy, legislation, and a national health care program has been significant: All have contributed to the goal of reintegrating persons with disabilities into mainstream society. However, only VR programs have employability as their stated aim.

Perhaps we need to rethink such basic questions as, In what ways are people with disabilities the same as, or different from, people without disabilities? and Can people with disabilities be appropriately served in generic settings, or is there something special about disability that requires unique programs? (Scotch, 2000)

The rehabilitation counseling profession places great value on the dignity of the individual, but it recognizes the importance of the Protestant work ethic, the value of individual independence, and individual satisfaction that can occur when a person obtains employment. In some cases, however, these values come into conflict, because of changes in, or indecision about, process or delivery issues, eligibility, and outcome policies.

In the 1990s, it was, and continues to be, virtually impossible for any one person to be current on all of the disability service programs that exist, let alone the ways in which they interact. Disability policy and new legislation should form a coherent rationale for rehabilitation counseling practice. It may be difficult to agree on a common definition of disability and, therefore, to create a disability policy that bridges the uniqueness of individual programs. Because these programs have been frequently conceived and administered in isolation from one another, they have perpetuated a service structure that has been described as stagnant and resistant to change. Rehabilitation counseling programs could be stimulated and made more effective, if the collection of insulated service programs were replaced by a cohesive disability policy that reflects the aspirations and values that people with disabilities have for themselves (Schriner, 1990).

The parameters that could influence the professional practice of rehabilitation counseling in the twenty-first century are thought provoking, comprehensive, and possibly overwhelming. The strength of professional practice is a commitment to the inherent value, dignity, and uniqueness of each individual with a disability. Rehabilitation counseling services are now being viewed as an economically profitable enterprise. Technological expertise, ability to communicate information and educate individuals quickly, and changes in private insurance planning, all contribute to the growth and optimism of individual potential and the elimination and prevention of major disability (Parker & Szymanski, 1998).

Integrated disability policy and well-conceived legislation, in concert with the development of comprehensive disability and health care systems, will foster a positive, optimistic future, desired by all individuals experiencing disability. The ultimate result will be more-responsive rehabilitation counseling services that reflect innovative, creative professional practices consistent with federal disability law and policies.

CHAPTER 6

Ethics

Vilia M. Tarvydas

Increased quality of life for clients with disabilities depends on professional counselors heeding the caution embodied in the words of Samuel Johnson: "Integrity without knowledge is weak and useless, and knowledge without integrity is dangerous and dreadful." The development of a strong professional identity rests on clear professional standards of practice. Clients need solution-focused, respectful, nonexploitative and empowering, and therefore ethical, relationships with their counselors.

Clearly, clients require the services of professionals who are grounded firmly in the awareness of their value-laden mission and who are willing and able to assist people, through appropriate knowledge and competencies (Gatens-Robinson & Rubin, 1995). The unusually strong tradition of explicit philosophical foundations is critical to the profession of rehabilitation and led to an early recognition of the value-based nature of rehabilitation counseling (B. A. Wright, 1983). This treasured legacy provides a strong basis for understanding the ethical principles at the heart of the ethical decision-making skills needed within the practice of rehabilitation counseling.

COMPONENTS OF PROFESSIONAL STANDARDS

The practice of counseling is both an art and a science, requiring the practitioner to make both value-laden and rational decisions. Rather than being incompatible stances, both facts and values must be considered in juxtaposition to one another, to engage in rational decisions (Gatens-Robinson & Rubin, 1995). Within ethical deliberation, the practitioner blends such elements as personal moral sensitivities and philosophies of practice with clinical behavioral objectivity and the quest for efficient care of clients.

The nature and complexity of standards of practice for all of the professions have changed and grown over the last several decades. The phrase *professional standards* no longer simply means specifically the ethical standards of the profession. This term is a general term meaning professional criteria indicating acceptable professional performance (Powell & Wekell, 1996) and may encompass ethical and/or clinical care standards. There are three types of standards relevant to describing professional practice: (1) the *internal standards* of the profession; (2) *clinical standards* for the individual practitioners within a profession; and (3) *external, regulatory standards*. Taken together, these professional standards increase the status of the profession and its ability for self-governance, as well as enhancing the external representation and accountability for the profession's competence with clients, the general public, employers, external regulators, and payers (Rinas & Clyne-Jackson, 1988). These types of standards, their major characteristics, and principal components are depicted in Figure 6.1.

Internal Standards

First, the internal standards of the profession form the underpinnings of the appropriate role and functions of the profession. Internal standards are characterized by being focused on advancing the professionalism of the group in question, having the intent of setting a profession-wide standard of practice, and assisting individual practitioners, through defining their professional identity and obligations. Prominent examples of mechanisms in this category are the profession's code of ethics and any guidelines for specialty practice relevant to the discipline.

Clinical Standards

The clinical standards for professional practitioners are close to the internal standards described, in that both are directly relevant to services delivered to the individual client or patient. Additional characteristics include focusing on single disciplinary or multidisciplinary standards of clinical care. These standards may be specific to a particular setting or client population, they evaluate the competency of individual professionals, based on the specific

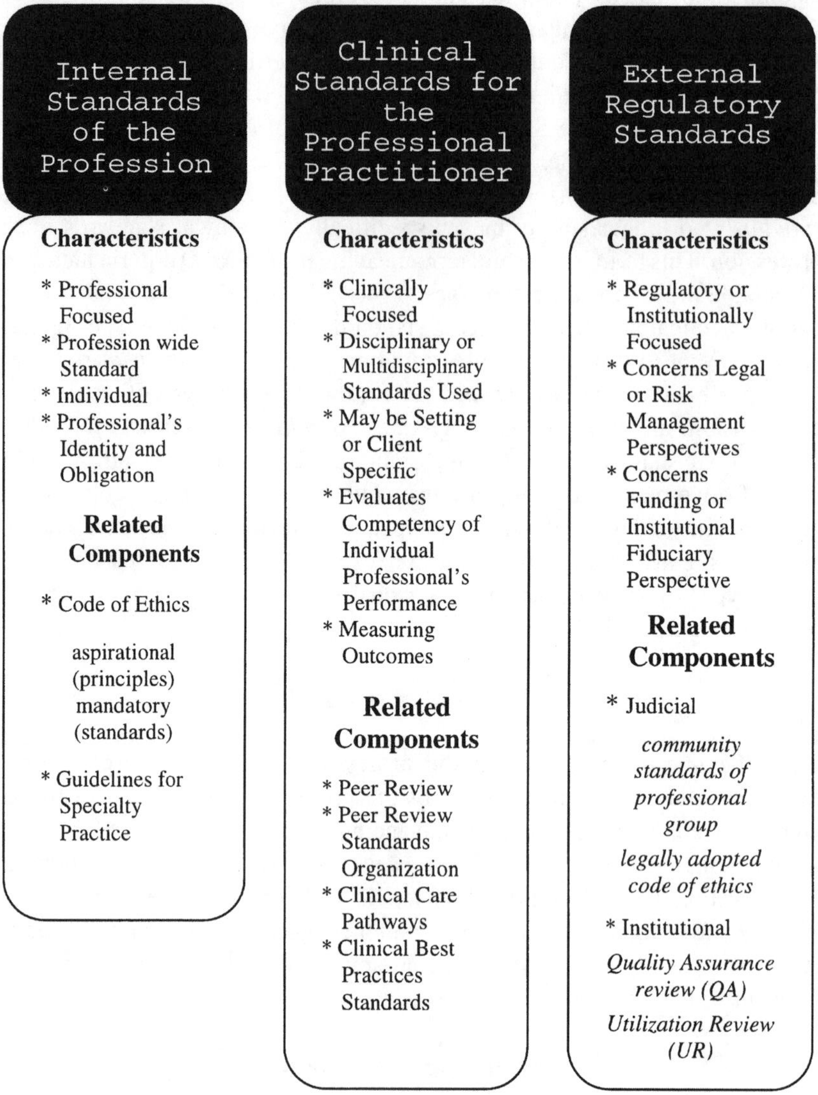

Internal Standards of the Profession

Characteristics

* Professional Focused
* Profession wide Standard
* Individual
* Professional's Identity and Obligation

Related Components

* Code of Ethics

  aspirational (principles)
  mandatory (standards)

* Guidelines for Specialty Practice

Clinical Standards for the Professional Practitioner

Characteristics

* Clinically Focused
* Disciplinary or Multidisciplinary Standards Used
* May be Setting or Client Specific
* Evaluates Competency of Individual Professional's Performance
* Measuring Outcomes

Related Components

* Peer Review
* Peer Review Standards Organization
* Clinical Care Pathways
* Clinical Best Practices Standards

External Regulatory Standards

Characteristics

* Regulatory or Institutionally Focused
* Concerns Legal or Risk Management Perspectives
* Concerns Funding or Institutional Fiduciary Perspective

Related Components

* Judicial

  community standards of professional group
  legally adopted code of ethics

* Institutional

  Quality Assurance review (QA)
  Utilization Review (UR)

FIGURE 6.1 The structure of professional standards.

care rendered; and they have a client or patient care outcome measurement focus. Peer review processes and standards, as well as clinical care pathways, are examples of this type of standard.

External Regulatory Bodies

The last component of the professional standards trio involves the standards of external regulatory bodies of diverse sorts. They are focused on regulatory or institutional-level concerns. They usually involve legal or risk-management questions and deal with funding or institutional fiduciary perspectives. There is a judicial type of component in which legal or quasi-legal processes are at play, such as community standards of a professional group being used in a malpractice suit or a code of ethics adopted by a licensure board to discipline licensees. General social values underlie both law and the values of the profession, making them generally compatible. The society would not long tolerate a profession that routinely operated in a manner significantly at variance with its core value structure. Corey, Corey, and Callanan (2003) noted that law and ethics are similar, because they both constitute guidelines for practice and, in some sense, are regulatory in nature. However, law can be seen as representing the minimum standards that society will tolerate, and ethics involves the ideal standards set by the profession itself. The law also informs the counselor of what is likely to happen if the professional is caught committing a prohibited act. The other component of external regulatory standards involves institutional standards used to judge the effectiveness and efficiency of an entire agency or institutional unit, as is typically done in quality assurance or utilization review. Such strategies have been common in medical settings and will become increasingly common in counseling, as the influence of managed care on the profession accelerates, through increasing demands for outcome-based treatment planning.

This chapter is concerned with the ethical standards of rehabilitation counseling, but it is important to note the synergistic relationship among the three types of professional standards described earlier. *Ethics* are the moral principles that are adopted by a group to provide rules for right conduct (Corey et al., 2003). The code of ethics for a professional organization is a specific document formally adopted by the organization, which is an attempt to capture the profession's current consensus regarding what types of professional conduct are appropriate or inappropriate. However, they are normative statements, rather than absolute dictates of situational guidance.

ETHICS GOVERNANCE

Effective processes to govern ethics practice are necessary, to give meaning to professional standards of practice and to enhance the societal stature of the profession. These governance processes guide the profession's practitioners, through education and socialization into the professional role, and subsequently discipline them if they do not practice within the proscribed standards established. Ethical components of the standards of practice can be thought of as being either mandatory or aspirational, in the level of direction they provide the practitioner (Corey et al., 2003). The most basic level of ethical functioning is guided by mandatory ethics. At this level, the individuals focus on compliance with the law and the dictates of the professional codes of ethics that apply to their practice. They are concerned with remaining safe from legal action and professional censure. The more ethically sophisticated level is the aspirational level. At this level, individuals additionally reflect on the effects of the situation on the welfare of their clients, and the effects of their actions on the profession as a whole.

These same concepts of mandatory and aspirational ethics can be applied to the overall structure of governance for a profession's ethical standards of practice as a whole. Codes of ethics are binding only on persons who hold that particular credential (e.g., certification through the Commission on Rehabilitation Counselor Certification [CRCC]), or have membership in that organization (e.g., member of the American Counseling Association [ACA]). Those professionals so governed must take ethical guidance, and sanctions may be applied, based upon the specific ethical codes and disciplinary process of this specific professional entity. The disciplinary process of CRCC is an example of such a process applicable to rehabilitation counseling practice. If a credential holder or member of a particular professional entity violates its code of ethics, the entity has the responsibility to provide a disciplinary procedure to enforce its standards. After due process, the entity applies an appropriate sanction to the violator. In the case of a professional organization, the ultimate sanction would typically be removal from membership, with possible referral of the findings to other professional or legal jurisdictions. For a credentialing entity such as CRCC or a counselor licensure board, the violator could face the more serious option of certificate or license revocation, thus possibly removing an individual's ability to practice. Less-serious levels of sanction, such as reprimand or probation, are also available. Often these statuses are coupled with significant educational or rehabilitative conditions, such as taking an ethics course or treatment of an addiction and supervised practice, to assist practitioners in regaining appropriate ethical standards of practice, while protecting their clients. A letter of instruction may be used when there is no ethical violation found, but the disciplinary body determines that information could be provided to the practitioner about the best ethical practices that might improve the future provision of services to consumers.

The assessment of the level of seriousness of the ethical violation will affect the actual choice of sanction, once the individual is adjudicated as being in violation of the code of ethics. Factors often considered include intentionality, degree of risk or actual harm to the client, motivation or ability of violator to change, and recidivism of the violator (Keith-Spiegel & Koocher, 1998).

Responsible practitioners supplement this basic mandatory level of practitioner ethics with advanced knowledge of the clinical wisdom and scholarly literature on best practices in ethics. In addition, they will gain guidance from other codes of ethics and specialty guidelines for ethical practice that are relevant to their practices. These sources should be sought, to supplement the required mandatory ethical standards with the more aspirational principles and ethical concepts to which the more sophisticated practitioner should aspire. In fact, for certain situations, the course of action suggested by the aspirational ethics perspective may contradict that required by the dictates of mandatory ethics. Such a situation leaves the practitioner in the stressful position of needing to responsibly reconcile the two directions.

The contemporary structure of ethics governance for counselors is presented in Figure 6.2. This representation depicts types of professional organizational entities in counseling, organized hierarchically in the shape of a pyramid. The levels of ethical functioning are represented by the vertical arrow to the side of the pyramid, depicting the entities as existing roughly on a continuum from a primarily aspirational to a primarily mandatory level of function.

Colleges and universities provide professional education and research services, doing so under the review of credentialing bodies such as the Commission on Rehabilitation Education (CORE) or the Commission on the Accreditation of Counseling and Related Educational Programs. As such, they are entities that have the broadest function to provide aspirational education and guidance in ethics, and that represent the foundation of the structure of ethics governance. Additionally, they build the theoretical and research base for understanding ethical issues, decision-making processes, and ethics educational methods. These aspects of the aspirational knowledge base are needed to support ethical development of the profession. Colleges and universities also ensure that proper preservice education and professional socialization occur, to inculcate future practitioners and educators with a proper ethics base from which to conduct their future practice of counseling. This obligation includes active role-modeling and supporting ethical analysis and ethical behavior in teaching, supervision, and actual clinical practice. Educational institutions also serve as a resource to other professional organizations and regulatory bodies, to provide teaching, research, and service, supporting aspirational and mandatory ethical practice in the community.

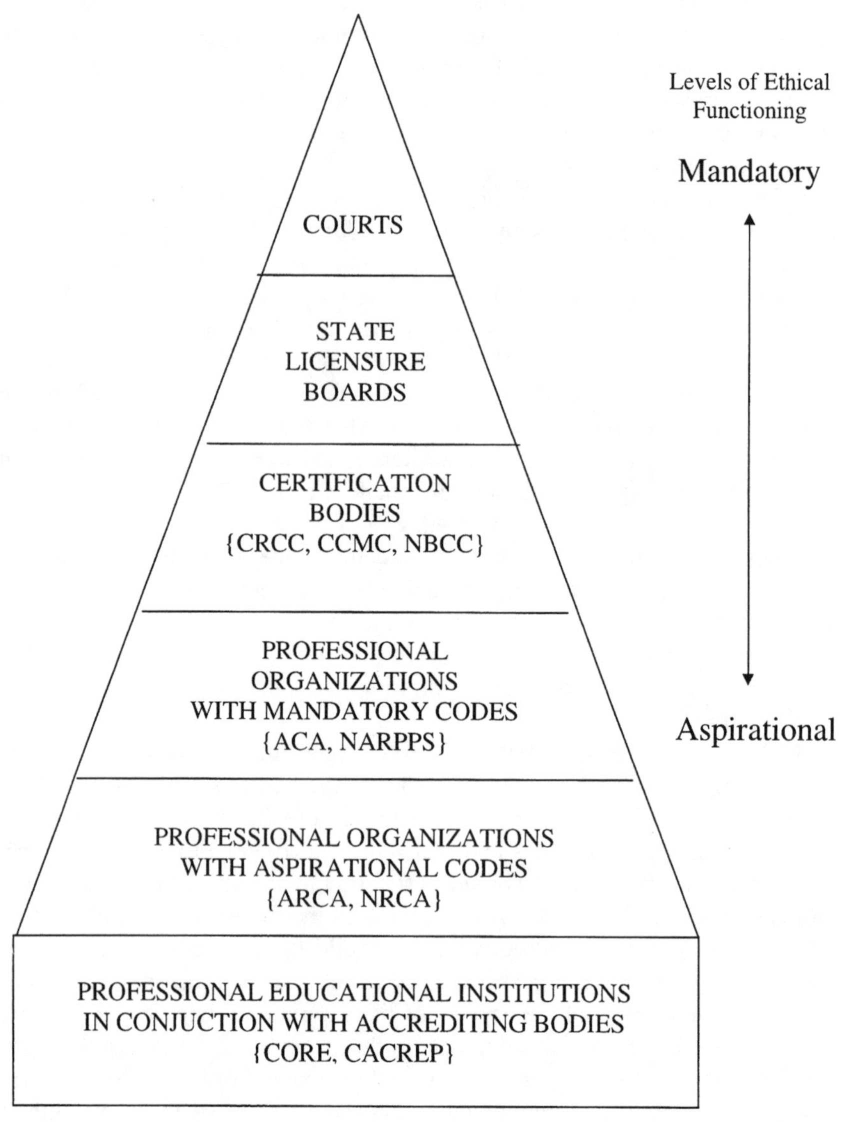

FIGURE 6.2 Model of ethics governance for rehabilitation counselors.

At the next level sit the professional organizations with aspirational codes of ethics, but with no internal mandatory enforcement mechanisms for them. For example, the Association for Specialists in Group Work and the American Rehabilitation Counseling Association (ARCA), as divisions of ACA, occupy this position. For such organizations, the primary task is to encourage aspirational ethical levels of function in their members. Mandatory enforcement tasks are not undertaken by such professional organizations, because of such factors as lack of appropriate consumer access and protection in the disciplinary process; appropriate remedies for serious infractions; and the substantial financial, staff, and professional resources necessary for responsible enforcement. In some cases, the mandatory enforcement function of the organization is referred to a parent organization (e.g., to ACA, in the case of ARCA members who are ACA members), or the complainant is referred to another appropriate jurisdiction, to initiate a disciplinary process.

Nonetheless, professional organizations with aspirational codes perform several significant functions within the ethics governance structure. They may provide supplemental, complementary codes of ethics for their members, which extend and explicate other more general codes of ethics. Such a document provides guidelines for ethical practice for special issues frequently encountered or of particular concern to these professionals. For rehabilitation counselors, examples of such issues might include assessment of persons with functional limitations caused by disability, interdisciplinary team practice relationship issues, managed care practice, and the responsibility of advocacy for persons with disabilities. A supplementary code may take the form of specialty guidelines for practice, which address specialty setting or function-specific issues. One example of this type of guideline is the *American Psychological Association Guidelines for Computer-Based Tests and Their Interpretation* (1986).

In addition to maintaining supplementary, specialty ethical standards for practice, some professional organizations, with an aspirational ethical level of function, collect information regarding ethical trends and needs for revision of either the specialty or generalist ethics codes. Their leadership also should participate in the code revision and writing processes for both types of codes. These organizations should identify and supply qualified professionals to serve on the various mandatory enforcement bodies. They provide educational programs to further knowledge and the quality of ethical practice, performing significant educational and socialization functions. An innovative role, yet one that is potentially most meaningful, is the provision of mechanisms and expertise to offer remediation or rehabilitation programs for impaired professionals who have been found in violation (or are at risk of violation) of ethical standards.

At the third level of ethical governance are professional organizations that maintain and enforce a mandatory code of ethics, such as ACA and the International Association of Rehabilitation Professionals in the Private Sector. These organizations provide an entry-level mandatory code of ethics and enforcement process for their members, and, in the case of ACA, the enforcement for referred complaints of its specialty memberships. This level of organization consults with certification and licensing bodies and the specialty professional organizations, to ensure active participation of all parties in the ethics enforcement process, and attempts to incorporate specialty viewpoints into a compatible and continually revised master code of ethics. They provide referral to other jurisdictions for complaints against accused parties, as appropriate. They may provide important educational programs to increase practitioner expertise in ethical practice, and may issue advisory opinions to members who inquire, to assist in proactively guiding ethical practice.

At the next two levels of ethics governance are professional regulatory bodies that either certify or license professionals, and that constitute the preeminent enforcers of the mandatory code. National certification bodies, such as CRCC and the National Board for Counselor Certification (NBCC), as well as the state counselor licensure boards, operate at this level. They perform a pivotal role in the promulgation and enforcement of ethical standards. However, they draw their specific codes of ethical standards from the professional organizations, because they do not constitute the profession, but rather regulate it, based upon the profession's own internal standards. They may provide information and consultation to professional organizations in revising and maintaining current the codes of ethics. Beyond the ethical regulatory function, the regulatory bodies encourage ethical proficiency of their licensees and certificants, through requiring preservice education and continuing education in the area of ethics.

As a practical matter, states that license professional counselors usually adopt the ACA Code of Ethics and Standards of Practice, as does NBCC, and a counselor licensed in a state that has adopted the ACA code would be governed by that code or one very closely related to it. Additionally, the 2002 revised CRCC Code of Professional Ethics for Rehabilitation Counselors (Appendix C in this book) is very similar to the ACA code of ethics (Tarvydas & Cottone, 2000), and this code has been adopted by ARCA and National Rehabilitation Counseling Association. In essence, this consistency provides rehabilitation counselors with a unified code of ethics within the profession, which is highly compatible with ethical standards of ACA and most counseling licensure boards.

At the pinnacle of the ethics governance hierarchy are found the civil and criminal courts and other legal jurisdictions that impact the ethical practice of counselors. For example, engaging in sexual intimacy with a client is a criminal offense in some states, including Colorado, Wisconsin, Minnesota, Missouri, Texas, Washington, Michigan, and Florida (Corey et al., 2003). However, one of the primary mechanisms of legal governance of ethics still is through the use of malpractice suits in civil courts. In malpractice actions, one of the central points is to establish a violation of duty, requiring determining the standard of what constitutes "good professional practice," as applied to the matter at hand. This issue is difficult to determine, because it is often ill-defined and requires many types of considerations. It is not unusual that various expert witnesses would be called to testify regarding such practices. Additionally, there might be an attempt to establish that a blatant violation of the general rules of the profession occurred, by reference to the profession's ethical standards (Thompson, 1990).

Another standard of practice that might be applied would be consideration of whether the action or service in question was both within the scope of practice of the profession and within the individual's personal scope of practice (see Appendix B of this book for the CRCC Scope of Practice). The profession of rehabilitation counseling has established its scope of practice, with which its practitioners must be familiar, to appropriately and ethically establish their personal scopes of practice (CRCC, 1994). Additionally, licensed professional counselors in many states are governed by the scope of practice described for counselors within their state's licensure regulatory language, and are often required to declare their personal scopes of practice at the time they are licensed, and to revise them as appropriate. Practitioners are ethically bound to limit their own scopes of practice to areas within the profession's scope, in which they are personally competent to practice, by virtue of appropriate types and levels of education, supervision, and professional experience (LaBuda, 1995).

Through these six levels, the various professional governance entities interact to provide a network of mandatory and aspirational ethics functions. Concern for the protection of consumers is very strong among these professional governance structures, and they have cooperated to share information about the most serious ethical infractions that are adjudicated within their organizations. All member counselor licensure boards and affiliate organizational members of the American Association for State Counseling Boards (AASCB) contribute such information to the Disciplinary Information Network, which facilitates enforcement of ethical standards across all these entities. ACA, CORE, and CRCC are affiliate members of AASCB and participate in this informational database by providing and receiving information about credential and membership revocations. In their totality, they are an interactive system of research, educational, and enforcement services to shape and regulate the ethical practice of counselors. Taken together, these systems of knowledge, traditions, rules, and laws form the regulatory content, but they do not provide the practitioner with possibly the most crucial tool for ethical practice—knowledge and experience in application of a decision-making process that can be applied to this form and content.

ETHICAL DECISION-MAKING PROCESSES

The intent of an ethics code is to provide rehabilitation counselors with guidance for specific situations they experience in their practices. However, authorities have long recognized that ethics codes must be written in general-enough terms that they apply across a wide range of practice settings. They also are reactive in nature; that is, they address situations that have already been part of the profession's experience (Kitchener, 1984; Mabe & Rollin, 1986). As a result, even with the knowledge of the profession's code of ethics, rehabilitation counselors may find that they do not have sufficient guidance to resolve the dilemma in question. They may find that the particular situation with which they are faced is not addressed in their code; that their practice is governed by more than one code, providing conflicting direction in the situation; or that conflicting provisions within any one code appear to apply to the situation. For that reason, the rehabilitation counselor must be prepared to exercise their professional judgment in ethics responsibly. This type of occurrence is not so much a failure of ethical codes, but rather a natural and appropriate juncture recognizing the importance and role of professional judgment. In other words, it is affirmation that one is involved in practice of a profession, rather than doing a job, however skilled. In order to exercise professional judgment, the rehabilitation counselor must be prepared to recognize underlying ethical principles or conflicts between competing interests, and to apply appropriate ethical decision-making skills to resolve the dilemma and act in an ethical manner (Francouer, 1983; Kitchener, 1984; Tarvydas, 1987). Fortunately, the professional is assisted in this task by examination and refinement of their ordinary moral sense, as well as by the availability of thoughtful models for the ethical decision-making process. Many components of ethical decision making involve teachable, learnable skills, to supplement the professional's developing intuitive professional judgment.

Several types of models exist, which seek to explain and structure the process of ethical decision making (Cottone & Claus, 2000). Some prominent examples view the ethics decision making process as: professional self-exploration (Corey et al., 2003); a moral reasoning discourse (Kitchener, 1984); the result of a moral developmental process (VanHoose & Kottler, 1985); a multidimensional, integrative psychological process (Rest, 1984); and involving a hierarchy of four contextual levels that affect the process of decision making (Tarvydas & Cottone, 1991). Generally, ethical decision-making models can be thought of as having the characteristics of either principal or virtue ethics (Corey et al., 2003). *Principle* ethics focuses on the objective, rational, cognitive aspects of the process. Practitioners who adhere to this perspective tend to view the application of universal, impartial ethical principles, rules, codes, and law as being the core elements of ethics. *Virtue* ethics considers the characteristics of the counselors themselves as the critical element for responsible practice. Thus, proponents of virtue ethics approaches would tend to concern themselves more with counselors reflecting upon and clarifying their moral and value positions. Additionally, they would examine other personal issues that might impact their ethical practice, such as unresolved emotional needs, which might negatively affect their work with their clients. Preferred approaches to ethical decision making should include both aspects (Corey et al., 2003; Meara, Schmidt, & Day, 1996). Among other positive contributions of such a synergistic approach, Vasquez (1996) has speculated that the addition of virtue ethical perspectives may improve ethical conduct in multicultural and diverse interactions and settings.

TARVYDAS' INTEGRATIVE DECISION-MAKING MODEL OF ETHICAL BEHAVIOR

The Tarvydas integrative decision-making model of ethical behavior builds on several well-known decision-making models widely used by professionals in the mental health and counseling communities. It incorporates the most prominent principle and virtue aspects of several decision-making approaches and introduces some contextual considerations into the process. The Tarvydas integrative model emphasizes the constant process of interaction between the principle and virtue elements, and places a reflective attitude at the heart of the process. The model also focuses on the actual production of ethical behavior within a specified context, rather than prematurely terminating analysis by merely selecting the best ethical course of action. The model is shown in Table 6.1. This approach respects the importance of setting and environmental factors, which are crucial in counseling. Indeed, in reviewing the various approaches to ethical decision making, Garcia, Cartwright, Winston, and

TABLE 6.1 Tarvydas Integrative Model for Ethical Behavior

Themes or Attitudes in the Integrative Model

Maintain an attitude of *reflection.*
Address *balance* between issues and parties to the ethical dilemma.
Pay close attention to the *context(s)* of the situation.
Utilize a process of *collaboration* with all rightful parties to the situation.

Stage I. Interpreting the Situation Through Awareness and Fact-Finding

Component 1. Enhance sensitivity and awareness.
Component 2. Reflect, to determine whether dilemma or issue is involved.
Component 3. Determine the major stakeholders and their ethical claims in the situation.
Component 4. Engage in the fact-finding process.

Stage II. Formulating an Ethical Decision

Component 1. Review the problem or dilemma.
Component 2. Determine what ethical codes, laws, ethical principles, and institutional policies and procedures exist that apply to the dilemma.
Component 3. Generate possible and probable courses of action.
Component 4. Consider potential positive and negative consequences for each course of action.
Component 5. Select the best ethical course of action.

Stage III. Selecting an Action by Weighing Competing, Nonmoral Values

Component 1. Engage in reflective recognition and analysis of personal competing values.
Component 2. Consider contextual influences on values selection at the collegial, team, institutional, and societal levels.
Component 3. Select preferred course of action.

Stage IV. Planning and Executing the Selected Course of Action

Component 1. Figure out a reasonable sequence of concrete actions to be taken.
Component 2. Anticipate and work out personal and contextual barriers to effective execution of the plan of action, and effective countermeasures for them.
Component 3. Carry out and evaluate the course of action as planned.

Borzuchowska (in press) observed that this model uses virtue ethics and behavioral strategies that are consistent with a multicultural approach to counseling and ethical decision making, and have proposed an integrative transcultural ethical decision-making model that is based primarily on the Tarvydas integrative model.

Themes and Attitudes

In addition to the specific elements or steps of the Tarvydas integrative model, there are four underlying themes or attitudes that are necessary for the professional counselor to enact. These attitudes involve mindfully attending to the tasks of (1) maintaining a stance of reflection concerning one's own conscious awareness of personal issues, values, and decision making skills, as well as extending an effort to understand those of all others concerned with the situation, and their relationship to the decision maker; (2) addressing the *balance* among various issues, people, and perspectives within the process; (3) maintaining an appropriate level of attention to the context of the situation in question, allowing awareness of the counselor–client, treatment team, organizational, and societal implications of the ethical elements; and (4) seeking to use a process of *collaboration* with all rightful parties to the decision, but most especially the client.

By adopting these background attitudes of reflection, balance, context, and collaboration, counselors engage in a more thorough process that will help preserve the integrity and dignity of all parties involved. This will be the case even when outcomes are not considered equally positive for all participants in the process, as is often true in a serious dilemma when such attitudes can be particularly meaningful. Indeed, Betan and Stanton (1999) studied students' responses to ethical dilemmas, analyzing how emotions and concerns influence willingness to implement ethical knowledge. They concluded that "subjectivity and emotional involvement are essential tools for determining ethical action, but they must be integrated with rational analysis" (p. 295).

Reflection is the overriding attitude of importance throughout the enactment of the specific elements of stages and components that constitute the steps of the Tarvydas integrative model. Many complex decision-making processes easily become overwhelming, either in their innate complexity, or in the real-life press of the speed or intensity of events. In the current approach, the counselor is urged always to "Stop and think!" at each point in the process. The order of operations is not critical or absolute, nor more important than being reflective and invested in a calm, dignified, respectful, and thorough analysis of the situation. Not until we recognize that we are involved in the process, and appreciate its critical aspects, can we call forth other resources to assist the process and persons within it. Such an attitude of reflection will serve the counselor well at all stages of this process.

Elements

The specific elements that constitute the operations within the Tarvydas integrative model have four main stages with several components, including the steps to be taken within each stage. The concepts summarized below are drawn, in the main, from the work of Rest (1984), Kitchener (1984), and Tarvydas and Cottone (1991).

Stage I: Interpreting the Situation Through Awareness and Fact-Finding

At this stage, the primary task of counselors is to be sensitive and aware of the needs and welfare of the people around them, and of the ethical implications of these situations. This level of awareness allows counselors to imagine and to investigate the effects of the situation on the parties involved and the possible effects of various actions and conditions. This research and awareness must also include emotional, as well as cognitive and fact-based, considerations. Three components constitute the counselors' operations in this stage.

Component 1 involves enhancing one's sensitivity and awareness. In *Component 2,* the counselor takes an inventory of the people who are major stakeholders in the outcome of the situation. It is important to reflect on any parties who will be affected and who play a major role in the client's life, as well as considering what their exact relationship is, ethically and legally, to the person at the center of the issue: the client. Imagine dropping a rock into a pond: The point of impact is where the central figure, the client, is situated; however, the client is surrounded by people at varying levels of closeness to them, such as parents, foster parents, intimate partners, spouse, children, employer, friends, and neighbors, all radiate out from the client in decreasing levels of intimacy and responsibility to the client.

Figure 6.3 depicts how the spheres of influence of these stakeholders in the client's life, as well as the stakeholders at each of the four levels in the professional world of the counselor, may be seen as intersecting. This way of thinking about the relationships among the different stakeholders in the situation allows for a fuller appreciation of the specific people and contexts of the counselor's practice and the client's situation.

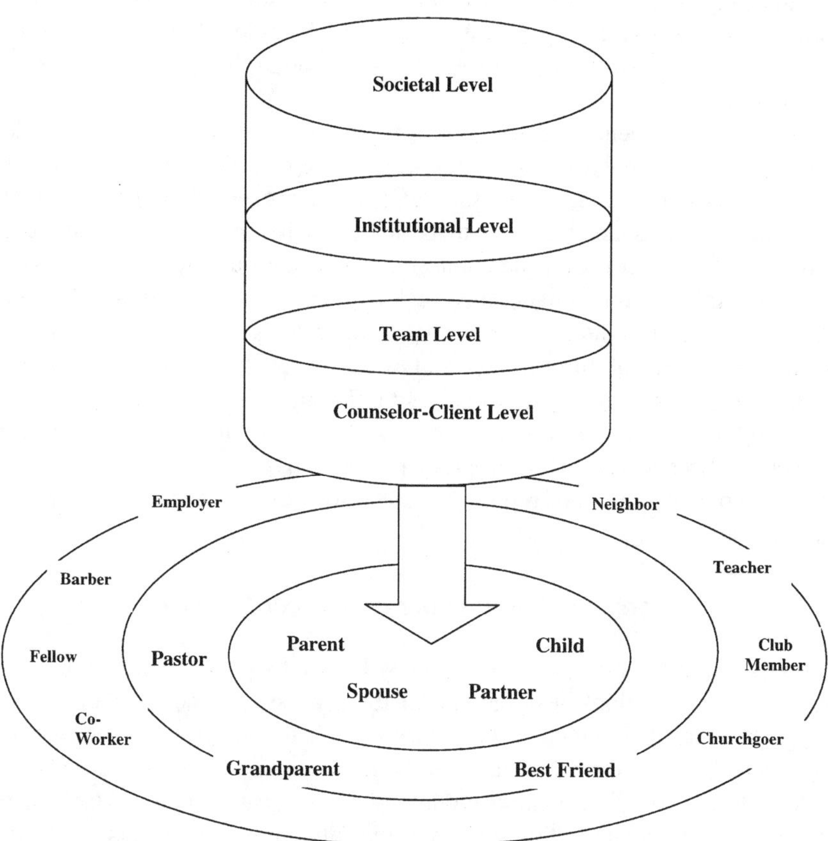

FIGURE 6.3 The intersection of the client's personal world with the counselor's professional hierarchical contexts.

A number of people and levels of the service hierarchy will (or should) play a part in the ethics decision. These social forces will create both positive and negative influences in the ethical situation, and should be taken into account in the ethical analysis. The ethical claims of these parties on the counselor's level of duty are not uniform. Almost all codes of ethics in counseling make it clear that the client is the person to whom the first duty is owed, but there are others to whom the counselor has lesser, but important levels of duty. It is always important to determine whether any surrogate decision makers for the client exist, such as a guardian or person with power of attorney, so that they may be brought into the central circle of duty early in the process. Sensitivity and proactivity are useful in working through situations in which the legal relationships involved do not coincide with the social and emotional bonds between the client and other people involved in the dilemma.

The final element in Stage I is *Component 3,* in which the counselor undertakes an extensive fact-finding investigation, with a scope appropriate to the situation. The nature of the fact-finding process should be carefully considered and is not intended to be a formal investigative or quasi-legal process. The intent is that the counselor should carefully review and understand the information at hand, then seek out new information. Only information that is appropriately available to a counselor should be involved. The scope and depth of information that would be rightfully available to the counselor is surprising, but it is often not fully utilized. For example, information might be gained from such sources as further discussion with the client, contacts with family (with appropriate permission of the client), case records, expert consultation and reports, legal resources, or agency policy and procedures.

Stage II: Formulating an Ethical Decision

This aspect of the process is most widely known by professionals, and many may erroneously think it is the end of the process. The central task in this stage is to identify which of the possible ethical courses of action appears to come closest to the moral ideal in the situation under consideration (Rest, 1984). Many decision-making models in other areas of counseling can be applied as a template at this stage, but the following components are drawn from the work of Van Hoose and Kottler (1985).

Component 1 suggests that the counselor review the problem or dilemma, to be sure that it is clearly understood in light of any new information obtained in Stage I. In *Component 2,* the counselor researches the standards of law and practice applicable to the situation. This component includes Kitchener's (1984) attention to ethical codes, laws, and ethical principles, and Tarvydas and Cottone's (1991) concern for the team and organizational context in the examination of institutional policies and procedures to make mention of other useful areas for consideration. The counselor would also analyze which of the five core ethical principles (autonomy, beneficience, nonmaleficence, justice, and fidelity) may be either supported or compromised by the types of actions that are being contemplated in the situation. This operation is formally known as *principle analysis* and is one of the most challenging, yet critical aspects of the ethical analysis of a dilemma. The core, or main, principle analysis concerns the ethical obligations owed to the client, rather than to other parties to the situation. *Component 3* initiates the process of formally envisioning and generating of possible and probable courses of action. As with all decision-making processes, it is important not to truncate this exploratory process by prematurely censoring the possibilities, or succumbing to a sense of being too overwhelmed, or too limited, in options. *Component 4* is the logical outgrowth of considering courses of action: Positive and negative consequences are identified and assessed in relation to risks, as well as to material and personal resources available. In *Component 5,* the counselor is reminded to consult with supervisors and trusted and knowledgeable colleagues for guidance, if this has not been done before this point. Professional standards of practice emphasize the importance of appropriate collegial consultation to resolve difficult clinical and ethical dilemmas. Research has also demonstrated that such consultations can have a significant influence on those seeking such consultation (Cottone, Tarvydas, & House, 1994). There is value in reviewing the reasoning employed in working through the ethical dilemma to this point, and the solutions and consequences envisioned, to be sure that all potentially useful and appropriate considerations have been taken into account. Finally, the best ethical course of action is determined and articulated in *Component 6.* The ethical decision at this stage of the model should be contrasted with the decision about what the counselor actually decided to do, which is the product of Stage III.

Stage III: Selecting an Action by Weighing Competing, Nonmoral Values, Personal Blind Spots, and Prejudices

Many people would think that the ethical decision-making process is concluded at the end of Stage II. This impression is limited in its realization of the many additional forces that may affect the counselor and result in the counselor not actually executing the selected ethical course of action. *Component 1* of Stage III interjects a period of reflection and active processing of what the counselor intends to do, in view of competing, nonmoral values (Rest, 1984). At this point, the counselor considers any personal factors that might intervene to pull them away from choosing the ethical action or cause that action to be substantially modified. Nonmoral values involve anything that the counselor may prize or desire, which is not in and of itself a moral value, such as justice. Such values may include such things as valuing social harmony, spending time with friends or working on one's hobby, or having personal wealth. In this component, counselors are also called upon to examine themselves, to determine if they have some personal blind spots or prejudices that might affect their judgment or resolve to do the ethical thing, such as a fear of HIV infection, or the conviction that gay men are also likely to molest children. This portion of the model provides an excellent opportunity for counselors to carefully evaluate whether they have adequately incorporated multicultural considerations and competencies in their work on this ethical dilemma and to be sure that they are not operating from a culturally encapsulated frame of reference.

Counselors must allow themselves to become aware of the strength and attractiveness of other values they hold, which may influence whether they will discharge their ethical obligations. If they are self-aware, they may more effectively and honestly compensate for their conflicted impulses, at this point. Counselors may have strong needs for acceptance by peers or supervisors, for prestige and influence, to avoid controversy, or to be financially successful. These value orientations may come into conflict with the course of action necessary to proceed ethically, and must be reconciled with ethical requirements, if the client is to be ethically served. On the other hand, counselors may place a high value on being moral or ethical, on being accepted as respected professionals with high ethical standards, or they may value the esteem of colleagues who place a high value on ethical professional behavior. Those forces should enhance the tendency to select ethical behavioral options (the influence of the ethical climate on the ethical behavior of the counselor is more fully explored in Tarvydas, O'Rourke, and Malaski [2003]). Therefore, the importance of selecting and maintaining ethically sensitized and positive professional and personal cultures should be recognized as critical to full professional functioning, as the next component would suggest.

In *Component 2,* counselors systematically inventory the contextual influences on their choices at the collegial, team, institutional, and societal levels. This is not a simple process of weighing influences, but it should serve as an inventory of influences, which may be either dysfunctional or constructive, for selecting the ethical course over other types of values present in these other interactions. Counselors may also use this type of information to think strategically about the influences they will need to overcome to provide ethical service in the situation. Beyond the immediate situation, counselors should control their exposure to contexts that consistently reinforce values that run counter to the dictates of good ethical practices. For example, rehabilitation counselors working in private practices where their employers consistently pressure them to favor the attorneys that hire them in their forensic evaluations run the risk of eventually succumbing to these pressures.

Component 3 is the final aspect of Stage III, in which the counselor selects the preferred course of action or the behavior that they plan to undertake.

This decision may be a reaffirmation of the intention to take the ethical course of action, as determined at the conclusion of Stage II. However, it may be some other course of action that may even not be ethical, or a modified version of the ethical course of action selected in Stage II. Whatever the choice, the counselor has selected it after this more extensive reflection on their own competing values and personal blind spots, as well as the contextual influences on them in the situation in question.

Stage IV: Planning and Executing the Selected Course of Action

Rest (1984) described the essential tasks of this stage as planning to implement and executing what one plans to do. This operation includes *Component 1*, in which the counselor figures out a reasonable sequence of concrete actions to be taken. In *Component 2*, the task is to anticipate and work out all personal and contextual barriers to effectively executing the plan. Preparing countermeasures for barriers that may arise is useful. Here, the earlier attention to other stakeholders and their concerns may suggest problems or allies to the process. Additionally, earlier consideration of the contextual influences in Stage III assist the counselor in this type of strategic planning. *Component 3* is the final step of this model, in that it provides for the execution, documentation, and evaluation of the course of action as planned. Rest (1989) noted that the actual behavioral execution of ethics is often not a simple task, frequently drawing heavily on the personal, emotional qualities and professional and interpersonal skills of the counselor. He mentions such qualities as firmness of resolve, ego strength, and social assertiveness. To this list could be added countless skills, such as persistence, tact, time management, assertiveness skills, team collaboration, and conflict-resolution skills. Considerations are limited only by the characteristics and requirements of the counselor and specific situation involved. Clear and thorough documentation of the entire plan, and the rationale behind it, and ethical decision-making steps taken in responding to the ethical dilemma as the process unfolds, are critical to protect the interests of both counselor and client. The information gained in this documentation process will prove critical to assisting in evaluating the effectiveness of the entire ethical decision-making process.

Practicing the Tarvydas Integrative Model. Just like the basic counseling microskills, the skills of ethical decision making, as described, do not come automatically, or even easily, after merely reading about the concepts in a book. Practice in solving mock ethical dilemmas; working to address actual ethical dilemmas under the supervision of an ethically knowledgeable instructor, clinical supervisor, master counselor, or mentor; and incorporating ethical analysis into your clinical training process, are all essential to gradual progression in gaining practical skills and sensitive, accurate ethical knowledge. A complex ethical scenario, with a full ethical analysis using the Tarvydas integrative model and all its stages and components, is presented in Table 6.2, to begin your exploration of how to use this rich approach to ethical decision making.

The following analysis does not represent the one and only correct answer to this dilemma. Sometimes, information discovered, or concerns raised by other reasonable people, can lead to important shifts in the elements of a case. Also, because reasonable professionals can judge and weigh even the same ideas or risks differently, there may be other valid conclusions to the same case. This process is not so much about getting the hidden, correct answer, but rather is about going through the process of decision making thoroughly and carefully, and exercising due care and good, reasonable professional judgement throughout. If you do this, in the end, you will be more likely to have arrived at an explicable judgment that minimizes risk to your client, yourself, and others. You will also benefit from increased confidence and peace of mind, assured that you have done your best in the situation, having used a thorough, thoughtful approach to solving a dilemma that may not have a solution that is satisfying to the parties involved.

CASE STUDY 6.1

CASE STUDY ILLUSTRATION OF THE TARVYDAS INTEGRATIVE MODEL FOR ETHICAL BEHAVIOR

NARRATIVE OF CASE EXAMPLE

John is a 43-year-old man who is meeting with a counselor at the Department of Correctional Services (DCS). He has recently been released from prison on parole, and is meeting with a counselor voluntarily to deal with some issues of depression. He is currently on medication for depression, and has made previous suicide attempts. He was married to a woman for nine years, and they had two children together, now 7 and 5 years old. She also had two children from a previous relationship, now 12 and 8 years old, which John also considers to be his children. He and his wife are recently divorced. At first, she would not allow the children to visit their dad, but just recently John says they have been talking again, and his ex-wife has started to trust him again and let the children visit whenever they wanted. Just recently, his youngest girl confided in him that their mom and her new friends are still using drugs, and are also selling them from the house. She had found a syringe at the home, which her mom had thought was hidden. John is very adamant that he does not want to contact the Department of Human Services (DHS) or any other similar agency about this. He had contacted DHS for a similar situation a few years ago, and had a bad experience. DHS had "done nothing," and his ex-wife had found out that he had made the report. She did not let him see the kids for a long time after the incident. He feels that, at this point, he can do the most good by keeping a close relationship with his children, and a civil relationship with his ex-wife. He is living a clean and drug-free life, and feels that he is his ex-wife's best hope right now to straighten out. He says that, if a report is made, the only thing he is sure of is that his ex-wife would not let him see the children, and he does not know if he could live without being part of his children's life. In this case, the client has his reasons for not wanting to contact DHS, and client autonomy needs to be respected. The client also raises the issue that maybe contacting the authorities really is not in the best interest of the children. He also made some statements regarding not being able to live without being a part of his children's lives, which need to be taken seriously, given the client's suicidal history and current state of depression. On the other hand, young children are involved in a dangerous situation. There is no report of physical or sexual abuse occurring, yet drug use in the home and young children coming across needles is dangerous and could be considered abuse. At this point, the counselor feels there may be a potential dilemma that needs to be explored further.

STAGE I: INTERPRETING THE SITUATION THROUGH AWARENESS AND FACT-FINDING

The primary task of the counselor in Stage I is to be sensitive and aware of the needs and welfare of the people around them, and of the ethical implications of these situations. This level of awareness allows counselors to imagine and to investigate the effects of the situation on the parties involved and the possible effects of various actions and conditions. This research and awareness must also include emotional as well as cognitive and fact-based considerations.

Component 1: Sensitivity and Awareness

At this point, the counselor talks to the client and gets his impression of who will be affected by this situation, and how they will be affected. The client clearly cares about his children, but firmly believes that the best chance they have is if he continues to be a part of their life. He has no guarantee what would happen if he did contact DHS, and he does not want to take that risk. Given what happened the last time he called, he is very distrustful of the system. He also expressed some concerns for his ex-wife, and, even though they parted on unfriendly terms, he still seems to care about her and wants what is best for her, also. He says that they are just starting to talk again, and he feels that he may be the only one who truly understands what she is going through with the drugs and might be able to help her kick the habit. Although he admits that he worries what kind of environment his children are living in, he feels that this is the best chance they have.

The counselor also notes that there are four children in the house, of varying ages. An 18-year-old might understand how dangerous finding a needle in the house really is, but a 5-year-old most likely would not. Even aside from needles being in the house, there is also the potential for danger with what kind of people are around the children. If their mother is dealing drugs from the home, many of those she sells to are probably in the house, also, and around the children.

The client says he understands all of this, but still feels that he is making progress with his ex-wife, and that he is the best chance for his children. He acknowledges that he is taking on a lot of responsibility, but says that he would do anything for his children and truly believes that he is doing the best for them in the long run.

Component 2: Major Stakeholders and Their Ethical Claims

The counselor identifies the parties who will be affected and what their exact relationship is, ethically and legally, to the person at the center of the issue. There are often others to whom the counselor has lesser, but important, levels of duty, such as parents, intimate partners, spouse, children, employer, friends, neighbors, guardian, or persons with power of attorney. List below all important parties with an ethical or legal claim in the situation.

Parties	*Ethical Claim*
The client	He does not want to contact any authorities.
The children	They may be in danger, may not know all of their options or how they could get help.
DCS	They are responsible for their counselors, and could be held liable for mistakes made by their employees.
The counselor	They may be held liable for any harm that befalls the children or the client.
The ex-wife	She could face an abuse investigation and the subsequent consequences.
Grandparents	If DHS did find abuse, they would most likely get custody of the children.

Component 3: Fact-Finding Process

The counselor undertakes an extensive fact-finding investigation, of a scope appropriate to the situation, by reviewing and understanding current information and seeking out new information. This investigation involves gathering information appropriately available to the counselor, either through professional records and channels (with appropriately obtained releases of information), or part of public domain information. Sources might include further discussion with the client, contacts with family (with client's permission), current and old client records in one's own or another agency, expert consultation and reports, legal resources, or agency policy and procedures. List below all facts or factual questions the counselor should reasonably be able to research or answer.

A call was made anonymously to DHS to find out if the situation in general fell under the guidelines for mandatory reporters, which it did not. DHS stated that it did not fall under mandatory guidelines, because it was third-party information.

The counselor talked to the supervisor and found out that they have an unwritten rule or policy at DCS. This policy is to convince the client to call authorities and report the situation.

The client stated that, if DHS was contacted, an investigation was conducted, and action was taken to remove the children from their mother, her parents would probably receive custody. The client stated that he has a good relationship with her parents. He thought that they would allow him to see the children, if they did get custody of the children.

The counselor was informed by a supervisor that one reason DHS may not have done anything the last time he reported was that there may have been some type of drug investigation going on. If there is a current investigation into drug trafficking or selling, they can postpone going into the house for a child abuse charge, because the house is under supervision as part of a larger investigation.

STAGE II: FORMULATING AN ETHICAL DECISION

The counselor's task in this stage is to identify which of the possible ethical courses of action appears to come closest to the ethical ideal in the situation under consideration.

Component 1: Review Problem or Dilemma

Review the problem or dilemma, to be sure it is clearly understood in relation to any new information.

Because this situation does not fall into the category of mandatory reporting, the counselor is not legally bound to break the client's confidence. However, we now know that the unwritten policy of the institution (DCS) is to try to convince or coerce the client to call DHS on their own. Thus, we must decide whether to respect the client's wishes not to call DHS or to try to coerce the client to call, in accordance with the institution's unwritten policy.

Component 2: Determine Ethical Codes, Laws, Principles

The counselor must determine and research the standards of law (in any and all applicable local jurisdictions) and professional practices applicable to the situation. The latter material includes ethical codes and related standards of care, laws, ethical principles, and institutional policies and procedures. List these below.

ETHICAL CODES

List any rules or canons from applicable ethics code(s) and provide a summary of the dictate. For counselors, the ACA Code of Ethics and Professional Standards, and any applicable specialty standards, are recommended. If the counselor is licensed or holds national certification, the codes of ethics that apply to that credential also must be consulted.

ACA Code of Ethics

Section A.1.a Primary Responsibility. The primary responsibility of counselors is to respect the dignity and promote the welfare of the clients.

Section A.1.b Positive Growth and Development. Counselors encourage client growth and development in ways that foster the client's interest and welfare; counselors avoid fostering dependent counseling relationships.

Section B.1.c Exceptions. The general requirement that counselors keep information confidential does not apply when disclosure is required to prevent clear and imminent danger to the client or to others or when legal requirements demand that confidential information be revealed.

Section D.1.c Negative Conditions. Counselors alert their employers to conditions that may be potentially disruptive or damaging to the counselor's professional responsibilities or that may limit their effectiveness.

Section D.1.l Employer Policies. The acceptance of employment in an agency or institution implies that counselors are in agreement with its general policies and principles. Counselors strive to reach agreement with employers as to acceptable standards of conduct that allow for changes in institutional policy conducive to the growth and development of clients.

LAWS/LEGAL CONSIDERATIONS

List any laws or legal considerations that may apply. Research those relevant to your own jurisdiction. The example is provided, based upon Iowa law, circa 2000. This example is not to be considered a legal opinion, only an example. For further information, consult legal counsel and resources in your own area.

Iowa Code

Section 232.69 Mandatory and permissive reporters-training required. [A counselor is considered to be a mandatory reporter] ". . . who, in the scope of professional practice or in their employment responsibilities, examines, counsels, or treats a child and reasonably believes a child has suffered abuse.

> Section 232.68 [Included in the definitions of child abuse:] An illegal drug is present in a child's body as a direct and foreseeable consequence of the acts or omissions of the person responsible for the care of the child.

ETHICAL PRINCIPLES

List all ethical principles that describe relevant obligations. Describe the courses of action, the principles upheld, the principles compromised, and the obligations. Sometimes this process is referred to as *principle analysis,* a process wherein ethical principles are specified and subjected to balancing considerations.

Each of the two courses of action can be supported by one or more ethical principles. Contacting authorities could fall under the category of beneficence on the part of the children. Keeping John's confidence could fall under the category of autonomy, for honoring the right to individual decisions. There is also the possibility that both scenarios could fit into the category of nonmaleficence. Not telling anyone could lead to harm for the children, in some way. Also, by telling, it is possible that John's fears could materialize and the ex-wife could keep the children away from him. In this way, it may be harmful to the client, and may be also for the children, if they are not allowed to see their father.

The ethical principles supporting the other course of action will be compromised. If the authorities are told, the counselor is not respecting the client's autonomy. If authorities are not told, the counselor may be compromising the principles of nonmaleficence toward the children and the concept of beneficence, in the same way.

This situation is an ethical dilemma, not just an ethical issue. An ethical issue has a fairly identifiable course of action that is appropriate, even if taking that action is not necessarily easy in practice (i.e., as in the case of involuntarily committing a seriously suicidal individual).

Action A. Pressuring the Client

Principles Upheld	*Principles Compromised*
Beneficence (to children)	Beneficence (to client)
	Nonmaleficence (to client)
	Autonomy (of client)
	Fidelity (to client)

Resultant Obligations: Work with client?*

Action B. Not Pressuring the Client

Principles Upheld	*Principles Compromised*
Nonmaleficence (to client)	Beneficence (to children)
Beneficence (to client)	Nonmaleficence(to children)
Autonomy (to client)	
Fidelity (to client)	

Resultant Obligations: Work with client?*

*Note: In principle analysis, the principle obligations owed to your client normally outweigh those to others. Therefore, frequently they are the only ones considered; or, if those obligations to others are considered, those owed to the client generally supercede them, because the counselor incurs these primary obligations by virtue of entering into a professional relationship with the client. The exception to this case would involve obligations to vulnerable others (e.g., small children), and/or those situations in which there a high degree of serious danger or risk. This reasoning is why this case is a particularly troublesome dilemma.

INSTITUTIONAL/AGENCY RULES OR POLICIES

List any institutional/agency rules or policies that may apply.

In the experience of the counselor, the unwritten policy of DCS is to try to coerce the client into reporting the possible child abuse to DHS.

Component 3: Courses of Action

List all possible and probable courses of action. If you can boil this selection down to two opposing options, this strategy is recommended.

Action A: Attempt to coerce the client into reporting.
Action B: Do not try to coerce the client into reporting.

Component 4: Positive and Negative Consequences

Consider potential positive and negative consequences for each course of action, in light of the risks.

Action A: Pressure the client

Positive Consequences	*Negative Consequences*
May protect the children from abuse Follows unwritten DCS policy Hurts client's trust of counselor DCS would not step in to coerce the client Less time for other pressing issues of client Protects DCS from liability	Does not respect client's autonomy or confidentiality Ex-wife may cut off child visitation Negative relationship with ex-wife May evoke suicidal thoughts

Action B: Do not pressure client

Positive Consequences	*Negative Consequences*
Respects client's autonomy and confidentiality Time for other client issues Does not evoke suicidal thoughts Child visitation is preserved Positive relationship with ex-wife	Does not protect children from possible abuse Counselor is defying employer (DCS) DCS might step in and coerce client anyway DCS might be liable (if child is harmed)

Component 5: Consult with Others

Consult with supervisors and other knowledgeable professionals. Review the reasoning employed so far in working through the ethical dilemma in consulting with others.

Individual	*Type of Consultation*
1. ACA Ethics Committee	Review situation, obtain suggestions and opinion.
2. Counselors from other corrections	Review situation, obtain agencies suggestions and opinion.
3. Other colleagues	Review situation, obtain suggestions and opinion.
4. DHS anonymously again	Review situation, obtain suggestions and opinion.
5. Attorney	Review situation, obtain suggestions and opinion.

Component 6: Determine Best Ethical Action

Select the best ethical course of action.

The best ethical course of action would be not to pressure the client to report to DHS, for the following reasons:

1. More ethical principles support this course of action, especially for client.
2. More positive than negative consequences are likely to result.
3. The Iowa Code does not consider this a situation of mandatory child abuse reporting, because the counselor is not working directly with the children, and the only information is "hearsay."

STAGE III: SELECTING AN ACTION BY WEIGHING COMPETING, NONMORAL VALUES, PERSONAL BLIND SPOTS, OR PREJUDICES

The counselor, in this stage, must realize the many additional forces that may affect the counselor and tempt the counselor to not actually execute the selected ethical course of action.

Component 1: Competing Values or Concerns

The counselor engages in a period of reflection and active processing of personal competing values (e.g., need to be liked by coworkers or their supervisor, or a desire to be seen as a team player, so as to be promoted by the supervisor), personal blind spots, or prejudices that may influence whether or not they will discharge their ethical obligations. These value orientations may either come into conflict with the course of action necessary to proceed ethically or enhance the tendency to select ethical professional behavior.

Conflicting Concerns	*Potential Effects*
1. Fear of a negative evaluation by DCS, if unwritten policy is not followed	Loss of job, license, respect Financial consequences
2. Feel the need to protect the children at all costs, no matter what the situation	Loss of reputation and seen as a confidential risk

3. Fear of legal repercussions if abuse situation is not reported to DHS	Children are harmed Loss of license of job
4. Fear of harm to DCS	Personal mental health Financial impact on agency/self
5. Fear of losing respect of colleagues	Personal mental health Future relationships
6. Feeling that client should not be pressured and has autonomy in the decision	Harm to children Increased client confidence
7. Feeling that counseling session should not be used to work on the client's problems (e.g., depression), rather than using all of the time trying to convince client to call DHS	DHS not contacted and children are harmed Client benefits from counseling

Component 2: Contextual Influences

The counselor systematically inventories the contextual influences, on their choices at the collegial, team, institutional, and societal levels. These influences might be either dysfunctional or constructive for selecting the ethical course over other types of values.

Level 1: Clinical

1. Counselor's professors/supervisors have recommended advocating for clients' autonomy in the past.

Level 2: Team

1. A few coworkers note that DHS, said that the counselor is not required to report the situation to DHS, because it is third-party information.

Level 3: Institutional/Agency

1. DCS has an unwritten policy of convincing the client to report abuse, on their own.

2. Counselor's supervisor and most colleagues support the institution's policy and feel that all counselors at DCS should adhere to both written and unwritten policies.

Level 4: Social Policy/General Cultural

1. Society values children and children's welfare.
2. Society has little tolerance for drug abuse or the selling of drugs, especially when children are involved.
3. There is a fear of transmitted diseases in society, especially HIV and AIDS, which can be passed through intravenous drug use.
4. Society has a prejudiced attitude toward ex-cons on parole, and makes little distinction between those who are successfully recovering and those who are not.

Component 3: Select Preferred Action

The counselor selects the preferred course of action.

This course of action is to attempt to convince the client to call DHS anonymously. Yet, he still respects the client's autonomy and will not coerce him to report the situation to DHS.

STAGE IV: PLANNING AND EXECUTING THE SELECTED COURSE OF ACTION

The counselor in this stage plans to implement and execute the selected course of action.

Component 1: Possible Sequences of Actions

The counselor figures out a reasonable, practical sequence of concrete actions to be taken. List the action steps to be taken.

1. Talk with client about the consequences of his reporting versus not reporting the situation (anonymously, at least) to DHS.
2. Attempt to convince the client to call DHS anonymously for information about what would happen if the situation were reported.

3. If the client does not call, do not continue to convince him any further.
4. If the client does call and receives the information, give support for what he decides to do next.

Component 2: Contextual Barriers and Countermeasures

The counselor will need to anticipate and work out all personal and contextual barriers to effectively execute the plan. It is useful to prepare countermeasures for any contextual barriers that may arise.

Possible Barriers	*Possible Countermeasures*
1. Client does not wish to call.	Document the attempts to get him to call and not press the issue any further.
2. Supervisor may want the counselor to continue to coerce the client to call.	Counselor could let the supervisor know what she is not comfortable doing and apprise someone in authority over the supervisor of the situation.
3. DCS may assign the case to someone else.	No countermeasure, unless client insists upon seeing the current counselor.
4. John's ex-wife may refuse to let him see the children, if he reports the situation to DHS.	Counselor could encourage the client to speak with an attorney about his rights with the children.

Component 3: Carry Out, Document, and Evaluate

This step provides for the execution, documentation, and evaluation of the course of action as planned. Describe here the planned goal(s) and potential types of measurements of plan effectiveness and sources of information.

The counselor would carry out the plan by talking to the client about the consequences of reporting versus not reporting the abusive situation to DHS and attempt to get the client to call for information. If the client decides to call, the counselor would support his next step. The counselor would document the ethical decision-making steps taken. Finally, the counselor would evaluate the effectiveness of the plan of action and the entire ethical decision-making process.

Goal	Measure
1. Review consequences of reporting or not reporting and attempt to get the client to call DHS for information.	Weigh benefits and costs of client's decision: assess client's level of comfort with either decision.
2. Support client if he decides to call.	Assess what client needs from counselor.
3. Prevent harm to children and help mother.	Follow up with treatment referrals for mother and on the children's welfare.

This Case Study was developed by Vilia Tarvydas, PhD, LMHC, CRC, and uses the Tarvydas Integrative Decision-Making Model for Ethical Behavior.

SUMMARY

Rehabilitation counseling continues to grow in stature and visibility, as a profession. As a result, contemporary rehabilitation counselors should anticipate the need to demonstrate high levels of competency in the ethical aspects of their practices. The profession as a whole has provided substantial tools to inform this process, including the revised 2002 ethical standards of practice (Appendix C of this book), mechanisms to educate and govern the practice of these ethical standards, and knowledge and wisdom for individual counselors, embodied within models of ethical decision making and behavior. With responsible utilization of these sizable assets for ethical practice, rehabilitation counseling should continue its leadership in the counseling professionalization movement.

CHAPTER 7

Qualified Providers

Michael J. Leahy

Among the various professionals (e.g., physiatrists, psychologists, social workers, medical case managers) who may provide services to individuals with disabilities during their individual rehabilitation process, the rehabilitation counselor represents a unique professional, who plays a central role in the extramedical phase of the rehabilitation process, for individuals with both acquired and congenital disabilities (G. N. Wright, 1980). Rehabilitation counseling emerged as a full-time occupation over 80 years ago. Unlike the beginnings of other counseling specialties and health-related occupations, rehabilitation counseling was mandated as a specific work role, through federal legislation (Smith-Fess Act in 1920), which established the public or state–federal rehabilitation program in this country. In the years following this landmark legislation, rehabilitation counseling practice in the public and private sectors evolved and expanded to provide a comprehensive array of vocational and independent living services to an everincreasing adult population of persons with a wide range of physical and mental disabilities (Leahy & Szymanski, 1995).

Although the occupational status of rehabilitation counseling was established in the 1920s, it was not until the mid-1950s, with the passage of the 1954 Vocational Rehabilitation (VR) Act Amendments, that the discipline embarked on a series of significant ongoing developments (e.g., preservice education, professional associations, code of ethics, regulation of practice), which have led, over time, to the professionalization of practice in this country, and to some extent internationally. Although initially a very heterogeneous group of practitioners, in terms of educational background and professional competencies, rehabilitation counselors today, as a result of the professionalization process over the past 45 years, represent a group of professionals with a much higher degree of commonalty in preservice preparation, practice, and professional identity than at any previous time in our professional history.

The purpose of this chapter is to review those elements of the profession that serve to uniquely identify and provide the foundation for rehabilitation counseling practice in today's health and human services environment. Particular attention is devoted to the scope and research-based foundation of practice, and to the definition of qualified providers. In addition, preservice and continuing education, regulation of professional practice (certification and licensure), and the professional associations in rehabilitation counseling are reviewed.

SCOPE OF PRACTICE

Rehabilitation counseling has been described as a process in which the counselor works collaboratively with the consumer to understand existing problems, barriers, and potentials, in order to facilitate the effective use of personal and environmental resources for career, personal, social, and community adjustment following disability (Jaques, 1970). In carrying out this multifaceted process, rehabilitation counselors must be prepared to assist individuals with disabilities in adapting to the environment, to assist environments in accommodating the needs of the individual, and to work toward the full participation of individuals in all aspects of society, with a particular focus on career aspirations (Szymanski, 1985).

Over the years, the fundamental role of the rehabilitation counselor has evolved (Jaques, 1970; Rubin & Roessler, 1995; G. N. Wright, 1980), with the subsequent functions and required knowledge and skill competencies of the rehabilitation counselor expanding as well. Regardless of variations in their employment setting and client population, most rehabilitation counselors (a) assess needs, (b) establish a working alliance with the individual to develop goals and individualized plans to meet identified needs, and (c) provide or arrange for therapeutic services and interventions (e.g., psychological, medical, social, behavioral), including job placement and follow-up services. Throughout this individualized process, counseling skills are considered essential components of all activities. The specialized knowledge of disabilities and of environmental factors that interact with disabilities, as well as the range of knowledge and skills required in addition to counseling, serves to differentiate the rehabilitation counselor from social workers, other types of counselors (e.g., mental health, school, career) and other rehabilitation practitioners (e.g., vocational evaluators, job placement specialists) in today's service delivery environments (Jenkins, Patterson, & Szymanski, 1992; Leahy & Szymanski, 1995).

In 1994, utilizing the long-standing tradition in rehabilitation counseling research of studying the role and functions of qualified practitioners, an official scope of practice statement was developed and adopted by the major professional, accreditation, and credentialing organizations. This statement, which is consistent with available empirical research, was required to more explicitly identify the scope of practice for the public, consumers of services, related professional groups, and regulatory bodies. The statement, which was originally constructed by members of the Examination and Research Committee of the Commission on Rehabilitation Counselor Certification (CRCC), also contains major assumptions and underlying values associated with the scope of practice. The statement was formally adopted in the mid-1990s by the following organizations: the American Rehabilitation Counseling Association (ARCA), National Rehabilitation Counseling Association (NRCA), Alliance for Rehabilitation Counseling (ARC), National Council on Rehabilitation Education, CRCC, and the Council on Rehabilitation Education (CORE). The official scope of practice statement for rehabilitation counseling reads as follows:

> Rehabilitation counseling is a systematic process which assists persons with physical, mental, developmental, cognitive, and emotional disabilities to achieve their personal, career, and independent living goals in the most integrated setting possible through the application of the counseling process. The counseling process involves communication, goal setting, and beneficial growth or change through self-advocacy, psychological, vocational, social, and behavioral interventions. The specific techniques and modalities utilized within this rehabilitation counseling process may include, but are not limited to:
>
> assessment and appraisal;
> diagnosis and treatment planning;
> career (vocational) counseling;
> individual and group counseling treatment interventions focused on facilitating adjustments to the medical and psychosocial impact of disability;
> case management, referral, and service coordination;
> program evaluation and research;
> interventions to remove environmental, employment and attitudinal barriers;
> consultation services among multiple parties and regulatory systems;

job analysis, job development, and placement services, including assistance with employment and job accommodations; and

the provision of consultation about, and access to, rehabilitation technology (CRCC, 1994, pp. 1–2)

RESEARCH-BASED FOUNDATION OF PRACTICE

Underlying the practice of any profession or professional specialty area is the delineation of specific knowledge and skill competencies required for effective service delivery. *Job analysis, role and function, professional competency, critical incident*, and *knowledge-validation research* are all terms that describe a process whereby the professional practice of rehabilitation counseling has been systematically studied, to identify and describe important functions and tasks or knowledge and skills associated with the effective delivery of services to individuals with disabilities.

Over the past 40 years, an extensive body of knowledge has been acquired through these various research methods, which has empirically identified the specific competencies and job functions important to the practice of rehabilitation counseling (e.g., Berven, 1979; Emener & Rubin, 1980; Harrison & Lee, 1979; Jaques, 1959; Leahy, Chan, & Saunders, 2001; Leahy, Shapson & Wright, 1987; Leahy, Szymanski, & Linkowski, 1993; Muthard & Salomone, 1969; Rubin et al., 1984; Wright & Fraser, 1975). This long-standing emphasis on the development and ongoing refinement of a research-based foundation in relation to practice, and the required knowledge and skills, has served to distinguish rehabilitation counseling from other counseling specialties that are also seeking to define and validate their scope of professional practice. These research efforts have also provided the profession with evidence of construct validity of rehabilitation counseling knowledge and skill areas (Szymanski, Linkowksy, Leahy, Diamond, & Thoreson, 1993b).

Although role and function approaches generally provide an empirically derived description of the functions and tasks associated with the role, the knowledge required to perform these functions is typically more indirectly assessed and inferred on the basis of the described functions and tasks. Roessler and Rubin (1992), in their review of major studies (Emener & Rubin, 1980; Leahy et al., 1987; Rubin et al., 1984), concluded that rehabilitation counselors have a diverse role requiring many skills, if they are to effectively assist individuals with disabilities improve the quality of their lives. They also concluded that the role of the rehabilitation counselor can be fundamentally described as encompassing the following functions or job task areas: assessment, affective counseling, vocational (career) counseling, case management, and job placement.

Conversely, knowledge validation and professional competency approaches provide an empirically derived description of the knowledge and skills associated with a particular role, but the actual functions and tasks are more indirectly assessed and inferred on the basis of the knowledge and skills needed by an individual to practice. Recent research by Leahy et al. (2001) provided empirical support that the following six knowledge domains represent the core knowledge and skill requirements of rehabilitation counselors: (1) career counseling, assessment, and consultation; (2) counseling theories, techniques, and applications; (3) rehabilitation services and resources; (4) case and caseload management; (5) health care and disability systems; and (6) medical, functional, and environmental implications of disability. A complete listing of the knowledge domains and subdomains from this study, sponsored by the CRCC, is provided in Table 7.1.

In terms of research utilization and applications, these empirically derived descriptions of the rehabilitation counselor's role, function, and required knowledge and skill competencies have assisted the profession in a number of important ways. First, they have helped define the professional identity of the rehabilitation counselor, by empirically defining the uniqueness of the profession and by providing evidence in support of the construct validity of its knowledge base. Second, the descriptions have been extensively used in the development of preservice educational curricula, in order to provide graduate training in areas of knowledge and skill critical to the practice of rehabilitation counseling across major employment settings. Third, the longstanding emphasis on a research-based foundation to practice has greatly contributed to the rehabilitation counseling profession's leadership role in the establishment and ongoing refinement of graduate educational program accreditation, through the CORE, and in individual practitioner certification, through the CRCC. Finally, this body of knowledge has also been useful in identifying the common professional ground (shared competency areas) and the uniqueness of rehabilitation counseling among related rehabilitation disciplines (e.g., vocational evaluators, job placement specialists) and other counseling specialties (e.g., career, school, mental health). This process of further definition in the area of occupational competence is a normal sequence in the professionalization process for any occupation seeking public recognition.

QUALIFIED PROVIDERS

According to the professional associations (ARCA, NRCA, and ARC), qualified providers of rehabilitation counseling services are those professionals

TABLE 7.1 Rehabilitation Counseling Knowledge Domains and Subdomains

Domain 1: Career Counseling, Assessment, and Consultation Services

Subdomain A: Vocational Consultation and Employer Services
Employer practices that affect employment or return to work
Ergonomics
Job modification and restructuring techniques
Job analysis
Consultation services available from rehabilitation counselors for employers
Methods and techniques used to conduct labor market surveys
Work-conditioning or work-hardening resources and strategies
Business/corporate terminology
Accommodation and rehabilitation engineering services
Marketing strategies and techniques for rehabilitation services
Workplace culture and environment

Subdomain B: Job Development and Placement Services
Employer development and job placement
Client job-seeking skills development
Client job-retention skills
Job placement strategies
Job and employer development
Follow-up/postemployment services
Occupational and labor market information
Vocational implications of functional limitations associated with disabilities

Subdomain C: Career Counseling and Assessment Techniques
Tests and evaluation techniques available for assessing client's needs
Computer-based counseling tools in rehabilitation counseling
Computer-based job-matching systems
Interpretation of assessment results, for rehabilitation planning purposes
Internet resources for rehabilitation counseling
Assistive technology
Theories of career development and work adjustment
Transferable skills analysis

Domain 2: Counseling Theories, Techniques, and Applications

Subdomain A: Mental Health Counseling
Mental health and psychiatric disability concepts
Rehabilitation techniques for individuals with psychological disabilities
Treatment planning for clinical problems (e.g., depression and anxiety)
Substance abuse and treatment
Human sexuality and disability issues
Wellness and illness prevention concepts and strategies

TABLE 7.1 *(continued)*

Subdomain B: Group and Family Counseling
Family counseling theories
Family counseling practices and interventions
Group counseling practices and interventions
Group counseling theories

Subdomain C: Individual Counseling
Individual counseling theories
Individual counseling practices and interventions
Behavior and personality theory
Human growth and development

Subdomain D: Psychosocial and Cultural Issues in Counseling
Psychosocial and cultural impact of disability on the family
Psychosocial and cultural impact of disability on the individual
Multicultural counseling issues
Gender issues
Societal issues, trends, and developments as they relate to rehabilitation
Techniques for working with individuals with limited English proficiency

Subdomain E: Foundations, Ethics, and Professional Issues
Design of research projects, program evaluation, and needs assessment
Basic research methods
Evaluation procedures for assessing the effectiveness of rehabilitation services and outcomes
History of rehabilitation
Philosophical foundations of rehabilitation
Ethical issues related to on-line counseling
Ethical decision-making models and processes
Theories and techniques of clinical supervision
Advocacy processes needed to address institutional and societal barriers that impede access, equity, and success for clients
Legislation or laws affecting individuals with disabilities

Domain 3: Rehabilitation Services and Resources

Supported employment strategies and services
School-to-work transition for students with disabilities
Services available for a variety of rehabilitation populations, including persons with multiple disabilities
Planning provision of independent living services with clients
Financial resources for rehabilitation services
Community resources and services for rehabilitation planning
Social Security programs, benefits, and disincentives
Organizational structure of the public vocational rehabilitation service delivery system
Rehabilitation services in diverse settings
Organizational structure of the not-for-profit service delivery systems

TABLE 7.1 *(continued)*

Domain 4: Case and Caseload Management

Case management process and tools
Case recording and documentation
Principles of caseload management
Professional roles, functions, and relationships with other human service providers
Clinical problem-solving and critical-thinking skills
Negotiation and conflict resolution strategies
The case management process, including case finding; service coordination; referral to, and utilization of, other disciplines; and client advocacy
Techniques for working effectively in teams and across disciplines

Domain 5: Health Care and Disability Systems

Managed care concepts
Health care delivery systems
Employer-based disability prevention and management strategies
Workers' compensation laws and practices
Techniques for evaluating earnings capacity and loss
Expert testimony
Life care planning
Organizational structure of the private, for-profit vocational rehabilitation systems
Health care benefits
Appropriate medical intervention resources

Domain 6: Medical, Functional, and Environmental Implications of Disability

Environmental barriers for individuals with disabilities
Physical/functional capacities of individuals with disabilities
Medical aspects and implications of various disabilities
Rehabilitation terminology and concepts
Medical terminology
Attitudinal barriers for individuals with disabilities

who have completed graduate degree training in rehabilitation counseling or a closely related degree program (e.g., counseling) at the master's level, have attained national certification as a Certified Rehabilitation Counselor (CRC), and have acquired the appropriate state licensure (e.g., Licensed Professional Counselor), in those states that require this level of credential for counseling practice. As an integral aspect of this professional identity, qualified providers, under this definition, are required to practice rehabilitation counseling within the guidelines and standards of the Code of Professional Ethics for Rehabilitation Counselors (2002) and to maintain ongoing professional development through relevant continuing education to maintain and upgrade their knowledge and skills related to practice. In addition to these professional requirements and responsibilities, qualified providers are expected to be members of a professional association and contribute, through professional advocacy, to the advancement of the profession.

In recent years, a series of studies were conducted to investigate the relationship between rehabilitation counselor education and service delivery outcomes, which has provided consistent support for the position that rehabilitation counselors, as qualified providers, need to obtain preservice training at the graduate level in rehabilitation counseling or a closely related field, prior to practice. Studies of the New York (Szymanski & Parker, 1989), Wisconsin (Szymanski, 1991), Maryland (Szymanski & Danek, 1991), and Arkansas (Cook & Bolton, 1992) state VR agencies demonstrated that counselors with master's degrees in rehabilitation counseling achieved better outcomes with clients with severe disabilities than did rehabilitation counselors with unrelated master's or bachelor's degrees. In another group of studies, involving rehabilitation counselors from a variety of employment settings, preservice education was linked to the rehabilitation counselors perceived (self-assessed) level of competency. Shapson, Wright, and Leahy (1987), and Szymanski, Leahy, and Linkowski (1993) demonstrated that counselors with master's degrees in rehabilitation counseling perceived themselves to be more competent or better prepared in critical knowledge and skill areas of rehabilitation counseling than did counselors with unrelated preservice preparation (Leahy & Szymanski, 1995).

During the past 25 years, there has been a growing expectation, among members of the profession, employers, and regulatory bodies, that rehabilitation counselors who provide services to people with disabilities have the appropriate preservice education and credentials (certification and licensure). Even today, however, there are individuals practicing as rehabilitation counselors in both the public and private rehabilitation sectors in this country who do not have this type of preservice preparation or appropriate credentials. Although this heterogeneity in professional background was once thought to be a natural consequence of a quickly expanding field, in more recent years the practice of hiring individuals without appropriate professional training and credentials has been heavily criticized by professional, educational, and regulatory bodies in rehabilitation counseling.

Recently, in probably one of the most substantive policy advances in relation to professionization in the history of the public rehabilitation program, the Rehabilitation Act Amendments of 1992 provided explicit guidance to state agencies about personnel requirements that may have a significant and long-lasting effect on professionalism at the practitioner level. In 1997, these new regulations regarding qualified providers of rehabilitation counseling services were implemented within the public rehabilitation program. In a commissioners memorandum (CM-98-12), dated May 29, 1998, Fredric Schroeder indicated that:

> Section 101(a)(7) of the Rehabilitation Act Amendments of 1992, commonly referred to as the Comprehensive System of Personnel Development (CSPD), requires state VR agencies to establish qualified personnel standards for rehabilitation personnel, including VR counselors, that are consistent with any national or State-approved or recognized certification, licensing, or registration that apply to a particular profession. To the extent that a State's existing personnel standards are not based on the highest requirements of the State, the State agency is also required to develop a plan to retrain or hire personnel to meet personnel standards that are based on the highest requirements. . . . The purpose of the CSPD provisions is to ensure the quality of personnel who provide VR services and assist individuals with disabilities to achieve employment outcomes through the VR program. (p. 1)

In most situations, state agencies will be required to upgrade and retrain existing personnel to the point at which they would be considered eligible for CRC certification. For new hires, this same standard would be used. What this does not mean is that these personnel would be required to be certified. In addition, only academic criteria will be used by the state agency to determine eligibility—not the typical process of evaluating both academic and work experience, as is the case with CRCC.

On the one hand, this represents a positive step forward in relation to upgrading the educational backgrounds of rehabilitation counselors practicing in state agencies throughout this country. On the other hand, although these provisions are viewed as highly constructive, the current interpretation of the provisions, as relating only to eligibility and not the attainment of the CRC credential, represents some real limitations in relation to individual practitioner accountability. As indicated previously, certification implies that the practitioner not only has appropriate education, but is able to successfully pass a knowledge exam, adhere and be accountable to the profession's code of ethics in delivering services, and continue the process of professional development, while being certified through continuing education (Leahy, 1999).

One of the key characteristics of any profession is regulation of practice (Rothman, 1987). Individuals who practice rehabilitation counseling outside of the profession are not accountable to, or included in, such regulation of practice, and are therefore not required to adhere to the profession's code of ethics or accepted standards of practice. Although this situation has improved over the years, it is still unacceptable. Clearly, however, in the years to come, the trend toward professionalization, and particularly the movement toward state licensure and certification in this country, will make it less likely that an individual will be able to practice as a rehabilitation counselor without appropriate training and credentials.

SPECIALIZATION AND RELATED PROVIDERS

Today, a majority of rehabilitation counselors practice in the public, private, and nonprofit rehabilitation sectors. In recent years, however, rehabilitation counselors have begun to practice in independent living centers, employee assistance programs, hospitals, clinics, mental health organizations, public school transition programs, and employer-based disability prevention and management programs. Although setting-based factors may affect the relative emphasis or importance of various rehabilitation counselor functions or may introduce new specialized knowledge requirements for the rehabilitation counselor, there remains a great deal of communality in the role and function among rehabilitation counselors, regardless of employment setting (Leahy et al., 1987, 1993, 2001). One aspect that is often affected by these various settings is the specific job title—rehabilitation counselor—used in most settings, but one can also find the use of the title *rehabilitation consultant* or *case manager* among today's rehabilitation counselors in practice. In addition, as one advances up the career ladder within these various settings, rehabilitation counselors can assume supervisory, management, and administrative roles.

Although the majority of rehabilitation counselors are viewed as generalists, another aspect of variation among practicing rehabilitation counselors is the degree to which they specialize their practice. One particularly useful model for viewing this issue was developed by DiMichael (1967), who suggested a two-way classification of horizontal and vertical specialization. In DiMichael's model, *horizontal specialization* refers to rehabilitation counselors who restrict or specialize their practice with a particular disability group (e.g., deaf, blind, head injury, substance abuse) that requires a significant amount of specialized knowledge or skill, specific to the type of disability. *Vertical specialization*, on the other hand, occurs when rehabilitation counselors attend to only one function in the rehabilitation process (e.g., assessment or job placement) in their work with consumers. Vocational evaluators and job placement specialists are examples of vertical specialists in this model.

The previous section, on qualified providers, does not imply that only rehabilitation counselors should provide rehabilitation services for persons with disabilities. In fact, there are numerous other related work roles that contribute to the rehabilitation process and complement the role and services provided by the rehabilitation counselor. In addition to vocational evaluators and job placement specialists, who can assist the rehabilitation counselor and client at critical stages in the rehabilitation process (assessment and job placement), other supportive resources could include physicians and physiatrists, physical and occupational therapists, psychologists, work adjustment trainers, job coaches, and various vocational training personnel. Oftentimes, a critical aspect of the rehabilitation counselor's role is the coordination of services provided by these various professionals within the context of a multidisciplinary team approach, to effectively address the multifaceted needs of the consumer in the rehabilitation process.

PRESERVICE EDUCATION AND PROFESSIONAL DEVELOPMENT

Throughout this chapter, the importance of appropriate preservice education in rehabilitation counseling has been emphasized. By the 1940s, three universities (New York, Ohio State, and Wayne State) had developed graduate training programs in rehabilitation counseling (Jenkins et al., 1992). In 1954, with the passage of the VR Amendments, federal grant support was provided, for the first time, to universities and colleges to develop graduate preservice training programs, to prepare rehabilitation counselors for employment in the public and private nonprofit rehabilitation sectors. This federal training support, which continues to this day, accelerated the design and development of graduate training in rehabilitation counseling, and can be viewed as the beginning of the professionalization process for the formal discipline of rehabilitation counseling (Leahy & Szymanski, 1995).

During this initial period of program development, a conference report by Hall and Warren (1956), which documented the findings of a comprehensive workshop sponsored by the National Rehabilitation Association (NRA) and the National Vocational Guidance Association (now the American Counseling Association [ACA]), provided the initial guidelines for curriculum planning by the new, federally funded rehabilitation counselor education programs (G. N. Wright, 1980). In the years that followed, empirical research, in the form of role and function and professional competency studies (covered earlier in this chapter), helped guide curriculum redesign efforts to ensure that critical knowledge and skill areas needed in the field were reflected in the preservice training content.

As rehabilitation counselor education programs expanded in colleges and universities, there was a need to devise a mechanism to standardize and accredit these training programs. In 1972, the CORE was established as the national accreditation body for rehabilitation counselor education programs "to promote the effective delivery of rehabilitation services to individuals with disabilities by promoting and fostering continuing review and improvement of master's degree level programs" (CORE, 1991, p. 2). Research conducted at the University of Wisconsin laid the foundation for a multistakeholder program evaluation process, which was recognized in 1975 by the National Commission on Accrediting, a predecessor of the Council on Postsecondary Accreditation, and, since 1977, the Council for Higher Education Accreditation, and is still in use today (Linkowski & Szymanski, 1993). Currently, there are over 85 accredited master's degree educational programs in rehabilitation counseling. As the oldest and most-established accreditation body among the counseling professions, the CORE process remains firmly grounded in research and regularly conducts a systematic review of the adequacy and relevancy of its standards.

Following graduate level preservice education, practicing rehabilitation counselors need to continue their professional development, to maintain and upgrade knowledge and skills associated with the delivery of rehabilitation counseling services to persons with disabilities. For example, CRCs are required to obtain a minimum of 100 hr of relevant continuing education, of which a minimum of 10 hr is required in ethics, during their 5-year certification period. With the rapid pace of change in the field and the continual dissemination of new knowledge and expanded skills associated with practice, the rehabilitation counselor needs to be aware of continuing educational opportunities available to them. Although there are numerous organizations and groups that provide this type of training (both face-to-face and distance education opportunities), the primary sources and sponsors of continuing education for the rehabilitation counselor are the professional organizations (e.g., ARCA, NRCA, NRA, ACA), the Regional Rehabilitation Continuing Educational Programs, research and training centers, and university-based outreach educational programs.

REGULATION OF PRACTICE AND CREDENTIALING

Regulation of practice, through professional certification and licensure, is an important characteristic of professions (Rothman, 1987). Rehabilitation counseling has been widely recognized as the leading counseling specialty in the development and pioneering of credentialing mechanisms through national certification and educational program accreditation, which serve as the cornerstones of the general counseling professionalization system (Tarvydas & Leahy, 1993). However, the order of credentialing development in rehabilitation counseling has also been widely observed to be atypical of the expected order of progression seen in other, more-established professions, such as medicine and law. The more-classic evolution of credentials, according to Matkin (1983), has been for the profession to initially achieve state licensure, then move to develop national specialty certifications or endorsements regulated by the professional organizations. In rehabilitation counseling, national certification was established first, followed by a long period of legislative advocacy, in which other counseling specialty groups took the lead role, along with rehabilitation counselors, to establish state counselor licensure laws in individual states (Tarvydas & Leahy, 1993).

In our field, the CRC credentialing process is the oldest and most-established certification process in the counseling and rehabilitation professions. The purpose of certification is to ensure that the professionals engaged in rehabilitation counseling are of good moral character and possess at least an acceptable minimum level of knowledge, as determined by the CRCC, about the practice of their profession. The existence of such standards is considered to be in the best interests of consumers of rehabilitation counseling services and the general public. From a historical perspective, the CRC credentialing program was an outgrowth of the professional concerns of the ARCA and the NRCA.

Since the inception of the credential and the subsequent development of the CRCC in 1973, over 30,000 professionals have participated in the certification process. Today, there are over 15,000 CRCs practicing in the United States and several foreign countries (Leahy & Holt, 1993). Certification standards and examination content for the CRC have been empirically validated through ongoing research efforts throughout the 30-year history of the commission. These standards represent the level of education, experience, and knowledge competencies (see Table 7.1) required of rehabilitation counselors, to provide services to individuals with disabilities (Leahy & Szymanski, 1995).

In terms of regulation of practice, the most powerful credential is licensure. As differentiated from voluntary national certification, licensure regulates the practice of a profession through specific state legislation. Beginning in 1976, with the passage of the first counselor licensure bill in Virginia, there has been a long struggle by advocates of the counselor licensure movement to enact legislation on a state-by-state basis to protect the title and regulate the practice of counseling. During the past 25 years, 48 states have enacted counselor licensure legislation. The trend has been toward the passage of general practice legislation (which covers various counseling specialty groups), which is consistent with the recommendations of the ACA's licensure committee in its 1995 model legislation for licensed professional counselors (Bloom et al., 1990; Glosofs, Benshoff, Hosie, & Maki, 1995). Reflecting this trend, the most commonly used title in counselor licensure bills has been that of the Licensed Professional Counselor.

Counselor licensure legislation has been intended to regulate the use of the terms by which the statute officially refers to professional counselors, as well as to protect the practice of professional counseling as set forth in its definition and scope of practice provisions. This combination of title and practice bill is the most stringent form of credentialing and would prohibit anyone from practicing counseling unless fully qualified, regardless of formal title. Title-only legislation, on the other hand, prohibits persons from using the specific titles restricted in the bill to those who have met the specified qualifications established by the bill and who have achieved licensure. It does not, however, restrict persons from providing counseling services, if their job titles avoid restricted language. Most title-only legislation was passed to avoid powerful lobbying efforts that would have been mounted to defeat the more restrictive title and practice bills. Clearly, this type of legislation was seen as a first stage, by counselor licensure advocates, in the overall drive toward eventual regulation of practice through future revisions of the initial legislation (Tarvydas & Leahy, 1993).

Although there are presently three states who have passed licensure laws specifically covering rehabilitation counselors (Texas, Louisiana, and Massachusetts), the majority of states have enacted general practice legislation covering all counselors. The professional associations in rehabilitation counseling (ARCA, NRCA, and the ARC) have taken the position to strongly advocate for the inclusion of rehabilitation counselors within general counselor state licensure, whenever possible. With this in mind, the LPC designation, combined with certification as a CRC, would represent the appropriate credentials for rehabilitation counselors working with individuals with disabilities, in states with general practice legislation.

PROFESSIONAL ASSOCIATIONS

Professional associations provide a forum for the exchange of information and ideas among professionals, reflect the philosophical bases of a profession, and, as political entities, are concerned with the organization of the profession and relations with external groups (Rothman, 1987). In rehabilitation counseling, professional associations also provide an organizational home for individuals with similar professional identities, interests, and backgrounds, who are committed to the further development and refinement of the profession.

Throughout the modern history of rehabilitation counseling, there have been two divergent models of the profession that have served to define the professional associations of the rehabilitation counselor. One model postulates that rehabilitation counseling should be viewed as a separate and autonomous profession, organizationally aligned with other related rehabilitation disciplines. The other model views the rehabilitation counseling profession as a specialty area of general counseling, organizationally aligned with related counseling groups. These early beliefs are presently reflected in the profession's two major professional associations, which also represent rehabilitation counseling's dual emphasis in counseling and rehabilitation.

The ARCA was founded in 1958 as a professional division of the American Personnel and Guidance Association (now the ACA). The NRCA was also founded in 1958 as a professional division of the NRA. The presence of these two organizations, with similar missions and constituencies, has been the topic of much discussion and debate over the years. The perplexing aspect of these discussions is that, depending on individual perspective, one can rationalize the efficacy of either organizational model. In fact, the argument can be made that formal organizational relationships, with both the counseling and rehabilitation communities, has, over time, served to strengthen, align, and confirm our dual orientations as rehabilitation counselors and has provided the profession with a unique identity and heritage (Tarvydas & Leahy, 1993).

Through the years, there have been serious discussions of organizational merger and unification (see Rasch, 1979; Reagles, 1981; Leahy & Tarvydas, 2001) and systems of collaboration (Wright, 1980; Leahy & Tarvydas, 2001), to repair the fragmentation and professional and public confusion created by the existence of two such organizations representing rehabilitation counseling (Leahy & Szymanski, 1995). To address these concerns, the ARCA and NRCA boards created the Alliance for Rehabilitation Counseling in 1993, as a formal collaborative structure to marshal the strengths of both organizations into a unified professional policy and strategic planning voice for rehabilitation counseling, while respecting the autonomy, heritage, and value of each of the individual organizations.

Although this collaborative relationship has only been in existence for 10 years, these two professional organizations have coordinated their respective strategic planning efforts and developed and approved joint policy statements on impending federal legislation, counselor licensure, and scope of practice. In addition, they have developed joint committees, which will meet, under the auspices of the Alliance, in the areas of licensure, standards of practice, and professional development (e.g., Annual Alliance Professional Development Symposium). The Alliance appears to have been a major step forward for the profession in developing comprehensive and coordinated professional advocacy efforts at the national level and in providing a mechanism under which all rehabilitation counselors in this country can unite, as we continue down the path of professionalization.

CHAPTER 8

Research

Fong Chan, Susan M. Miller, Gloria Lee, Steven R. Pruett, and Chih Chin Chou

One of the ultimate goals of rehabilitation counseling research is utilization, by professionals and people with disabilities. Bolton (1979) emphasized that rehabilitation professionals must be aware of contemporary research. He stressed that counselors need to incorporate research-based knowledge into their practices, in order to assure that people with disabilities receive effective services. In today's era of accountability, rehabilitation professionals are also increasingly concerned with accurately assessing and documenting vocational rehabilitation (VR) changes, in people with disabilities, that can be attributed to rehabilitation interventions (Rubin, Chan, & Thomas, in press). One area of rehabilitation education that will continue to require significant attention is the preservice and in-service training of rehabilitation counselors as intelligent research consumers.

Although research utilization is a desirable goal, it is also quite elusive. Rehabilitation counseling research is probably the least-popular course in the master's level rehabilitation counselor education curriculum. The same negative attitudes toward rehabilitation research prevail among rehabilitation counselors in professional practice (Bolton, 1979). This challenge can be attributed to several negative perceptions about rehabilitation research, including a weak theoretical foundation, lack of practical relevance for practitioners and consumers, a dearth of well-designed experimental design studies aimed at validating the efficacy of rehabilitation counseling interventions, and the underutilization of qualitative research methodologies (Bellini & Rumrill, 2002; Berkowitz, Englander, Rubin, & Worrall, 1975, 1976; Parker & Hansen, 1981; Rubin & Rice, 1986).

To train master's level rehabilitation counseling students and professional counselors to be intelligent consumers of research, it is important, although not sufficient, to teach them the basic concepts of research design and statistical methods. They need to see clearly how research can be a practical and integral part of their professional practice. This chapter discusses the importance and relevance of rehabilitation counseling research within the framework of evidence-based practice. Specifically, we (a) review current major findings in counseling and rehabilitation that are significantly related to positive counseling and rehabilitation outcomes, (b) present a rehabilitation counseling model incorporating salient features of current-outcome research findings and discuss how this model can be validated to meet the requirements of evidence-based practice, and (c) discuss current developments in rehabilitation outcome measurements using a quality-of-life (QOL) framework.

MAJOR FINDINGS IN COUNSELING AND REHABILITATION OUTCOME RESEARCH

In today's climate of cost-containment and managed care, the measurement of outcomes is important for rehabilitation service providers (Chan & Leahy, 1999; Chan, Lui, Rosenthal, Pruett, & Ferrin, 2002). Outcome measurement allows rehabilitation agencies to demonstrate the level to which treatment and services are effective and cost-effective. Specifically, rehabilitation outcomes are changes associated with the provision of rehabilitation services to consumers (Fuhrer, 1987; Rubin, Chan, & Thomas, in press). Outcome research seeks to relate the type of service or intervention provided to a range of positive or negative outcomes, in order to identify what works best, and for whom (Pransky & Himmelstein, 1996a). Outcome research helps inform practitioners about the optimal services that will result in positive outcome for people with disabilities.

A weak theoretical base and poor quality are two major criticisms of rehabilitation research. These two criticisms are interrelated. Bellini and Rumrill (2002) contended that rehabilitation counseling operates essentially atheoretically, with no general theory to account for a significant proportion of the knowledge content of rehabilitation counseling. Their observations are consistent with many rehabilitation scholars (e.g., Arokiasamy, 1993; Cottone, 1987; Hershenson, 1996). However, the view that rehabilitation counseling has a deficient theoretical base may also result from our failure to adequately distinguish between theories and models. According to Bellin and Rumrill, theories are more general than models: "Models typically operate at an intermediate level of conceptualization. . . . Model-generated hypotheses are often tied to practical concerns in the role performance of rehabilitation counselors and delivery of services to persons with disabilities" (p. 127). They concluded that the use of rehabilitation models to validate the effectiveness of different rehabilitation counseling practices might be more fruitful than a theory-building approach for an applied discipline such as rehabilitation counseling. The development of competing models of rehabilitation counseling, using salient and empirically supported constructs, would allow researchers to validate the effectiveness of these models, using a true experimental research design, which is an important indicator of research quality.

Recent topical research areas that have been found to enhance rehabilitation and counseling outcomes, which can be used to develop a rehabilitation counseling intervention model, are reviewed in the following section.

Working Alliance

There is strong empirical support in the recent literature for the effect of working alliance on counseling outcomes. Specifically, Wampold (2001) used meta-analysis to review thousands of studies, in order to examine the efficacy of counseling interventions on client outcomes. He found that at least 70% of psychotherapeutic effects are caused by general effects (i.e., the effects caused by common factors), but only 8% result from specific ingredients (i.e., specific factors), with the remaining 22% partially attributed to individual client differences. Common factors are defined in the literature as ingredients that all forms of counseling have in common, which exist across all forms of counseling as typically delivered. These ingredients include goal setting, empathic listening, allegiance, and therapeutic alliance. Wampold defined *allegiance* as the degree to which the therapist is committed to the belief that the therapy is beneficial to the client. *Therapeutic alliance* is related to (a) the client's affective relationship with the therapist; (b) the client's motivation and ability to accomplish work collaboratively with the therapist; (c) the therapist's empathic response to, and involvement with, the client; and (d) client and therapist agreement about the goals and tasks of therapy.

Separately, Chan, Shaw, McMahon, Koch, and Strauser (1997) described a conceptual framework for enhancing the counselor–consumer working relationship in VR counseling. They focused their research on counseling expectancies as the underlying factor for working alliance. It is widely believed that there is a relationship between counseling expectancies and help-seeking behavior by consumers. For example, low expectancies may explain why many people, particularly minority individuals, tend to seek help from close friends, family members, or ministers, instead of counselors, when they are in need of counseling (Tinsley, de St. Aubin, & Brown, 1982).

Several studies in counseling (e.g., Tinsley, Bowman, & Ray, 1988) have indicated that consumers' decisions to discontinue therapy after the first few sessions result mostly from a discrepancy between the consumers' expectations for counseling and what actually occurs in therapy. In particular, minority individuals and international students consistently have been found to have different expectations about counseling than European Americans (Kenny, 1994; Kunkel, 1990; Yuen & Tinsley, 1981). For example, Kunkel reported that Latino consumers expect their counselors to be directive and solution-oriented. Byon, Chan, and Thomas (1999) found that Korean international students would terminate counseling quickly, if the process was viewed as unpleasant or did not seem to be immediately helpful. Korean students expected to approach counseling like a classroom-learning situation, in which they could present problems, ask questions about the problems, and work on assignments to solve the problems. These studies illustrate the need to identify and discuss any misperceptions that consumers in counseling may have, related to expectations about the counseling process.

Al-Darmaki and Kivlighan (1993) reported that congruence in consumer–counselor expectations about the counseling relationship is positively related to ratings of the working alliance, and the quality of the working alliance is related to counseling outcomes. Because the relationship between the rehabilitation counselor and the consumer shares many similarities to that of similar dyads within psychology, counseling, marriage and family therapy, and other disciplines, differences between rehabilitation counselors and consumers in their expectations about the VR process can be assumed to negatively impact working alliance and rehabilitation outcomes. Conversely, convergence in rehabilitation counseling expectancies will enhance working alliance and rehabilitation outcomes.

Recently, Chan, McMahon, Shaw, and Lee (in press) reported the development of a psychological instrument, the Expectations About Rehabilitation Counseling Scale (EARC), to measure discrepancy in rehabilitation counseling expectations between counselors and consumers. They found that consumers and counselors differed significantly on two counseling expectancy factors: consumer behavior and clinical and support services. Consumers tend to rate themselves as more responsible and motivated than their counselors rate them. Consumers also expect to receive more clinical and support services than counselors expect to provide, but the sole focus of counselors is on vocational services. Discrepancies in counseling expectancies between counselors and consumers are inversely related to working alliance. Shaw, McMahon, Chan, and Hannold (in press) reported a process of assessing discrepancies in counseling expectations, using the EARC scale, and employing the conflict resolution approach to enhance communication and working alliance. They believe that disagreement in counseling expectations must be addressed early in the rehabilitation process. Schelat (2001) surveyed 255 state VR clients, who were closed successfully or unsuccessfully in August 1988, and found that all factors of working alliance (i.e., goal, task, and bond) are predictive of rehabilitation outcomes, with high scores strongly predictive of successful outcomes. Similarly, Donnell, Lustig, and Strauser (2002) surveyed 305 individuals with mental illness, to assess their reported level of working alliance and rehabilitation outcomes. They also reported that working alliance is related to employment outcomes and job satisfaction. Therefore, working alliance appears to be a key ingredient to positive rehabilitation outcomes.

Stages of Change

Researchers and practitioners in counseling and health promotion services have been searching for the most effective interventions to maximize successful outcomes in their clients. Over the past decade, the transtheoretical model (Prochaska & DiClemente, 1983), popularly known as the stage of change (SOC) model, has become the most prominent and popular model, providing a comprehensive framework with which to understand and describe the behavioral change process of clients. The SOC model posits that clients can be categorized into different stages of change, based on their readiness or motivation to change, and that interventions should be tailored according to their level of readiness for change. Having originated from smoking cessation research, the SOC model has been empirically validated numerous times and has been applied to various counseling settings, ranging from smoking cessation to treatment for unsafe sexual behaviors (Prochaska, 1994). Because of its compelling nature and applicability to diverse populations, it has come to be recognized as a general model of change (Peterocelli, 2002), with practical applications to the practice of rehabilitation counseling.

Having emerged from analysis of various psychological and behavioral theories, the SOC model conceptualizes the behavioral change process as a sequence of stages through which people typically progress. These stages consist of precontemplation, contemplation, action, and maintenance. For most individuals, progressing through these stages is not a liner process. Commonly, individuals cycle through certain stages several times before they can successfully conquer the behaviors they want to change (Prochaska & DiClemente, 1983). Furthermore, the SOC model identifies perceived self-efficacy and decisional balance as predictors of stage movement: *self-efficacy* is defined as confidence in ability to perform specific tasks, and *decisional balance* refers to the evaluation of pros and cons related to the performance of specific tasks (Prochaska, DiClemente, & Norcross, 1992). Studies specific to a variety of problem behaviors have indicated that clients in the precontemplation stage have the lowest self-efficacy and weighed cons heavier than pros; clients in the maintenance stage have the highest self-efficacy and weighed pros heavier than cons (DiClemente, 1986; Prochaska, 1994). Increasing levels of self-efficacy and positive decisional balance can help clients to progress through stages. Interventions should be designed to build self-efficacy and positive decisional balance, through specific coping strategies and skills training tailored to clients' specific stages of change. These stage-matched interventions should help clients move forward to the next stage of change.

Various studies have reported more favorable outcomes related to stage-matched interventions than traditional non-stage-matched interventions. For example, clients in smoking cessation, receiving stage-matched interventions, reported 100% higher success in an 18-month follow-up than those who received non-stage-matched interventions (Prochaska, DiClemente, Velicer, & Rossi, 1993). Research in other areas, such as safe sexual behaviors (Parsons, Huszti, Crudder, Rich, & Mendoza, 2000), healthy diet (Campbell et al., 1994), and exercise acquisition (Marcus et al., 1998) also supported the superiority of the stage-matched interventions. One particular stage-matched intervention shown to be effective is the motivational interviewing (MI) technique, which is a counseling style that involves assessing client motivation, promoting self-efficacy, and exploring pros and cons related to goal achievement (Miller & Rollnick, 1991). As a result, motivational interviewing can help to resolve clients' ambivalence about change and to increase their motivation to move along the path to change (Rollnick, Heather, & Bell, 1992).

Research in rehabilitation counseling has noted the importance of increasing clients' motivation to change, in order to reduce premature termination and increase active participation. The significance of preparing clients for change during the rehabilitation process suggests that the SOC approach would be applicable to the practice of rehabilitation counseling. Preliminary studies have supported the SOC model for state VR clients with physical disabilities (Mannock, Leveque, & Prochaska, 2002) and psychiatric disabilities (Rogers et al., 2000). In addition, researchers have suggested that applying MI strategies, along with SOC, can help clients identify rehabilitation goals and improve insight and treatment adherence in psychiatric rehabilitation (Corrigan, McCracken, & Holmes, 2001; Rusch & Corrigan, 2002). The results of these studies suggest that rehabilitation counseling clients can be classified into different stages of change, based on their different levels of motivation; yet, these studies have not addressed the issues of how to help clients progress through stages. Although further research is needed, it is possible to say that, by understanding that clients vary in the degree to which they are ready to adapt a rehabilitation counseling approach, and that interventions should be tailored to the particular stages clients are in, rehabilitation counselors can devise and deliver more appropriate, individualized, and effective interventions.

Skills Training

According to Corrigan, Rao, and Lam (1999), people with persistent and severe mental illness struggle with a variety of disabilities. They may have deficits in cognition, social skills, hygiene and personal management, coping skills, interpersonal support, symptom management, and motivation. Comprehensive psychiatric rehabilitation programs, combined with appropriate medication management, help such persons meet the variety of needs and challenges imposed by their psychiatric disabilities (Corrigan et al., 1999). Rehabilitation programs are designed to help persons with psychiatric disabilities to diminish psychiatric symptoms, learn and use interpersonal skills, learn and use coping skills, avail themselves of community resources, and avail themselves of community supports. Corrigan et al. summarized the full range of typical services provided to assist people with psychiatric disabilities to function in the least-restrictive environment. These include instrumental and social support, family education and support, skills training, transfer training, cognitive rehabilitation, and behavioral incentives. Skills training is still the centerpiece of psychiatric rehabilitation, but the skills identified as important for people with persistent and severe mental illness, to function effectively in community living and employment settings, are also important in varying degrees to people with other disabilities. Benton and Schroeder (1990) examined the efficacy of social skill training for people with schizophrenia, using meta-analysis. Their meta-analysis yielded a significant effect size, indicating that 69% of the people receiving social skill training are better off than people without social skills training. People with alcohol dependence, receiving social skills training and coping skills training, were also found to maintain a higher number of abstinent days than people without such training (Drummond & Glautier, 1994; Erikson, Bjornstad, & Gotestam, 1986).

EVIDENCE-BASED REHABILITATION COUNSELING PRACTICE: A MODEL FOR RESEARCH AND PROFESSIONAL PRACTICE

In the previous section, we reviewed literature that can be used as the foundation for the development of a rehabilitation model, to enhance rehabilitation outcomes by using salient and empirically supported constructs. Rehabilitation counseling researchers have developed assessment instruments and treatment protocols to help counselors incorporate these evidence-based counseling components into their practice (e.g., Rubin, Chan, & Thomas, in press; Rubin, Chan, Bishop, & Miller, in press; Chan, McMahon, et al., in press). Some of the factors identified as positively related to counseling outcomes include working alliance, counseling expectancies, SOC/MI, and skills training. However, the model is flexible enough to allow other components, which might be found to contribute significantly to counseling or rehabilitation outcomes, to be incorporated into practice. Counselors who incorporate these components into their practice might reasonably be expected to have more successful rehabilitation outcomes. This will occur by assisting counselors to improve their working relationship with people with disabilities, to match counseling focus (e.g., motivational and outcome expectancy enhancement versus skills training and self-efficacy) with the SOC of rehabilitation consumers, and to use proven curriculum and format to provide social skills and coping skills training for people with disabilities. The effect of each specific outcome enhancement strategy on rehabilitation counseling outcomes can be tested on an individual basis. The overall effect of the enhanced model of rehabilitation counseling can also be tested. Rubin, Chan, and Thomas (in press) presented a model for evaluating positive changes in people with disabilities, which can be attributed to the effect of VR services. They advocated the use of a QOL framework for rehabilitation planning and program evaluation.

QOL as a Framework for Assessing VR Changes

The ultimate goal of rehabilitation is to promote the economic self-sufficiency and community integration of each individual (Murphy & Williams, 1999).

Rehabilitation services have been held accountable to this goal since the passage of the Rehabilitation Act of 1973. This mandate requires rehabilitation service programs to demonstrate that they have met expected service outcome goals and have done so in an efficient manner (Rubin & Roessler, 2001). Meeting and exceeding expected service outcome goals is one method of demonstrating the success and effectiveness of services provided and of justifying the continued funding of rehabilitation services.

Pransky and Himmelstein (1996a, 1996b) conceptualized medical care outcomes with a model that is also applicable for evaluating rehabilitation outcomes. They defined *medical outcomes* as the results or effects of medical care on QOL domains such as social functioning, mental health, and personal well-being, as well as on general perceptions of health, functional, and physical status. In rehabilitation, the focus is on resolution of symptoms, return to normal functioning at home, and return to full and long-term functional capacity and earning capacity in the workplace.

Pransky and Himmelstein (1996a, 1996b) suggested that, in measuring outcomes, considering a broad range of outcome dimensions is important. In their opinion, the more restricted the range of outcomes, the less credible the results. They argued that paying attention to many life and societal domains is crucial to achieving resolution of conditions and symptoms. Function in daily activities must be assessed and monitored. Such activities may include household and family responsibilities, transportation/driving, sexual activity, sleep patterns, social and recreational activities, health perceptions, ongoing medical care requirements, and so on. They also identified components of the vocational situation, such as work status, lost work time, comparison of the postinjury job with preinjury job, short- and long-term job retention, productivity, quality, and flexibility at work, all to be important indicators of service outcome. Consumer satisfaction was also identified as a key variable influencing case outcomes.

Historically, however, evaluation of the effectiveness of rehabilitation services has been primarily focused on short-term employment outcomes. Yet, it becomes difficult to determine the meaning of short-term employment outcome data as an index of service effectiveness, without information about how the life skills and QOL of each individual have changed following participation in rehabilitation services (Chan & Rubin, 1999). Consumers are motivated to participate in rehabilitation services by the anticipated effects that those services will have on their QOL. Most rehabilitation services focus directly on decreasing deficits in skills that prevent the consumer from fully integrating into society or reaching some personal goal. As significant deficits in life skills diminish, the individual's capacity for independent functioning and level of self-esteem are likely to increase. As those gains are experienced, the subjective perception that the individual has of their QOL is likely to become more positive (Cronin, 1996). Therefore, to the extent that rehabilitation services are effective, one should be able to see a reduction in significant life skills deficits of the individual, which, in turn, can lead to greater self-esteem and capacity for independent functioning. Ultimately, the process should be associated with a more positive perception of one's QOL (Dennis, Williams, Giangreco, & Cloniger, 1993).

This conceptual shift has led to an increased focus on QOL in assessment of service outcomes among rehabilitation researchers. *Quality of life* is a term typically used to describe an individual's perceived well-being (Murphy & Williams, 1999; Zautra, Beier, & Cappel, 1977). The World Health Organization definition of QOL refers to "individuals' perceptions of their position in life in the context of the culture and value systems in which they live and in relation to their goals, expectations, standards, and concerns" (WHOQOL Group, 1995). Through the use of a valid system for assessing changes in QOL resulting from rehabilitation services, professionals can obtain feedback on which services are most effective, somewhat effective, or least effective, for meeting the needs of their consumers (Chan & Rubin, 1999). Over time, such a system may further provide a differential blueprint of effective service provision, depending on the characteristics of the person with a disability served. Overall, such a system can help identify the best practice in the rehabilitation service delivery process, information which in turn can play a major role in facilitating the upgrading of rehabilitation services (Cronin, 1996).

QOL is generally referred to as a multidimensional construct, and this may influence its reputation for being ambiguous and difficult to define (Bishop & Feist-Price, 2002). Broad definitions of QOL tend to address freedom of action, sense of purpose for one's life, achievement regarding work, family or social/recreational life, self-preservation of esteem and integrity, and physical and material well-being (Flanagan, 1978; Goodinson & Singleton, 1989; Murphy & Williams, 1999). Dimensions typically included in QOL measures include psychological well-being (such as life satisfaction and happiness), physical well-being, social and interpersonal well-being, financial and material well-being, and functional ability. In addition, given that "work is still the overarching value and that research indicates that there is a dynamic interaction between quality of work life and quality of life in general" (Murphy & Williams, 1999, p. 3), QOL assessment should include occupational or career development, as well.

When assessing QOL, the level of importance placed by the consumer on well-being, in various aspects of their life should be the key consideration

(Felce & Perry, 1995; Zahn, 1992). Assessment of one's QOL should address life satisfaction in relation to personally determined standards of what the consumer considers desirable or undesirable for their life. Such an assessment should suggest the services that are needed to restore, maintain, or enhance aspects of the individual's functioning or life situation necessary for optimizing QOL.

In 1999, Chan and Rubin received a field-initiated project grant from the National Institute on Disability and Research, to develop a multidimensional rehabilitation planning and program evaluation system. Specifically, they advocate the inclusion of QOL in the framework for assessing rehabilitation counseling outcomes, to broaden and improve the definition of successful rehabilitation beyond the use of status code 26 in state VR agencies. The theoretical framework underscores the concept of measuring well-being, as well as functioning, in order to examine the relationship between improvement in functioning and changes in the well-being of consumers as indicators of successful outcomes. The operational framework involved the use of several instruments (the Life Skills Inventory for functioning, the Sense of Well-Being Inventory for well-being, and a demographic questionnaire to collect data on disability, severity, health care costs, government benefits received, and earnings, etc.), to help enhance counselor–consumer involvement in the rehabilitation planning and program evaluation process. Ideally, achievement of the goal of full integration of individuals with disabilities into mainstream society, in a state of optimal economic self-sufficiency, can be expected to result from a process in which deficiencies in life skills are accurately diagnosed and reduced or removed via targeted rehabilitation services. To the extent that goal is achieved, the recipient of rehabilitation services should also experience improvement in their QOL. Therefore, changes in the QOL of the individual with a disability, from pre- to postrehabilitation services, can be considered as a valid index of the level of effectiveness of those services.

SUMMARY

We have reviewed selected rehabilitation and counseling literature related to outcomes, in order to demonstrate that knowledge of current research is relevant to the professional practice of rehabilitation counseling. We propose a flexible model, which rehabilitation counselors can use to incorporate components that are found to contribute significantly to counseling or rehabilitation outcomes into their own practices. For counselors who are interested in incorporating the evidence-based counseling components identified in this chapter into their own practices, they are encouraged to take into consideration some of the concepts, such as improving their working relationship with people with disabilities, matching counseling focus (e.g., motivational and outcome expectancy enhancement vs. skills training and self-efficacy) with the stages of change of rehabilitation consumers, and using proven curriculum and format to provide social skills and coping skills training for people with disabilities. In addition, Chan and Rubin (1999) have developed a rehabilitation planning and program evaluation model that will allow counselors to evaluate the added effect of using these enhanced counseling components in helping people with disabilities improve their QOL.

Finally, rehabilitation professionals must also develop a thorough understanding of research designs and statistical analysis techniques (both quantitative and qualitative approaches), so that they can become intelligent consumers of rehabilitation counseling research and will have the ability to evaluate the relative quality of the voluminous research available in the literature. This knowledge will help them to identify the best components to incorporate into their practices.

ACKNOWLEDGMENTS

Preparation of this manuscript is supported in part by a National Institute of Disability and Rehabilitation Research Field-Initiated Research Grant funded to the Foundation for Rehabilitation Education and Research.

CHAPTER 9

Counseling For Diversity

Brenda Cartwright and Michael D'Andrea

In a previous edition of this book, formerly titled *Rehabilitation Counseling*, Flowers, Griffin-Dixon, and Trevino (1997) noted that:

> The profession of rehabilitation counseling has undergone various changes since its inception in the early 1900s. The services it provides and the people it serves has expanded considerably. Amid all the transformations in the profession, however, one concept has remained constant—the philosophy and practice of diversity. That is, the rehabilitation profession is diverse and practices pluralism as a system. (p. 124)

Over the past several years, the rehabilitation counseling profession has increased attention to diversity issues. Like the counseling profession in general, much of this attention has focused on the unique needs of persons in the five major racial/ethnic groups in the United States (i.e., African Americans, Asian Americans/Pacific Islanders, Latino/Latina Americans; Native Americans/Native Alaskans, and European Americans). While this attention has led to an increased understanding of some of the unique psychological strengths and needs of persons in these groups, several researchers stress that mental health practitioners continue to do a poor job in effectively meeting the psychosocial and personal needs of clients who come from culturally diverse groups, including clients from non-White populations, poor persons, and gay/lesbian/bisexual individuals (Surgeon General Report, 2001). Additionally, rehabilitation counselors have not provided services equitably to traditionally underrepresented groups, including clients from non-White populations, as well as persons from specific disability groups, such as deaf/hearing-impaired individuals and those with psychiatric illnesses (Atkins & Wright, 1980; Bowe, 1984; Jacobs, Wissusik, Collier, Stackman, & Burkeman, 1992; Moore, 2001; Patterson, Allen, Parnell, Crawford, & Beardall, 2000; Rimmerman, Botuck, & Levy, 1995; Wilson, 2002). Rehabilitation counseling practitioners are beginning to become more aware of some of the ways that their clients' diverse cultural contexts impact their lives, but many practitioners fail to effectively implement this knowledge in ways that result in maximized employment, economic self-sufficiency, independence, inclusion, and integration.

This chapter is designed to increase rehabilitation counselors' awareness and knowledge of a broad range of diversity issues and different contexts of practice that need to be addressed when serving persons from culturally diverse groups and backgrounds. Particular attention is directed to (a) the multidimensional nature of clients' development and (b) the need for rehabilitation counselors to assess how various historical/cultural/contextual factors have impacted their own development.

Several theorists have argued that counselors need to take time to conduct this sort of self-assessment so that they might then more fully understand how historical/cultural/contextual variables impact the different preferences, values, and biases that are manifested in their own counseling practices (Lewis, Lewis, Daniels, & D'Andrea, 2003). Although this kind of personal assessment might be useful prior to working with any client, ethical counseling practice requires practitioners to conduct this sort of self-evaluation prior to working with individuals who come from cultural groups and backgrounds that are different from their own (Ivey, D'Andrea, Ivey, & Simek-Morgan, 2002; Lewis et al., 2003). Without being aware of the ways in which historical/cultural/contextual factors influence their own development, counselors are likely to manifest various preferences, values, and biases in the counseling process that unintentionally conflict with culturally different clients' preferences, values, and biases. The counseling model that is presented in this chapter specifically focuses on a host of diversity and contextual issues that rehabilitation counselors are encouraged to consider as they strive to work more effectively, ethically, and respectfully with persons from diverse client populations. Definitions of key terms and concepts included in the counseling model are presented. Case studies demonstrate the practical utility of assessing the various components in rehabilitation counseling practice.

THE RESPECTFUL COUNSELING MODEL

The RESPECTFUL counseling model represents a new, comprehensive, and integrative way of thinking about the persons who are directly involved in the counseling process. This includes (a) those individuals who seek assistance with various problems and challenges that they are encountering in their lives (e.g., clients) and (b) professionals (counselors, psychologists, psychiatrists, and social workers) who are trained to assist clients in acquiring the knowledge and skills that will enable them to lead more effective and satisfying lives.

The RESPECTFUL counseling framework is rooted in two theoretical assumptions. The first assumption rests on the belief that the ultimate goal of all counseling is to promote clients' psychological and personal development. Counselors routinely use their knowledge and skills to achieve this broad goal by:

1. fostering the development of more effective decision-making and problem-solving competencies, which can be used by clients who are not necessarily in crisis, but are in need of acquiring more effective life skills;
2. providing crisis counseling services that are designed to help clients develop more effective coping strategies during times of heightened stress; and
3. utilizing more intensive, long-term psychotherapeutic interventions that are aimed at stimulating qualitative changes in clients' personality development.

The second assumption that underlies the RESPECTFUL counseling model involves the importance of understanding the unique and complex multidimensionality of human development and the need to intentionally address the multiple factors that impact clients' development in rehabilitation counseling practice. The counseling profession in general, and the field of rehabilitation counseling in particular, are beginning to demonstrate a greater awareness of the ways in which various cultural/contextual dimensions of a person's life affect their sense of psychological well-being. This increased awareness has mostly been spurred by the development of new theoretical insights and a host of research findings that have helped professionals reconstruct and expand their thinking about human development.

The RESPECTFUL counseling model addresses the multidimensional nature of human development, by directing attention to ten factors that are known to significantly impact the psychological development of both counselors and their clients. As is discussed later in this chapter, this theoretical framework can be used by rehabilitation counselors to (a) assess their own development, (b) identify their own cultural/contextual biases, (c) assess some of the factors that impact their clients' development, and (d) help these practitioners understand how to more effectively and ethically address the interface of multiple cultural/contextual factors in rehabilitation counseling practice. The 10 factors that comprise the RESPECTFUL counseling model include:

Religious/spiritual identity;
Economic class background;
Sexual identity;
Psychological maturity;
Ethnic/racial identity;
Chronological/developmental challenges;
Trauma and other threats to one's well-being;
Family background and history;
Unique physical characteristics; and
Location of residence and language differences.

Religious/Spiritual Identity

The first component in the RESPECTFUL model focuses on the way in which individuals personally identify with established religions or hold beliefs about extraordinary experiences that go beyond the boundaries of the strictly objective, empirically perceived world, which characterizes Western, modern, psychological thought (D'Andrea & Daniels, 2001). Kelly (1995) notes that the terms *religion* and *spirituality* are both grounded in an affirmation of transcendental experiences that are typically manifested in religious forms that extend beyond the boundaries of the ordinary and tangible. As used in the RESPECTFUL counseling framework, *religion* and *spirituality* generally refer to a person's belief in a reality that transcends physical nature and provides individuals with an "extra-ordinary" meaning of life in general and human existence in particular.

Although the terms *religion* and *spirituality* include the affirmation of a transcendental dimension of reality, they also hold different meanings as well. As D'Andrea and Daniels (1997) explain:

> While the term spirituality is often used to refer to a person's belief and affirmation of a transcendental connectedness with the universe, religion is typically used to denote the specific ways in which the belief is manifested institutionally within the creeds and dogmas of different religious groups and denominations. As used in the RESPECTFUL counseling model, the term religious/spiritual identity refers to a person's beliefs about the afterlife and the interconnectedness of all things in the universe as well as one's views about the meaning of such concepts as "God," "enlightenment," and "grace" to name a few. (p. 30)

Because clients' religious/spiritual identity may play an important role in the way they construct meaning of their life's experiences, it is important that rehabilitation counselors take time to assess the degree to which this factor impacts an individual's psychological development early in the helping process. Equally important, rehabilitation practitioners must take time to consider how their own religious/spiritual identity and beliefs may positively or negatively impact the work they do with clients who embrace different perspectives than their own in these areas. This is important, because, when left unexamined, counselors' own religious/spiritual identity and beliefs (or lack of) may result in inaccurate interpretations and misunderstandings of clients' development and their views about mental health and personal well-being.

Economic Class Background

Despite the tremendous impact that an individual's socioeconomic class standing has on his/her personal, psychological, and career development, counselors and psychologists frequently fail to adequately take this important factor into consideration when working with persons from diverse economic backgrounds. One of the reasons why many contemporary rehabilitation practitioners fail to direct more attention to socioeconomic factors, and their impact on human development, lies in the overuse of terms that have little relevance in accurately describing many clients' economic group identities. The overreliance on general categories, such as lower-, middle-, and upper-class backgrounds, represents an inadequate and, in many instances, an irrelevant way of describing this dimension of our clients' lives. To help rehabilitation counselors gain a greater understanding about the different economic classes or groups of which many clients are a part, D'Andrea and Daniels (2001) have extended the three general classes that have been traditionally used by social scientists, by describing six socioeconomic classes or categories into which most persons in the United States can be classified. Those researchers believe that this new classification system more accurately describes the different positions individuals hold, in terms of their economic class standing and background in the United States today.

This classification system includes: (1) *poor persons* (e.g., unemployed individuals with less than a high school degree, who are in need of economic assistance to meet their basic living needs); (2) *working poor persons* (e.g., individuals who have a high school or equivalency degree and/or some college experience, are employed as unskilled workers, and whose annual incomes fall below the federal poverty guidelines); (3) *working-class persons* (e.g., individuals who have a high school degree, some college experience, or have received a certificate or license in a particular trade, whose annual incomes fall above the federal poverty guidelines); (4) *middle-class nonprofessionals* (e.g., persons with at least a high school degree, but who more likely have an advanced degree or specialized training in a given vocational career, whose annual incomes are above the national average); (5) *middle-class professionals* (e.g., individuals with at least a college degree, but more likely with an advanced degree in some professional field, such as education, law, medicine, etc., whose annual incomes are above the national average); and (6) *persons in the upper class* (e.g., individuals whose annual income falls within the upper 10% of the national average).

Numerous researchers have explained how a person's economic class standing and background impacts their attitudes, values, worldview, and behaviors (Alkinson, Morten, & Sue, 1993; Scheurich, 1993). Recognizing the influence that this aspect of clients' multidimensionality has on their development, practitioners need to be attentive to the ways in which this factor contributes to an individual's identified strengths and expressed problems during counseling. Because counselors are also likely to have integrated inaccurate and negative views and prejudices about persons who come from economic backgrounds that are different from their own, rehabilitation professionals must evaluate their own class-based assumptions, biases, and stereotypes when working with individuals who come from diverse economic class groups.

Sexual Identity

One of the most complex, although often understudied, aspects of an individual's psychological development involves the development of sexual identity of persons who come from diverse groups and backgrounds in our society. As used in the RESPECTFUL counseling model, the term *sexual identity* relates to a person's gender identity, gender roles, and sexual orientation. The term *gender identity* refers to an individual's subjective sense of what it means to be either male or female. A person's gender identity is clearly impacted by the different roles men and women are expected to play within a given cultural/ethnic context. Savin-Williams and Cohen (1996) note that the type of gender identity that one develops is markedly influenced by "those behaviors, attitudes, and personality traits that a society designates as masculine or feminine, that is, more 'appropriate' for or typical of the male or female role" (p. 72).

A person's sexual identity can be manifested in a broad range of ways, which extend beyond the narrow notion of masculinity and femininity. Transsexuals, for example, are described as individuals who are convinced that they were born the wrong biological sex. Thus, the term *transsexualism* refers to those persons who experience discordance between their gender identity and their anatomical sex (Bailey, 1997).

A person's sexual identity is also influenced by one's sexual orientation. There are a number of ways to conceptualize this dimension of a person's sexual identity. Generally speaking, it includes such concepts as *bisexuality*, *heterosexuality*, and *homosexuality*. *Bisexuality* refers to individuals who demonstrate a sexual interest in both males and females. *Heterosexuality*, in contrast, refers to individuals whose sexual interest is directed toward persons of the opposite sex. A third way of viewing this dimension of one's sexual identity involves the concept of *homosexuality*, which is a term that has been used to identify individuals whose sexual preference involves persons of the same sex. Because of the negative stereotypes that have historically been associated with the term *homosexuality*, words like *gay males, gays,* and *lesbians* are considered more acceptable and respectful terms to use in describing this dimension of a person's sexual identity (D'Andrea & Daniels, 2001). Rehabilitation counselors must recognize the important impact that clients' and practitioners' sexual identity has in counseling and psychotherapeutic settings and the tremendous impact that feminist theories are having in the fields of counseling and psychology, as well.

From the perspective of the RESPECTFUL counseling framework, it is vital that rehabilitation counselors conscientiously assess the ways in which the interaction of multiple factors of this framework influence their clients' and their own development. A number of case studies are included in this chapter to help the reader better understand how the interaction of multiple factors in the RESPECTFUL counseling model might be manifested among clients with whom they work and to emphasize the need for counselors to continually assess the ways in which these multiple factors may impact their own development and ways of approaching clients from diverse groups and backgrounds. In the following case study, the reader is encouraged to think about the ways in which the interplay of three factors contained in the RESPECTFUL counseling model (religious/spiritual identity, economic class background, and sexual identity) may affect the content and process of the counseling services that are offered to Douglas.

CASE STUDY 9.1

Douglas is a 24-year-old, openly gay male who is so excited that Jehovah has blessed him that he shares *Awake* and *The Watchtower* (religious publications) with everyone with whom he comes in contact, even while waiting to be seen by his new VR counselor, Linda. He is currently a Supplemental Security Income recipient, but wants to be self-supportive and to become a vendor under the Randolph-Sheppard Program and, therefore, arrives one-half hour early for his counseling appointment. The receptionist informs Linda that her 11:00 a.m. appointment arrived early and is causing chaos in the waiting room by eliciting other clients to read his religious materials.

Linda agrees to see him early, but makes a quick note that she must address appropriate work behaviors with Douglas, including consideration of schedules and imposing personal religious beliefs on others. At the same time, she realizes that she must consider her own biases about Jehovah Witnesses and recognize that his religious conviction may be used as a strength in acceptance of his disability.

As Linda greets Douglas, she is struck by his effeminate gestures and mannerisms and thinks to herself, "Oh my, another issue to be addressed," but recognizes that her own attitude toward gay males also needs to be addressed.

Psychological Maturity

Rehabilitation counselors often work with clients who share common demographic characteristics (e.g., age, gender, socioeconomic and cultural/racial backgrounds, etc.), but appear to be very different in psychological terms. In these situations, we might refer to one client as being "more psychologically mature" than another client who is the same age, identifies with the same cultural/racial reference group, and shares a similar sexual identity. Some descriptors that are commonly used by counseling professionals to describe this immature client include statements such as "He demonstrates limited impulse control in social interactions" or "She has a low capacity for self-awareness." Statements that are commonly used to describe more mature clients include the following: "He is able to discuss his problems with much insight;" "She is highly self-aware;" and "She has developed a much broader range of interpersonal and introspective skills than many of the other clients with whom I am working."

Over the past three decades, there has been a tremendous increase in our understanding of the developmental stages that individuals pass through as they mature psychologically. Much of this knowledge comes from the work of a variety of structural-developmental psychologists, who have presented numerous models that help explain the process of psychological maturity. This includes the work of Piaget (1977) (cognitive development), Perry (1970) (ethical development), Kohlberg (1981) and Gilligan (1982) (moral development), Selman (1980) (social/interpersonal development), and Loevinger (1976) (ego development).

Structural-developmental theories view psychological development as a process in which individuals move from simple to more complex ways of thinking about themselves and their life experiences. This movement can be traced along a set of invariant, hierarchical stages that reflect qualitatively different ways of thinking, feeling, and acting in the world (Sprinthall, Peace, & Kennington, 2001). According to Young-Eisendrath (1988), each developmental stage represents a uniquely different frame of reference for meaning-making. She goes on to point out that developmental stages "are not entirely dependent on chronological maturation. . . . Stages evolve with aging up to a point. However, when further development is not supported by environmental factors, a person may stop developing" (p. 71).

By assessing clients' levels of psychological maturity, rehabilitation counselors are better positioned to more effectively design interventions that are tailored to meet their unique personal strengths and needs. It is also important that rehabilitation counselors take time to reflect on their own psychological development. The therapeutic process can easily be undermined when practitioners are matched with clients who are functioning at a more complex level of psychological maturity than they themselves.

Ethnic/Racial Identity

The term *ethnic* is derived from the Greek word meaning *nation*. Thus, the concept of ethnic identity refers to persons who identify with, and are distinguished from others by, the unique social/cultural characteristics, values, and traditions that have evolved within the nation-states in which a person lives or has descended. Although individuals are commonly associated with large cultural/racial groups (i.e., African Americans, European Americans, Native Americans, etc.), people commonly demonstrate strong personal identification with specific ethnic groups (i.e., Italian-Americans, Irish-Americans, etc.), whose values and traditions have had a substantial impact on their development and view of the world.

Historically, the term *race* has been used to connote both biological and social differences. From a biological perspective, people of different races have been classified into three major groups: Caucasoid, Mongoloid, and Negroid. These three categories have frequently been used to broadly distinguish racial differences in the past, but they have recently been criticized as being misleading and superficial, in terms of classifying persons according to phenotypic variations in skin color (Helms & Cook, 1999). The long-standing history of miscegenation in the United States (e.g., persons born to parents from different racial groups) has rendered such biologically based explanations of race as relatively useless. The theory of miscegenation simply suggests that, if everyone in the United States were able to accurately track their biological lineage back in time, they would find that each of us comes from a mixed racial blood lineage (Helms & Cook, 1999).

Another major problem associated with using externally manifested biological traits to define racial differences is that, although researchers readily acknowledge that phenotypic differences (e.g., differences in skin color, hair texture, etc.) are apparent among many people in our society, there is actually greater genotypic variation (e.g., differences in a person's genetic makeup) among individuals who come from the same racial groups than individuals who have historically been identified as belonging to different racial groups in this country (Allen & Adams, 1992; Helms & Cook, 1999; Zukerman, 1990).

Because scientific evidence clearly negates traditional definitions of race that are rooted in biological/genetic differences, one might question the usefulness of thinking about human differences in racial terms at all. Given the ambiguity and confusion that surrounds the definition of the term *race*, from a biological perspective, it is reasonable to ask why this construct continues to be used to categorize people in our society. In attempting to answer this question, Helms and Cook (1999) suggest that, rather than being thought of in biological terms, the word *race* can be more meaningfully defined as a social construction that is designed to assure that certain societal privileges are maintained among persons in particular racial groups in our society. This includes a broad range of privileges, such as easier access to education and employment opportunities, health care resources, housing, and personal loans, as well as differential sentencing for criminal acts and treatment by law enforcement personnel, to name a few (Jones, 1997). When racial factors are taken into consideration, numerous researchers have reported that these and many other social privileges continue to be disproportionately bestowed among persons from middle- and upper-class White European backgrounds (particularly male persons) in our nation (Helms & Cook, 1999; Jones, 1997; Scheurich, 1993).

The various privileges, discrimination, and types of oppression that have been, and continue to be, bestowed among persons who are associated with different racial groups have a profound psychological effect on the way individuals construct meaning of the world and of themselves. Over the past 15 years, numerous researchers have helped shed light on some of the ways persons from diverse groups develop a personal sense of identity that integrates reactions to one's racial background and experiences. The interested reader is encouraged to review Cross's (1995) model of Black identity development, as well as Helm's (1995) model of White identity development and her racial identity development framework for people-of-color, to learn more about the different developmental statuses/stages and unique psychological characteristics that distinguish persons who operate from the various levels of these theoretical models.

Clearly, tremendous psychological differences exist among persons who come from the same ethnic/racial group. This variation is commonly referred to as "within-group" differences. Given the within-group variation that is notably manifested among persons from the same ethnic/racial groups, it is important that rehabilitation counselors develop the knowledge and skills that are necessary to accurately assess these differences and respond to them in effective and respectful ways in rehabilitation counseling settings. Rehabilitation counselors must understand how their own ethnic/racial experiences have impacted their psychological development, the way they construct meaning of the world, and the types of biases they have acquired toward others in the process.

Chronological/Developmental Challenges

Besides the types of developmental changes that are discussed under the "Psychological Maturity" section (see earlier), individuals also undergo systematic changes that are chronologically based. These age-related, developmental changes represent what are referred to as chronological challenges, which individuals face at different points across the life span. Rehabilitation practitioners are familiar with many of these challenges, because they represent the characteristics that we normally associate with infancy, childhood, adolescence, and adulthood.

Theorists who explain human development from a chronological perspective are commonly referred to as life-span development (Craig, 1992; Havighurst, 1953; Shaffer, 1993) or maturational theorists (Erikson, 1968). Unlike the structural-developmental theorists, who tend to look at a particular aspect of a person's psychological maturity (e.g., intellectual, moral, social development), life-span development theorists examine a person's growth from a more holistic perspective, which includes taking into account the types of physical, cognitive, and psychological changes that predictably occur at different times in an individual's life (D'Andrea & Daniels, 2001).

The specific changes that life-span researchers have noted individuals normally undergo, as they develop from infancy through adulthood, include physical growth (e.g., bodily changes and the sequencing of motor skills), the emergence of different cognitive competencies (e.g., the development of perceptual, language, learning, memory, and thinking skills), and the manifestation of a variety of psychological skills (e.g., including the ability to manage one's emotions and the demonstration of more effective interpersonal competencies) that occur over time (Shaffer, 1993). The ways in which individuals successfully negotiate the chronological challenges that are commonly associated with infancy, childhood, adolescence, and adulthood mostly determine the degree to which they develop a positive sense of self-esteem, lead productive lives, and experience personal satisfaction in life.

Human development researchers have greatly helped rehabilitation counselors refine their thinking regarding the unique challenges individuals face at different points across the life span. Practically speaking, this knowledge enables practitioners to work more effectively with persons who face difficult chronological challenges in their lives, by implementing age-appropriate intervention strategies in different counseling settings. It also allows practitioners to be mindful of the unique challenges that they are likely to encounter when significant chronological differences exist between themselves and their clients. D'Andrea and Daniels (1997) suggest that many young practitioners are likely to encounter major challenges, in terms of gaining a high level of trust, respect, and sense of professional legitimacy, when working with some clients who are much older than themselves.

Trauma and Other Threats to One's Well-Being

Trauma and threats to one's well-being are included in the RESPECTFUL counseling and development model, to emphasize the complex ways in which stressful situations put people at risk of psychological danger and harm. Such harm typically occurs when the stressors individuals experience in their lives exceed their ability to cope with them in constructive and effective ways. An individual's personal resources (coping skills, self-esteem, social support, and the personal power one derives from their cultural group) may be overtaxed when one is subjected to ongoing environmental stressors for extended periods of time. When individuals experience similar stressors for lengthy periods of time, they are commonly referred to as a vulnerable or an at-risk group (Lewis et al., 2003).

Rehabilitation counselors are frequently called upon to work with persons in various vulnerable, at-risk groups, including poor, homeless, and unemployed people; adults and children in families undergoing divorce; pregnant teenagers; individuals with HIV or AIDS; persons with cancer; and individuals who are victimized by various forms of ageism, racism, sexism, and cultural oppression. Although persons in these vulnerable populations greatly differ from one another, they all routinely experience high levels of environmental stress that tax their personal resources and coping abilities. Heightened, prolonged, and historical stressors often result in more-severe and adverse psychological outcomes for many persons from oppressed cultural/ethnic/racial groups in our contemporary society. These stressors can and do result in traumatic life experiences, which underlie many of the intergenerational problems that are manifested among many persons from diverse and vulnerable groups in our nation (Salzman, 2001).

To be effective, rehabilitation practitioners must accurately assess the different ways in which environmental stressors adversely impact clients' lives and must develop intervention strategies that help to ameliorate these problems. Rehabilitation counselors, who work with persons from diverse client populations, need to be knowledgeable of the ways in which intergenerational trauma is sustained over time and need to implement interventions that are intentionally designed to address such threats to clients' psychological health and sense of well-being. These practitioners must also consider how various life stressors and traumatic events may have had a lasting impact on their own psychological development.

The following case study is presented to again highlight the importance of taking into consideration multiple contexts of diversity that impact both clients' and rehabilitation counselors' psychological development. In this case study, the reader is encouraged to think about the ways in which the interplay of three factors contained in the RESPECTFUL counseling model (ethnic/racial identity, chronological challenges, and trauma) may affect the content and process of the counseling services that are offered to Geraldine.

CASE STUDY 9.2

A community advocate referred Geraldine to the local VR agency to be evaluated for the supported employment program. Geraldine is a 27-year-old African American with severe mental retardation, who has been working in a sheltered workshop for the past 8 years. David, a European American counselor, has just received her medical reports indicating that she is HIV positive. Because of Geraldine's mental-versus-chronological maturation level, he must contact her legal guardian to share this news and determine the next steps. At the same time, he must confront possible biases and assumptions he may have regarding her sexual behavior.

Family Background and History

The rapid cultural diversification of the United States includes an increasing number of families that are very different from the traditional notion of family that many rehabilitation counselors have historically used as a standard for determining "normal family life" and "healthy family functioning." The different types of families (e.g., the increasing number of single-female-headed families, blended families, extended families, families headed by gay and lesbian parents, etc.) that counselors increasingly encounter in their work challenge practitioners to reassess the traditional concept of the nuclear family, which has been used as a standard to which all types of other families were compared.

Rehabilitation counselors will be increasingly pressed to understand the unique strengths that clients derive from these different family systems and to implement counseling strategies that are intentionally designed to foster the healthy development of these diverse familial units. In addition to learning about the personal strengths that individuals derive from these different types of family systems, rehabilitation practitioners are encouraged to assess biases and assumptions that they may have developed about family life, as a result of their own family history and experiences. This is important to do, because, when left unexamined, these biases and assumptions may adversely impact the counseling relationship one has with clients who come from families that are very different from that of the counselor's.

Unique Physical Characteristics

The RESPECTFUL counseling framework emphasizes the importance of being sensitive to the ways in which our society's idealized images of physical beauty negatively impact the psychological development of many persons whose physical nature does not fit the narrow views of beauty that are fostered by our modern culture. McWhirter (1994) notes that "one of the most disheartening and frightening phenomena in our society is the relentless and all-consuming desire for physical beauty" (p. 203). This obsession is rooted in an idealistic image of persons who are thin and muscular. In reality, few persons match this idealistic image, and many experience a sense of reduced self-esteem and increased feelings of personal inadequacy as a result of not living up to this socially constructed view of a beautiful person (McWhirter, 1994). In other instances, persons who possess certain unique physical characteristics, which have traditionally been referred to as "physical, mental and emotional disabilities," have also suffered from various forms of discrimination and stigmatization, whose genesis is rooted in misperceptions and stereotypes about physical beauty and health.

When working with clients whose unique physical characteristics may be a source of stress and dissatisfaction, rehabilitation counselors need to reflect on the ways in which the idealized myth of physical beauty may have led them to internalize negative views and stereotypes about persons who do not fit this myth. When these sorts of internalized views go unchecked, they may lead to inaccurate assessments and misinterpretations of our clients' personal strengths. Also, when working with women and men whose psychological development has been negatively impacted by some aspect of their own unique physical nature, practitioners need to be able to assist them in understanding the ways in which gender role socialization contributes to irrational thinking about their own sense of self-worth (D'Andrea & Daniels, in press).

Location of Residence and Language Differences

Location of residence refers to the geographical region and setting where one resides. D'Andrea and Daniels (2001) identify five areas that many persons commonly refer to when talking about the major regions in the United States: northeastern, southeastern, midwestern, southwestern, and northwestern regions of our nation. These geographical areas are distinguished by the types of persons who reside in these areas, as well as by differences in terms of climate patterns, geological terrain, and, to some degree, the types of occupations and industry that are available to workers who reside in these areas. These geographical locations are also often characterized by their own unique subcultures, which reflect the types of values, attitudes, and language/dialects that are commonly manifested by many of the individuals who reside in these areas.

Location of residence also includes the type of setting in which a person resides. Rehabilitation practitioners are probably familiar with three major types of residential settings in which clients live: rural, suburban, and urban settings. As defined by the U.S. Bureau of the Census (1990), rural populations consist of people who live in places or towns of less than 2,500 inhabitants and in open country outside the closely settled suburbs of metropolitan cities. In contrast, urban areas consist of cities with 50,000 or more inhabitants (U.S. Bureau of the Census, 1990). When rehabilitation practitioners work with persons who come from geographic regions or residential settings that are different from the ones in which they were raised, they need to reflect on the possible stereotypes and biases they may have developed about individuals who come from these different areas. This is particularly important when working with persons who use a different dialect/language in interpersonal interactions. As is the case with the other components of the RESPECTFUL counseling model, this sort of self-assessment is important, because possible stereotypes and biases that rehabilitation counselors may have developed about persons whose residential background and language/dialect is different from their own may lead to inaccurate assumptions and clinical interpretations within rehabilitation settings.

CASE STUDY 9.3

Maria is a 35-year-old, single mother of two young children. She recently became deaf after a blow to her head by an abusive husband, and fled from Texas to Florida. Her case worker referred her to VR for employment assistance. Maria shares with Chari, her VR counselor, that she is considering returning to Texas, where she at least can get support from family members. Considering that she is not accepted by the deaf community, whose members primarily use American sign language, nor the hearing community members, with whom she experiences frequent communication difficulties, Maria is manifesting signs of depression.

Although Chari is eager to assist Maria to meet the psychosocial and employment challenges that characterize her client's life, this counselor recognizes that her own professional biases and failure to recognize the importance of this client's family support are vital considerations that need to be addressed, before the counselor can work ethically and respectfully with this individual.

We anticipate that the comprehensive diversity framework of the RESPECTFUL model will help expand rehabilitation counselors' thinking about the various considerations that underlie a culturally competent approach to rehabilitation counseling practice. We also recognize that the components contained in this model do not represent an exhaustive listing of all the factors impacting human development; therefore, we expect that practitioners and researchers will work collaboratively, to continue to add to a better understanding of the multidimensional nature of human development, personally and professionally.

CHAPTER 10

Advocacy

William M. Liu and Rebecca L. Toporek

The notion of advocacy in rehabilitation counseling is not new. Rehabilitation counselors, in many professional practices, often find themselves at the forefront of helping clients, in multiple ways, to creating optimal environments for growth and development (Maki & Riggar, 1997). Yet finding literature, empirical and theoretical, concerning the practice of advocacy in rehabilitation counseling is difficult. Moreover, the notion of advocacy may conjure up images of social activism or empowerment movements. These images reflect the confusion that surrounds advocacy in rehabilitation practice. Thus, in building a case for advocacy within rehabilitation counseling, one possible area in which some understanding may be gained is from multicultural counseling.

The multicultural counseling literature has critiqued traditional counseling practices, research, and training, for their cultural bias toward individualism, middle-classness, and, certainly, ability (Olkin, 1999, 2002; Prilleltensky, 1997). Typically, the denial of power systems that perpetuate the marginalization of minority peoples has been a problematic theme in many of our theoretical orientations (Toporek & Liu, 2001). Consequently, the failure to be self-actualized and productive is often considered to be the fault of the client, rather than of context, history, or access to resources. In order to correct these issues and more fully integrate context into therapy, many in our counseling professions have taken upon themselves the responsibility to work beyond the confines of the therapy space and to engage, directly, in social action and advocacy. Through sustained efforts of practice, research, and training, some changes have been noted in the profession. Within the American Psychological Association, the recent passage of the *Guidelines on Multicultural Education, Training, Research, Practice, and Organizational Change for Psychologists* (2002) is one example of efforts to change a profession that is having a discernable outcome.

Hence, the focus of this chapter is to enhance the discussion about advocacy in rehabilitation counseling by attending to the contribution of multicultural counseling perspectives. To meet this goal, we first discuss the relevance of incorporating multicultural competency into the definition of advocacy in rehabilitation counseling. Second, we discuss the issue of politicizing the profession through advocacy activities, and we describe various models and definitions of advocacy. Finally, we discuss training and practice implications, with particular attention to the professional responsibilities of rehabilitation counselors and the challenges that they face as they attempt to advocate for their clientele.

MULTICULTURAL COUNSELING COMPETENCIES

By now, many counselors understand the necessity of multicultural competencies. The best-known framework for multicultural competencies, as articulated by Sue, Arredondo, and McDavis (1992), state that counselors need to have knowledge, awareness, and skills in the three areas of understanding their biases, clients' worldviews, and culturally congruent interventions. The argument for the integration of multiculturalism into counseling has rested on the changing racial and ethnic demographics of the United States (Ridley & Kleiner, in press). Problematically, however, this argument often overlooks other existing aspects of diversity (e.g., sexual orientation, women, and ability), and situates multiculturalism with race and ethnicity. On the contrary, multiculturalism must be defined in general and overarching cultural dimensions—to be expansive and inclusive (Stone, 1997). There are two works that may contribute to the relevance of multicultural competencies to rehabilitation counseling. First, Arredondo et al. (1996) discussed an inclusive perspective of multiculturalism and elaborated the competencies within the framework of personal dimensions of identity. Those authors suggested that counselors must consider the multiple ways that individuals define themselves and the multiple communities of importance to clients and that counselors strive for competence in these different realms. In keeping the expansive definition of multiculturalism, it is easy to understand how advocacy, multiculturalism, and rehabilitation counseling can form a strong partnership. In the second work that contributes to our discussion, Toporek and Reza (2000) used the base of multicultural counseling competencies, provided by Sue, Arredondo, and McDavis (1992), to assert that multicultural competencies should include attention to institutional dimensions, as well as to professional and personal realms. They described *institutional cultural competence* as actions that counselors may need to take in addressing institutional issues that impact the well-being of clients. Counselors may do this through administrative roles, coordinator roles, as members of an organization, or in a variety of other functions. This attention to institutional competence directly suggests that advocacy, of one form or another, may be critical in working in culturally competent ways, beyond one-on-one work with clients.

Focusing on rehabilitation counseling specifically, we see that this counseling specialty is very appropriate for an integration of advocacy and multiculturalism. Hershenson's (1990) "C-C-C" model of rehabilitation counseling may be used as a framework for considering how advocacy may be an integral part of the role. In this model, the rehabilitation counselor's role includes three primary functions: coordinating, counseling, and consulting. Within each aspect of this role, the counselor may find that some form of advocacy is an appropriate intervention. Multiculturalism, in general, encourages institutions and individuals to seek out transformation of systems, rather than to settle for additive changes or superficial reorganizing (Liu & Pope-Davis, in press). As such, advocacy becomes an implicit activity of those who identify as multiculturally competent counselors. In a similar manner, rehabilitation counselors may find themselves in situations in which they must facilitate client self-advocacy or advocate for client welfare, with, or on behalf of, the client, in order to make environments accommodate and change for the client. This advocacy activity is congruent with the aims of multiculturalism, since nonadaptive or nonaccommodating environments may be construed as marginalizing and oppressive milieus for clients. As a function of their role, rehabilitation counselors acting, as advocates in promoting changes in a client's environment, are engaging in multiculturally competent work for the betterment of their clients.

Although there may appear to be a dichotomy between counseling and advocacy, Lerner (1972) believed that this perception results in a false dichotomy between social action and counseling. For some counselors, the idea of advocacy is perceived as a confluence between the personal and private world of counseling versus the public and political world of social action. Consequently, reluctance toward advocacy may be construed as a fear of politicizing counseling (Pope-Davis, Liu, Toporek, & Brittan, 2001). This fear, of course, assumes that counseling is a nonpolitical activity (Liu & Pope-Davis, in press).

Advocacy in counseling, especially rehabilitation counseling, challenges many of the values inherent in traditional counseling and psychotherapy (Toporek & Liu, 2001). Among these conflicts are the value of individualism, insight as a cure, and ableism (Olkin, 2002). It also challenges the notion of time-limited or brief therapy, psychological distance between the client and counselor, and dual relationships. Advocacy confronts the notion that clients are, by themselves, responsible for their situation (i.e., that it is their distorted perceptions that are creating the problem) and that only they can change their environment. Often, many of these values are implicit in the way clients are treated (i.e., diagnosed) in counseling (Follette & Houts, 1996). Rehabilitation counseling, by its nature, tends to recognize that the environment significantly impacts their clients. However, the controversy in rehabilitation counseling is often about the extent to which counselors use their own power for the benefit of their client. Consequently, advocacy actions risk and threaten the status quo on which the counselor may depend. That is, rehabilitation counselors may be at risk of losing their job, if their advocacy actions challenge the system in which they exist. Although self-advocacy is certainly an important counseling goal, we also believe that the counselor may need to consider situations in which it is appropriate to intervene directly with organizations or systems. Within the model presented by Hershenson (1990), the roles of consultation or coordination may represent such examples.

One of the principles in multicultural counseling is the idea of collaboration with clients. Rather than become mired in the ambiguity between what we do with or for a client (Lerner, 1972), the focus needs to be always upon what we can do along with clients, in order to better their environment, situation, or condition (e.g., Freire, 1989). In traditional psychotherapy, clients tend to be disempowered and may feel a lack of agency, because of the assumptions many counselors may have of clients, for example, that the counselor knows what is best for the client, not including clients in decisions, and stigmatizing individuals through deficit-oriented labels (Prilleltensky, 1997). In rehabilitation counseling, working collaboratively with clients is particularly important to identify the part of the problem that is internal (intrapsychic) and the part that is external (systemic), as well as actions that the client may take to change the systemic issues. In addition, we argue that there are times when it is appropriate for counselors to recognize their responsibility in addressing systemic issues. For example, when the help-giving organization is one that is perpetuating barriers, not only must clients voice their concern, but the counselor's responsibility, as a member of the organization, is to actively facilitate change within the organization. If the counselor does not take such action, they are in danger of colluding with the problematic system. Additionally, the client may sense the counselor's implicit collusion and may interpret counselor–client discourse as a double-bind message of "I'll help you only if I don't risk anything on my part." Consequently, the counselor's credibility and ability to conduct therapy may be jeopardized.

Because counseling must be seen as an interactional process, the client and counselor are conceived as collaborators. The counselor is open to change as much as the client, and they both must envision potential changes within their environment. Because the client or consumer should be construed as a participant in their own change, we would like to posit that the consumer language often used in rehabilitation counseling be challenged for not fully incorporating the notion of client agency in the environment. Although the consumer label for clientele is popular, because it puts the potential power within the consumer and not necessarily with the service provider, the marketplace metaphor still resonates with an adversarial theme. If the consumer is unhappy with a particular service, then the service provider is to change and meet the new demands. Yet, implicit in this notion of the consumer and the market is also a "bottom line." Based upon cost–benefits, some agencies may not change at all, and, eventually, clients may find themselves without adequate services altogether. The notion of collaboration or equality is not inherent in an economic model of service provision (e.g., Eriksen, 1997, 1999). Consequently, we here use the language of collaboration to denote the role of the client and counselor, rather than using the common language of the consumer in this chapter.

Before continuing further, the role advocacy has in counseling and in the counseling profession must be understood. Additionally, we discuss the various models from which advocacy can be operationalized. The following section is a brief overview of these two facets of advocacy in counseling.

ADVOCACY IN COUNSELING

Politicizing the Profession

For us, the issue of advocacy is partly a professional identity issue and not solely a practical concern. Actions that benefit clients, by eliminating or diminishing institutional and cultural barriers, may have a secondary effect of empowering clients and encouraging future social action by clients and counselors. Many sentiments toward institutional and cultural change were elements of advocacy and community organizing in the 1970s, when changing structural inequities was considered an appropriate professional role (Lewis & Lewis, 1983). Yet, through the 1980s and 1990s, the advocacy perspective seemingly lost its prominence (McClure & Russo, 1996; Toporek & Liu, 2001). McClure and Russo (1996) speculate that a change of focus by the counseling profession, toward credibility and individualism, has contributed to the decreasing emphasis on advocacy as a legitimate professional role.

With the increasing emphasis on multiculturalism and multicultural competencies, the pendulum may be swinging back toward advocacy. With the advent of multiculturalism and feminist orientations, traditional notions of psychotherapy and counseling are being challenged to become relevant for historically marginalized groups (Toporek & Liu, 2001). Because multiculturalism is concerned with social justice, especially for disenfranchised and marginalized groups, and because advocacy also is typically aligned with combating marginalization (Chesler, Bryant, & Crowfoot, 1976), advocacy is becoming an important professional concern. Recognizing that counseling has been differentially effective, and sometimes biased, against minority individuals, there have been increasing challenges to the profession to explore the individual, cultural, and institutional barriers that perpetuate oppression (Ridley, 1995; Sutton & Kessler, 1986). Some oppression can be acted upon in dyadic interactions, but some can only be targeted through advocacy (Atkinson, Thompson, & Grant, 1993). For instance, a client expressing a negative sense of self-related to internalizing negative stereotypes of their racial group (i.e., internalized racialism) (Cokley, 2002), can be a pertinent dyadic issue in individual counseling. But, if a client reports that they cannot gain access to a building because of wheelchair restrictions to doorways and steps, then in-session therapy is likely to be unsuccessful in ameliorating client distress, anger, and frustration. Only through appropriate advocacy—out-of-session actions—will clients start to build a sense of efficacy and empowerment (McWhirter, 1994). Gruber and Trickett (1987) posit that advocacy operationalizes the privileges and power of the advocate, which are the intimate knowledge of rules, norms, and systems that are the resources that counselors can use to work with clients, in a concerted and effective way for change. In the latter case, the counselor is the most effective agent to start the change process, to make the agency more accessible.

The movement toward advocacy within the counseling professions is not without its detractors. Some argue that counselors cannot be involved in clients' environments and that advocacy is an unrealistic expectation (Weinrach & Thomas, 1998), or that it is a dangerous ideology (i.e., social justice)

(Ramm, 1998). This attitude, of course, assumes that the counseling profession is value-neutral and that we are not constantly practicing our politics in session (Pope-Davis et al., 2001). In fact, counselors are constantly negotiating their values in session, and practicing their worldviews out of session.

Others argue, correctly, that, in an effort to be an effective advocate, counselors need to be intentional and cautious in their activities, so as to not create unrealistic dependencies (Pinderhughes, 1983) or disempower clients (McWhirter, 1994). Again, this dependency-building is a type of value and worldview imposed by the counselor upon the client, a noncollaborative relationship, in which the counselor retains their position as "healer" and the client's position as that of the "sick person." Both are examples of nonadvocacy relationships and are more likely traditional therapy relationships masquerading as advocacy.

Definitions and Models

Although we focus specifically on advocacy in this chapter, one of the confusions that can occur is among the definitions of advocacy, empowerment, and social action. Sometimes, all three labels can be used synonymously to describe a particular activity, but we would draw some distinctions that may not be apparent. For us, *advocacy* is "the action a mental health professional, counselor, or psychologist takes in assisting clients and client groups to achieve therapy goals through participating in clients' environments" (Toporek & Liu, 2001, p. 387).

Historically, authors have sought to refine the overall idea of advocacy to include a variety of activities. Lewis and Lewis (1983) distinguish *case* advocacy, which is advocacy on behalf of a client, and *class* advocacy, which is advocacy on a systemic level. They also describe three types of advocacy: *here and now* advocacy, or responding to a situation; *preventative* advocacy, or actions to create a just environment; and *citizen* advocacy, or action encouraging others to challenge social issues. Chan, Brophy, and Fisher (1981) elaborate further on the concept of advocacy and suggest three types of advocacy that may be used. First, *representative* advocacy, in which a counselor takes on the issues of their client, because the client is unable to express or act upon their needs. This is similar to the counselor–advocate model of Atkinson, Morten, and Sue (1993), in which the counselor "speaks on behalf of the client, often confronting the institutional sources of oppression that are contributing to the client's problem" (p. 301). Second, *group* advocacy in which a "group seeks to intervene in a problem situation in order to achieve a goal consistent with the interest of the members of the group or others"

(Chan et al., 1981, p. 195). Finally, there is *self*-advocacy, when the individual is taught agentic knowledge, actions, and behaviors. In this last case, Chan et al. (1981) illustrate their self-advocacy by presenting cases in which clients are faced with a problematic situation. Counselors, working in this model, help clients define the problem and develop a list of possible actions from which the client chooses an alternative.

In considering advocacy in counseling, we have found it useful to describe advocacy as a continuum of activity on which empowerment and social action reside (Toporek & Liu, 2001). For us, *empowerment* is considered to be at one end of the agentic continuum. In this model, empowerment implies that counselor and client work to develop efficacy within the client's and counselor's sociopolitical world (McWhirter, 1994, 1997; Toporek & Liu, 2001). Thus, empowerment encompasses a specific action and behavior, with a specific client. As a result of empowerment, clients are able to cope with specific situational problems and concerns, and they have a sense of self-efficacy to contend with similar problems in the future. *Social action*, on the other hand, means that the counselor is constantly working on removing institutional and cultural barriers for a community or population. Social action implies advocacy on a societal level, on such issues as legislation or public policy that affect all clients. Thus, social action implies broad-based action and not specific activities for one individual. Within this model, there is a range of behaviors that counselors may engage in to remove barriers and address injustice. We assert that all these activities may be considered under the umbrella of advocacy and that each of these behaviors may be appropriate at various times in work with clients.

Although advocacy, empowerment, and social action are sometimes conflated, our belief is that any action, along all these dimensions, may be positive for clients and counselors alike. In all of these cases, changing environments for the optimal growth and development of the client is the goal. These actions are necessary and important in the professional lives of rehabilitation counselors, but it is unclear how counselors can learn or train to be effective advocates for their clients.

PRACTICE

Advocacy, in practice, may take many forms, as suggested by the continuum model we described earlier. Because the practice of rehabilitation counseling also takes many forms, we now address examples and possible advocacy roles throughout counseling, coordination, and consultation.

The counseling function of rehabilitation counseling lends itself to advocacy in relation to individual issues. Chan et al. (1981) provide some excellent examples of self-advocacy and a model for working with individual clients to facilitate their knowledge and agency in addressing barriers. In addition to self-advocacy, there are other examples of advocacy behaviors in counseling. For example, advocating for clients in their presence can serve as a model of agentic behavior for clients, as well as serve an advocate function. With this type of behavior, it is critical that the counselor and client collaboratively decide on what action the counselor might take, including goals and strategy for the action. This type of behavior may be appropriate in a situation in which the power and privilege of the counselor's role lends something that is not attainable by the client. The modeling involved in this action can provide a visible demonstration for situations in which self-advocacy is more important.

The coordinating function of rehabilitation counseling also lends itself to advocacy. Advocacy at this level may address individual or group concerns. Within the coordination function, counselors may be participants in decision- and policy-making bodies, such as clinical and administrative management teams, and, as such, may have access at a level different from that available to the client or client groups. Advocacy at the coordination level may also include actions such as identifying client needs that are not being met by the institution, then working to establish funding and institutional support for programs that may meet the needs of a special population.

The consultation role provides a noteworthy avenue for advocacy. As with coordination, advocacy in this role may serve individuals or groups. One example of advocacy at this level would be to engage legislators as consultees around issues that represent barriers to clients from marginalized groups. Other examples might include consulting with social service agency staff to provide training around multicultural competence, prejudice, and discrimination, or consulting with faculty to ensure that new curriculum includes issues related to disabilities. A final example of this would be lobbying the institution to include a permanent advocate on planning committees for access issues in remodeling or construction.

Considering the multifaceted role required in the practice of rehabilitation counseling, effective training for advocacy is a complex endeavor.

TRAINING

Advocacy training is one of the most contentious issues in counseling training. Along with course work, counseling training implies the need for face-to-face work with clients, as well as for competent supervision. But how does one go about receiving competent supervision for advocacy work? One possible answer may come from the advocacy work, as well as training strategies, described within multicultural competencies.

First, a distinction needs to be made between advocacy self-efficacy and specific competent behaviors. For example, multicultural competency can be perceived as the sense of self-efficacy that counselors may have about working with diverse peoples and groups, and multicultural competencies may be the specific proficiencies counselors have in working with diverse peoples. Although counselors sometimes have a high sense of self-efficacy (competency), they may not have the exact proficiencies that allow them to work effectively with diverse peoples and groups (Ridley & Kleiner, in press). For instance, counselors who perceive themselves to be multiculturally competent may not be experienced as such by their clients (Pope-Davis et al., 2002). This issue is pertinent to advocacy in rehabilitation counseling, because counselors may have a sense of competency in being an advocate for their clients, but may find themselves at a loss when it comes to the real behavior and action of advocacy. Thus, training and supervision become integral aspects of rehabilitation counseling advocacy.

Another training issue for rehabilitation counselors is that the very environment that they are challenging for their client may be the one that employs them. Hence, as rehabilitation counselors seek to engage and transform environments for their clients, they may become acutely aware that their jobs may be threatened. Training would be useful regarding ways of identifying and resolving this dilemma.

One model that may provide a good guide is that of a portfolio approach to advocacy training. Coleman and Hau (in press) provide a model of using portfolio assessment to evaluate and support student development around multicultural issues. A similar model may be applied for advocacy in rehabilitation counseling training. Using this type of model, students would develop a portfolio of training and practice activities related to advocacy work that they have completed throughout the program. The portfolio may include examples of specific cases within practicum, papers they have written, workshops they have attended, and so on. This would provide the student with more comprehensive training and the program faculty with more data on which to evaluate the student's progress.

Currently, the primary problem with advocacy in rehabilitation counseling may be that there is not enough training on the issue of being an advocate for clients (Collison et al., 1998; Eriksen, 1997, 1999). Effective training would include skills in identifying problem situations and determining which type of advocacy might be appropriate. In addition, it would be important for counselors to be able to identify the consequences of advocacy actions for both clients and themselves, for example, living with a changed system, or, less optimistically, the ramifications of challenging a hostile system. Although advocacy issues are not new for rehabilitation counseling, there is a need for more attention to coursework, curriculum, and supervision necessary to be an effective rehabilitation counseling advocate.

CONCLUSION

Rehabilitation counseling provides a natural forum for integrating advocacy into practice and training. However, there are some philosophical issues that must be dealt with, in order for counselors and training programs to effectively use this approach with clients. These issues include concerns about creating dependency, balancing client agency with counselors' responsibilities to address systemic barriers, dilemmas regarding conflict of interest between counselor and their home institution, and many others. Training will be critical in providing rehabilitation counselors an avenue for developing appropriate skills in resolving these issues and identifying appropriate times and strategies for advocacy. Multicultural counseling competencies can provide useful guidance in terms of training models and the establishment of competency standards that recognize issues faced by clients who are marginalized and impeded by systemic barriers. We hope that this chapter provides a useful framework, as well as tools that may help rehabilitation counselors and educators in integrating advocacy thoughtfully and effectively.

CHAPTER 11

Assessment

Norman L. Berven

Assessment is a fundamental practice in rehabilitation counseling and related helping professions, because it serves to direct all actions taken by counselors and the clients or consumers with whom they work, in attempting to meet client needs. As discussed in the *Standards for Educational and Psychological Testing*, published by the American Educational Research Association (AERA), American Psychological Association, and the National Council on Measurement in Education (1999), assessment may be defined as "systematic procedures to obtain information from a variety of sources to draw inferences about people" (p. 172). The systematic procedures used include not only the traditional standardized tests that are usually associated with assessment, but also other procedures, such as interviews, observations, medical examinations, and job tryouts, and the sources may include consumers or clients themselves, other professionals, and other people who know the individual, including family, friends, and previous employers. Finally, inferences may be drawn about abilities, interests, personality characteristics, likely behavior and satisfaction in different work and living environments, and likely responsiveness to intervention strategies that might be selected for use.

The scope of assessment is broad, extending well beyond the description of individuals, their functioning, and needs, to identifying and conceptualizing (a) concerns and problems experienced by individuals seeking assistance who might require intervention; (b) goals and objectives for rehabilitation programming, including career and life goals, along with the barriers that may stand in the way of accomplishing those goals; and (c) intervention strategies and related rehabilitation programming that might assist in resolving problems and achieving goals, including the organization of the strategies into a comprehensive service or treatment plan (see Vocational Evaluation and Work Adjustment Association, 1975). Assessment focuses not only on the person, but also on situational or environmental contexts in which an individual functions. In addition, assessment occurs at many different levels in rehabilitation counseling. At a macro level, assessment forms the basis for overall service plans, guiding the rehabilitation counseling process with a particular individual; at a more specific level, assessment forms the basis for the identification of appropriate strategies to follow in response to an unexpected crisis; and, at an even more specific level, assessment at a particular moment in time forms the basis for determining a verbal response or action to take at that moment, which will be consistent with the individual's needs, producing a desired response in a counseling session.

The purpose of this chapter is to discuss the assessment process and contemporary assessment practices in rehabilitation counseling, including assessment methods used, the synthesis and interpretation of assessment information, and the types of decisions and determinations for which assessment is commonly used. In addition, current trends and future developments in assessment are briefly discussed.

REHABILITATION COUNSELOR AND CONSUMER ROLES IN THE REHABILITATION PROCESS

The roles of rehabilitation counselors, in relation to clients or consumers served, may be conceptualized along a continuum of control over decision making. At one extreme, in the more traditional service delivery model, the rehabilitation counselor maintains control of the process and serves as the primary decision maker in service delivery. Midway along the continuum, the rehabilitation counselor and consumer function as a team, assuming joint control and collaborating in the decisions to be made, through an effective working alliance (Chan, Shaw, McMahon, Koch, & Strauser, 1997). At the other extreme, the consumer assumes control as the primary decision maker, and the rehabilitation counselor serves as a consultant, providing information and opinions to the consumer to facilitate his or her independent decision making. A move along the continuum toward greater consumer control of the rehabilitation process has been advocated by many, as a move away from a medical model of service delivery, toward an approach that is less paternalistic toward people with disabilities and that is more empowering (e.g., Holmes, 1993; National Institute on Consumer-Directed Long-Term Services, 1996; Nosek, 1998). Kosciulek (1999) has developed a consumer-directed theory of empowerment, and Kosciulek and Merz (2001) have documented the hypothesized relationships among consumer direction, community integration, empowerment, and quality of life.

Whether service delivery and treatment decisions are to be made by the professional, the consumer, or through collaboration between the two, assessment provides the information base for decision making, and the rehabilitation counselor has special expertise to bring to the process in developing that information base. To the extent that consumers assume greater control over decision making, they need to be involved as active participants in assessment planning, and the information that is accumulated needs to be communicated to consumers in a form that can be effectively used by them to facilitate their own decision making.

ASSESSMENT PROCESS

Assessment begins when the first information is received by a rehabilitation counselor about an individual to be served, perhaps through a phone call from the individual, a written referral, or a phone call from another professional, sometimes accompanied by previous treatment or service records. From the time that this initial information is obtained, the rehabilitation counselor begins to form impressions about the individual and his or her needs, as well as about goals that might be appropriate and services or intervention strategies that might be indicated. As additional information is accumulated, it is interpreted and synthesized with the information previously obtained, to develop an increasingly sophisticated and complex understanding of the individual and his or her needs, which can be used to predict how the individual might behave in different situations or respond to different intervention strategies. These predictions, in turn, facilitate the decisions to be made in treatment and service delivery. The assessment information is shared with the client or consumer, facilitating self-understanding, predictions about the future, and collaboration in treatment and service decisions.

BASIC CONCEPTS

Cronbach (1990) has distinguished between indicators of maximum performance and indicators of typical performance, and this distinction can be useful in understanding the purposes of various assessment methods in rehabilitation counseling (Berven, 1980; Maki, McCracken, Pape, & Scofield, 1979). Indicators of maximum performance are used to predict the behavior of an individual when performing at his or her best, for example, in training or employment, and may be further categorized into indicators of ability or aptitude and indicators of current skills or achievement. Although aptitude and achievement indicators are widely thought to measure developed abilities and to be influenced by learning histories (Anastasi, 1992), they may be conceptualized as having somewhat different purposes in assessment. Indicators of aptitude assist in determining the potential to develop skills, if given appropriate opportunities through training or other experiences; in contrast, indicators of current skills or achievement can assist in determining current mastery of skills. For example, a measure of mathematical aptitude might be used to determine one's potential to learn math skills; a measure of mathematical achievement might be used to determine whether an individual already possesses the math skills required for a particular type of employment or training (e.g., carpentry) or whether some further training in math might be required to improve skills. Indicators of typical performance are used to determine how an individual might typically behave in various situations and may be further divided into indicators of interests, facilitating predictions about likely satisfaction in different work and life situations, and indicators of personality characteristics.

With all assessment methods, it is important to consider reliability and validity of the scores or other information provided. According to the AERA et al. (1999) *Standards*, *reliability* refers to "the degree to which test scores are . . . dependable and repeatable for an individual test taker; the degree to which scores are free from errors of measurement" (p. 180), and *validity* refers to "the degree to which accumulated evidence and theory support specific interpretations of test scores entailed by proposed uses of a test" (p. 184). As an example, the reliability and validity of the "weight score," provided by a bathroom scale, might be assessed by having an individual step onto and off the scale, each time recording the weight indicated. Reliability of the scale as an assessment device would be reflected by the extent to which the scale consistently indicated the exact same weight on each occasion, and, if the weights indicated were highly inconsistent, the scale would have little value in measuring weight. In contrast, validity would be reflected in the extent to which the weight indicated provided an accurate measure of the individual's true weight, and, if the weight indicated was considerably different from the true weight, the scale would have little value, even if the weight indicated was highly consistent. With any assessment procedure, the reliability and validity of scores or other information produced are mostly responsible for determining its value as an assessment method or device.

Standardization is another concept that is important in understanding the variety of standardized or norm-referenced assessment devices that are commonly used in rehabilitation counseling practice. A standardized assessment procedure is a test, instrument, or procedure that has been administered to one or more large groups of individuals, referred to as the standardization or normative sample, according to carefully specified procedures. When the device is then used in assessment applications, it is administered according to the same standardized procedures, and the individual's performance can be compared to the standardization or normative samples when interpreting scores. However, the comparison of performance to the normative samples can be made only if the standardized procedures have been strictly followed, but the presence of limitations associated with disability may render standardized administration procedures impossible, and the accommodations required will serve to complicate the interpretation of scores and other performance measures (e.g., see Berven, 1980; Ekstrom & Smith, 2002; Holzbauer & Berven, 1999; Nester, 1993; Sherman & Robinson, 1982; Willingham et al., 1988). In addition, the presence of functional limitations can influence the meaning or inferences to be drawn from test scores in other important ways (e.g., see Berven, 1980; Holzbauer & Berven, 1999).

ASSESSMENT PRACTICES

A wide variety of assessment information is typically used in the rehabilitation process. The information obtained includes scores and other quantitative data from standardized tests and related instruments and procedures, as well as qualitative data obtained through such methods as interviews or direct observations. Sources of assessment information include the individuals themselves, other people who have known or have worked with them, and physicians and other professionals who may be called upon to conduct examinations or evaluations of current functioning or potential. Although assessment is heavily concentrated in the initial stages of the rehabilitation process, it continues throughout the entire process. Some of the methods utilized are the same as those used in other counseling and human service specialties and settings; others have been specifically developed to meet the needs of people with disabilities in rehabilitation settings.

Interviews

Berven (2001) has discussed the use of interviews for assessment in rehabilitation settings, and, as in virtually all counseling and human service disciplines, the interview is probably the most widely used of all assessment methods. It is often the first point of contact between a rehabilitation counselor and an individual seeking assistance and serves to initiate assessment. The interview provides a rich source of self-reported information, as well as an opportunity to observe the individual. Observations may include interpersonal skills, thought processes, affect, deficits in memory, and follow-through on plans and commitments made. Unlike standardized tests, the interview is not restricted to prespecified questions and directions of inquiry: the counselor is able to move the information-gathering process in whatever directions seem to be most productive as the interview unfolds.

There are many potential sources of error in information obtained through interviews (see Berven, 2001; Kaplan & Saccuzzo, 1997), including subjectivity on the part of the counselor in interpreting statements and observations during the interview; intentional or unintentional distortions in information reported by the individual; the manner in which questions are asked by the counselor, which can influence the responses obtained (e.g., leading, closed-ended questions); and the relationship established between the counselor and the individual, which can influence openness in responding. In addition, observations made during interviews may be situation-specific and may not generalize to other situations in which predictions regarding the behavior of the individual need to be made. Critics of traditional testing and assessment procedures may advocate interviews and observational procedures as viable alternatives. However, based on reviews of research (e.g., Garb, 1998; Groth-Marnat, 1997), Berven (2001) concludes that "reliability and validity of interview assessments tend to be poor relative to those of standardized tests and related assessment tools," and, further, they depend substantially on "interviewing skills and clinical judgment, which tend to vary considerably among practitioners" (p. 211). Thus, information obtained through interviews may be highly inconsistent, and the information and observations obtained may not be particularly useful in making good inferences and predictions about future behavior.

There are a number of ways to enhance the usefulness of interviews in assessment (Berven, 2001). Training in interviewing, and other methods to facilitate awareness and sensitivity to potential sources of error in information obtained through interviews, can encourage greater vigilance in identifying and attempting to counter sources of error. In addition, reliability and validity of information obtained can be enhanced through the use of more highly standardized interview procedures. Such standardization, if carried too far, however, can reduce some of the advantages of interviews, particularly their flexibility and individualization. Some standardized interview protocols have been developed specifically for use in rehabilitation settings, including the Preliminary Diagnostic Questionnaire (Moriarty, Walls, & McLaughlin, 1987), the Vocational Decision-Making Interview (Czerlinsky, Jensen, & Pell, 1987), and the Employability Maturity Interview (Morelock, Roessler, & Bolton, 1987). In addition, attempts have been made to comprehensively identify important questions and lines of inquiry that can facilitate direction and comprehensiveness of initial interviews in rehabilitation settings (e.g., Esser, 1980; Roessler & Rubin, 1992; Rubin & Roessler, 2001).

Standardized Tests and Inventories

Standardized psychological and vocational tests and inventories include a wide variety of paper-and-pencil, apparatus, and computer-administered instruments, which are widely used in rehabilitation settings. Tests of maximum performance include achievement tests and batteries, particularly those focusing on academic skills such as reading and mathematics. Also included are aptitude tests and batteries, focusing on intelligence and other cognitive and neuropsychological abilities, along with a wide variety of vocationally relevant aptitudes, including clerical, mechanical, and manual dexterity. Tests of typical performance include vocational inventories that focus on vocational interests, attitudes, and values, which may be used to predict likely satisfaction in different occupations and vocational situations and, consequently, the likelihood of persisting in those occupations. Also included are personality inventories and related instruments, designed to measure a wide variety of emotions, motives, values, beliefs, attitudes, and related characteristics, which are used to facilitate predictions about the ways in which individuals are likely behave in situations of interest.

Literally thousands of tests and inventories have been developed, many available through a number of different commercial publishers and distributors, and textbooks on testing and assessment typically focus primarily on these types of instruments. Reviews of available instruments are provided through a number of sources, including the *Mental Measurements Yearbook* (Plake, Impara, & Spies, 2003), which reviews widely used instruments and is also available in electronic form on CD-ROM, with individual instrument reviews available online at the Buros Institute Web site (http://frontier-s.unl.edu/BUROS/trolpage1a.html). Of all assessment methods, reliability and validity tend to be most extensively documented for standardized tests and inventories; however, the reliability and validity of even the best available instruments tend to be more limited than is commonly believed, and a great deal of caution should be used in interpretation of scores and other performance measures. Reliability and validity of tests of maximum performance tend to be more positive than for tests of typical performance (e.g., see Parker, 2001). In a review of research on the validity of psychological tests, Meyer et al. (2001) concluded that the validities are generally comparable to those of medical tests, but this conclusion was challenged by others, who viewed the findings as much less positive in supporting the validity of psychological tests (e.g., Garb, Klein, & Grove, 2002; Hunsley, 2002; Smith, 2002).

Simulations of Work and Living Tasks

Simulations of tasks actually performed in specific occupations or clusters of occupations, known as work samples, have been widely used in rehabilitation counseling practice. In a similar manner, physical functioning and daily-living tasks are also often simulated to assess physical capacities, self-care, and independent-living skills, and these assessments are often conducted by occupational therapists and related allied health professionals. Traditionally, the term *work sample* has been used to refer to a simulation of the tasks in a particular job or cluster of jobs, thus having a direct, one-to-one correspondence with that job or cluster (Dowd, 1993). For example, a work sample could be developed to simulate an entry-level occupation that individuals who successfully complete a particular training program may often pursue, and performance on the work sample may then indicate potential to pursue the training and, ultimately, employment in the occupation. Alternatively, work samples are often conceptualized and used as performance aptitude tests, assessing a combination of aptitudes that are important to performance in many different occupations (e.g., the combination of clerical perception and manual dexterity), and inferences may be drawn from scores and other performance indicators, regarding potential for a variety of occupations requiring that combination of aptitudes.

Work samples, like tests, are typically standardized and are administered to individuals served under those same standardized conditions, with scores compared to norm groups or to industrial standards established through engineering time studies. In addition to assessment of potential, the completion of a variety of work samples can provide opportunities for career exploration, allowing individuals to try a variety of occupational tasks in a short period of time, in order to explore and identify potential interests. A number of commercially available work sample and related vocational assessment systems are commonly used, and Brown, McDaniel, Couch, and McClanahan (1994) have provided reviews of a number of the available systems. According to Brown et al., evidence regarding reliability and validity of many of the available systems is limited and sometimes totally nonexistent, and considerable caution is thus warranted in drawing inferences from scores and performance observed. Patterson (2001) and Power (2000) provide more recent summaries of a number of commercially available systems.

Simulated and Real Environments

In contrast to work samples, which involve the simulation of tasks in a particular occupation or cluster of occupations, entire work environments may also be simulated. Similarly, a kitchen or entire apartment may be simulated in a hospital rehabilitation unit, to assess independent living skills, behaviors, and potential. Historically, work environments have been simulated in sheltered employment settings, in order to assess work behaviors and potential for employment and to identify behaviors to target for intervention, in order to facilitate employability. Although such applications of situational assessment are still practiced, contemporary thought has questioned the validity of such assessments, because of the contrived nature of the simulated environments, differing in many important ways from real work environments, and the dramatic influence that these differences can have on the behaviors observed.

Observations of individuals functioning in real work or living environments, such as job tryouts, can be viewed as the most definitive of all assessment approaches, in determining potential, skills, and behavior related to functioning in that specific environment or other similar environments. For example, individuals may be placed in the same environment in which they worked prior to the onset of a disability, or in a new occupation and work environment being considered for the future; accommodations can be implemented, training can be provided in vivo, and observations can be made to assess both maximum performance (i.e., aptitudes, skills, and behaviors in relation to the demands of that work environment) and typical performance in that specific environment. Similarly, an individual recovering, in an inpatient rehabilitation unit, from the recent onset of a physical disability, can be observed during short stays in the home environment, to assess independent living skills and to determine needs for further training in activities of daily living, aids and appliances that might improve independent living skills, and the accommodations that might be required in the home environment.

Behavioral observations of individuals in simulated and real environments, as well as in other assessment situations (e.g., work samples and interviews), can be facilitated through the use of systematic behavioral assessment methods and a variety of rating scales (see Galassi & Perot, 1992; Silva, 1993). Many rating scales commonly used in rehabilitation settings are homemade scales that are loosely constructed, with little or no reliability or validity data available. Several scales are available through commercial publishers, however, and reviews of available rating scales have been provided (e.g., Esser, 1975; Harrison, Garnett, & Watson, 1981; Power, 2000).

Ecological assessment emphasizes the use of real environments and has been advocated as a preferred method of assessment for individuals with severe disabilities (Browder, 1991; Parker & Schaller, 1996; Parker, Szymanski, & Hanley-Maxwell, 1989). Ecological assessment minimizes the use of traditional standardized tests and simulations of tasks and work environments, in favor of interviews and observations with clients or consumers and others who have had opportunities to observe them in various situations, along with careful analysis of potential work and living environments, in relation to individual characteristics identified. A key component of ecological assessment is observation of individuals in real environments of interest, where congruence between the individual and the environment can be assessed, in order to identify methods of accommodation and otherwise resolve discrepancies between environmental demands and the capacities, skills, and other characteristics of the individual.

Functional Assessment

Functional assessment may be defined as any systematic approach to describing an individual's functioning, in terms of skill (what an individual can do), current behavior (what an individual does do), or both (Brown, Gordon, & Diller, 1983). Functional assessment is typically conducted with the aid of scales, with the items representing comprehensive listings of areas of functioning, so that each can be comprehensively rated, evaluated, or described. Some scales produce summary scores and score profiles; others rely on checklists and narrative descriptions of an individual's functioning in each area included in the scale. In most cases, multiple sources of information are integrated in the completion of functional assessment measures (e.g., interviews, client self-report, direct observation, and examinations, evaluations, and reports completed by other professionals); in fact, any of the assessment methods described earlier may contribute information relevant to functional assessment. A number of functional assessment measures are available for use in rehabilitation settings, and reviews and discussions of instruments have been provided (Crewe & Dijkers, 1995; Halpern & Fuhrer, 1984; Tenth Institute on Rehabilitation Issues, 1983). Crewe (2001) provides a recent review of available measures of independence and function, organized according to the body systems and structure, activities, and participation categories of the World Health Organization's revised *International Classification of Impairments, Disabilities, and Handicaps* (1980). Functional assessment measures have been widely used in rehabilitation counseling practice, and their use will probably continue to grow.

INTERPRETATION AND SYNTHESIS OF ASSESSMENT INFORMATION

As information is gathered regarding a client or consumer, the meaning of the various bits of information must be determined, any inconsistencies with other available information must be resolved, and information gathered must be organized and synthesized into an overall picture of the individual. This process of making sense of diverse bits of information, in order to understand individuals and their needs, is much like the process of research, which involves the discovery of the order underlying the phenomena under study (Sundberg & Tyler, 1962).

Interpretation of Assessment Information

Several authors have described the process of interpreting assessment information, in which they identify different levels of interpretation, each characterized by different degrees of inference (Sundberg, 1977; Sundberg & Tyler, 1962). At the lowest level of inference, items of assessment information can be viewed as samples of behavior in their own right, with full consideration given to the situational context in which the behaviors occurred. At the next higher level of inference, items of information are interrelated in search of consistencies and generalizations. At the next higher level of inference, a hypothetical construct (e.g., depression, motivation, self-esteem) may be used to describe the essence of the consistencies or generalizations identified. When making such interpretations, remember that inferences are often far removed from the observations on which they are based, and, consequently, interpretations must be made with caution, remaining tentative and open to revision as new information emerges.

Organization of Information According to Assets, Limitations, and Preferences

In order to make sense of the myriad of information typically available in working with clients or consumers in rehabilitation settings, the information must be organized in ways that will facilitate the assessment process. The information accumulated includes not only information about the individual, but also information about the environmental context surrounding the individual, including barriers to improving the quality of life and resources that may be available to the individual. Relevant information may include such diverse elements as personal characteristics described in terms of hypothetical constructs (e.g., flat affect, positive self-esteem, perseverance in the face of obstacles to progress), credentials held by an individual (e.g., a driver's license or a high school diploma), and resources available (e.g., social support, financial resources, or stable living arrangements). All such information may have a great deal of relevance to the rehabilitation process, in assisting individuals in finding their place in society and improving the quality of their lives.

One approach to making sense of the mass of information typically available is to organize the information in a continuing process, as it is accumulated, according to assets, limitations, and preferences. Assets include the strengths of the individual and his or her surrounding situation, which may facilitate the accomplishment of rehabilitation goals and thus may be relevant to rehabilitation planning; limitations represent those characteristics that may serve as barriers. Preferences represent the individual's likes and dislikes, interests, and needs, which are significant in developing rehabilitation plans that will result in outcomes that will be satisfying to the individual. As assessment information is accumulated, interpreted, and organized, increasingly sophisticated statements can be formulated regarding assets, limitations, and preferences, which can facilitate rehabilitation planning.

Synthesis of Information Into a Comprehensive Working Model of the Individual

A number of authors have described the process by which counselors and other professionals process information and conceptualize individuals with whom they work, along with their problems and needs (e.g., Goldman, 1971; McArthur, 1954; Pepinsky & Pepinsky, 1954; Strohmer & Leierer, 2000; Strohmer, Shivy, & Chiodo, 1990). In general, effective clinicians systematically construct a working model or conceptualization of an individual, then use that working model as a basis for clinical or service decisions. The process of building the working model begins with inductive reasoning, in which inferences are drawn about individual bits of information and apparent consistencies among them. To the extent that inconsistencies appear, inferences are revised, in an attempt to resolve the inconsistencies, seeking broader inferences to incorporate more and more of the information available and building an increasingly sophisticated working model of the person. Deductive reasoning is then used to formulate and test hypotheses regarding the usefulness of the working model in accounting for already available information and for making future predictions. To the extent that hypotheses tested do not account for the information or do not result in accurate predictions, the model of the person is revised to account for the new information. In this manner, a comprehensive working model or conceptualization of the individual is derived, which can then be used to make predictions about the behavior and outcomes likely to be achieved by the individual in a wide variety of situations.

Potential Sources of Bias in Interpretation and Synthesis of Information

Tversky and Kahneman (1974) and Kahneman, Slovic, and Tversky (1982) described judgmental heuristics or cognitive processing strategies that are used in processing information and making judgments that lead to biased inferences, and Nezu and Nezu (1993), among others, have applied these heuristics to understanding sources of bias in clinical inferences. The *availability heuristic* is invoked when a previous experience, which is readily called to mind, exerts an undue influence on the inferences of a counselor; for example, a counselor may have recently attended a training program on alcohol and other drug abuse, which may lead to a quick judgment or inference that an individual is abusing alcohol or other drugs, and the counselor may fail to consider other possible explanations for the behaviors observed. The *representativeness heuristic* is invoked when individuals who share one characteristic are also believed to likely share another characteristic; for example, stereotypes about women, African Americans, or people with a particular type of disability may lead to inferences, from behaviors observed, that an individual is depressed or unmotivated, again failing to give adequate consideration to other possible explanations or inferences. The *anchoring heuristic* is invoked when quick determinations are made about an individual on the basis of initial impressions, and these determinations are resistant to change, because any subsequent information that is inconsistent with those impressions will be ignored or discounted, but information that is consistent will be given more weight, resulting in a confirmatory bias. A number of authors have empirically examined and discussed these sources of bias in counseling and the importance of recognizing and avoiding them in making inferences in assessment (e.g., Morrow & Deidan, 1992; Turk & Salovey, 1985).

In addition to heuristics, Garb (1998) identified related cognitive processes that can influence the validity of clinical judgments, cognitive biases, and knowledge structures. One of the most common cognitive biases is confirmatory bias. As an example, counselors may tend to formulate hypotheses very early in their work with a client or consumer, and, because of confirmatory bias, they may seek and attend to only that information that supports those hypotheses, while ignoring information that is inconsistent (Haverkamp, 1993; Strohmer et al., 1990). Knowledge structures include knowledge and theory about problems and behavior held by counselors, as well as stereotypes, prototypes, and scripts. For example, stereotypes related to race may lead counselors to misdiagnose pathology and other problems (Lopez, 1989) or to underestimate the educational and vocational potential of clients (Rosenthal & Berven, 1999).

MAKING CLINICAL AND SERVICE DECISIONS AND DETERMINATIONS

The final phase of assessment involves the translation of information into any of a number of different clinical decisions and determinations, which vary, depending on the purposes of the assessment. The most common decisions and determinations in rehabilitation counseling practice include selection for service, establishment of vocational objectives, identification of needed interventions and formulation of case service plans, and disability determinations. In making all of these decisions and determinations, the working model of the individual, which has been developed through synthesis and reasoning, is used to make predictions corresponding to the decisions and determinations to be made.

Selection for Service

Virtually all rehabilitation agencies and human service programs have established criteria for determining who will be served. Some criteria may be relatively objective and easily established, such as the presence of a particular diagnosis or type of disability or the presence of a prespecified level of financial need. Others rely on more subjective determinations. Perhaps the most universally used criterion concerns the perceived benefits that are likely to occur, if treatment or services are provided, and whether these probable benefits are sufficient to justify whatever time, effort, and expense would be required to achieve them. In making such determinations, the working model of the individual is projected into the future, to predict the likely outcomes of the rehabilitation process if services were to be provided, the extent to which those outcomes would be considered successful, and the costs that would be associated with the services required to achieve those outcomes. These determinations are highly subjective and are based in part on the experience of the counselor with other individuals judged to be similar to the individual being assessed and the outcomes achieved with those individuals. A decision regarding selection for service requires that a value judgment be added to the determination, concerning whether it is worthwhile to proceed with the provision of treatment or service.

Establishing Career or Vocational Objectives

Career or vocational objectives are some of the most common goals established in rehabilitation counseling practice, and interventions and services are then directed toward achieving those objectives. To establish career or vocational objectives, the working model of the individual is projected into work environments associated with different occupations, in order to predict likely functioning and, consequently, likely satisfactoriness and satisfaction (Lofquist & Dawis, 1969). To the extent that assets, limitations, and preferences of the individual have been comprehensively identified in developing the working model of the individual, the process will be facilitated, because a suitable vocational objective will capitalize on the assets of the individual, will minimize the impact of limitations, and will be consistent with preferences. Assets and limitations must be considered in terms of any changes that are expected to occur as a result of intervention and service, along with potential accommodations that may be provided. In addition, as the working model of an individual is projected into a potential work environment and likely functioning is predicted, other assets or limitations may be identified that are specific to that particular environment. Information about the ability requirements and sources of satisfaction provided can be found in printed sources of occupational information, such as the O*NET occupational information system (Hansen, Matheson, & Borman, 2001), as well as through job analyses and other direct observations of work environments. Finally, similar procedures can be used in establishing other types of life objectives and plans to be pursued, such as the identification of a suitable living arrangement that is consistent with an individual's assets, limitations, and preferences.

Treatment and Case Service Plans

The comprehensive listing of assets, limitations, and preferences of an individual provides the basis for developing treatment and case service plans; problems or barriers that need to be targeted for intervention will be found among the limitations identified. In those instances in which a career or vocational objective is being pursued through the rehabilitation process, the working model of the individual is projected into work environments consistent with that objective, and the impact of the individual's limitations on functioning in those environments can then be predicted (employability determinations). Similarly, the impact of limitations identified can be determined on obtaining employment in that occupation (placeability determinations) and in functioning in whatever environments might be required in preparing for that occupation. Those limitations that are predicted to pose barriers to accomplishment of the objective are then targeted for intervention. Limitations targeted might include skill deficits (e.g., specific vocational, academic, social, independent travel, test-taking, and job-seeking), inconsistencies between typical behavior and environmental expectations (e.g., punctuality, mannerisms, and speed), lack of credentials (e.g., degrees, diplomas, and licenses), or a wide variety of other limitations that may pose barriers (e.g., limitations in self-confidence, social support networks, finances, and transportation).

For each limitation that is targeted for intervention, one or more treatment intervention strategies or services must be identified. Possible interventions would include counseling or other strategies provided directly by the rehabilitation counselor; other agencies or professionals would be called on to provide other interventions or services. The technique of brainstorming, which involves the identification of as many alternative intervention strategies as possible, while temporarily suspending judgment about their appropriateness, can serve to stimulate creativity in identifying a comprehensive array of alternatives. Decisions regarding the interventions of choice can then be achieved by projecting the working model of the individual into the future, to predict the likely outcomes of each alternative intervention, while also considering the practical costs associated with each alternative, including monetary costs, time, and effort. Intervention strategies selected are then organized into a comprehensive, integrated treatment or service plan, which is then implemented.

Disability Determinations

Rehabilitation counselors are often called on to provide expert opinion regarding the vocational implications of disability in Social Security, workers' compensation, personal injury, and related proceedings. Lynch (1983) has conceptualized vocational expert opinion as including both employability and placeability opinions. Employability opinions require the identification of occupations that are compatible with an individual's residual capacities. Formulation of those opinions would involve procedures similar to those described in establishing vocational objectives, in which the working model of the individual is projected into work environments associated with different occupations, to predict likely functioning. Placeability opinions concern the likelihood of actually obtaining employment in particular occupations, and are influenced by the opinions of individuals empowered with hiring decisions regarding the suitability of candidates for employment. To formulate placeability opinions, the working model of the individual is projected into the hiring process, to predict the likelihood of a favorable hiring decision. In addition, the availability and competition for jobs in a geographically defined labor market must be determined.

The determinations required of rehabilitation counselors, serving as vocational experts, vary, depending on the type of proceeding (Field & Sink, 1981; Rothstein, 1991). In Social Security proceedings, determinations must be made about whether or not an individual is prevented by disability from engaging in substantial and gainful activity in jobs that are available in significant numbers in the national economy. In workers' compensation and personal injury proceedings, a determination must be made regarding the loss of earning capacity resulting from a disability; this requires a comparison of earnings in jobs available to the individual in the local labor market, prior to the onset of the disability, with earning from those available following onset. The Vocational Diagnosis and Assessment of Residual Employability system provides one step-by-step systematic procedure to facilitate such determinations (Field, 1993; Havranek, Grimes, Field, & Sink, 1994; Weed & Field, 1994).

FUTURE PERSPECTIVES

Assessment devices and resources have grown substantially in numbers and types in past years, and this growth seems likely to continue in the years ahead. The number of assessment devices available is so large that it is virtually impossible for any practitioner to be knowledgeable about all available alternatives for a particular assessment purpose. For example, a total of 2,780 standardized tests and inventories, available through commercial publishers, are indexed in *Tests in Print VI* (Murphy, Plake, Impara, & Spies, 2002), and another 10,209 instruments, which are not commercially available, are indexed in the *Directory of Unpublished Experimental Mental Measures*, culminating in Volume 8 (Goldman & Mitchell, 2002). Brown et al. (1994)

review 18 work sample and related assessment systems and 12 job-search software systems, and these systems represent only a sampling of those used in rehabilitation settings. Finally, a wide variety of functional assessment measures, rating scales, and other related assessment devices are available.

Rehabilitation counselors have a wide range of assessment devices from which to choose, and identifying the available alternatives will continue to become increasingly difficult. In addition, the interpretation of assessment reports completed by psychologists, vocational evaluators, and other professionals will frequently include scores and other performance measures on tests and systems that are unfamiliar to counselors. If counselors are to be effective consumers of such assessment information and avoid deferring completely to the judgment of professionals conducting the outside assessments, they will need to maintain access to sources of information on new tests and systems and to be diligent in consulting those sources of information when needed.

The application of computer technology in assessment is another trend that will certainly continue in future years, along with greater use of Web-based assessment methods (e.g., see Drasgow & Olson-Buchanan, 1999). Bunderson, Inouye, and Olsen (1989) have discussed four generations of computer applications in assessment, and only the first generation—computerized conventional tests—has been applied extensively in rehabilitation counseling practice. Burkhead and Sampson (1985) identified the following assessment applications of computers in rehabilitation settings: standardized testing; structured interviews; vocational evaluation systems, including work samples; job matching systems, which may stand alone or be integrated with vocational evaluation systems; and computer-assisted career guidance systems. Computers may be used to score responses to tests and other assessment devices, with answer sheets sent to a computer-scoring service or entered or scanned into a microcomputer, for computation and profiling of scores or the generation of narrative interpretive reports. Computers may also be used in administration of assessment devices, with immediate scoring and reporting of results.

The second generation of computer applications discussed by Bunderson et al. (1989), which has not been widely used, to date, in rehabilitation settings, but which holds much promise for the future, is computerized adaptive testing (Embretson, 1992; Wainer, 2000; Weiss, 1985; Weiss & Vale, 1987). Computerized adaptive testing involves the construction via computer of an individually tailored test for each person taking a particular test by oversampling test items near the individual's level of the characteristic being tested (e.g., ability level), while excluding items that are either well above or well below that level (e.g., items that are too easy or too difficult). Anastasi (1992), among others, has suggested that adaptive testing is one of the most significant current trends in testing. One example of a computer-based adaptive test, available for use in rehabilitation settings, is the *Differential Aptitude Tests: Computerized Adaptive Edition*. In the third and fourth generations of computer applications, discussed by Bunderson et al. (1989), continuous measurement of dynamic changes and intelligent measurement, along with computerized adaptive testing, could serve to revolutionize assessment in rehabilitation counseling practice, in the years ahead.

Despite the central role of assessment in rehabilitation counseling practice, the empirical basis for assessment is often lacking (see Berven, 1994). For example, in a review of vocational evaluation systems commonly used in rehabilitation settings, Brown et al. (1994) found no evidence whatsoever regarding reliability and validity for 4 of the 18 systems reviewed, and they indicated that the available evidence for several of the other systems was either extremely limited or equivocal. Similarly, there is little empirical basis underlying use of the interview as an assessment tool, sources of bias that influence the judgments of rehabilitation counselors, and the processes by which they make clinical judgments and determinations. Given the importance of assessment to all aspects of rehabilitation counseling, the improvement of assessment methods and practices should be given a high priority, if rehabilitation counselors are to effectively assist individuals with disabilities in maximizing quality of life.

CHAPTER 12

Placement

Robert Stensrud and Dennis D. Gilbride

INTRODUCTION

Placement has been identified consistently as one of the fundamental functions of rehabilitation counselors in public (Berven, 1979; Muthard & Salomone, 1969; Parker & Szymanski, 1992; Rubin et al., 1984; Sink & Porter, 1978) and private for-profit (Collignon, Barker, & Vencill, 1992; Gilbride, 1993; Lynch & Martin, 1982) organizations. Because of its central role in the practice of rehabilitation counseling, placement is an important knowledge base for professional development. The practice of placement generally includes the following activities: contacting and developing ongoing relationships with employers; educating consumers regarding job seeking, resume writing, interviewing, and job selecting; collaborating with consumers and employers to make workplace accommodations; and following consumers to ensure satisfaction with placements. This chapter discusses the impact of legislation on public and nonprofit placement, private rehabilitation, current public policy trends, model's of placement, understanding employers, education for placement competency, and placement in the future.

THE IMPACT OF LEGISLATION ON PLACEMENT

The delivery of placement services to people with disabilities can be initially traced to two pieces of legislation: the Smith-Hughes Act of 1917 (Pub. L.

64-347) and Soldier Rehabilitation Act of 1918 (Pub. L. 65-178). These acts, which supported vocational education and rehabilitation, provided the legislative foundation for today's state-federal partnership. Early legislation mandated vocational education, vocational guidance, occupational adjustment, and placement services. The goal of services was employment: All services had to clearly relate to a feasible vocational goal and an employment outcome.

The federal government was addressing clear social needs when they legislated this vocational focus. Dislocated workers were traveling from rural areas to cities without the necessary skills to enter the labor force. Many wounded veterans survived, returning with significant disabilities that limited their employment options. The legislation was not intended to correct some societal wrong or please a vocal interest group. It was intended to use the available human resources efficiently and move the nation into the mainstream of the Industrial Revolution.

Vocational Rehabilitation (VR) service providers formed a professional association, the National Civilian Rehabilitation Conference (now the National Rehabilitation Association [NRA]), in 1924. Shortly after that, an interest group called the National Vocational Guidance Association was formed within the American Personnel and Guidance Association (now the American Counseling Association [ACA]). Not until 1954, with passage of the Vocational Rehabilitation Act Amendments (Pub. L. No. 83-565), were these employees recognized as professional rehabilitation counselors. This act provided money for training rehabilitation professionals, including counselors. It also supported research and demonstration projects to develop and extend new knowledge. Despite years of developing a professional association and additional years working as rehabilitation providers, only the 1954 act finally provided the foundation for the profession of VR counseling.

Shortly after passage of the 1954 act, debate over the professional role of rehabilitation counselors entered the professional literature. Patterson (1957, 1966, 1967) argued that professional rehabilitation counselors should provide psychological counseling and that less professional rehabilitation coordinators should provide, among other things, placement services. This distinction had little effect on the actual practice of VR counseling in the public sector. Studies of how VR counselors spent their time suggested they were generalists, rather than specialists (Muthard & Salomone, 1969) and performed all the functions Patterson recommended for counselors and coordinators. But, as well as professionalizing counselors, the act professionalized the activity of counseling. After the act, face-to-face counseling assumed a more important role than other activities, until services directly related to placement consume only a fraction of counselors' time (Vandergoot, 1987; Zadney & James, 1977). Placement is recognized by practitioners as one of the most important areas of competency, but counseling is considered the most important skill (Wright, Leahy, & Shapson, 1987). This leaves rehabilitation counseling and placement, as presently practiced, as overlapping, but often separate, skill domains.

The act of 1954 also promoted the expansion of nonprofit rehabilitation facilities as community-based centers for work adjustment training. During the 1950s and 1960s, these facilities provided services to people with severe disabilities, especially people with developmental and psychiatric disabilities. Facilities were more apt than public agencies to employ specialists for specific tasks. Starr (1982) suggested that is because they followed a hospital-type organizational structure for service delivery and employed people in more diverse positions. Although public VR counselors worked as generalists, providing all things to all people, facility personnel worked within more tightly defined job descriptions, providing only specialized services.

In terms of overall personnel, rehabilitation counseling, in both the public and private non-profit sectors, grew tremendously through the 1950s and 1960s. Funding increased, the types of disabilities approved for services increased, and the number of rehabilitation professionals subsequently increased. A growing economy provided more jobs than there were applicants, so the idea of equal employment was widely accepted. People with disabilities came for services, counseling and training were provided, and people found jobs. The one place where this was not the case in was facilities where the majority of consumers had severe disabilities. For these people, placement was more difficult. This may be why the movement for placement specialization originated among facility personnel.

On October 9, 1963, Robert Eddy, the manager of handicapped placement services for Goodwill Industries of Chicago, brought together several people who worked as job placement specialists, to form a professional association. Participants in this meeting agreed that placement specialists, and the services they provided, would be better served by creating a professional division within the NRA. This meeting resulted in the formation of the Job Placement Division (JPD) of NRA and recognition of job placement as a specialized profession (Tooman, 1986). This group elected an *ad hoc* committee that worked to make the division official within NRA. The division held its first organizational meeting on November 10, 1964, at the NRA Annual Conference in Philadelphia. The first president of JPD was Louis Ortale, who worked for the state VR in Des Moines, Iowa.

JPD sought to enhance its professionalism through several means. Members were recruited, and the role of the division was clarified. JPD established conferences and training programs, including the Louis Ortale Memorial Lecture at the annual NRA conference (he died in 1967 when he was immediate past-president). The forerunner of the *Journal of Job Placement* began as an intradivisional communication device. Finally, the division sought to establish standards and competencies for placement professionals.

The initial professional competencies and standards were proposed by William Usdane, who was employed by the Rehabilitation Services Administration (RSA), during his presentation at the fourth Louis Ortale Memorial Lecture in 1973. The lecture included a statement of scope of practice which said placement professionals should be given responsibility for job development, job solicitation, economic job forecasting, labor market information, job engineering, job placement, and post-job adjustment. From this description of the role of placement professionals, the National Rehabilitation Job Placement/Job Development Institute at Drake University was developed, to design the competencies for a master's degree based on Usdane's lecture. Howard Traxler, who was director of that program, gave the Ortale Lecture in 1978, laying out competencies and a training agenda for graduate degree programs in placement and rehabilitation counseling.

These competencies remained central to the role of job placement specialists in public and non-profit rehabilitation agencies, through the 1970s and 1980s. Rehabilitation counselor education programs, still driven by Federal funding to prepare people for public sector jobs, included these competencies in their program requirements, but did not emphasize them. Placement was important: There just were not many people doing it. The people who were supposed to do it often put a higher value on providing counseling (Emener & Rubin, 1980; Neely, 1974).

In 1992, consumers sent a new message in the form of the Rehabilitation Act of 1973 as Amended (Pub. L. 102-569). The consumer involvement mandated by the 1973 Act was important, but employment outcomes needed to be reemphasized. With the 1992 reauthorization, the initial focus of vocational rehabilitation—employment—had returned to the central position it held at the beginning of the century. Employment remained the fundamental purpose of disability services, but consumers' expectations had changed over 70 years. Consumers expected to be actively involved in a rehabilitation process that assisted them to achieve their own personal and career goals. They also expected a high standard of quality in the services and outcomes they received from VR. This emphasis continued, with the 1998 reauthorization of the Rehabilitation Act and its inclusion with the Workforce Investment Act (WIA) discussed later.

PRIVATE REHABILITATION

Placement as a cluster of professional activities evolved in a sector of the workforce that, until recently, was separate from public and nonprofit rehabilitation. This other sector is the private for-profit sector, which serves industrially injured workers and people receiving private long-term disability insurance payments. The increasing cost of medical care and workers' compensation insurance, gave rise to private (insurance) rehabilitation in the mid-1970s. Growick (1993) stated that rehabilitation and workers' compensation were "made for each other," because both viewed return to work for people with disabilities (albeit for different reasons) as their primary goal.

Because private for-profit rehabilitation needed to meet the needs of both employers and people with disabilities, it traditionally focused more on employment and return to work than did public rehabilitation (Collignon, Barker, & Vencill, 1992; Gilbride, 1993; Gilbride, Connolly, & Stensrud, 1990; Matkin, 1983; Matkin, 1987). During the late 1970s and early 1980s, there was a movement toward state-legislated rehabilitation, as states viewed private rehabilitation as a cost-effective way to help injured workers return to work.

In recent years, however, there has been a major reduction in mandatory rehabilitation services for people with work related injuries (Lui, 1993). Spiraling costs of workers' compensation insurance provided impetus for many state legislatures to repeal the mandatory rehabilitation provisions of their workers' compensation systems (e.g., Colorado, Kansas, Minnesota) or to dramatically constrain the provision of rehabilitation services (e.g., California). At least part of this backlash resulted from private rehabilitation providers' inadequate documentation of their effectiveness in returning injured workers to employment (California Workers' Compensation Institute, 1991; Washburn, 1992). However, the continued use of rehabilitation in nonmandatory states, and the limited extant empirical data, suggest that appropriate rehabilitation services often are successful at putting injured workers back on the job, while saving employers money (Collignon, Barker, & Vencill, 1992; Growick, 1993).

Private for-profit rehabilitation, like private nonprofit rehabilitation, held placement as a central component of the service delivery system. Structurally, for-profit rehabilitation was more like public rehabilitation, in that a single counselor managed a single case (but much smaller total caseload) from beginning to end. In the case of for-profit rehabilitation, however, payment mechanisms made employment outcomes more critical than in public rehabilitation, and careful documenting of activities less important (Growick, 1993).

Public rehabilitation agencies provided involvement-oriented counseling to people with disabilities, but offered few placement services. Community Rehabilitation Programs (CRPs), which are private nonprofit agencies, provided a specific focus on placement services, primarily to people with severe disabilities, but low compensation limited the professionalization of the industry. Private for-profit rehabilitation companies focused on placement, but the intense outcome orientation resulted in limited systemic documentation of effectiveness. Each sector evolved somewhat separately and with its own strengths and weaknesses. The question became, How do we attain the focus of private nonprofit rehabilitation, the documentation capabilities of public rehabilitation, and the outcome orientation of private for-profit rehabilitation? But no one asked this question, because there were no incentives to do so, until recently.

CURRENT PUBLIC POLICY TRENDS

In the mid 1990s, federal budget deficits, concern over the size and influence of the federal government, and questions about the effectiveness of the state federal VR program (General Accounting Office, 1993), led to a general rethinking regarding the manner in which public VR services were delivered. The Rehabilitation Act amendments of 1992 and 1998 again underscored the centrality of employment outcomes, and RSA directives discussed quality placements, but many consumer groups and policy makers remained skeptical. Their input to state plans, federal administrative activities, and federal legislation focused on having these concerns addressed by rehabilitation providers.

This contributed to the federal government engaging in a major overhaul of the way it addressed employment, especially employment of people with disabilities. The Department of Labor (DOL) and the Bureau of the Census revised how they collected employment data. Legislation was enacted to dramatically modify how people with disabilities were served. A presidential work group, from agencies across the federal system, was convened specifically to streamline how employment services were provided to people with disabilities. These initiatives resulted in a renewed focus on consumers with the most significant disabilities and an increase in the use of supported employment as a central placement strategy (Gilbride, 2000).

The DOL also began the process of replacing the venerable Dictionary of Occupational Titles (DOT) with O*NET (http://online.onetcenter.org/). While the DOT focused on how tasks were performed, O*NET focused on the skills needed to obtain a job. O*NET reviewed the contemporary labor market and updated the jobs it included, how jobs were classified, and how skill were clustered. In this way, the central mechanism by which jobs were categorized was made more relevant to a twenty-first century workforce.

Once O*NET replaced the DOT, other classifications were seen to be obsolete. The older Occupational Employment Statistics (OES) was replaced by the Standard Occupational Classification (SOC). This updated jobs and made the classification more relevant to the contemporary workplace. A job seeker could go to the O*NET-SOC "crosswalk" and search for information on any job listed in the system. They could search by job title, skills, and related occupations. From there they could link to the *Occupational Outlook Handbook* and learn more detail regarding the job's future.

The DOL also serves as the central resource for America's Job Bank (*http://www.ajb.org/*). This is an Internet-based clearinghouse of job openings posted by employers. Job seekers can search for openings nationally or through the Web sites of individual states. The combination of these resources offers a comprehensive job selection, search, and application service to job seekers.

Employer data also were updated by the Bureau of the Census. The older Standard Industrial Classification (SIC) system was replaced by the North American Industry Classification System (NAICS). This updated information on how industries had evolved over the past decades and gave a more clear sense of how jobs were clustered within industries.

Together, O*NET, the SOC, America's Job Bank, and the NAICS brought data gathering into the twenty-first century. Job seekers could go on-line with O*NET and examine their skills and interests, examine potential careers, and look for work anywhere in the country, with the new Internet-based system. Job seeking went high-tech.

Two major pieces of legislation that were passed in the 1990s were the Workforce Investment Act (WIA) was passed in 1998, which was designed to create broad participation across agencies that provide employment related services, and sought to streamline services, so consumers could experience a seamless system, while feeling empowered through choice and flexibility. The act created locally driven One-stop agencies, which included as partners all agencies that provided employment services, including services to people with disabilities (*http://www.doleta.gov/usworkforce/Runningtext2.htm*).

The Rehabilitation Act was included in WIA under Title IV. While maintaining their administrative and funding independence, VR agencies were mandatory partners within One-stops and were expected to collaborate in creating a seamless system of employment services for people with disabilities.

The second major piece of legislation was the Ticket to Work and Work Incentives Improvement Act of 1999 (TWWIIA). This legislation was passed to increase choices for people receiving Social Security disability benefits, as they sought rehabilitation and vocational services, remove barriers that force consumers to choose between employment and health insurance, and provide incentives for people receiving public benefits to enter the workforce. Its major impact has been through providing tickets or vouchers by which people receiving Social Security Disability Insurance and/or Supplemental Security Income (SSI or SSDI) could seek training and placement assistance from an array of vendors, rather than be restricted to VR. The other major impact was to create a mechanism by which people could earn more, while maintaining their public health care benefits.

TWWIIA provided a mechanism by which potential vendors, called Employer Networks, could take tickets from Social Security recipients and provide services that would be reimbursed by the Social Security Trust Fund. Individuals or organizations could apply to become an EN and be listed by the government as approved to receive tickets. State VR agencies were encouraged to become ENs, but were not required to do so. During 2002, the first tickets were sent to consumers in a number of pilot states. It may take until the middle of the decade to determine the effectiveness of this important new service delivery strategy.

Combined, these data collection and dissemination revisions and new legislation dramatically altered the job seeking environment for people with disabilities. More accurate and accessible data allowed greater access to information by people with disabilities. They could, if they wished, access these services on-line, without the assistance of rehabilitation professionals. They could access One-stop services without requesting assistance. They also could access a VR system that could assist in job searches anywhere in the country, simply by using the Internet.

The promise of One-stop and independently managed tickets is there, but the complexity of these changes are tremendous. Employment personnel may not be familiar with the new resources, consumers may not have access to Internet-based resources, and agencies may not work together as the legislation intends. To determine how best to facilitate this, a Presidential Work Group on Employment of People with Disabilities engaged in a series of meetings, and it awarded several systems change grants to study how to streamline employment services for people with disabilities, how to better address the needs of people with disabilities who were on public assistance, and how to make return to the workforce more enticing for people receiving Social Security benefits. One of the major consequences of this group's actions was the creation of the Office of Disability Employment Policy (ODEP) within the DOL. This was the first time a single entity within DOL focused resources on improving employment opportunities for people with disabilities.

MODELS OF PLACEMENT

Although these current initiatives will continue to influence delivery of placement services, at present, most placement is still provided within one of six models (Gilbride, Stensrud, & Johnson, 1994): Counselor provided placement, placement specialist services, contracted services, supported employment, marketing, and demand-side placement.

The two most common models have been VR counselor provided services and placement professional provided services. Both approaches offer the same services, which are similar to those described by Usdane in 1973. These services include job seeking skills (clarification of job goals, preparation of resumes and portfolios, job hunting strategies, interviewing skills, and job search support), and employer development (contacting employers, matching employers with consumers, and providing post-placement follow-up). These activities account for most of the placement services provided to rehabilitation consumers (Gilbride, 2000).

In a recently released study of VR services, the RSA found that 32.8% of all state VR consumers received employment-related services. Almost all of those who did (32.5%), received these services from rehabilitation counselors. The report also found that rehabilitation counselors spent a mean of 18.6 hours per month on employment related activities ([RTI] Research Triangle Institute, 2002).

Contracting for placement services has been used for several years in different forms. One form of contracted services is Projects with Industry (PWI), funded by legislation in 1968. In this approach, placement is contracted with organizations that are administered by employer councils. Such an approach moves placement responsibility closer to employers and involves them as collaborators in the rehabilitation process (Baumann, 1986; Kaplan & Hammond, 1982). PWIs exist as separate corporate entities that form a bridge between rehabilitation providers and employers. Because they are part provider and part employer, they understand the needs and concerns of both, thus making transition to work more effective.

Contracting also is used directly by rehabilitation agencies to secure outside entities that provide direct placement services. These services can be provided by any entity that markets itself as having placement capabilities such as PWIs, nonprofit agencies, for-profit companies, or self-employed individuals. Because placement specialists have no professional credentialing process, there are no clear criteria that can be used to determine who is suitable to provide these services nor any standard compensation for the service. The RSA report found that, of the 32.5% of consumers who received employment services, 72.5% received purchased services (RTI, 2002).

Supported employment was authorized by the 1986 amendments to the Rehabilitation Act. Supported employment varies from other traditional models, because it applies a "place and train" approach rather than a "train and place" approach. This model is used most often for consumers with significant disabilities. Supported employees are assisted to secure employment with a cooperating business. On-site training and support are provided to the employee by a job coach, who helps the employee learn how to do the job and how to function in different work roles. Job coaches may also work with employers to help them develop the capacity to effectively assimilate the supported employee into the workforce. Gilbride (2000) found that supported employment currently comprises 11.5% of state agency placement activity, with a range from .5% to 50%. Sixty-nine percent of state administrators anticipated that supported employment would increase over the next 3–5 years.

The marketing model of placement derived mostly from the efforts of the JPD of NRA. Members of JPD, in cooperation with some Regional Rehabilitation Continuing Education Programs and Drake University, disseminated a marketing model of placement in the early and mid 1980s. This model was designed to go beyond the traditional sales calls made by job developers and to create lasting relationships between placement specialists and employers. It offered the potential for rehabilitation personnel to target companies likely to employ people with disabilities and to build long term relationships that were in the best interests of consumers and employers. This was the first model to recognize that placement has two equally important clients: rehabilitation consumers and employers. Each has needs and expectations. Placement specialists who can effectively address the needs and expectations of both clients will provide quality placements. They also will open opportunities for future consumers to easily find jobs with those satisfied employers (Vandergoot, 2002).

Demand-side placement recognizes that employers are the people most directly responsible for employing people with disabilities. Placement is seen as a consulting relationship with employers that increases their enthusiasm for hiring people with disabilities (Gilbride & Stensrud, 1992). As employers learn how to easily select and accommodate qualified applicants with disabilities, and as they learn to trust rehabilitation personnel as resources to their business, they should be more willing and better able to select people on the basis of job-related competence rather than contextual issues such as gender, ethnicity, or disability. Demand-side placement rests on the assumption the employment settings have a far greater need to be rehabilitated than do people with disabilities. sues such as gender, ethnicity, or disability.

There is little empirical data on any of these models except supported employment. For this reason, the utility of each is uncertain. Gilbride, Stensrud, and Johnson (1994) hypothesized that each model should be viewed as being appropriate in certain situations. Given that assumption, the appropriate situations for each model would resemble the following table:

Counselor Provided Placement
This model may be most appropriate when:

- Counselors have smaller caseloads
- Clients require formal training or education, and some placement will be coordinated by the training program
- Rehabilitation counselors have placement training and have weekly time scheduled for employer development
- Clients live in rural areas in which other services are not available
- There are few employers available in the area
- Counselors have specialized case loads (i.e., learning disabilities, psychiatric disabilities)
- Placement may involve self-employment, purchasing equipment, and subsequent technical assistance

Placement Specialist Provided
This model may be most appropriate when:

- The specialist works from a large centralized office with a steady influx of placement-ready clients
- The area has a number of employers and varied industries
- The placement professional is specifically trained in placement and employer development
- Clients are geographically clustered

Contracted Placement
This model may be most appropriate when:

- Rehabilitation counselors have large case loads
- There are well trained rehabilitation professionals in the private sector with whom to contract
- VR agencies do not have adequate personnel to engage in consistent and ongoing employer development
- Referrals are made to services specializing in serving a specific group of consumers (such as clubhouses)

Supported Employment
This model may be most appropriate when:

- Case loads consist of clients with severe disabilities
- Transition assistance is coordinated among rehabilitation and educational programs
- Rehabilitation professionals have the capacity to train and supervise paraprofessionals, and do employer development
- Ongoing funds and services are available to support clients post-placement

Marketing
This model may be most appropriate when:

- Employers are generally not aware of rehabilitation services
- There is a major commitment of time, resources and personnel by the agency to placement
- There are a number of varied businesses and industries in the area

Demand-Side Placement
This model may be most appropriate when:

- A large number of employers are forced by events such as government regulation to consider employing people with disabilities
- There is a high demand for trained employees and an inadequate supply of applicants in the local labor market
- Employers are unfamiliar with hiring workers with disabilities, so they need access to technology and assistance in recruitment and accommodation

- Rehabilitation professionals are trained as business consultants and placement specialists
- There is a potential for a large and varied supply of placement-ready clients (Gilbride et al., 1994, pp. 229–230)

The range and complexity of these models indicates that the practice of placement has advanced substantially since its origin in the early twentieth century. Placement was initially a simple train-and-place activity, but innovative approaches are improving the practice of placement in several ways. Place-and-train approaches are making better use of worksite-based education as a way to assist people with significant disabilities to develop work skills. Employer development has evolved to include approaches that offer innovative ways to involve employers in placement, build relationships between business and placement specialists, and show companies how they can benefit from the consulting expertise of rehabilitation personnel. These innovations offer promise to improve employment outcomes, consumer and employer satisfaction with rehabilitation services, and the impact of rehabilitation on society.

There is an unfortunate lack of empirical research on different placement models, which makes it difficult to determine how best to structure services. Despite the promise of recent innovations, too little is known about which model works best with specific consumers in specific labor markets. Gilbride et al. (1994) proposed an "aptitude-treatment interaction" approach to assess placement models. This research strategy would compare different models in specific consumer labor market combinations, to determine the situation specific effectiveness of each. From this research, rehabilitation counselors and placement professionals could have better information on which to base rehabilitation plans and employer development strategies.

UNDERSTANDING EMPLOYERS

Millington and others (Millington, Asner, Linkowski, & Der-Stepian, 1996) proposed a method for conceptualizing placement from the perspective of employers. This approach derived from the work of Vandergoot (1987, 1992) and extended his emphasis on rehabilitation professionals as "labor market intermediaries."

In the employer-focused model, the employer is a management role within a business organization, responsible for maximizing the productivity of the business's labor resources (Sartain & Baker, 1978). Employers manage change in the workforce or the marketplace through planning functions. They manage worker relationships through organizing functions, such as establishing a formal structure for the organization. They motivate workers to perform in predetermined ways, through directing or leadership functions. They manage process and product standards, through control functions. Most central to placement, employers manage the movement of applicants into the business organization, and the movement of workers within the business organization through staffing functions (Millington, Asner, Der-Stepanian, & Linkowski, 1996).

The staffing function includes recruitment, selection, and career development and support. Staffing activities are initiated when the employer perceives a long- or short-range labor need (Meyer & Donaho, 1979). This projection is based on analyses of market trends, available technologies, cost per hire, vacancy rates, and turnover patterns within the organization. Once the need has been assessed and the staffing objective defined, the employer implements a selection process that recruits, screens, and hires applicants. Before external employment selection, managers look for other ways to use existing resources, consolidate work, automate activities, and make internal transfers.

The purpose of recruitment is to attract a pool of applicants who have self-selected the company, based on meaningful criteria. Factors that affect recruitment are labor markets targeted for recruitment, demand for labor, budget constraints, immediacy of results, number of applicants desired, and company affirmative action goals. Employers have two basic intervention strategies available in planning recruitment efforts: They can diversify the structure of the job, making it more flexible to accommodate target markets; or they can differentiate the avenues for disseminating information (advertising). Job diversity strategies include flex time, telecommuting and home-based work, temporary employment, supplemental workforces, work sharing, and independent contracting (Arthur, 1991). Differentiating advertisement strategies include in-house job posting (Gutteridge, Leibowitz, & Shore, 1993), word-of-mouth, school recruitment, job fairs, open house, broad commercial media (want ads, radio, television) (Half, 1985) and market-specific media (trade journals, professional publications), and private and governmental agencies.

The purpose of screening is to eliminate the false positives in the most economical way possible. Screening is not always formally defined in the selection process, but it becomes necessary when the number of applicants in the recruitment catchment presents an unacceptably high drain on the employer's resources. Because the objective is to expediently thin the applicant pool, screening criteria are negatively weighted and the decision-making process is kept simple. Screening strategies include structured phone interviews, application or resume review, reference checks, and objective testing (Swan, 1989).

The purpose of hiring is to negotiate the best labor investment from the remaining applicants. The objective is to make thoughtful distinctions between desirable candidates, so the criteria are generally positively weighted, and the process is more complex. The most prevalent method of hiring is the interview, which is often centered around three concerns: ability to do the job, motivation, and manageability (Yate, 1987). Interviews may be structured or informal. In practice, interviews tend to be rather informal, and the decision process is relegated to subjective interpretation of the interviewer. Most hiring decisions are made by people conducting interviews only one or two times per year, thus causing decisions to be less objective (Half, 1985).

When the applicants have been ranked according to desirability, the employer will approach the most desirable candidate and negotiate the close. This strategy is the employer's attempt to make the job attractive to the applicant, within the economic considerations of the business. Employers have offering strategies and may negotiate salary, perks, moving expenses, and other incentives (Wendover, 1989).

The final staffing function is career development and support. This function is controlled by a different set of decision-making and intervention strategies. By the time the employee enters the worksite, the organization has invested a considerable amount of resources and has established certain expectations for performance. Career development practices include training and development, job matching, and individual counseling (Gutteridge et al., 1993). Systems of rewards, in-house training and orientation programs are generally seen as effective interventions available to the employer, which increase the productivity of their workers (Gutteridge et al., 1993).

This staffing knowledge base can improve our understanding of how rehabilitation professionals can effectively prepare consumers for employment. For example, the initial experiences of new workers suggest specific placement services that could improve job selection and retention. Cox (1993) found that new hires must integrate into the work culture via formal and informal socialization processes. Feldman (1981) identified three factors that enhance organizational socialization: developing work abilities, engaging in appropriate work role behaviors, and acquiring the values and beliefs of the workplace culture. Given this information, these would be the points at which placement efforts could design effective interventions. Rehabilitation placement plans, using one of several different placement models, could identify characteristics unique to an organization's culture and systematically prepare consumers to perform specific essential functions and demonstrate specific work role behaviors, and do so in organizations whose values and beliefs are consistent with those of the consumer.

This information also demonstrates the importance of good consumer employer matches. If, for example, the values of a consumer and an employer are inconsistent, we may be of better service by looking elsewhere for a placement, rather than promoting a match that will lead to dissatisfaction by either client. Especially when some employers are less open to diversity, this matching of values and beliefs seems important for successful placements (Gilbride, Stensrud, Vandergoot, & Golden, 2003; Stensrud & Gilbride, 1994).

By combining the literature on rehabilitation placement and the literature on employer selection, new models and theories of placement should evolve. Research that tests these factors is critical, if we are to improve our understanding of the placement process and deliver the employment outcomes expected by consumers and legislators.

EDUCATION FOR PLACEMENT COMPETENCIES

Neither of the two major accrediting bodies that impact rehabilitation recognize placement specialists as having independent professional status. The Council on Rehabilitation Education (CORE), which accredits rehabilitation counselor education programs, and the Commission on Rehabilitation Counselor Certification (CCRC), which accredits individuals, both recognize rehabilitation counselors, but not placement specialists. Both CORE and CRC include placement competencies in their evaluation criteria, which recognizes its importance for rehabilitation counselors. But the lack of any credentialing mechanisms has limited the growth of placement as a separate profession. Further, rehabilitation providers in the state federal program must be qualified which is generally defined as being Certified Rehabilitation Counselor. Only a few graduate programs in the country offer education in placement as a specialization. This also limits the growth of the practice, because few people with recognized graduate degrees in placement are available to work in rehabilitation.

Rehabilitation counselor education programs, although they include placement competencies in their curricula, often provide only one class on the subject during a 2-year degree. This does not leave students with much understanding of how placement is done or how they can apply various placement strategies in their work as rehabilitation counselors. Rehabilitation educators, without graduate degrees in rehabilitation (roughly 25% of all faculty) indicate they feel less competent to teach content related to placement (Ebener, Berven, & Wright, 1993). This also limits students' possible expertise in placement.

PLACEMENT IN THE FUTURE

Placement always will be a central component of the rehabilitation counselor's role. The study by RTI for the RSA (2002) showed that counselors spend more time on employment-related activities (18.5 hours per month) than on any activities other than file management (43.8 hours per month) and counseling (37.9 hours per month). Placement services for people with disabilities assumed a special role for state VR agencies, with passage of WIA. Although all job seekers are expected to enter the One-stop system, a form of triage should be in place, by which people with disabilities are seamlessly referred to VR for services. This means that rehabilitation counselors must assume a role of consultant to One-stops, because they are the people best prepared to ensure One-stops and their partner agencies are accessible and accommodating to people with disabilities.

Within One-stops, there are two clients: job seekers and employers. Some One-stop partners, such as state DOL agencies, provide some services to both of these, many gaps remain. People with disabilities may not be effectively served by One-stop services that move people through a single service system without recognition of individual needs. Some evidence suggests this is the case (Stensrud, 2001). When employers were asked what barriers they saw to continued employment of people with disabilities, a major concern was the lack of post-employment follow-up, when disability-related barriers arose, and the need for ongoing support to hire and accommodate employees with disabilities (Gilbride et al., 2003). Among One-stop partner agencies, VR is the only agency with postemployment services among their repertoire of expertise.

Another barrier to One-stops involves their political sensitivity. Many One-stops confront barriers when they seek to determine whether a job opening is appropriate for a specific job seeker. This may put job seekers with disabilities in a vulnerable position when they apply for work with employers who are not open to accommodating the barriers they face (Gilbride et al., 2003).

However governmental legislation proceeds, and One-stop operations evolve, certain placement competencies will remain critical for rehabilitation professionals. Many of these, such as occupational and labor market information, job analysis, job modification and restructuring, job placement strategies, understanding employers, and client job seeking and job retention skills development already are known. Others will emerge as further research is conducted on the placement process.

CHAPTER 13

Private Sector Practice

Linda R. Shaw and Chad Betters

Rehabilitation services in the private sector include a wide array of services provided by rehabilitation counselors and other rehabilitation professionals, who are employed by private businesses, rather than by publicly funded agencies. The term *private sector rehabilitation* encompasses the work of a wide array of rehabilitation personnel within both for-profit and not-for-profit businesses, but this chapter focuses more narrowly upon the work of rehabilitation counselors employed in the private for-profit sector.

The types of services provided by rehabilitation counselors in the private sector include many of the same type of services offered by rehabilitation counselors anywhere, regardless of work setting. These practices may include vocational and affective counseling, case management, job development and placement, and/or vocational assessment and evaluation. What makes the work of the private sector rehabilitation counselor unique is the business environment in which this occurs. Regardless of the mission, product, or services that characterize any given business, the business must make a profit. The profit-producing "bottom line" is a business's "raison d'etre," and without it no business will long survive. Consequently, the goals, business practices, and all functions of the business's employees must be attuned to this underlying fact. While the services provided by private sector rehabilitation counselors may be substantially the same as those provided by any rehabilitation counselor anywhere, there are a few key differences. Lynch and Lynch (1998) identified several differences in the services provided in the private sector, asserting that they are (1) more versatile; (2) quicker to initiate; and, most important, (3) cost-effective. The private sector is the world of business, and these distinctions serve to address companies' needs to generate profits.

This chapter examines the emergence of private sector rehabilitation. Additionally, it provides a brief review of several of the most common settings in which a rehabilitation counselor may work while providing for-profit services. These settings include insurance case management, internal case management, disability management, and forensic rehabilitation. This chapter also discusses the relevance of various credentials and discusses the professional development needs of the practicing rehabilitation counselor in the private sector.

EMERGENCE OF REHABILITATION IN THE PRIVATE SECTOR

Private sector rehabilitation is a relatively young field, having emerged during the late 1970s (Shaw, Leahy, & Chan, 1999). Those authors assert that two concurrent phenomena opened a door for private rehabilitation to emerge. The first was a growth spurt in private rehabilitation facilities, as a result of the expanding population of individuals with disabilities and the availability of government funding for rehabilitation services. Because rehabilitation units and centers were exempt from the prospective payment system, which characterized health care reimbursement at the time, many tertiary care centers established rehabilitation units, and freestanding rehabilitation centers evolved. Many of these programs began to focus on issues related to community integration, including vocational rehabilitation (VR), in addition to medical rehabilitation (McCourt, 1983). Concurrently, a report published by the National Commission for State Workers' Compensation Laws brought the concept of VR as a cost-containment strategy to the attention of the individual state workers' compensation (WC) boards, who were struggling to control their escalating costs. The idea that the initiation of VR services might effect a more rapid return to work, thereby resulting in substantial cost savings, resulted in a rapid acceleration in the development and utilization of VR services within the WC arena (Lynch, Lynch, & Beck, 1992; Matkin, 1995). Although many WC insurance companies initially relied upon the state–federal VR program to provide services to their injured claimants, they soon became disenchanted with the services provided within this arena, which were generally seen as too slow, too focused on training rather than placement, and insufficiently focused on cost-effectiveness (Habeck, Leahy, Hunt, Chan, & Welch, 1991; Weed & Field, 2001).

In 1979, George Welch formed International Rehabilitation Associates (IRA; (later changed to Intracorp), a fee-for-service, independent case management business, which provided both medical and vocational case management services to WC claimants. Increasingly, WC insurance carriers began to contract with IRA and similar companies, and to hire their own rehabilitation personnel to provide WC case management services to their industrially injured claimants, with the goal of cost-effective service provision and rapid return to work (Lauterbach, 1982; Shaw, 1995; Shrey, 1979).

From these beginnings, the practice of private sector rehabilitation has taken a toehold, not only within the insurance industry, but also within such settings as large self-insured corporations, the health care system, courtrooms, and in individual private practices. Although practitioners within these varied arenas share many commonalities of function, they differ in their areas of specialization and, subsequently, in their focus and specific activities.

SPECIALIZATIONS WITHIN THE PRIVATE SECTOR

Insurance Rehabilitation

Insurance rehabilitation, often referred to as insurance case management, employs the largest number of private rehabilitation providers. A survey conducted in 2000, by the Case Management Society of America (CMSA), found that approximately 68% of the estimated 80,000 case managers in the United States work in the insurance rehabilitation arena (Adkins, 2001). Rehabilitation counselors who practice in insurance rehabilitation are often called "insurance case managers," because case management constitutes a substantial portion of their professional functions. *Case management* is defined as a "collaborative process which assesses, plans, implements, coordinates, monitors and evaluates options to promote quality, cost-effective outcomes" (CMSA, 1994, p. 59). Although case management, as defined above, is practiced in a variety of settings by many different professionals within the health care and rehabilitation service delivery systems, it is primarily practiced within the insurance industry by rehabilitation counselors and nurses. The two professional groups' respective foci are reflective of their training, with nurses more inclined to provide medical case management and rehabilitation counselors more typically practicing vocational case management (Leahy, Chan, & Shaw, 1999). More recently, however, there has been considerable blending of these two traditional roles, with rehabilitation counselors providing substantial case management and nurses becoming more involved in the vocational arena (Shaw, Leahy, & Chan, 1999). The two most common types of claims that require the services of insurance case managers are WC and long-term disability (LTD) (Matkin, 1985).

WC Insurance. WC is a state-regulated insurance system that provides coverage to individuals whose injuries or illness are work-related. The WC system was developed in order to ensure that injured workers would receive financial and medical assistance while unable to work because of an illness or injury sustained on the job. Each state's WC statutes differ, and, consequently, no two states' systems are the same; however, certain guiding principles are found within all states' WC laws. WC statutes are no-liability laws; therefore, neither the employer nor the employee is deemed responsible for the injury (Matkin, 1985). Employers are required by law to maintain WC insurance compensation insurance coverage for their employees, in the event of a job-related injury. Many states provide services within a state VR agency, which employs rehabilitation counselors, provides VR services exclusively to injured workers with WC claims, and also oversees the activities of private insurers who provide WC coverage to workers within its state.

WC case managers perform a variety of functions in the process of assisting the injured individual to return to work (RTW). Generally, the counselor must perform a thorough assessment of the individual which may include a thorough record review; consultation with other medical, vocational, and rehabilitation professionals; scheduling and coordinating medical and vocational evaluations; and conducting an initial interview. The counselor must also thoroughly assess the injured worker's work setting, with the following questions in mind: Can he/she be returned to the old job? Are modifications necessary? Are there other jobs within the company that may be possibilities for the injured worker? Does the employer have modified duty positions available? How eager is the employer to welcome the injured worker back?

The WC case manager must synthesize all pertinent medical, vocational, psychosocial, and other information, to determine an appropriate vocational goal and to identify the services required in order to help the individual achieve that goal. The WC case manager, in cooperation with the injured worker, develops a plan, which includes all of the services necessary to return the individual to work. The claims manager, on behalf of the insurance company, must approve any plan. Consequently, the plan must be developed while keeping in mind the priority of the insurer, that is, a rapid and cost-effective return to work (RTW). Plans that involve lengthy retraining, or long and costly treatment programs, are likely to be rejected in favor of brief, focused therapies and RTW strategies. Most WC case managers keep in mind the well-known hierarchy of placement goals preferred by WC insurance carriers (Matkin, 1985):

1. same employer, same job;
2. same employer, different job;
3. different employer, same job;
4. different employer, different job; and
5. formal training for new job.

In implementing the rehabilitation plan, WC case managers provide a number of services. One of the most critically important functions is that of "coordination and service delivery," identified by Leahy (1994) as a key factor in the knowledge requirements of rehabilitation case managers. Case coordination services require the ability to "effectively communicate with all members of the patient/client's treatment team to facilitate cost-effective case resolution" (p. 6). The case manager reviews progress reports; accompanies injured workers to their medical appointments; arranges and monitors medical, vocational, and rehabilitation services; and monitors the progress of the individual, being mindful that other needs may arise during the process, necessitating changes in the rehabilitation plan. For example, it is not unusual for claimants to become depressed or anxious as the process unfolds, necessitating psychotherapy or supportive services. Again, the insurance carrier must approve any revisions to the plan. Claims managers may or may not be inclined to approve such changes, depending upon such considerations as the extent to which the needed services are directly related to the original injury or to the cost or complexity of requested services. Consequently, the ability to skillfully negotiate needed services is seen as an invaluable case management tool.

Mullahy (1995) has attempted to summarize the skills that are necessary for case managers, as follows:

- Apply problem-solving techniques to the case management process.
- Assess variables that impact on health and functioning.
- Interpret clinical information and assess implications for treatment.
- Develop an individualized case management plan that addresses singular physical, vocational, psychosocial, financial, and educational needs.
- Negotiate competitive rates, to maximize available funding for individual care.

- Understand insurance policy language.
- Present various health care options.
- Document case management activities.
- Maintain confidentiality regarding the release of information, according to legal and ethical requirements and guidelines.
- Maintain familiarity with disease processes, available resources, and treatment modalities, assessing their quality and appropriateness for specific disabilities, illnesses, and injuries. (p. 10)

An additional area of emphasis for WC vocational case managers is the general area of vocational placement-related activities. WC case managers must know how to interpret vocational evaluation data and, often, how to perform limited vocational assessments themselves. They must be able to synthesize such information with functional capacity and medical information and to perform such functions as labor market surveys, job development activities, and direct placement activities at the worksite.

LTD Insurance. The second type of claim for which case management services are often provided is LTD. LTD is a type of insurance coverage that provides benefits in case of a serious injury or illness that would prevent an individual from working (Lui, Chan, Kwok, & Thorson, 1999). The injury or illness itself may or may not be work-related. The claimant is covered, regardless of the setting in which the injury or illness occurred, as long as the injury prevents the individual from working. LTD insurance is intended to assist the injured individual, while a decision is made about his/her ability to RTW in the occupation in which he/she was employed at the time of the injury. Should it be determined that the individual will not be able to return to his/her former occupation, benefits generally continue for a specified period of time or until the individual is returned to work in another capacity (DeVinney, McReynolds, Currier, Mirch, & Chan, 1999). Because benefits are paid out until a return to work is achieved, the services of a vocational case manager are critical. The sooner an LTD claimant can return to work, the sooner the insurance company may discontinue individual benefits (Gann & Moreland, 1992). Insurance case managers working in LTD are usually employed by insurance companies that issue this type of insurance policy. They may also work outside the insurance company, either as an employee of a case management company or as an individual contractor, and contract their services to the insurer, as needed. The services provided are very similar to those described earlier for WC claims, with identical goals: a rapid return to work and discontinuation of benefits.

Disability Management

Despite the increased use of case managers to contain costs in the WC arena, costs to employers have continued to spiral upward, because of a variety of social and economic reasons. Kreider (1996) asserts that employers have become increasingly concerned about lost work time caused by illness or injury, noting that the costs associated with work-related disability extend beyond direct WC benefits, and include indirect costs, such as recruitment and training of replacements and increased WC rates. He notes that many employers are now demanding proactive, early intervention and case management, rather than reactive claims management. In order to gain better control over the management of their injured workers, and to ensure earlier and more effective intervention, many large self-insured employers have begun to bring case management services in-house and to integrate them with other risk-management and human resource functions. Such programs, termed *disability management programs*, attempt to control costs associated with industrial injury or illness by assuming responsibility for its management at the workplace. Habeck and Kirchener (1999) distinguish between the term *disability management* (DM), as applied to the organizationally focused initiatives aimed at bringing about the management of employee disability on a large, management-oriented scale (referred to as "Big DM"), and the specific interventions provided to the injured worker at the individual level, designed to manage the individual's disability in the most cost-effective manner possible (referred to as "little dm"). They note that rehabilitation case management is an essential and commonly used little dm intervention that may play a critical role in the big DM effort.

DM attempts to minimize the work-related effects of a disability by managing the interaction between the worker and the workplace, so that productivity can be maximized and costs minimized (Shrey, 1995). This is distinguished from private sector WC case management, in that it is characterized by "direct access to the workplace and by intervention at the onset of work-related injury or illness" (Currier, Chan, Berben, Habeck, & Taylor, 2001, p. 133). Furthermore, DM programs are generally seen as proactive, in that they include such functions as wellness programs, safety awareness, and injury/illness prevention, rather than being limited to reactive interventions, such as case management, transitional work programs, and job modification/restructuring, although the reactive interventions are still integral parts of the overall DM program (Currier et al., 2001; Sawisch, 1989).

Habeck, Hunt, and VanTol (1998) were interested in distinguishing the key characteristics that differentiated employers who were able to successfully manage the occurrence and management of disability in the workplace from those that were less successful. They examined the performance of employers on a number of outcome measures, including lost workday cases, WC wage-loss claims, and total lost workdays, and found better performance on these measures to be associated with higher degrees of achievement of certain company policy and practice dimensions, particularly safety diligence, safety training, and proactive RTW programs. A study by Habeck, Scully, VanTol, and Hunt (1998), focusing on employer strategies, using the same sample, found that

> employers who work in partnership with their employees, their insurance administrators, and their health care and rehabilitation providers can substantially prevent and control work disability and achieve more productive and cost-effective outcomes through a proactive process of injury prevention, injury management, and return to work. (p. 159).

A successful DM program, then, must be proactive, with a focus on prevention; must feature aggressive RTW interventions; and, perhaps most important, must acknowledge the responsibility of the employer to work collaboratively with employees, providers, and administrative personnel, to manage the incidence and impact of disability within the workplace.

The role of the rehabilitation counselor within DM programs may vary, depending on the structure of a given program. Generally speaking, however, the rehabilitation counselor plays a critical role in RTW activities, including development and utilization of transitional work programs, job analysis, worksite modification, and job restructuring. Involvement in occupational health and safety awareness and education programs is common. The rehabilitation counselor also generally plays a key role in coordinating the services of various providers and effecting a successful interface between the injured employee, medical and rehabilitation providers, and stakeholders within the workplace (e.g., unions, supervisors, human resource personnel, risk management or safety personnel, employee assistance programs, etc.). Rumrill and Scheff (1996) observed that rehabilitation counselors, with specific training in employer relations and case management are ideally positioned for positions as coordinators of DM programs, and cited the following key responsibilities for counselors acting in that capacity:

1. assessment of employee's functional capacities and limitations;
2. identification of RTW options;
3. implementation of reasonable accommodations;
4. consideration of retraining needs;

5. coordination of external services;
6. development of an interdisciplinary RTW plan;
7. consultation with other service providers;
8. development of transitional work options during employee's recovery from initial injury; and
9. training for all employees regarding WC policies and DM programs.

Disability managers may be employed directly by the employer or may be outsourced to independent case managers or case management companies (Drury, 1991; Thessellund & Cox, 1996; Habeck & Kirchner, 1999).

Internal Case Management

The sudden burgeoning of rehabilitation centers in the 1980s created a new rehabilitation function: that of internal case manager. As rehabilitation facilities began to admit individuals who had increasingly complex and catastrophic disabilities, a greater number and variety of types of medical and rehabilitation specialists were required, in order to provide adequate care. Many of these rehabilitation specialists were employed directly by the centers (e.g., physical and occupational therapists, neuropsychologists, etc.); others were commonly referred to on an as-needed basis (e.g., neuro-ophthalmologists, prosthetists, etc.). The interdisciplinary team philosophy was also gaining hold during that time, resulting in a critical need for a manager of the team (Melvyn, 1980). The role of the team manager had traditionally been seen as the physician, but the number and complexity of care providers created a strong need for someone to fill a case management function, including the team assessment, planning, coordinating, monitoring, and communication functions typical of case managers, rather than physicians.

Dixon, Goll, and Stanton (1988), referring to case management in brain injury rehabilitation facilities, asserted that "one of the major goals of using a case management system is to reduce fragmentation by placing the responsibility for directing and monitoring comprehensive services on one person" (p. 338). Malkmus (1993) emphasized the impact of case management on outcomes and costs, because of the case manager's critical role in facilitating and overseeing admission, assessment and evaluation, outcome progression, conferencing, reporting, consumer support, discharge, and follow-up procedures within facility-based case management. The case management function that occurs within health care and rehabilitation settings is often referred to as *internal case management*, to distinguish it from the external case management role of the insurance case manager (Wulff, 1994).

Rehabilitation facilities experimented with various models of internal case management, many settling upon the creation of an independent position termed *case manager*, in which the focus was on the coordination and management of services provided by an interdisciplinary team, rather than on a clinical role. The National Head Injury Foundation (NHIF; now known as the Brain Injury Association) advocated the increased use of case management for individuals with brain injuries (NHIF Insurance Committee, 1988), and, by the late 1980s, the use of the case management model within rehabilitation facilities was beginning to become commonplace. Outcome studies have consistently demonstrated the benefits of case management within rehabilitation programs, both in terms of costs and patient outcomes (Strickland, 1996; Hosack, 1998; Musco, 1995).

More recently, case management has been extended to primary health care facilities and long-term care facilities, as managed care has created a demand for earlier intervention and better coordination of multidisciplinary health care services (Howe, 1999; Lui, Chan, Kwok, & Thorson, 1999). Although the majority of case managers employed in such settings tend to be nurses, the rehabilitation counselor's training and experience in medical case management has created opportunities for them within these settings (McMahon, Shaw, & Mahaffey, 1988). Additionally, as rehabilitation services are increasingly offered in outpatient, community-based, and/or home-based settings, opportunities for case managers in these settings have evolved accordingly (Choppa, Shafer, Reid, & Kiefker, 1996).

Forensic Rehabilitation

Black's Law Dictionary refers to *forensic rehabilitation* as the practice of rehabilitation principles in legal settings (Black, 1990). Rehabilitation counselors may become engaged in a variety of legal and quasi-legal settings, including WC and Social Security hearings, civil court proceedings, and family court hearings (Shaw, 1995; Weed & Field, 2001). Rehabilitation counselors may serve as fact witnesses or expert witnesses. The remainder of this section focuses on the role of the rehabilitation counselor as an expert witness, as well as on the role of the life care planner.

Life Care Planning

Paul Deutsch and Frederick Raffa developed life care planning in the early 1980s, as an ideal legal document that plans health care services for an individual with a catastrophic injury or disability (Weed & Riddick, 1992).

The life care plan (LCP) is a comprehensive document that delineates the disability-related services that will be required by a catastrophically injured individual over his/her life span. The plan is designed to be modified as needed, because of such circumstances as a change in the individual's health status, new medical technology, or economic changes (Weed & Field, 2001). The LCP is a useful tool in forensic rehabilitation, because it may serve as a guideline to juries in assessing damages in personal injury or medical malpractice cases. The LCP includes cost figures attached to the various lifetime care needs, as projected by an economist, and can therefore result in a total cost figure that can be presented in a courtroom. Because the LCP is based upon a comprehensive examination of the needs of a person with a particular disability, a fairly accurate dollar amount can be assessed at any given time (Weed & Field, 2001). Deutsch (1995) has emphasized the importance of using a consistent and valid methodology in the development of LCPs, which incorporates consideration of the individual, family, and geographic needs of the person. Reid, Deutsch, Kitchen, and Aznavoorian (1999) have provided a comprehensive review of the process of LCP development, which is summarized below:

1. Interview the individual who is the focus of the LCP, along with his/her family, whenever possible.
2. Obtain and thoroughly review all available medical, psychological, educational, vocational, and rehabilitation-related information.
3. Communicate and consult with members of the rehabilitation treatment team, as appropriate.
4. Systematically analyze the individual's needs, including projected health-related professional evaluations, projected therapeutic modalities, diagnostic testing and educational assessments, wheelchair needs, wheelchair accessories and maintenance, orthopedic equipment needs, orthotic or prosthetic requirements, disability-related home furnishings and accessories, aids for independent function, drug and medical supply deeds, home care or facility-based care needs, projected routine future medical care, projected future surgical treatment or other aggressive medical care, transportation needs, required architectural renovations, leisure time or recreational equipment requirements, and specific VR needs. Additionally, a section of the LCP should address potential complications, for informational purposes only.
5. Provide specific dates and frequencies of needed services, along with costs associated with those services.

The plan should always be accompanied by a written report that explains the rationale and basis for the information contained in the LCP. Applications for LCPs have spread beyond the courtroom, however. They are currently used as tools for the provision of case management services (Reid, Deutsch, & Kitchen, 2001), discharge planning (Deutsch, 1990), patient and family education, reserve-setting by insurance companies, and the development of structured settlements and special-needs trusts (Reid et al., 1999).

Expert Witnesses

Rehabilitation counselors are most often retained by attorneys as expert witnesses, to render opinions regarding the needs of individuals with disabilities in civil court. In order to qualify as an expert witness under the Federal Rules of Evidence, a witness may establish his or her qualification as an expert by reason of "knowledge, skill, experience, training, or education" (Gunn & Gunn, 1999, p. 382). Additionally, in 1993, *Daubert v. Merrell Dow* established the requirement that expert testimony "must be founded on a methodology or underlying reasoning that is scientifically valid and can be properly applied to the facts of the issue" (Weed, 1999, p. 354). Consequently, rehabilitation counselors who have specialized experience or training with the disability population and a thorough understanding of the process of preparing for and developing opinions, rooted in sound methodologies, are well positioned for expert witness work.

In addition to expert witness work associated with life care planning, rehabilitation counselors often serve as vocational experts for Social Security disability hearings. The vocational expert assists the administrative judge in determining the vocational potential of an individual, which is a crucial determination in the Social Security system. If an individual can be considered to be employable, Social Security disability benefits are typically denied. However, if the vocational expert cannot identify any occupation that will provide the individual with "substantial gainful activity," the individual may become eligible for Social Security disability benefits. Consequently, Social Security vocational experts must be proficient with transferable skills analyses, job analyses, and labor market surveys. The vocational expert must have an in-depth knowledge of the nearby job market to determine whether the individual could reasonably be expected to secure employment in his/her geographic locale. Additionally, the vocational expert must also be knowledgeable in understanding information about functional limitations and physical restrictions.

Rehabilitation counselors are also retained to provide services related to other legal proceedings, including the provision of expert opinions and/or testimony in personal injury, medical malpractice, the Americans with Disabilities Act (ADA), and civil rights litigation, as well as marital dissolution proceedings (Sleister, 2000; Smith & Growick, 1999; Weed & Field, 2001). Rehabilitation counselors' combined knowledge of disability, vocational evaluation, loss of earning capacity assessment, and rehabilitation principles, ideally position them to serve as expert witnesses in these venues.

PROFESSIONAL DEVELOPMENT

Regardless of the type of private sector setting or role in which rehabilitation counselors function, they must establish themselves as competent, credible professionals with the requisite skills, knowledge and/or experience for their role. Credibility can be established in a number of ways. Weed and Field (2001) assert that the primary factor in determining credibility is a review of credentials, which suggest competency, professionalism, and an adherence to a system of regulation to maintain the credential. Credentials are awarded only after the rehabilitation counselor has successfully met specified criteria that demonstrate possession of the necessary knowledge and skills to practice in the profession. The most crucial credential for rehabilitation counselors in both the private and public sector is the Certified Rehabilitation Counselor (CRC) credential, which is administered by the Commission on Rehabilitation Counselor Certification (CRCC). CRCs must have a master's degree in rehabilitation counseling from an education program accredited by the Council on Rehabilitation Education (CORE) and a passing score on the CRC examination. Alternatively, there are several other eligibility categories that require various combinations of related degrees, specified coursework, supervised internships, and supervised experience. In every case, the certificant must pass the CRC exam. Continuing education units (CEUs) are required to maintain the CRC credential, which can be obtained by attending seminars, workshops, formal classroom training, or engaging in other specified educational activities that focus on emerging issues in disability, such as technology, ethics, legal implications, and other pertinent topics in rehabilitation practice. Individuals may also maintain their CRC credential by re-taking and passing the certification examination.

Other credentials that may prove beneficial to private sector rehabilitation counselors, depending upon the type of rehabilitation services they provide, include Certified Case Manager (CCM), Certified Disability Management Specialist (CDMS), Certified Vocational Evaluator (CVE), Certified Life Care Planner (CLCP), Certified Disability Examiner (CDE), Licensed Professional Counselor (LCP), Licensed Mental Health Counselor (LMHC), and the National Certified Counselor (NCC). There are also a number of other specialty certifications available to rehabilitation providers (Weed & Field, 2001). In many states, individuals interested in providing private WC rehabilitation services may need to obtain some type of state-issued credential, to show competence in this practice. A listing of selected certification and licensure organizations is included in the Table 13.1, along with website addresses.

Rehabilitation counselors also benefit from membership in professional associations and organizations, which provides opportunities for obtaining continuing education credits, networking with other rehabilitation professionals, access to professional journals and emerging research in the field, and an overall sense of identity with the profession. There are a number of professional rehabilitation organizations that are specifically geared toward private rehabilitation, including the International Association of Rehabilitation Professionals (IARP), the National Association of Service Providers in Private Rehabilitation (NASPPR), and the Case Management Society of America (CMSA). Other organizations of interest to both private and public rehabilitation counselors may include the American Counseling Association (ACA), the American Rehabilitation Counseling Association (ARCA), the National Rehabilitation Association (NRA), the National Rehabilitation Counseling Association (NRCA), and the Vocational Evaluation and Work Adjustment Association (VEWAA). The International Academy of Life Care Planners (IALCP) addresses the professional needs of life care planners. Web sites for these organizations are also provided in the table.

THE FUTURE OF PRIVATE REHABILITATION

The future for rehabilitation counselors working in the private sector is unclear, at best (Dunn, 2001). A major concern for rehabilitation professionals is the constriction of referrals, because of managed care intrusions into the WC and other disability insurance systems (Howe, 1999). Rehabilitation counselors and other practitioners in the private sector will need to focus on demonstrating their cost-effectiveness and justify expenditures for case management and vocational services.

Although it is impossible to predict the changes in health care and the rehabilitation landscape, rehabilitation counselors have, historically, been adept at being attuned to the trends and quickly reacting to the signals in the marketplace (Prestin & Havranek, 1998). Perhaps it is their entrepreneurial spirit or their training that emphasizes the importance of adapting themselves to the needs of the moment, but private sector rehabilitation counselors have

TABLE 13.1 Selected Credentialling and Professional Organizations

Selected Certification and Licensure Organizations

Certified Rehabilitation Counselor (CRC)—The Commission on Rehabilitation Counselor Certification (CRCC). *www.crccertification.com*

Certified Case Manager (CCM)—The Commission on Case Manager Certification (CCMC). *www.ccmcertification.org*

Certified Disability Management Specialist (CDMS)—The Commission on Disability Management Specialist Certification (CDMSC). *www.cdms.org*

Certified Vocational Evaluator (CVE)—The Commission on Certification of Work Adjustment and Vocational Evaluation Specialists (CCWAVES). *www.ccwaves.org*

Certified Life Care Planner (CLCP) and Certified Disability Examiner (CDE)—The Commission on Health Care Certification (CHCC). *www.cdec1.com*

National Certified Counselor (NCC)—The National Board for Counselor Certification (NBCC). *www.nbcc.org*

Licensed Mental Health Counselor (LMHC) or Licensed Professional Counselor (LPC)—This will differ, depending by state, because licensure regulations and state government determine requirements.

Selected Professional Organizations

International Association of Rehabilitation Professionals (IARP). *www.rehabpro.org*

National Rehabilitation Association (NRA). *www.nationalrehab.org*

National Rehabilitation Counseling Association (NRCA).[a] *www.nrca-net.org/*

Vocational Evaluation and Work Adjustment Association (VEWAA). *www.vewaa.org*

National Association of Service Providers in Private Rehabilitation (NASPPR).[a] *www.nationalrehab.org/website/divs/nasppr*

American Counseling Association (ACA). *www.counseling.org*

American Rehabilitation Counseling Association (ARCA).[b] *www.nchrtm.okstate.edu/ARCA*

Case Management Society of America (CMSA). *www.cmsa.org*

International Academy of Life Care Planners (IALCP). *www.internationalacademyoflifecareplanners.com/*

[a]National Rehabilitation Counseling Association (NRCA), and National Association of Service Providers in Private Rehabilitation (NASPPR) are specialty divisions within the National Rehabilitation Association.

[b]American Rehabilitation Counseling Association (ARCA) is a specialty division within the American Counseling Association.

proven amazingly tenacious throughout all of the ups and downs of the health care marketplace. Rehabilitation counselors' broad skill set, their demonstrated outcomes, and professional flexibility seem to point to a future filled with possibilities for rehabilitation counselors within the private sector.

CHAPTER 14

Caseload Management

Jack L. Cassell and S. Wayne Mulkey

The practice of rehabilitation counseling rests on the confluence of two professional forces: counseling and management. Systematic practice by a professional in this arena is the result of these two professional forces working in synergy. No single professional force can be said to predominate, because synergy is only established through concepts and practice intrinsically linked to a balance principle. To espouse a "one foundation" profession is tantamount to preaching without a gospel or practicing without a guiding credo.

Although counseling and management come with equal forces directed toward building a competent professional practice, this chapter is confined to elaborations on the exposition of only the management force of the synergy. The counseling force is thoroughly detailed in another chapter. The systematic practice of rehabilitation counseling, then, is anchored in several elements and skills within a management paradigm. As noted by Cassell and Mulkey (1985), "It is evident that even *the most counseling-oriented rehabilitation practitioner cannot survive without implementation of at least minimal skills in management*" (p. xiv).

THE PARADIGM

The practice of rehabilitation caseload management (CLM) is founded on a five-point model: *boundary definitions* (defines actions, micromanagement, macromanagement); *skill clusters* (planning, organizing, coordinating, directing, controlling); *personal control* (drives the system); *action decisions* (set objectives, be proactive, be outcome focused); and a *systems approach* (politically mandated). When regularly practiced actions consistently emanate from these defining areas, the rehabilitation professional will be an effective caseload manager. This paradigm relies on guiding premises. Clearly, rehabilitation practitioners must:

- develop and become cognizant of the operational definitions that direct their job performance;
- develop competent responses in basic skill clusters that form the nucleus of a management approach dealing with a complex caseload of persons with disabilities;
- develop and rely on an internal referent for personal control, when attempting to keep job parameters within manageable limits;
- become adept at issuing progressive, proactive action decisions that enhance success, with stated objectives and projected outcomes; and
- develop a systems mentality for keeping complex array of information and data under management control.

BOUNDARY DEFINITIONS

Boundary definitions are terms and concepts that provide a quality of comprehension, wholeness, and objectivity to systematic practice. These terms provide a basic grounding on which to guide one's present understanding of practices and enhance direction for ongoing development. Every individual in every profession creates and operates from sets and subsets of definitions. Personal and professional definitions of identity and purpose set psychological conditions that translate into boundaries and limitations that can facilitate or hinder outcomes. That is to say, because everyone at all times is forced to operate from a wide gamut of definitions, the kinds of definitions held by individuals have a direct influence on actions.

Consequently, a professional, guided by accurate, unambiguous, descriptive definitions, is much more likely to produce higher levels of performance. Conversely, ambiguous, negative-laden, incomplete definitions will produce a confused and stressed professional whose performance will be diminished.

Manager

Rehabilitation counselors are managers, even though many do not think of themselves as such. Reeves (1994) notes there are managers without titles, and states, "You may not think of what you do as 'managing.' But if you are working through other people to achieve a purpose or goal, you are managing" (p. 4). Indeed, at one time in history, the rehabilitation practitioner was titled a rehabilitation administrator, rather than a counselor.

This definition, or lack of it, in rehabilitation counseling can be problematic. There is a premise in the field of management: If you do not *think* like a manager, you cannot *act* like a manager. Rehabilitation professionals who resist, repudiate, and expunge a management definition for themselves will experience system reprimands, practice disarray, and workforce disharmony. Regardless, systematic practice will be unlikely.

Rehabilitation practitioners are counselors and managers (Cassell & Mulkey, 1985). This "two-hat" philosophy is vital to developing a complete, systematic approach to practice. For example, various case management functions would emerge from the counseling role, but CLM functions essentially emanate from a managing role (Greenwood, 1992). The appropriate merging of counseling and managing skills results in outcomes that can be measured as actual performance.

Proactive Not Reactive

In a broad sense, one's practice can be viewed as a flow of actions from a dichotomous behavior base, that is, proactive or reactive behaviors. Definitions have a key role in establishing this behavior base. Remember, every practitioner operates from an array of definitions that guide ongoing behavior. Thus, a person operating from a reactive definition would likely be low in initiative, nonanticipatory, and experience low personal control over the various aspects of managing a caseload. Such a person is likely to be stuck in a procrastinating mode.

Conversely, the practitioner who operates from a proactive definition will likely be one who anticipates problems and deals with them before they become crises. A proactive definition produces a professional who is assertive, in charge, a risk taker, and, wherever possible, a problem preventer (as opposed to merely a problem solver).

Case Management

The term *case management* has often been confused with the term *caseload management*. In fact, these terms are sometimes used synonymously, without attempting to distinguish any real difference. Peterson (2000) made note of a two-level construct to identify functions as macromanagement (i.e., CLM) and micromanagement (i.e., case management). Mullahy (1998) describes the roles and functions of a case manager with a comprehensive knowledge base as part general practitioner, social worker, psychologist, and minister or rabbi. Thus, case management is proclaimed as a collaborative process that focuses on individualized service provision for effective outcomes.

Grech (2002) provides insight into the evolution of case management and identifies several models that are being utilized in response to social and political factors focused on outcomes. The disciplines of case management and disability management continue to escalate, even as defining parameters are developing (Mullahy, 1998; Shrey & Lacerte, 1995). Clearly, the practice of case management and/or disability management continues to expand as a method of assisting individual consumers, through an array of health care support services, to identify individualized service needs. Indeed, case managers began credentialing in 1993 (Cassell, Mulkey, & Engen, 1997), when the Certified Case Manager (CCM) credential was introduced, sponsored by the Certification of Insurance Rehabilitation Specialists Commission (CIRSC). Then, at the 1996 annual meeting, the CIRSC approved a change of name for the commission to Certification of Disability Management Specialists Commission. Consequently, the designation of the certification changed. Formerly known as Certified Insurance Rehabilitation Specialist, the credential became Certified Disability Management Specialist. The *CCM Certification Guide* states, in the revision of July 2002, the philosophy of case management as:

> Case management is not a profession in itself, but an area of practice within one's profession. Its underlying premise is that when an individual reached the optimum level of wellness and functional capability, everyone benefits: the individuals being served; their support systems; the health care delivery systems; and the various reimbursement sources.
>
> Case management serves as a means for achieving client wellness and autonomy through advocacy, communication, education, identification of services resources, and service facilitation. The case manager helps identify appropriate providers and facilities throughout the continuum of services, while ensuring that available resources are being used in a timely and cost-effective manner in order to obtain optimum value for both the client and the reimbursement source. Case management services are best offered in a climate that allows direct communication between the case manager, the client, and appropriate service personnel, in order to optimize the outcome for all concerned.
>
> Certification determines that the case manager possesses the education, skills, and experience required to render appropriate services based on sound principles of practice.

Since there are numerous texts, articles, and other literature specific to the needs of case managers and/or case management, the reader is referred to those sources regarding the importance of, and further elaboration on, case management. Remember, the focus of this chapter is to define elements related to macromanagement or rehabilitation CLM.

Caseload Management

Definitions of CLM are not plethoric. Some have ventured to define CLM as being distinct from case management (Cassell & Mulkey, 1985; Gaines, 1979; Riggar & Patrick, 1984; Willey, 1978). For our purposes, CLM can be defined as the systematic process of organizing, planning, coordinating, directing, and controlling for effective and efficient counselor and manager decision making, to enhance a proactive practice. Indeed, CLM is a *process*. There are beginning stages, mid-stages, and ending stages. Beginning stages involve, for example, case-finding, fact-finding, and eligibility determination. Mid-stages involve service provision, and case closure activities take place in the end stages. These aspects are true for nonprofit and private for-profit rehabilitation practices; often, however, the actual tasks and duties differ. CLM involves application of at least the five listed management functions. Effective CLM is achieved through counselor and manager role interactions resulting in decision-making activity.

Henke, Connolly, and Cox (1975) described CLM without defining it. Their description of CLM reads:

> . . . how to work with more than one case at a time, how to select which case to work with, how to move from one case to another, how to establish a system to insure [*sic*] movement of all cases, and how to meet the objectives one has established, in terms of numbers served. (p. 218)

Contrary to some conceptualizations (e.g., Greenwood, 1992), case management is developed within the larger context of CLM, not vice versa. This misunderstanding of case and CLM extends to a wider scope and is perpetuated in some education/training arenas. For example, Cassell and Mulkey (1992) surveyed the catalog-listed course offerings of Council on Rehabilitation Education–approved rehabilitation counselor education programs in the nation, regarding the inclusion of CLM in their basic curricula. The finding revealed that less than 2% of the programs had a course devoted to CLM. Many reported CLM concepts were subsumed in case management instruction. Case management courses were available in 39% of the programs. If these findings represent instructional reality, graduates entering the field are probably doing so without the benefit of an orientation to systematic practice. To reiterate, CLM is the gestalt; case management is an element within CLM.

The caseload manager, then, draws from successes in dealing with case management parts, to achieve levels of outcomes.

The broader scope is evident when one considers that CLM involves a macromanagement perspective, dealing with multifarious, related elements. For example, related elements focus on case development (Szufnarowski, 1972), multicultural issues (Sheppard, Bunton, Menifee, & Rocha, 1995), and case management (Riggar & Patrick, 1984).

In summary, key concepts characterizing CLM practice for the rehabilitation counselor include:

- focus on the total caseload, the relationship and issues between and among the various cases;
- coordinating counselor practices with consumer and support service demands;
- coordinating counselor practices with agency/organization policies and procedures;
- taking multiple cases to logical conclusions in a timely manner; and
- accountability for outcome measures, based on organizational standards and goals.

SKILL CLUSTERS

Skill clusters are patterns of actions that revolve around central themes or axes. A skill, of course, is a learned ability for doing something in a competent manner. Often, the execution of one skill relies on another prerequisite skill. Thus, skills often occur in clusters, each skill relating to the other. Each cluster gathers together sets of specific actions that the caseload manager relies on for consistency of personal practices and for fulfilling organization standards. For managers of caseloads, there are five major clusters: *planning, organizing, coordinating, directing,* and *controlling.*

Planning

Planning skills assist the caseload manager in anticipating future demands and help guard against the exogenous influences that interfere with daily efforts to produce desired outcomes. Webber (1975) declares that rationale for planning "... is not to show how precisely we can predict the future, but rather to uncover the things we must do today in order to have a future" (p. 268). Being in charge of the future (in a management sense) begins with good planning skills today.

Planning is intrasystemic, which means that planning develops its own internal system properties. Planning must be approached in a systematic way. Planning is neither ordinary insight nor foresight. The complete caseload manager is one who is adept at taking obscure or incomplete information, then anticipating future developments of a case through "best-bet" hypotheses or guesses. There are numerous planning methods, techniques, or skills. Four are listed below.

Skill One: Use a Calendar

Consistently use a calendar or scheduling device. A rehabilitation practitioner is confronted with a multitude of elements and variables to keep within satisfactory operating limits (after all, this is what management is about). Therefore, a calendar of events is essential to observe and track the development of a case. Calendars or scheduling devices can follow the typical diary system, using a week-at-a-glance notebook or the more sophisticated computer software available today. The Tickler System, mentioned later, is a planning method utilizing the calendar approach.

Skill Two: Use Anticipatory Decision Making

Ackoff (1970) affirms that planning is anticipatory decision making. When acquired, this skill assures the professional a future position of control and a higher level of ability to enact the proposed plans. Thus, anticipatory decision making is a crucial precursor to readying the professional for making decisions and acting on them.

Skill Three: Make a Habit of Planning

Planning done daily, and at the same time each day, establishes consistency of actions. Thus, habitual planning takes on energizing characteristics that systematically stimulate a caseload manager into do-it-now responding. Like any habit, time and consistency are the key factors for building a response pattern that will withstand the onslaught of other "priority thieves." The skilled practitioner will soon be adept at utilizing the habits of successful people (Covey, 1989).

Skill Four: Follow Strategic Planning

Planning is strategy, not mere foresight. Strategy implies a weighing of best-bet alternatives and invoking actions to satisfy systematic intentions.

Planning has long been a basic strategy for managers. Recently, the focus has become strategic planning (e.g., Cook & Fritts, 1994; Gibson & Mazur, 1995; Luther, 1995; Schoemaker, 1995; Tombazian, 1994), which means planning that is critical, vital, crucial, and essential. Webber (1975), prophetically, recognized that dreams and visions are important to planning. Thus, a sense of the present developmental phase of the caseload, and where one should be with it, is a part of strategic planning. An extension to this last perspective is Ackoff's (1970) contention that planning is anticipatory decision making. Although projected, again primarily on an organizational level, the strategic-planning process is applicable to the individual process as well. The steps projected for the individual level are to (1) develop a personal vision; (2) write assumptions that shape a caseload; (3) from the assumptions list, state issues facing a caseload; (4) state objectives you want to achieve; (5) develop measures for objectives; and (6) choose strategies to satisfy objectives.

Finally, systemic planning requires the perspective that a common purpose exists among the activities to be accomplished in CLM, which are interlinked by personal, professional, and organizational philosophies of service. These philosophies, of course, direct themselves to all concerns, in a timely fashion. Planning is intrinsically linked with goal-setting activities. Remember, planning is not one goal, but, instead, is a common direction in which the caseload manager, the consumer, and the program are moving. Planning is not the setting of one plan, but the conscious selection of successive plans, one building inherently on the other.

Organizing

The cluster of skills involved in organizing all have a central focus of establishing the next priority to engage the caseload manager. The intersystemic nature of the five skill clusters (i.e., planning, organizing, coordinating, directing, and controlling) is evident, when one considers the basic question that must be posed for the organizing function of management, which is, What are the activities that must be accomplished? This question is, of course, answered through the enumerations of skills from the planning stage (e.g., through a constructed list of activities to be accomplished).

Organizing, then, is priority setting. How chaotic it would be for a caseload manager to complete an activity and not have a next priority work activity. How self-deceiving and stress-producing it is for caseload managers to be working on an activity a very short time, switch to another set of actions, switch again a few minutes later, all the while falsely assessing themselves to be working on the next priority each time.

Skill One: Set ABC Priorities

Lakein (1973) suggests an effective manager will take demands confronting the individual and divide them into ABC levels of immediacy. "A" actions require primary focus and need to be responded to systematically. "C" actions are low in priority and should be left to solve themselves or should be done in a block-timing effort (i.e., save and deal with all at one time). "B" priorities should be put into either an "A" or "C" category. Activities are either worth a manager's time or not. "B" actions will translate into procrastination if not dealt with in a timely manner.

Skill Two: Learn to ICE CLM Problems

There are at least three elements that help the rehabilitation practitioner become skilled at establishing priorities. The acronym *ICE* is formed from these elements: *Insulate:* The practitioner must be in charge of controllable time and be selectively unavailable, to be in a position to do all the things required to manage a caseload; *Concentrate:* In light of the 80–20 principle, the practitioner must concentrate efforts on the vital few, or 20%, of activities that will produce the greatest outcomes, and practitioners must consolidate their activities with a skill, such as block timing; *Eliminate:* Avoid nonessential activities, selectively neglect low-priority activities, and sometimes practice saying "No."

Skill Three: Use the Tickler System

Some form of a tickler system is important for organizing. A tickler system is a device or method for jogging one's memory. This can be a file system or calendar system that serves as a stimulus to bring an activity to one's attention in a timely manner. There are several variations on the tickler system approach. One effective strategy is discussed later in this chapter.

Coordinating

Since C. H. Patterson (1957) first posed the question, rehabilitation professionals have long wondered whether they are counselors or coordinators. Patterson, of course, was solely interested in skill clusters focused on counseling. Therefore, those educators and trainers who followed this lead (even to the present day) disparage management functions, when, in fact, these are crucial to the counselor–manager equation. Without either, the equation deteriorates and the rehabilitation professional is lost in a myriad of confusing priorities.

The skills necessary for coordinating assist the practitioner in recognizing community resources and becoming the link between consumer needs and the wide range of possible services available to meet those needs. Coordinating skills involve being competent with public relations, in order to interpret organizational philosophies, policies, programs, and practices of managers to the various rehabilitation constituents (Seitel, 1984).

Patterson's lack of a gestalt perspective is hardly excusable. Present-day educators and human resource developers likewise must share the burden of providing the complete rehabilitation practitioner with comprehensive skills that enhance performance and personal functioning.

Skill One: Continuity

Skills within clusters take on many forms. Continuity as a skill is the learned ability of competently bringing together the assessed needs of consumers and the developed resources available to meet the needs. Continuity connotes smoothness, flow, and progression of the case from the last developed stage to the next logical stage. Caseload managers who do not have a systematic approach to bringing together numerous other professionals and services, to satisfy rehabilitation program requirements, will find themselves unable to fulfill the timeliness principle of effective CLM.

Skill Two: Concatenation

Although continuity skills satisfy urgency or timeliness elements, concatenation skills function to satisfy linking elements. That is, the professional must be knowledgeable and alert to the many rehabilitation entities that will cost-effectively meet the established objectives for the various program strategies on the caseload. This potent skill cluster has historically served as the inclusive descriptor of the functioning of the rehabilitation professional. As a link between and among the myriad responsibilities required of a present-day rehabilitation practitioner, credence for such a premise is established.

Skill Three: Power Communication

Coordination and linking activities bring the professional into contact with numerous persons in a wide variety of positions within other organizations. Many of these individuals are accustomed to interacting at high levels within their organizations. Therefore, powerful communication interactions are abundant. The rehabilitation professional must be equipped with the basic patterns and skills that contribute to power communications.

Finally, a clear threat to systematic CLM exists when incorporating coordinating skill clusters into practice. The threat arises from the application of the strength of these skills in excess, that is, coordinating is a process of paving rehabilitation roads for consumers to travel on (i.e., doing for others). At times, the "counselor hat," with all its devotion to the helping behaviors, attempts to be all things to all people. Thereby, professionals coordinate themselves into system suicide, as they rob the consumer of self-initiation development, through doing too much for each consumer in an overcrowded caseload.

Directing

Once again, the system and synergy aspects of these skill clusters become evident, when one considers that planning plus organizing gives the practitioner the bases for making and enforcing decisions. Directing-skill clusters provide the action from which the previous skill clusters operate.

The best-bet estimates from planning are acted on through the directing skills. Directing is probably the weakest of the skill clusters, in a population of rehabilitation caseload managers. Logically, this is evident, because directing skills, endowed with pointing, steering, leading, instructing, regulating, and administering behaviors, are perceived as an antagonist to counseling orientations, imbued with helping, supporting, and empathic behaviors. The subtle power of directing a consumer to become their own powerful self, through internally generated goal setting and objective achievement, is overlooked by professionals heavily weighted by a pure counselor orientation.

Skill One: Assertiveness

Experience advises that one of the most pervasive concerns of professionals working with individuals on their caseloads is the inability to say No appropriately. A common phrase in the assertiveness field rings true: "Too much 'yes' leads to stress." If the coordinating skill clusters are not functioning at a high level, the caseload manager will attempt to be all things to all people. This, of course, is the unbalanced equation, in which the counselor role is practiced at the expense of the managing role.

Skill Two: Do It Now!

Much of the time, true management of a caseload is simply overcoming action inertia. Professionals often get caught in a maelstrom that stymies motivation and direction. Analogous to overcoming inertia in the physical sciences, psychological inertia must be surmounted. Rehearse the command to "Do It Now!" (Lakein, 1973), until it becomes automatic, then act on the command with aggressive action. This self-initiating stimulus will lead to action chaining, until the task is accomplished.

Skill Three: Five Levels of Initiative

Oncken and Wass (1974) instruct the manager concerning the effective guiding of initiative on the part of individuals on a caseload. The rehabilitation caseload manager must learn how to transfer initiative to consumers. There are five levels of consumer initiative (Oncken & Wass, 1974; W. C. Parker, 2002):

1. waiting to be told what to do;
2. asking, What is the next thing to be done?;
3. recommending a course of action, then taking some form of action;
4. actually taking action on one's own, but reporting immediately to the caseload manager the initiatives taken; and
5. acting on one's own and only reporting on a routine basis.

The focus of directing actions, on the part of the caseload manager, is to guide the consumer to achieve Level 5. Caseload managers with 20% to 40% of individuals on a caseload in levels 1 and 2 are involved in excessive doing-for-consumers, rather than doing-with-consumers, in a counselor–manager–consumer interaction cycle. Once Level 5 is achieved, the consumer is very close to the closure stage in the rehabilitation process.

Directing involves other patterns of action, as well. These include effective communicating, appropriate leading, and motivating consumers of services. Directing is a style that can be learned. However, directing often requires a paradigm shift, from pure counseling orientations to instructing and channeling constructive actions on the part of the consumer or patient. This permits the consumer or patient to experience the rewarding opportunity of establishing internal control over their own processes, thereby enhancing stable, lasting rehabilitation results.

Controlling

Controlling is the last of the skill clusters and works to keep the previous skills within operational boundaries. Controlling is drawn out as a separate entity in the paradigm, but this aspect of managing operates to weave among the previous skill clusters and pull them together into a system of codependent patterns of choice making, action initiating, results assessing, and ensuring consistent repetition of the cycle. Control is a strong variable, which many rehabilitation professionals believe lies outside their parameters of practice. With this key element of management missing, attempts at systematic practice become woefully inadequate. Control is given more attention later.

A Tickler System

An excellent example of how the skill clusters just described translate into practice come with the use of tickler systems (Elliott & Santner, n.d.). Again, a tickler system can be an organized way to jog memory, to serve as a reminder to bring matters to one's attention in a timely manner.

Presently, individual desktop computers and some rehabilitation state agency systems are making inroads in assisting rehabilitation professionals with this aspect of CLM. However, from the author's awareness, several of these systems do not, in and of themselves, address the caseload manager's needs. Most often, such systems merely bring to the professionals' attention when case actions (e.g., eligibility or closure) are required, but rarely is there adequate opportunity to manage the caseload on an ongoing basis. Needed is the opportunity to have in hand a means to bring timely needed actions to the caseload manager's attention.

One common tickler that has been implemented in many rehabilitation offices is the planning tickler system. This system is implemented in the following manner:

Step 1. Prioritize cases as follows: (1) cases needing immediate attention; (2) cases in which the caseload manager has been receiving many outside calls; (3) cases needing to be closed; (4) cases needing more than 1 hr of attention at one time; (5) cases on the fringes, which are not seen or contacted frequently; (6) cases long-established and that may need follow-up only every 60 or 90 days.

Step 2. Set up a weekly cycle for the entire caseload. Take the total number of cases, and divide by a number that will give approximately 15. This figure gives the number of weeks for a caseload to become completely cycled. For example, for a caseload of 120, this yields a system of three cases tickled up per day for 8 weeks. Thus, in an 8-week cycle, every case will have been tickled up and processed to some degree. The 8-week cycle and 3 per day can be adjusted for larger or smaller caseload sizes. Steps 1 and 2 are preparatory. These should be done only once, that is, at the initial setup stage.

Step 3. Initiate the tickler system. Obtain a week-at-a-glance type of calendar. Fill in all scheduled activities presently known to the caseload manager. Now, spread the cases from the priority order in Step 1 throughout the calendar as follows: (a) Spread cases in (1) and (2) into the first 2 weeks (these are high-priority cases needing immediate attention); (b) schedule (3) next (schedule early in the month); (c) schedule (4) (put an asterisk by these cases; this avoids scheduling too many of these in a single week); (d) date the cases in (4) and (5) (make time for a call or write a letter to make contact with these long-term cases).

Step 4. Initiate a cycle and keep the cycles going. On the first day of the week, have an assistant pull cases for necessary action. Work these cases into the week, along with the other appointments first entered in Step 3. When a case is tickled up, be sure all cases have a specific activity toward achieving goals set for the case. When finished with the case, redate it and put it on the calendar, according to the need to accomplish the next objective. Finally, write a narrative for activities that will be accomplished by the next tickler date.

There are recognizable benefits to the caseload manager for implementing such a planned tickler system. Elliott and Santner (n.d.) argue that a tickler system (a) establishes a regularly occurring cycle for the entire caseload, (b) prevents "loss" of cases on large caseloads, (c) copes with tendencies toward overscheduling, (d) thwarts the urgency-equals-emergency syndrome (every case will be tickled up and given its due attention over time), (e) makes plans for systematic closing of cases that are not moving (helps manage caseload size), and (f) affords high concentration, which should translate to quality case work.

This specific tickler system can be used in its entirety, or caseload managers can use it as a model to develop their own systems. The concept relied on is that there must be a system, if the caseload manager is to manage large, complex caseloads in a quality manner.

PERSONAL CONTROL

Personal control is a key ingredient in the systems paradigm. If skill clusters are the mechanical works of an entity termed *professional practice*, then personal control is the fuel needed to drive the entity. Personal control is the energy or force required to take charge of elements poised to go in divergent directions, contrary to intended and anticipated end results. Personal control may be illustrated as those intrapersonal processes that allow the practitioner to take charge of situations and events that would override the practitioner's assessed best-bet actions, that is, actions that would produce the desired outcome to benefit the consumer on that professional's caseload. Control as an organizational/structural variable does not fall within the purview of the present discussion.

In this chapter, focus on personal control is identified with internal versus external control orientations (Rotter, 1966, 1975). Rotter termed this the *locus of control*, and, since its first appearance in literature, research has continued to the present (e.g., Livneh, 2000; Key, 2002; Strauser, Keim, & Ketz, 2002). This extensively researched area provides a broad-based set of concepts from which the caseload manager can operate. In general, the perception that one's own behavior produces the majority of outcomes experienced defines an internal control expectancy, but the belief that outcomes and happenings are not the result of one's own actions leads to expectancies that one has little effect on those outcomes. The caseload manager who cannot develop the perspective that their actions had a significant effect on outcomes will not be in a position to exert managerial actions through the previously described skill cluster.

The person with an internal orientation is more able to take charge, take risks, manage time appropriately, respond assertively, and apply self-motivation and rewards for outcomes. The person with an external orientation is likely to experience greater confusion over which priorities to act on, procrastinates in making choices, is not a risk taker, can be manipulated by assertive or aggressive others, and is unable to establish systematic CLM. Further, with control localized within the caseload manager, this individual is more likely to be in a position to model the kind of control orientation that will be teachable to consumers, who can draw on this orientation to stabilize themselves at the conclusion of strategic programs of rehabilitation.

Action Decisions

Business-related or personal making of decisions is all about how to choose (Freemantle, 2002). Freemantle (2002) makes the point that increased awareness of choices, combined with a wider range of possibilities from which to choose, equals a higher probability of achieving outcomes. One source (*http://tip.psychology.org/decision.html*) notes that decision making (judgment and choice) is one of the most important human skills. In reality, rehabilitation caseload managers perform consistently at two decision levels (i.e., case management actions and CLM actions). Once specific actions are completed at the case management level, CLM decisions become appropriate regarding movement toward successful outcome(s).

There are basic common threads (Marshall & Oliver, 1995) to the decision-making problems encountered by rehabilitation caseload managers. To achieve a desired objective or rehabilitation outcome, the decision maker must select from any number of alternative choices of actions. The *apex decision* (Cassell & Mulkey, 1985) is the initial choice (decision) between doing nothing and doing something. Procrastination (i.e., doing nothing) is the greatest threat to any action decision.

Action decisions require rehabilitation caseload managers to (1) set objectives, (2) be proactive, and (3) maintain an outcome focus. This process can be visualized through a travel analogy. When one determines the destination of a city to visit (objective), anticipatory action (proactive response) dictates the necessary planning, and keeping on the road in a timely manner seeks completion of the trip (outcome focus). Action decisions provide a means for evaluating competing demands (desired side roads, or stops) and potential alternatives (change directions or city), to assure effective results.

An everincreasing emphasis is placed on assisting caseload managers to make decisions on the basis of accurate and adequate information (Cassell & Mulkey, 1985; Mittra, 1986; Brooks, Barrett, & Oehlers, 2002). Compromise is an important concept relative to understanding the selection of decision variables. Caseload managers must represent a philosophy or viewpoint that integrates or separates decision variables that influence the outcome focus. Thus, the decision approach used by any caseload manager determines the adequacy of case-by-case movement.

To illustrate, it is important to set obtainable objectives initially. These objectives must be *S*pecific, *M*easurable, *A*chievable, *R*elevant, and *T*ime-specific. Thus, the acronym *SMART* can also translate into structural events for all participants who will experience the decision. Objectives and intentions must never be determined as equal. It is critical that achievable objectives be established at the initial stage of planning. Remember, before event outcomes can reach fruition, action decisions must be selected. There will always be levels of uncertainty, but the effective caseload manager will act on the best possible (again, adequate and accurate) information for yielding desired and appropriate results.

ELECTRONIC CLM

Although chapter 15 addresses the role of technology in the field of rehabilitation, this chapter would be remiss if no mention is made of CLM in the "brave new workplace" (Gephart, 2002). Gephart (2002) notes that the "new age" is upon us, in which organizations are undergoing profound changes. Professionals are beginning to engage in "telework" to accomplish ever-increasing objectives and diminishing personal and in-house resources. Stensrud and Ashworth (2002) make this same point for the field of rehabilitation.

In a recent article, J. B. Patterson (2000) describes how the Internet can be incorporated into each stage of the rehabilitation process. Further, the report on the 26th Institute on Rehabilitation Issues, entitled "Using the Internet as a Resource to the Work of the State VR Counselor" (Dew, McGuire-Kuletz, & Alan, 2002), has sweeping implications for electronic CLM.

The most prevalent value of the electronic surge, for CLM purposes, comes from the fact that rehabilitation professionals have far greater control over information flow than ever before (Billingsley, Knauss, & Oehlers, 2002; Brooks, Barrett, & Oehlers, 2002; Patterson, Knauss, Lawton, Raybould, & Oehlers, 2002). Giving added focus to electronic CLM, J. B. Patterson et al. (2002) state that "all phases of the rehabilitation process, from case-finding to post-employment services" (p. 10), are involved in creative and practical applications of professional practice.

Reinforcing the key elements of the manager aspects of a caseload in the electronic age, Brooks et al. (2002) elaborate on a counselor's information literacy, which is "defined as the ability to access, evaluate, organize, and use information from a wide variety of sources" (p. 30), and we might add to this list the ability to plan, coordinate, direct, and control. Oehlers and Billingsley (2002) place further emphasis on the need for systematic CLM practices, with their discussion of rehabilitation as a Web-based distributed organization and the counselor's distributed work environments.

Both professionals and consumers are also noted beneficiaries of the electronic age in the management of a caseload (Sarno & O'Brien, 2002). With the consumer electronically involved in the rehabilitation process, the caseload manager is freed for more actual counseling with consumers. Sarno and O'Brien (2002) note that the consumer has access to all program publications and details about eligibility; information about vendors, service options, the rehabilitation process, and agency policies; developing effective resumes; and locating accurate primary and secondary labor market information, all of which facilitate informed choice in the rehabilitation process.

The consumer wins with technological approaches such as videoconferencing-based counseling (Glueckauf et al., 2002). This approach is especially useful for consumers located in rural settings. New concepts in treatment also emerge, with telehealth addressing chronic medical conditions (Liss,

Glueckauf, & Ecklund-Johnson, 2002). Puskin (2003) defines telehealth as "the use of electronic information and telecommunications technologies to support long-distance clinical health care, patient and professional health-related education, public health and health administration." Liss et al. further note that this telecommunications-based approach has implications for saving caseload service funds, with the reduction of spiraling costs of specialty services. Those authors go on to state that their finding "suggests that Internet, telephone, and videoconferencing may be effective and efficient modes of treatment for people with chronic, disabling conditions" (p. 25). But, at least one drawback to the utilization of the Internet by consumers is noted by Clawson and Skinner (2002), when their study found some information sources exclude some persons with disabilities.

The rehabilitation organization itself is strengthened by inclusion of the new technology. Luthans (2002) calls for a proactive, positive approach to emphasizing strengths in organizations, rather than attempting to fix weaknesses. J. B. Patterson (2002), then, notes that, with the advent of intranet communication in rehabilitation organizations, job satisfaction and the counselor's sense of belongingness to their agencies is enhanced. Within this latter context, organizations gain with the advent of distance education, when counselors spend more time in the office and clients gain by experiencing greater quality time with their counselors (Dew & Alan, 2002).

Finally, as consumer empowerment and streamlining issues emerge, more-advanced technological approaches will likely be incorporated into rehabilitation CLM practices. Certainly, service delivery demands and consumer informed choice will continue to shape electronic approaches in the field.

SYSTEMS APPROACH

A systems approach within this paradigm signifies that, without an adopted or self-constructed system of operations, effective practices will never evolve. All successful caseload managers employ a system or series of interconnected subsystems on which to base action and practice. A systems approach runs the gamut from something as simple as a diary system of appointments and timely scheduled actions, all the way to elaborate computer-based management information systems. Regardless, having a systems frame of mind is the only approach that will sustain a caseload manager in the face of multiple demands in the profession of rehabilitation.

In an environment crowded with a diversity of variables, many of which cannot be controlled but must be managed, the rehabilitation professional cannot survive without a modus operandi emanating from a systems perspective. "By the seat of the pants" CLM is asynchronous with a politically mandated rehabilitation environment. Demands on the rehabilitation caseload manager are multifarious and competing. For example, the rehabilitation organization has goals and objectives to be served, then consumer populations have advocate forces readily questioning the efficacy of professional decision making. Also, adjunctive sociolegal groups and organizations, which consumers apply to and/or hire, contend for the caseload manager's action decisions. All this suggests that priority setting and action initiating can only come from some systematic weighing and sometimes juggling of competing demands. If there were only one guiding principle of an effective caseload manager, it would be this: *The rehabilitation professional must operate from a self-constructed system of operations.* The rehabilitation professional must construct, adopt, or retool a system for doing CLM. Of course, this system must interface with the parameters of organizational policy. There is no other alternative to survival in an environment in which quantity of demands significantly outstrips quality responses. For CLM and case management practices, consistency and effectiveness are synonymous with system ideology.

CHAPTER **15**

Technology

Marcia J. Scherer and Caren L. Sax

What does every rehabilitation counselor need to know about technology? Ask a dozen rehabilitation professionals and you may get a dozen different answers. One thing is certain: It is no longer a question of whether or not they should learn, but rather Where do they begin to catch up. All rehabilitation counselors need to know about technology, including instructional or educational technology, as well as assistive technology (AT). Consider the uses of each. According to the popular press, at least 500 million people are connected to the Internet, with more signing on daily. Rapid advances in technology have become the status quo, but many individuals still struggle with integrating and applying it effectively in business, education, and everyday life.

For rehabilitation counselors, use of computers and access to the Internet are essential tools for assessment, job exploration, resource development, record keeping, and communication. As counselors partner with consumers to explore the vast resources available on the World Wide Web that will benefit them in the rehabilitation process, knowledge about on-line accessibility standards becomes more significant. Similarly, rehabilitation professionals should consider AT as an equally important tool for the consumers they serve. Mandated by years of legislation (e.g., Technology-Related Assistance to Individuals with Disabilities Act, 1988; Americans with Disabilities Act [ADA], 1990; Individuals with Disabilities Education Act, 1990; Assistive Technology Act, 1998), access to AT equipment and services increases the opportunities for many individuals with disabilities to participate more fully in vocational, educational, and community environments. Knowledge of AT, and how to identify, acquire, and integrate appropriate devices, is fundamental for effective rehabilitation counselors.

This chapter addresses the uses and applications of technology for rehabilitation professionals, by presenting a number of perspectives: the historical and legislative context, an overview of technology-related content areas, and recommendations for roles of consumers and professionals in the AT process. Although the focus is primarily on AT, the use of instructional and educational technology must also be considered. The nature of work and the composition of the workforce are changing, requiring different approaches for educating and training workers. Distance or distributed technologies, as a vehicle for rehabilitation preservice and inservice education, are becoming increasingly prevalent (Dew & Alan, 2002). Current and future rehabilitation professionals should have a basic understanding for evaluating and utilizing these important resources for professional development.

Few rehabilitation counseling graduate programs offered by American universities currently list required coursework in AT. As of October 2002, fewer than eight master's degree programs require students to take a course in AT (National Council on Rehabilitation Education, 2002). Yet, every rehabilitation counselor is expected to consider its use when talking with consumers about their goals. One way to bridge the gap from education to practice is by including a chapter on AT, or rehabilitation technology, in an introductory textbook such as this one.

UNDERSTANDING THE CONTEXT

The definition of AT most frequently cited first appeared in the Technology-Related Assistance of Individuals with Disabilities Act of 1988 (Pub. L. No. 100-407) as "any item, piece of equipment, or product system, whether acquired commercially off the shelf, modified, or customized, that is used to increase, maintain, or improve functional capabilities of individuals with disabilities." This is the generally accepted definition of AT, internationally.

ATs are meant to help people in their primary functional tasks. Wheelchairs, scooters, walkers, and canes are ATs for mobility; related products include lifts on vehicles and portable ramps. But, although AT for mobility is the largest single group of AT products, there are many others. There are environmental aids to daily living, as well as technologies for personal care and household management, augmentative/alternative communication devices, and technologies to compensate for sensory (hearing, eyesight) loss.

In October 2002, ABLEDATA (*http://www.abledata.com*), the AT product database sponsored by the Institute on Disability and Rehabilitation Research, U.S. Department of Education, lists 28,000 AT products, over 19,000 of which are currently available.

In spite of the assistance and promise of independence offered by many ATS and the growth in AT options, the rate of technology nonuse, abandonment, and noncompliance remains high (Scherer, 2000; Scherer & Galvin, 1996). Studies of abandonment reveal that, on average, about one third of all devices provided to consumers end up stored in the closet, basement, or drawer. The single most important reason devices are not used by consumers is lack of consumer involvement in selection. This is an issue which can be addressed appropriately in a comprehensive evaluation process (Scherer, 2000, 2002). Individuals with disabilities, who are involved in the decision in a meaningful way, will generally be more satisfied with services overall.

The Assistive Technology Act of 1998 highlights the importance of AT services, as much as the devices themselves. AT services have been defined as:

> Any service that directly assists an individual with a disability in the selection, acquisition, or use of an AT device, including evaluation, purchasing, leasing, or otherwise providing for the acquisition of an AT device; selecting, designing, fitting, customizing, adapting, applying, maintaining, repairing, or replacing AT devices; training and technical assistance.

Although AT devices and services are recognized, in several key pieces of legislation, as critical to the attainment of independent living and employment, technology abandonment, nonuse, or inappropriate use are common outcomes of far too many AT referrals. Mismatches of consumers with the most appropriate AT for their use is caused, in large part, by incomplete assessment, inadequate consultation with the consumer regarding goals and preferences, and the failure to delineate consumer strengths, as well as limitations, for their participation in society (Scherer, 2000, 2002). There are critical shortages in the numbers of professionals with people skills trained to interview and match individuals with accessible AT that can and will be used. For this reason, rehabilitation counselors are in a unique position to develop a broad knowledge of AT and to help individuals with disabilities identify the most appropriate options and obtain technology and other supports that match with their lifestyle, needs, and participation in work and community life.

UNDERSTANDING THE CONTENT

Rehabilitation counselors need not become experts in the field of AT; however, they must learn to ask important questions, be willing to listen to the answers, and become aware of the possibilities that AT offers individuals with disabilities in meeting personal and vocational goals. Before any of this can happen successfully, rehabilitation professionals must feel comfortable with the process of gaining knowledge about technology and its benefits and limitations.

The ability to pursue lifelong learning, or a process of continuing inquiry, is a skill that all professionals require. As individuals are faced with increasingly rapid changes in the world, the most important skill is "learning how to learn and acquiring the skills of self-directed inquiry" (as cited in Knowles, 1990, p. 167). Faced with the task of mastering educational technology, in order to access the information about AT, rehabilitation counselors in the twenty-first century are being challenged, especially if they are unfamiliar or lack comfort with technology. To help adult learners feel more comfortable in pursuing additional knowledge via technology, it is useful to ensure that the outcome is clear and that the benefits will have a positive effect on all those involved.

EXAMPLE OF A SUCCESSFUL AT COURSE

In order to give the reader a better idea of the basic competencies that rehabilitation professionals require, the content of an introductory course in AT, in a Council on Rehabilitation Eduction (CORE)–accredited graduate program for practicing rehabilitation counselors, is described. This content has been taught in a traditional face-to-face course, an Internet-based course, a hybrid version of the two, and has been redesigned as an undergraduate course. Portions of the content have also been organized into modules for 1- and 2-day training sessions. Activities for introducing areas of AT and familiarizing students with the process of matching appropriate technologies to an individual's needs are provided. The underlying philosophy that is emphasized is holistic, person-centered, and utilizes a multidisciplinary team strategy. Included in this process may be acknowledging some resistance to AT; therefore, it may be helpful to first assess the comfort level of students, both at the preservice and continuing education or inservice levels. A simple survey, such as the one shown in Appendix A of this chapter, can easily measure knowledge, experience, and comfort levels with AT.

Ideally, information about the access to, and use of, AT should be addressed throughout education and training for rehabilitation professionals. The CORE is reviewing its standards, to require that accredited academic programs address at least the following educational outcomes related to AT (CORE, 2002):

- E.2.5 Facilitate an individual's independent decision making and personal responsibility.
- E.3.2 Integrate cultural, social, economic, disability-related, and environmental factors in planning.
- E.3.3 Plan a comprehensive individual assessment (e.g., personality, interest, interpersonal skills, intelligence, and related functional capabilities, educational achievements, work experiences, vocational aptitudes, personal and social adjustment, transferrable skills, and employment opportunities).
- E.3.12 Identify and plan for the appropriate use of assistive technology, including computer-related resources.
- E.5.10 Assess an individual's need for rehabilitation engineering/technology services throughout the rehabilitation process.
- E.6.4 Modify and restructure jobs, and use assistive devices, where appropriate.
- E.6.5 Consult with experts to increase the functioning of individuals.
- E.6.6 Educate prospective employers about the benefits of hiring persons with disabilities including providing technical assistance with regard to reasonable accommodations in conformance with disability-related legislation.
- E.6.7 Assist employers to identify, modify, and/or eliminate architectural, procedural, and/or attitudinal barriers. (CORE, 2002)

Many of these outcomes were in the 1997 version of the standards, with the addition of E.2.5, E.3.2, E.3.3, and E.6.5, which cumulatively add emphasis on comprehensive assessments, the integration of various relevant influences (cultural, social, economic, disability-related, and environmental), consultation with experts, and consumer empowerment. In order for rehabilitation counseling students to realize these outcomes, the following activities can be easily inserted into required coursework or postemployment training for rehabilitation professionals, or can be used in designing a course such as the one described in this chapter.

AT Discovery

Simply stated, AT provides the means for individuals with disabilities to move, speak, read, see, and hear, and, generally, to be able to participate more and control their environment. Students and professionals may not be aware of the wide variety of devices, services, and strategies that fall under the category of AT. Raising the interest level about AT can be effective in adding to someone's comfort level, as well as building enthusiasm for the topic. Introducing the latest AT inventions goes a long way in helping "technophobes" become more comfortable with AT. One instructional strategy requires students to search for the latest developments in AT. In the on-campus graduate course on AT, students sign up for a specific class period to bring a description of a new AT device or a new use of technology by individuals with disabilities. They may use the Internet, newspaper, magazine, television, radio, or other source that can be documented. Most class sessions begin with this shared discovery, providing updated information about AT research and development. Similarly, students in the on-line class are required to find an AT solution and post their discoveries on a discussion board, so that others can read, and engage in a dialogue, about them. In this way, students become much more aware of current trends in AT and learn how creative thinking and collaboration can ultimately increase access and participation for individuals with disabilities.

Adapting this exercise as an opening activity for an in-service training seminar provides a way for participants to introduce themselves. AT discovery articles are handed out to pairs of participants, who are asked to read and summarize the information to share with the group. Featuring little-known uses of AT piques the interest of the participants and provides real-life demonstrations of technology transfer, multidisciplinary research and development, and success stories of individuals accessing technology as a tool to increase their participation in work, school, recreation, and community.

Webliographies

Another way to build knowledge about the wide range of AT devices is to identify examples in specific areas of functional use, including:

- aids for activities of daily living,
- alternative/augmentative communication,
- computer access,
- electronic aids to daily living/environmental controls,
- ergonomics,
- mobility,
- prosthetics,
- recreation,
- robotics,
- seating and positioning,
- switch use,

- transportation,
- universal design and access, and
- work-related accommodations.

Each of these areas constitutes a field of research, development, and application on its own and cannot be thoroughly addressed in one course. Therefore, the goal is for students to become familiar with the range of devices and services available within each area. In order to begin the inquiry, each student chooses one of these areas via the Internet, so that all topics are covered. Every student finds at least five Web sites related to the topic area and, for each site, describes the primary purpose of the site and provides a summary of its content, its source, and related links. Compiling the sets of URLs into one annotated list provides a useful tool for everyone. Through this activity, students become familiar with low-tech, high-tech, and customized devices within each AT specialization, together with the latest research and development. This assignment also requires that students become well-versed in techniques for searching the Internet.

In addition to examining the content, students can determine the level of Web site usability and accessibility, in order to become familiar with the latest standards. One tool to check the accessibility of Web sites is the Bobby guidelines (*bobby@watchfire.com*). Bobby tests Web pages, using the guidelines established by the World Wide Web Consortium's Web Access Initiative, as well as Section 508 guidelines from the Architectural and Transportation Barriers Compliance Board (Access Board) of the U.S. government. In September 2002, the U.S. Department of Education's Learning Anywhere Anytime Partnerships program supported a collaboration among international players in the on-line learning field, resulting in a set of guidelines for Web site accessibility, particularly in the area of distance education. The *IMS Guidelines for Creating Accessible Learning Technologies* are available on the Web in a screen-reader-friendly format, as well as in PDF (*http://ncam.wgbh.org/salt*). The *IMS Guidelines*, jointly published by the IMS Global Learning Consortium and the CPB/WGBH National Center for Accessible Media, are expected to be a comprehensive source on accessibility. Other Web resources relevant to this chapter are provided in Appendix B.

Local AT Site Visits

Whether accessing information in a traditional course, via a Web-based medium, or through a training session, rehabilitation professionals must become familiar with local AT resources and with those who can offer expertise in rehabilitation engineering, occupational and physical therapy, speech and language issues, and specific AT applications for education, employment, and living. A variety of activities can be designed to help students become more aware of local and virtual resources. Students may visit a recommended site to find out about services, referral processes, funding implications, timelines, and more. They may also choose to interview a professional in one of these related service areas, to clarify their role in the AT process. Students learn how to access these resources for future AT needs and explore funding options that are applicable to each source. Practicing professionals learn how to better integrate these services, as they build confidence in playing a more active role in the AT process.

ADA Accessibility Awareness

Since the ADA was passed in 1990, American businesses, transportation systems, communication corporations, and federal administrations have responded by making our communities more accessible for individuals with disabilities. Many improvements are visible, but more work needs to be done. One way for future and current rehabilitation professionals to develop a better awareness of the status of accessibility in their own communities is by completing an exercise in conducting an ADA accessibility survey. Students may choose a local restaurant, hotel, retail business, or other facility, to conduct the survey. They are required to measure doorways and ramps, count accessible parking spaces, identify signage, evaluate passageways for mobility within a facility, analyze provisions for emergency exits, and check the accessibility of bathrooms, drinking fountains, and other common spaces. Rehabilitation professionals have used this activity as an introduction into a one-stop employment center, offering to analyze the location for accessibility and make recommendations for improvements. In some cases, these activities have led to new partnerships, and in other cases, students have advocated for changes.

The variety of activities and assignments presented thus far provide an introduction for rehabilitation professionals to become familiar with AT, through a user-friendly and peer-supported approach. Whether through coursework or in-service training, participants learn about low-tech solutions, that is, devices that are simple and/or homemade, without many mechanical or electronic components. These include devices that enable an individual to grip eating or writing utensils, reach books from a high shelf, or perform daily living activities associated with dressing, eating, grooming, and self-care. Low-tech devices offer easy access for individuals to acquire more control over their environments and can build a comfort level in first-time AT users, who may be hesitant to consider high-tech equipment. High-tech devices, that is, expensive and complex electronic, hydraulic, and/or computer-related equipment, may be appealing or intimidating, depending on the individual's experiences. Ranging from power wheelchairs to eye-gaze-controlled computer operations, high-tech equipment can be very life-enhancing for AT users, because it provides the means for both accessing and controlling more of their environment. The key thing to remember is that each situation is different, and every individual has unique needs, experiences, and expectations.

UNDERSTANDING THE ROLES OF CONSUMERS AND PROFESSIONALS

The most notable area of awareness, which has been demonstrated in the AT education and training mentioned in this chapter, is the importance of the AT user's role in presenting their preferences and goals, then in identifying appropriate technology solutions.

Student comments often suggest that, in spite of knowing the value of a good and comprehensive assessment that involves the consumer in the AT selection process, they often view the task as a time burden. This attitude rarely changes, until they experience firsthand how a person-centered approach results in better outcomes and time-saving in the longer run.

Problem-Based Learning

The use of real-life scenarios in training and coursework promotes opportunities for rehabilitation professionals and consumers to clarify their understanding of their roles. Professionals and consumers work in partnership to frame the right questions, access appropriate resources, and brainstorm solutions. In a course or sequence of training modules, this instructional strategy builds on the use of the resources identified through the initial activities already described. For those participating in an ongoing sequence, participants have the opportunity to apply knowledge to practice by experiencing the process of matching individual needs with appropriate technology. The activity described here, the Tech Team process, includes steps that rehabilitation professionals should address throughout the rehabilitation process. It emphasizes the value of a comprehensive assessment that promotes consumer participation, decision making, and personal responsibility, as well as the utilization of appropriate expertise.

Tech Team Process

Langton and his colleagues first developed strategies for integrating AT questions into the rehabilitation process in the early 1990s, in the South Carolina Department of Vocational Rehabilitation. The latest version of *Integrating Rehabilitation Technology: The TECH Point Process* (Langton, 2000) prompts professionals to consider the possibility of AT, when first meeting with potential rehabilitation consumers, as well as for every step of the rehabilitation process.

Based on this approach, the Tech Team process consists of four phases:

- identifying an individual who might benefit from the use of AT and working with that individual to identify other needed members of the Tech Team;
- conducting a person-centered assessment to identify a goal or activity and target an intervention;
- researching and recommending possible AT devices to meet the identified need; and
- exploring possible funding options, so that the individual can acquire the AT.

The Tech Team may include family, friends, employer, coworkers, or others who can contribute expertise in specific areas related to the specific AT need, for example, rehabilitation engineer, occupational therapist, physical therapist, or speech and language specialist. The guiding principle is that the AT user is at the center of the team, researching and exploring options, alongside the team members. The rehabilitation professional often serves as the glue to hold the team together, following up on leads, contacting different experts, and ensuring that the AT user's interests are being heard and considered.

The Matching Person and Technology (MPT) assessment process is used most often in these courses (Scherer, 1998), along with the textbook that discusses the principles behind the development of the MPT process (Scherer, 2000). This process was developed from the experiences of technology users and nonusers, through participatory action research, and it consists of a series of forms to guide exploration, while taking advantage of the skills that both the rehabilitation counselor and consumer bring to the process. The counselor completes a series of survey forms, most typically in an interview format, to determine the AT user's perspective of incentives and disincentives to integrating AT into their lives. Three primary areas assessed are (a) determination of the environment/milieu factors influencing use (including the physical/architectural, culture, social, and economic aspects of the environment), (b) identification of the consumer's needs and preferences, and (c) description of the functions and features of the most desirable and appropriate AT.

In keeping with the World Health Organization's recently approved *International Classification of Functioning, Disability, and Health*, as well as to encourage consumer empowerment and social participation, the Assistive Technology Device Predisposition Assessment is divided into subscales, which assess:

1. physical capabilities;
2. subjective quality of life;
3. psychosocial characteristics:
   a. Mood and self-esteem,
   b. Self-determination,
   c. Social support,
   d. Adherence to recommendations from rehabilitationists; and
4. Device comparisons (up to three devices).

In general, counselors admit that, traditionally, the size of their caseloads has often precluded them from getting to know their consumers as much as they would like. When they used the MPT process, they became keenly aware of how much information they were missing and why, as a consequence, their recommendations were often unheeded or not used, and they were not given the respect from their consumers that they felt they deserved.

As soon as the students or counselors complete the assessment surveys, they find that they have the direction needed to move forward in the process. After they identify the area of AT that might be appropriate, they research types of equipment available to meet the needs of the individual. In collaboration with the AT user, they prioritize a list of at least three recommendations, including as many details as possible (prices, interface options, pictures, etc.). They may include commercially available items, items to be modified, or design ideas for a customized adaptation. During these first two phases, AT experts, or professionals from other disciplines, for example, physical and/or occupational therapy, speech, engineering, are consulted.

The next step is to investigate possible funding sources and their availability. This may include funding from the individual, department of rehabilitation, department of developmental disabilities, private insurance, Medicare, or funds raised through private or community groups. The final phase of the project requires students to reflect on the process from beginning to end and on the impact on their role as a professional. They explore such questions as:

- Was the individual comfortable with the whole Tech Team process?
- Were you comfortable with the process?
- Were you able to match their needs?
- Did the individual acquire any of the recommended devices/equipment?
- Did you discover new resources that you may use in the future?
- What can you take from this project into your current or future professional role? Any recommendations for next time?

Evaluating the Education

Evaluations from the Web-based graduate course described in this chapter indicated that the course information, interaction, and activities were practical and effective for rehabilitation professionals (Sax & Duke, 2002). A survey was conducted at least 1 year after course completion, to determine if these professionals continued to use the resources and strategies offered in the course and if they were more likely to recommend AT or consult with AT specialists, since completing the course. Of 102 requests, 71.5% were completed and returned by respondents ($N = 73$). Overall, the answers indicated that these rehabilitation professionals had increased the frequency of their professional practices related to AT in all areas, including recommendations for AT devices (74%), referrals for AT services (68.5%), consultations with AT experts or providers (57.5%), provision of AT resources to colleagues (63%), use of person-centered approach to assessment (72.6%), and use of on-line resources (74%). A much smaller percentage reported that these practices stayed the same, and none indicated that their practices had decreased, except in one case. When asked to rate their comfort level with recommending AT to their consumers, 87.7% indicated an increase. Although 79.5% indicated an interest in attending more training in the uses of AT, only 16.4% had taken any. This no doubt results from the lack of availability of continued training.

Cross-tabulations were run to determine the correlation between the increase in their practices and their comfort level in recommending AT. As might be expected, the correlation was high. For example, 80.6% and 78% of those who reported an increase in recommending AT devices and referring individuals for AT services, respectively, indicated that their comfort level had also increased. The follow-up survey results indicate that, at least from their own perceptions, rehabilitation counselors have integrated AT information, strategies, and resources into their work routines. At the time of this writing, results of matched precourse and postcourse surveys for the latest cohort of students were compared, to examine more closely the way in which students integrated the information about AT into their everyday activities as rehabilitation counselors. Again, the initial results indicate that participation in these activities and assignments have increased their comfort level with AT, as well as their participation in the AT process.

Embracing Technology

Although a national review of distance education has not been undertaken since a U.S. Department of Education survey in 1999, the Council for Higher Education Accreditation (2002) collected data in December 2001–January 2002, to learn about distance learning in 17 accrediting regional and national organizations. They found that, "of the 5655 accredited institutions, 1979 of them offered a form of distance-delivered programs and courses, some of which lead to the degree acquisition" (p. 4). The focus on assuring quality, from the accreditors' perspective, requires that programs demonstrate competence in offering alternative instructional designs, as related to curriculum, faculty support, and student learning outcomes. As colleges and universities increase their offerings in on-line courses and degrees, research has focused on the credibility of this type of instruction. According to a literature review undertaken by the 28th Institute on Rehabilitation Issues (IRI; Dew & Alan, 2002), "supporters of distance learning cite an abundance of research that shows no significant difference in the effectiveness of distance education compared with the traditional classroom experience" (p. 26). But the study group found evidence from critics stating the opposite opinion, as well as other information from those who claim to need more information to judge the effectiveness of the medium. Clearly, there is no definitive answer as yet.

The IRI study group (Dew & Alan, 2002) also examined distance education in relation to public vocational rehabilitation programs. These rehabilitation professionals addressed guiding principles in three areas related to distance learning: learning-based, learning-focused, and system-based: "The synergistic relationship between these three sets of guiding principles serve as the basis for distance learning and the systemic infusion of education and training experiences for rehabilitation practitioners, administrators, and consumers" (p. 31). These guidelines offer a foundation for future development and improvement of distance education as an educational model that can respond to the changing needs of those who represent the rehabilitation field.

Regardless of the questions still held about this vehicle for learning, distance education is gaining momentum within higher education (Coombs, 1998; Eldredge et al., 1999; Sax, 2002a; Sax, 2002b; Smart, 1999). Given the tremendous need for AT training, this medium is well suited to providing access to Internet-based instruction 24 hr a day, thus expanding educational opportunities to those who cannot easily access traditional education because of geographical location, time constraints, work and family responsibilities, or other individual access issues.

This chapter began by noting that all rehabilitation counselors need to know about instructional or educational technology, as well as AT. Technology is used by rehabilitation counselors for many essential job functions, for example, assessment, job exploration, resource development, record keeping, and communication. We addressed the uses and applications of technology for rehabilitation professionals, by presenting an overview of technology-related content areas and legislation, recommendations for roles of consumers and professionals in the AT process, and examples of integrating AT information into coursework and training for rehabilitation counseling. All current and future rehabilitation professionals should have a basic understanding of these resources, for their own professional development and for improving the services they provide to consumers. By offering this contribution to the volume, we hope we have contributed to the development of such an understanding.

APPENDIX A

AT Web Survey

On-line Course

- ❒ How many years have you been a rehabilitation professional? ______ years

- ❒ Have you recommended AT devices for individuals with disabilities?
  ____ no ____ yes

  If yes, what types of devices do you recommend most often? (Number types of AT in order of 1 [most often] to 8 [least often])

  - ❒ mobility
  - ❒ communication
  - ❒ compute- related (hardware, software)
  - ❒ adaptations for daily living
  - ❒ environmental controls
  - ❒ job-specific (either commercial or customized)
  - ❒ switches
  - ❒ seating and positioning

- ❒ How would you rate yourself in knowing about the uses of AT?

  1. I am very knowledgeable about AT.
  2. I am somewhat knowledgeable about AT.
  3. I have very limited knowledge about AT.
  4. What's AT?

- ❒ How would you rate your experience in accessing AT information? (May circle more than one answer)
  Frequency:

  - ❒ I seek AT information on a regular basis.
  - ❒ I seek AT information occasionally.

- ❒ I never seek AT information.

  Source:

- ❒ I seek AT information from a variety of sources.
- ❒ I seek AT information primarily from one source.
- ❒ I never seek AT information.

❒ Have you ever enrolled in any coursework regarding AT? If so, please name the course and the institution: ______________________________

❒ Have you ever attended any in-service training regarding AT? If so, who sponsored the training sessions? _____________________________

❒ How many hours of training have you completed since you have been a rehabilitation professional? ______

❒ What type(s) of assessment tools do you use when recommending AT devices? ____

❒ Do you consult with other professionals when determining the appropriate needs for assistive technology devices?
____ Yes ____ No
If yes, who do you ask? (Check all that apply)

- ❒ Occupational therapist
- ❒ Physical therapist
- ❒ Speech/language therapist/pathologist
- ❒ Rehabilitation engineer
- ❒ Ergonomics specialist
- ❒ Vendors of AT
- ❒ Other

❒ Is this your first experience taking an on-line course?
____ Yes ____ No
If no, what other class(es) have you taken? _______________________

❒ Are you currently enrolled in the on-line master's degree program?
____ Yes ____ No

APPENDIX B

Assistive Technology Web Resources

www.abledata.com

Sponsored by the National Institute on Disability and Rehabilitation Research, U.S. Department of Education, to provide a comprehensive source of information on assistive technology (AT). Products, books, and other resources are included.

http://disabilityinfo.gov/

The comprehensive federal Web site of disability-related government resources and the New Freedom Initiative's on-line resource for Americans with disabilities. Under the tab for technology, links are provided for AT, accessibility, communication, technology rights, and disability-related organizations.

http://www.ncddr.org/rpp/techaf/lrp_ov.html

The National Institute on Disability and Rehabilitation Research (NIDRR) Long Range Plan—Technology for Access and Function Research: In this document, NIDRR identifies research priorities in engineering and technology that will help improve functional outcomes and access to systems technology in sensory function, mobility, manipulation, cognitive function, information communication, and the built environment. The priorities also will promote business involvement and collaboration.

http://www.ed.gov/offices/OSERS/RSA/Research/studies/index.html

Evaluation studies conducted by the Rehabilitation Services Administration for purposes of improving program management and effectiveness. Focus is on their general effectiveness in relation to their cost, their impact on related programs, and their structure and mechanisms for delivery of services, using appropriate methodology and evaluative research designs.

http://www.ncd.gov/index.html

The National Council on Disability is an independent federal agency making recommendations to the president and Congress on issues affecting 54 million Americans with disabilities. Many excellent reports can be downloaded.

www.resna.org

The Rehabilitation Engineering and Assistive Technology Society of North America (RESNA) is an interdisciplinary association of people with a common interest in technology and disability. RESNA's membership ranges from rehabilitation professionals to consumers. There are sister organizations in Australia, Europe, and Japan.

http://ncam.wgbh.org/salt/

The Specifications for Accessible Learning Technologies Project is a collaboration with the IMS Global Learning Consortium, to make on-line learning resources accessible to people with disabilities, by developing and promoting specifications and effective models that will help level the playing field for learners with disabilities. Guidelines available: *http://ncam.wgbh.org/salt/guidelines/*

http://www.interwork.sdsu.edu

San Diego State University's Interwork Institute offers information on distance learning opportunities for rehabilitation counseling and related projects coordinated by faculty and staff.

CHAPTER 16

Clinical Supervision

James T. Herbert

Clinical supervision is an evaluative process that extends over time by which supervisors focus on supervisee professional and personal development so that client services meet organizational goals and professional standards (Bernard & Goodyear, 1998; Rich, 1993). Within rehabilitation counseling practice, clinical supervision is a necessary professional activity that results in rehabilitation counselors becoming effective service providers (Ross, 1979) and, as noted in the general counseling literature, without competent, ongoing clinical supervision, counselors may experience declining counseling skills (Spooner & Stone, 1977; Wiley & Ray, 1986). Clinical supervision that is harmful or counterproductive not only hinders professional growth resulting in a weakened supervisory relationship but also results in the counselor feeling disempowered and hesitant to self-disclose mistakes when providing client services (Gray, Ladany, Walker, & Ancis, 2001). Within the counseling psychology literature, reports of counterproductive supervision have resulted in supervisees experiencing little support for autonomy (Wulf & Nelson, 2000), emotional neglect (Kozlowska, Nunn, & Cousins, 1997), extreme stress and self-doubt (Nelson & Friedlander, 2001), and/or leaving the supervisee with unworkable solutions to resolve client problems (Moskowitz & Rupert, 1983). Poor supervision can therefore result in supervisee conflicts that are associated with high anxiety levels, supervision dissatisfaction, and ultimately work dissatisfaction (Olk & Friedlander, 1992). Extending these research findings to rehabilitation counselor settings both at pre-service and post-employment levels is virtually unknown, as there has been no specific study of counterproductive or harmful supervision. There is support, however, that staff turnover is partially influenced by the nature of supervision received (e.g., Riggar, Hansen, & Crimando, 1987). Finally, despite the reported importance of clinical supervision to pre-professional training (Herbert & Ward, 1989), continued professional development (Herbert & Richardson, 1995; Maki & Delworth, 1995) and service delivery (Herbert, 1997), it is a topic that has been generally ignored in the rehabilitation counseling literature (Herbert, Ward, & Hemlick, 1995). Consequently, much of what is known about clinical supervision is borrowed from other allied counseling and psychology disciplines (Stebnicki, 1998) and, as applied to rehabilitation practice, the focus has been on pre-professional training (Herbert, 1995).

During the past 23 years, there have been two studies that have investigated clinical supervision aspects among experienced counselors within the public sector vocational rehabilitation program. English, Oberle, and Bryne (1979) conducted the first and only nationwide study investigating rehabilitation counselor supervision of experienced counselors. The study investigated both administrative (concern for agency policy, procedures and efficiency) and clinical (concern for counselor skill development that achieves successful client outcomes) supervision aspects such as supervisory background, evaluation, practices, selection and training. Relevant to this discussion, the study found that supervisors (a) devoted most of their efforts towards administrative and case consultation, (b) used case review and field observation methods primarily when supervising counselors, and (c) did a "poor job in many functional areas of counselor consultation and counselor evaluation" (p. 11). In general, rehabilitation counselors were "critical about all aspects of supervision and least hopeful that supervision can be improved" (p. 12). Unfortunately, the results reported 23 years ago seem consistent with current practice. A recent study by Schultz, Ososkie, Fried, Nelson, and Bardos (2002) that investigated current supervisory practices and the nature of those practices on the supervisory relationship within two state VR programs identified similar problems. First, most supervision occurs on "as needed" basis and, as a result, this approach "eliminates the opportunity for engaging in proactive activities focused on counselor development" (p. 219). Second, less than one in three counselors reported having a regularly scheduled time to meet with their supervisor. Third, there exists a "severe lack of understanding" regarding the purpose, practice, and potential benefits of clinical supervision. Given the limited research available, it seems that clinical supervision represents an unknown phenomenon with respect to current professional development within the state public vocational rehabilitation program. With regard to the private non-profit and proprietary sectors, research in clinical supervision is nonexistent (Herbert, in press). In these practice settings, we know nothing regarding how clinical supervision occurs, its impact on professional development and client service delivery.

TRAINING IN CLINICAL SUPERVISION

Within rehabilitation counselor education, specific training in clinical supervision is one usually reserved for doctoral-trained personnel (e.g., Allen, Stebnicki, & Lynch, 1995; Schultz, Copple, & Ososkie, 1999). At the master's level, clinical supervision consists of providing students with a recipient rather than a provider perspective. As beginning counselors, master's level students learn about the helping process and, with appropriate structure and support, develop increasing autonomy and confidence in their skills (Maki & Delworth, 1995). Given initial supervisor-supervisee interactions, graduate students in accredited rehabilitation counseling programs receive some understanding of the nature and mechanics of clinical supervision through participation in practica and internship experiences. To what extent this understanding extends to later professional development depends on the skills and training of the clinical supervisor as well as interactions with subsequent supervisors. Most rehabilitation supervisors do not have specific training in clinical supervision (Thielsen & Leahy, 2001) and, in fact, are uncertain about the nature, goals, and process (Schultz et al., 2002). Given lack of training at the preprofessional level and recognizing that many counselors will eventually assume roles as supervisors and administrators (Crimando, Hansen, & Riggar, 1986; Riggar & Matkin, 1984), training in clinical supervision should occur at both preparatory and subsequent professional development.

Although graduate training in clinical supervision has not been typically included as part of the curriculum required by the Council on Rehabilitation Education, a new proposal recognizes that this content be covered (CORE, 2002). This proposal requires that master's level students demonstrate knowledge in "supervision theories, models and techniques" and be able to "provide basic consultation and supervision." The proposed standards, if implemented, may adequately prepare students for later supervisory roles. A recent study by Thielsen and Leahy (2001), however, suggests that these standards may need to be broadened to address knowledge domains unique to rehabilitation counseling practice. In terms of specific curriculum, Herbert and Bieschke (2000) proposed a graduate course in clinical supervision for advanced master's or doctoral students intended to address supervision theories, techniques and practice concerns. Relevant to this discussion, individual learning units on how to develop and maintain an effective supervisory relationship both within individual and group practice, establish ethical and legal supervisory practices, and understand administrative functions related to clinical supervision are content areas that graduate students should receive training. Interested readers may want to examine specific readings and learning assignments associated with these aspects as well as others not mentioned in this chapter but are described in the proposed course. It should be noted that the course designed by Herbert and Bieschke did not provide students with opportunities to work as clinical supervisors. Although models exist where more experienced master's students provide peer supervision to less experienced students (e.g., Bernard, 1992), they are intended to broaden one's understanding of the clinical supervision process and not necessarily develop competence as supervisors. As noted earlier, most master's-level students are developing their professional identity as counselors and therefore it would be inappropriate and unethical to assign them as primary supervisors of other beginning counselors. The benefit of formal coursework in clinical supervision is that it allows students to become "informed consumers." When students leave the academic setting and venture into professional practice, they take with them a foundation of what hopefully constitutes effective clinical supervision and, in turn, may influence subsequent interactions with their clinical supervisors who lack this knowledge. Most importantly, didactic coursework in clinical supervision provides students with a foundation that may be applied when they later serve as clinical supervisors.

As noted earlier, there seems to be a general dissatisfaction within the state-federal vocational rehabilitation program concerning how clinical supervision is provided. If findings from the limited studies that have investigated clinical supervision (English et al., 1979; Schultz et al., 2002) are representative of current practice, it seems that sufficient training in providing effective clinical supervision is unlikely to occur under the present system. Historically, the primary focus of supervision within the state-federal program deals more with administrative rather than clinical aspects of supervision. As Lewis (1998) noted, this focus may be partly attributable to the philosophy held by front-line supervisors who implement a "command-and-control" orientation rather than one of "serving and supporting" counselors. Under the control orientation, supervisors are more concerned with enforcing agency policies and practices that emphasize successful rehabilitation outcomes (i.e., obtaining and maintaining employment). In contrast, a supporting framework emphasizes counselor development to work more effectively within the client–counselor relationship that also ultimately leads to successful rehabilitation outcome. Although available studies have criticized the delivery of clinical supervision in the state-federal program, it provides an indication of what needs to be done to improve practice. Insight regarding other non-profit rehabilitation settings or proprietary settings is very speculative given that we know nothing about how clinical supervision occurs in these settings. As a result, one can neither criticize nor applaud what might exist in actual practice, as there has been no formal study of clinical supervisions in these settings.

THE STRUCTURED DEVELOPMENTAL MODEL

It is necessary to have a conceptual framework to understand the developmental process involved in becoming and maintaining competence and integrity as a professional rehabilitation counselor. Prior to presenting such a model, however, a definition of clinical supervision is required. The following definition has been suggested as functional and appropriate for our profession and this discussion. Clinical supervision is defined as:

> an intervention provided by a more senior member of a profession to a more junior member or members of that same profession. This relationship is evaluative, extends over time, and has the simultaneous purposes of enhancing the professional functioning of the more junior persons(s), monitoring the quality of professional services offered to the client(s), she, he, or they see(s), and serving as a gatekeeper for those who are to enter the particularly profession. (Bernard & Goodyear, 1998, p. 6)

Clinical supervision as defined above is therefore a distinct intervention that requires a trained supervisor. Specialized education in the area of clinical supervision is thus essential. Such supervision is critical at the preservice level as well as continuing education and professional practice levels, however. To not engage in appropriate clinical supervision does a disservice to the counselor and potentially places the client at risk.

Maki and Delworth (1995) have proposed the Structured Developmental Model (SDM) as a robust and relevant paradigm for understanding counselor development. The SDM refines the Integrated Developmental Model (IDM) proposed by Stoltenberg and Delworth (1987) through an organization of the eight domains that reflect counseling practice. Stoltenberg and Delworth assumed that progression from Level-1 counselor to Level-3 Integrated proceeds in a relatively systematic manner through eight domains, or areas of professional competence. The SDM categorizes these domains into two main categories: (1) three primary domains, and (2) five process domains. The primary domains, essential for every counselor, are sensitivity to individual differences, theoretical orientation, and professional ethics. These first three domains serve as metadomains and will continue to be addressed as counselors work through the levels as well as through each of the remaining five process domains.

The five process domains parallel the functions of the rehabilitation counselor and are presented in the traditional sequence of case service delivery as follows: (1) interpersonal assessment, which uses the counseling relationship to evaluate the social skills, personality characteristics, and interaction style of the client, (2) individual client assessment in his or her environment, which focuses on the person and the functional impact of disability and incorporates psychometric procedures and medical consultation, (3) case conceptualization, which requires the integration of interpersonal assessment and individual client-assessment data to generate a working image of the client as a whole person, (4) treatment goals and plans, and (5) intervention strategies. Each of these process domains contains specific knowledge and skills that are interrelated and become integrated as the counselor reaches the fourth and final level proposed by this model, Level-3 Integrated. The model presented herein provides the supervisor with a format for achieving the dual goals of clinical supervision: enhancing the therapeutic competence of the counselor while simultaneously monitoring the client's welfare.

The following is a brief description outlining a model developmental sequence defining the levels referred to previously. It is believed that a shared understanding of these levels and the developmental process involved will be of benefit to both the supervisor and counselor-in-training or in-practice who may be in the role of supervisee. This conceptual framework may serve to normalize and make more efficient the complex and often difficult process of supervision.

The developmental model assumes that counselors-in-training progress through four levels while learning to function clinically. According to Stoltenberg and Delworth's (1987) Integrated Developmental Model, as individuals progress across these levels, change occurs in a continuous manner with regard to the following: self and other awareness, motivation, and autonomy. As the individual moves through the levels, increased competence in each domain can be observed.

At Level One, counselors are both highly dependent on their supervisor and highly motivated to learn. They are concerned with their counseling performance to such an extent that they seem largely self-focused on their own behavior instead of on their clients. Counselors at this level are also influenced by their supervisor's method or technique and will most likely function from an imitative or recipe-oriented approach to counseling.

At Level Two, the counselors are less method-bound, more client-focused, and concerned with investing his or her own personality style into the counseling work. Counselors begin to experience in greater depth the emotional and cognitive states of their clients. Developing insight and differentiating personal reactions from client realities are recurrent struggles during this level. This dynamic may result in the counselors' vacillating motivational level. Because of the increase in skill base, Level-Two counselors also seem to vacillate between the need for supervision and the need for autonomy.

Level-Three counselors are more likely to assume a collegial relationship with their supervisor and other professionals. At this level, counselors is able to ask for what he or she needs without feeling inadequate or that his or her competency will be called into question through such requests. Supervision becomes consultative in nature and counselor-initiated. The Level-Three counselor also tends to have developed the ability to be empathetic with clients and to have a simultaneous sense of self-awareness, which allows for clear, professional boundaries. Having developed a balanced sense of personal and professional identity usually reflects itself in a fairly stable level of motivation.

The goal of a CORE-accredited rehabilitation counselor education program is to provide the preservice foundation for the counselor to become a Level-Three Integrated professional who is able to function independently. It is believed that this level can occur with supervised experience and continuing education after graduation.

PRACTICE ISSUES IN CLINICAL SUPERVISION

Perhaps an initial consideration when providing clinical supervision is to have a clear understanding regarding the nature and purpose of supervision. Beginning counselors who have received clinical supervision as part of their pre-professional training are not likely to find the same type of supervision instituted in their work settings. The nature and delivery of clinical supervision in rehabilitation settings will vary as a function of training and experience of clinical supervisors as well as the commitment by administrative personnel to this process. In situations where counselor licensure is an important consideration, one might expect a greater commitment to clinical supervision, as this aspect is often a necessary requirement for licensure (Stebnicki, 1998). In other public and private rehabilitation settings where rehabilitation counselors are not required to be licensed professional counselors, obtaining clinical supervision may be more difficult to achieve. In these instances, rehabilitation counselors may have to actively seek out supervision within or outside their work settings.

Selecting the Right Supervisor

An initial problem for rehabilitation counselors seeking clinical supervision is determining, "Who is an appropriate clinical supervisor?" In most instances, the existing agency or facility has already established a "chain of command" in place as more experienced counselors perform clinical supervision duties. Usually, persons promoted through the ranks that, as a result of successful job performance as rehabilitation counselors, assume supervisory roles (Crimando et al., 1986). Working as an effective counselor does not mean that one will work as an effective supervisor, however (Herbert, 1997; Riggar, Crimando, Bordieri, & Phillips, 1988). Rehabilitation counselors who have choice and desire clinical supervision may want to consider other criteria when selecting an appropriate supervisor. As a start, counselors should consider: (a) length of time the person has been a Certified Rehabilitation Counselor, (b) extent of training received in clinical supervision (both at graduate and post-employment levels), (c) length of time providing direct clinical supervision, and (d) type of supervised work provided. In recognizing specific training and experience required to be an effective supervisor, the Commission on Rehabilitation Counselor Certification (CRCC) recently developed a new designation—Certified Rehabilitation Counselor–Clinical Supervisor [CRC-CS] (CRCC, 1999). Due to lack of professional interest, this designation no longer exists, however (S. Gilpin, personal communication, September 2, 2002). This development is unfortunate as it provided a professional mechanism that rehabilitation counselors could use to identify appropriately trained clinical supervisors. Interested rehabilitation professionals seeking further credentials as a clinical supervisor may wish to pursue the Approved Clinical Supervisor (ACS) designation from the National Board of Certified Counselors (2002). Persons would have to fulfill the requirements needed to become a National Certified Counselor, a licensed or certified mental health provider or a licensed or certified clinical supervisor however. Finding a rehabilitation counselor supervisor who completed graduate coursework in clinical supervision as part of one's master's degree program will be highly unlikely. As noted earlier, recent proposed changes requiring coursework in supervision have been suggested by the Council on Rehabilitation Education. Should these proposed changes be enacted, it will serve as a foundation for future students completing accredited rehabilitation counseling programs. Until such time, counselors who want formal training in clinical supervision will have to acquire it through professional seminars and workshops. These types of training activities are often sponsored through the Association for Counselor Education and Supervision (ACES). Training in clinical supervision sponsored by the major rehabilitation counseling associations such as the American Rehabilitation Counseling Association or the National Rehabilitation Counseling Association will occur with greater frequency as this topic generates further research and professional interest.

Beginning the Supervisory Relationship

In addition to having an appropriate clinical supervision experience, it is often the case that a major consideration in selecting the "right" supervisor is the ability to form a good working relationship. The working relationship or alliance that each supervisor and supervisee forms is characterized by three elements: (a) the bond or relationship between both individuals, (b) the degree to which both agree on supervision goals, and (c) the extent to which both agree on the supervision tasks to reach those goals (Bordin, 1983). Bieschke and Herbert (2000) described a pre-professional training model designed to promote an effective working alliance that could be applied to post employment settings as well. As part of the initial process, both supervisee and supervisor should discuss expectations each person has of the other as well as an idea of how the supervision process will evolve. Supervisors may wish to describe their theoretical orientation, supervisory style, evaluation process, and credentials related to supervision practice. Supervisees may want to outline their preferred counseling theoretical orientation(s), describe skill areas or client issues that they perceive as needing help with to work more effectively, and review past supervisory experiences and outcomes. There should also be a clearly written plan that describes the nature and process of supervision. This plan is particularly important as a way of addressing ethical and legal considerations that sometimes emerge during supervision.

Ethical and Legal Considerations

Clarity of how supervision is provided becomes an important aspect not only in specifying the nature of supervision but serves as a mechanism in reducing claims of professional malpractice. Issues regarding malpractice (negligence) should be addressed before any supervision occurs because supervisors assume vicarious liability or *respondeat superior* for the client. Although it is the counselor providing direct services, it is the supervisor monitoring this work and, in effect, the supervisor serves as the "gatekeeper" in assuring that quality services are provided (Herbert, 1997). Within the supervisory relationship, malpractice exists as a function of four elements: legal duty of care, standard of care, harm, and proximate cause (Guest & Dooley, 1999). Legal duty of care refers to the existence of a supervisory relationship where accordingly there is an implied contract between supervisor and supervisee. When applying this standard, supervisors assume responsibility of care that is often specified by a particular professional code. For example, the *Code of Professional Ethics for Rehabilitation Counselors* (CRCC, 2001) describes several ethical standards related to supervision. Under Section G: Teaching, Training, and Supervision, there are five standards that specify rehabilitation counselors will: (a) "maintain clear ethical, professional, and social relationship boundaries with students and supervisees" (p. 13), (b) avoid sexual relationships with supervisees and not subject them to sexual harassment, (c) supervise in areas in which they demonstrate competence through training and professional experience, (d) ensure that supervisees provide rehabilitation counseling services to clients that are adequate and do not cause any harm, and (e) endorse only those candidates who meet appropriate requirements for certification, employment, licensure, and/or program completion. It should be noted that lack of knowledge or competency in a particular area or other deviation from established ethical standards would constitute a breach of care and, in essence, provide legal justification for malpractice. Given the potential power differential between supervisor and supervisee (especially if both are affiliated with the same employer), potential injury or harm as a result of the relationship can also occur. Supervisors may be liable in situations where they go beyond their level of expertise or when supervisees provide services for which they are not qualified thereby harming themselves and their clients. Finally, proximate cause means that supervisor actions were the primary reasons for harm done to a client or supervisee.

Clinical supervisors must recognize the litigious society in which we practice and, as such, exercise preventative measures to reduce the potential for malpractice. A sound strategy would be to develop a written disclosure statement that is reviewed and agreed to by both supervisor and supervisee. This statement could include aspects such as the nature of supervision services, evaluation procedures, description of supervisory areas of competence, fee schedule, and related supervisor/supervisee responsibilities. Blackwell, Strohmer, Belcas, and Burton (2002) describe an excellent example of a professional disclosure statement. Providing rehabilitation counselor supervision in a professional and ethical manner consistent within one's area of competence is a fundamental responsibility of all clinical supervisors (Tarvydas, 1995). Ultimately, supervisors must be mindful in balancing counseling needs of the client with the professional development of their supervisees.

Supervisee Evaluation

By definition, clinical supervision requires an ongoing evaluation of counselor performance and, within the context of supervision, both supervisor and supervisee must agree on the evaluation methods used to assess this performance. In order to evaluate one's professional work, supervisors must evaluate rehabilitation counseling competencies and related case management skills. Central to the supervisory process is an understanding of client–counselor interactions that impact rehabilitation outcome. Typically, this awareness comes from observing counseling sessions. This observation may require delayed methods using audio- or videotape of recent client–counselor sessions or involve active methods where the supervisor observes or participates in the client–counselor process. For example, during live supervision, the supervisor may take a direct and active role such as a "co-counselor" or an indirect role where feedback is given to the supervisee without the supervisor being physically present (e.g., "bug-in-the-ear" technique). Supervisors may also rely on written documentation or verbal accounts of what transpired during counseling sessions (i.e., case review methods). As it can be inferred from these methods, the extent of client–counselor interaction will depend on the preferred supervisory method(s) used. For example, if delayed-indirect supervision using audio- or videotape of client-counselor sessions is used, will the entire tape be evaluated or only certain sections? If certain sections are reviewed, what rationale is applied and what evaluation structure will be used when reviewing selected segments? The supervision process may also consist of multiple supervisors and other supervisees within the same discipline (i.e., group supervision) or persons from multiple disciplines (i.e., team supervision). If group supervision formats are used, how will this process evolve? What procedures will be used in evaluating supervisee performance? Given the variety of models and related tasks used when conducting group supervision (e.g., Borders, 1991; Newman & Lovell, 1993), supervisors must structure how feedback is provided to various group members, develop procedures for case presentations, institute procedures that assure client confidentiality and review policies that group members must follow. Although clinical supervision offers a melange of approaches each with inherent strengths and limitations, in the final analysis, the method(s) selected are dependent on supervisee need, supervisor competence, and client informed consent (Herbert, in press).

The methods supervisors use to develop counselor (supervisee) competence, while important, are not as critical as the manner in which the clinical supervisor conducts supervisee evaluation. Bernard and Goodyear (1998, p. 156–159), in their review of the literature on conditions for conducting effective evaluation, identified several important aspects among them were:

1. Recognize that the supervisor-supervisee relationship is unequal. Since supervision involves evaluation there may be resulting negative consequences for the supervisee. Supervisors must be sensitive to the supervisee's position.
2. Supervisee defensiveness that occurs during evaluation must be addressed openly. Avoiding supervisee defensiveness only compounds the problem of being vulnerable to constructive criticism. Supervisors must examine and process helpful and unhelpful defensive behaviors that supervisees use during supervision.
3. Supervisors must serve as professional role models for their supervisees. Inviting supervisee comment, sharing appropriate self-disclosure, and reminding supervisees that the counseling profession is not one of facts but of concepts serves as reminders that supervisors are constantly evaluating their professional development.
4. Supervisors who do not enjoy supervision should avoid it. Supervisors who characterize supervision as frustrating, difficult, unrewarding, and/or painful would be better served not supervising others. As the authors note, "Whenever a trainee is denied appropriate supervision and evaluation, the professional community is diminished" (p. 159).
5. Everything that transpires during supervision is a function of the supervisory relationship. Ineffective or weak relationships may result in withholding important evaluation information that impact on supervisee professional development. Similarly, situations that result in supervisory relationships that are strained or too close can also negatively impact supervisee evaluations (pp. 156–159).

When providing verbal and/or written evaluations to supervisees, Larson (1998) proposed that supervisors focus on being accurate, provide specific feedback, and address issues that supervisees have the capacity for change. These suggestions are especially apropos for new rehabilitation counselors who are developing their sense of how to help persons with disabilities. As new counselors, they have not yet formed a firm sense of counselor self-efficacy or the belief that one is an effective counselor in assisting clients with particular concerns. For example, a rehabilitation counselor may perceive strong counselor self-efficacy as it relates to assisting a client in conducting information interviews with potential employers. This same counselor may not however perceive efficacy as it relates to dealing with grief issues associated with psychological adjustment for someone with a recently acquired disability. Although these examples may be unique to a particular counselor, a common self-efficacy problem expressed by many beginning counselors is associated with client confrontation. Often, beginning counselors will express a desire to confront clients but avoid such because by doing so it could result in greater emotional distance from their clients (Young, 1998). In order to avoid any potential alienation, the counselor will avoid confrontation. As inferred in these examples, counselor self-efficacy beliefs are important because they relate to expressed counselor anxiety and therefore impact counselor performance. It has been shown that lower counselor self-efficacy is more likely to occur among inexperienced counselors who encounter novel situations or past instances that have produced counselor anxiety (Larson & Daniels, 1998). In these instances, supervisors would have to exercise greater sensitivity and formulate positive responses to enhance counselor self-efficacy. The importance of providing positive feedback, as Daniels and Larson (2001) found, is especially critical for new counselors as this approach can significantly alter counselor self-efficacy. For this reason, it is important that clinical supervisors consistently ask supervisees about areas of perceived competence and those needing improvement. In contrast, more experienced and competent counselors appreciate supervisors who respond in a more direct, collegial manner. This difference in knowing how to respond effectively to supervisees with varying levels of self-efficacy simply demonstrates the developmental process that counselors experience when moving from a Level 1 or novice counselor to a Level 3I or "Integrated" counselor (Maki & Delworth, 1995). The effective supervisor must recognize supervisee needs vary as a function of each counselor's unique professional development level and respond accordingly. By doing so, the supervisor can impact counselor self-efficacy and ultimately counselor skill development.

Working with an Ineffective or Impaired Supervisor

Earlier commentary examined characteristics that supervisees may consider when selecting an appropriate supervisor. As noted previously, unless the counselor contracts for supervision independent of their work setting, it is more than likely that supervision will be provided where the counselor works. Whether the on-site supervisor understands and practices effective clinical supervision is something that is often unknown until the process begins.

Rehabilitation counselors may be assigned supervisors who are ineffective or impaired. Ineffective supervisors are characterized by disinterest when providing supervision, resistance to seeking further training or consultation, low empathy, and an intolerance and defensiveness when interacting with supervisees (Watkins, 1997). Impaired supervision occurs when the individual cannot perform supervisory roles as a result of supervisor behavior or the working environment (Muratori, 2001). Unlike the incompetent supervisor (who does not currently possess sufficient skills to supervise but could do so with additional training), the impaired supervisor did, at one time, possess sufficient skills to function effectively but now does so in a reduced capacity. While there are anecdotal reports of ineffective and unethical supervisory behavior in rehabilitation counseling clinical practica (Herbert & Ward, 1989; Stebnicki, Allen, & Janikowski, 1997) to what extent similar occurrences exists in counseling practice is unknown. It is certainly possible that new professionals who experienced the benefit of effective supervision as part of graduate training may enter into situations that are not conducive to receiving beneficial clinical supervision.

Although the literature concerning impaired supervisors is very limited, Muratori (2001) described a useful decision-making model that supervisees could implement if confronted with an impaired or ineffective supervisor. Key aspects of the model require the supervisee to identify maladaptive supervisor behaviors and discuss how these impact the supervisee. Once problems are clarified, supervisees should consult the appropriate professional ethical code to see what standards of practice apply to issues of supervisor impairment. Consultation with other colleagues regarding any breaches of ethical conduct may also be warranted and, in the case of certified rehabilitation counselors (CRCs), it is a professional obligation.

> Standard K.2.a. Consultation, requires when another CRC may be suspected of a code violation, there is a professional obligation to seek consultation to determine whether in fact a code violation has occurred. In these cases, consultation must ensue with "other rehabilitation counselors who are knowledgeable about ethics, with colleagues, and/or with appropriate authorities, such as CRCC, state licensure boards, or legal counsel." (CRCC, 2001, p. 19)

This professional code only pertains to CRCs, however. Should the supervisor not be a CRC, the student should continue to seek consultation with an experienced and trusted colleague. After consultation, the supervisee should generate a list of possible action steps; the first being to consider addressing issues of concerns directly with the supervisor. Muratori makes an important point should supervisees want to confront supervisors regarding their professional behavior. Recognizing the power differential between supervisor and supervisee (especially during pre-professional training), it is possible that retribution could result. As a preventative measure, it was recommended that consulting with a colleague of equal or greater power as the clinical supervisor within the same work setting might be a reasonable option. If one pursues this option, it was recommended that supervisees describe each situation with as much detail and objectivity as conceivable and avoid judgment or accusatory statements. In all instances, the communication regarding the behavior(s) in question should be presented in a "dispassionate fashion without attacking the character of the supervisor" (p. 53). Regardless as to whether the supervisee confronts the supervisor, careful thought will have to consider the options available and the risks associated with each option. In deciding which option may be best to pursue, Muratori suggests that several questions be applied. First, how comfortable will the supervisee be once others know his or her actions? Second, would the decision be one the supervisee advocates to other supervisees in a similar situation? Third, will there be any lingering doubts after making this decision? Fourth, would the same course of action be taken if a different supervisor who was similarly impaired acted in the same manner? Whatever course of action is taken or not taken, the final recommendation is to keep written documentation of all supervisory incidents and conversations with other colleagues. Although one would hope that no supervisee would experience impaired or ineffective supervision, given the probability that similarly impaired and ineffective rehabilitation counselors currently practice, it is incumbent for both supervisees and supervisor colleagues to take the appropriate actions to remediate this problem. While difficult and uncomfortable, ignoring this problem is both unethical and unprofessional.

FINAL COMMENT

The importance of training rehabilitation counselors in clinical supervision is receiving greater awareness in terms of professional preparation and an increasing commitment to research. In fact, within the past 5 years, there has been more attention devoted to this topic than at any time previously. Within rehabilitation counseling, it is imperative that we examine current clinical supervision practices in various settings (non-profit, proprietary, state–federal) so that effective supervision practices can be identified and models can be developed, evaluated, and implemented effectively. It is also imperative that future research efforts examine to what extent clinical supervision impacts rehabilitation service outcome. Although the relationship between having qualified personnel and successful rehabilitation outcomes has been documented throughout the literature (e.g., Szymanski, Herbert, Parker, & Danek, 1992), we have no understanding as to how rehabilitation counselor supervision contributes to this outcome. An important step is to understand specific knowledge and skills needed to work as an effective clinical supervisor as well as supervisor and situational variables that impact knowledge and skills (Thielsen & Leahy, 2001). At this point in our professional development, clinical supervision remains an important aspect of rehabilitation counseling practice but one that we are only starting to understand.

CHAPTER 17

Administration, Management, and Supervision

William Crimando

Management is involved in every stage of the modern rehabilitation organization. Fulmer (1988) referred to management as the process by which goals are achieved, as well as the body of knowledge needed to achieve them and the persons in the organization actually guiding the process. In rehabilitation organizations, administrators, managers, and supervisors are responsible for designing and maintaining the infrastructure, obtaining and using financial, human, and technological resources, and ensuring quality service delivery. Without administrators, managers, and supervisors to work with direct service staff, the important missions of rehabilitation organizations—to help persons with disabilities obtain employment, better physical and emotional health, and a better quality of life—could surely not be accomplished.

Although it may seem strange to some to find a chapter on administration in a book about rehabilitation counseling, there are two important reasons for its inclusion: First, research has shown that there is only a short time, ranging from just over 14 months to a few years, before counselors step up to supervisory roles (cf. Herbert, 1997). Unfortunately, they do so, generally, with no preparation to be supervisors (Edwards, 1999). This forces them to fall back on personal experience and the resources of the culture for guidance (Frieberg, 1991), as well as on "learning by doing." They either do what they have learned to do as counselors, which is often counterproductive, or copy the behavior of their former supervisors, who also may not have been adequately trained. Herbert's (1997) words still ring true: "Given the current political climate, which demands that rehabilitation service delivery and supporting programs be scrutinized . . . , it is especially important that rehabilitation administrators, managers, and supervisors find ways to ensure quality service delivery" (p. 246). However, as Thompson (1992) asserted, "When supervisors lack the knowledge and skill to create and maintain a positive work environment, quality of work life is compromised. The result? Absenteeism, tardiness, turnover, poor productivity, low morale . . . " (p. 16). In this chapter, it is hoped that expert counselors will be encouraged to seek out both management positions and the knowledge, skills, and abilities to assume those positions.

Second, this chapter is important, even if the reader has no specific plans to go into administration or supervision. Matkin (1982) proposed that training in supervisory and management functions become part of the preprofessional curriculum for all rehabilitation counselors. Herbert (1997) suggested that such training would make counselors better "informed consumers" of management, that is, better able to take advantage of the direction, coaching, counseling, and other services management has to offer. It is hoped that this chapter will start the development of the informed consumer of management.

This chapter provides an introduction to rehabilitation administration, management, and supervision, and will serve to supplement chapter 16, "Clinical Supervision." In the process of describing administration and supervision, the levels of management are first detailed, providing the background to discuss the functions of management and providing examples of activities at the various levels. Recent research and reportage on behavioral characteristics found in successful administrators, managers, and supervisors are introduced. Finally, given the importance, yet infrequency, of counselors receiving training in supervision before their first supervision jobs, a long section is included on education and training needs and resources.

LEVELS OF MANAGEMENT

Rehabilitation organizations differ in their number of levels of management. The classic management principle, "span of authority," suggests that the larger the organization, the more levels of management needed to work efficiently. A state vocational rehabilitation (VR) system, for example, needs to serve tens of thousands of consumers each year, and thus tends to be a very large organization, with numerous levels of management. These start, at the top, with central administration, including the state director, one or more deputy directors in charge of client/field services or administrative services, the budget director, planning director, and assorted other top administrative staff positions. The middle level of line management includes one or two levels of regional or area managers, who are responsible for coordinating the activities of supervisors in a large, geographically contiguous area. Finally, there are those field office or casework supervisors who are responsible for the day-to-day operations in one or more local field offices.

At the other end of the spectrum lies the small community rehabilitation program, which tends to have a flat organizational structure (an organization with few levels of management relative to its size is referred to as "flat"; those with more levels relative to size are referred to as "tall"). They may go from corporate executive officer directly to unit supervisors, omitting the middle levels found in larger organizations. Additionally, there have been efforts to flatten some state VR systems, because of financial exigencies or because of the more recent trend in the larger business community toward flatter organizations, as a matter of principle.

In general, the activities and behaviors of those in top administration tend to be broader in scope, longer-term in their implementation, and to have a wider impact on the organization than those in the lowest level of supervision; this is demonstrated in the following section on functions of management. Nevertheless, because supervisors are the closest level of management to consumers, their activities are every bit as important as those of higher levels.

FUNCTIONS OF MANAGEMENT

Although there have been a number of rubrics for categorizing management activities, the one provided by Crimando, Riggar, Bordieri, Benshoff, and Hanley-Maxwell (1989; cf. Riggar, Crimando, & Bordieri, 1991), although similar to the others, is more unambiguous. It is also more useful in the human services. Crimando et al. and Riggar et al. suggested that all management activities can be classified as one of five functions: planning, organizing, leading, evaluating, and staffing. These functions are defined and demonstrated as follows:

Planning

Planning is the process through which decisions are made about the results an organization expects to achieve and about courses of action most likely to lead to their achievement. Planning activities include conducting needs assessment; developing long- and short-range goals and objectives, as well as plans for achieving them; budget planning; and evaluation planning. As implied previously, the planning activities engaged in by top administrators differ in their scope and impact from those of supervisors. Top administrators generally engage in long-term strategic planning for the overall organization, as well as developing budgets and budget priorities; supervisors contribute to the development of goals, objectives, and operational plans, as well as make budget requests for their unit. These individual supervisory efforts are then combined by top administrators, who ensure that (a) the combined plans will indeed meet the strategic plan, (b) individual unit plans are not inconsistent with each other, and (c) individual plans are reasonable and within mission-related, ethical, legal, and fiscal restrictions.

Organizing

Organizing is the grouping of activities necessary to attain objectives, the assignment of each grouping to a manager with authority to supervise it, and the provision of coordination horizontally and vertically in the enterprise of structure. Organizing activities of frontline supervisors tend to be restricted to assigning work to individual staff and to assisting in the coordination of the unit with other units. Activities for top administration include developing the organizational chart. This is much more than a paper exercise, because it requires dividing up the work of the organization into jobs, positions, and units; determining lines of communication and authority and monitoring the organization, to make sure units are operating together. Recent literature (e.g., Kinney, 1996; Montgomery, Hendricks, & Bradley, 2001; Morgan, 1997) espouses viewing the organization as a system and using systems' principles (Kim, 1999) and proposes that to not do so would be to deny the growing complexity of modern organizations and the environments in which they must compete.

Leading

Leading in an organization is an implicit or explicit social contract involving two or more people, in which one person is able to influence the others' behavior toward the accomplishment of organizational goals. Recent literature has differentiated *transactional leadership* from *transformational leadership*. The former is defined as providing rewards or discipline contingent on employees' performance (Bass & Avoglio, 1994). Transformational leadership is exhibited when leaders

> stimulate interest among colleagues and followers to view their work from new perspectives, generate awareness of the mission or vision of the team and organization, develop colleagues and followers to higher levels of ability and potential, and motivate colleagues and followers to look beyond their own interests toward those that will benefit the group. (Bass & Avoglio, p. 2)

Recent literature has also differentiated leadership and management, until they are now treated as two ends of a dichotomy. Examination of the behaviors of effective rehabilitation administrators, managers, and supervisors, however, gives the lie to the dichotomy: They are both transformational and transactional, both leaders and managers. Everyone in the organization can be a leader, from the top administrator to the lowest-level counselors, employees, and even consumers. One of the tasks of top administrators is to make sure that leaders throughout the organization are leading in the same direction.

Evaluating

Sometimes referred to as "controlling," evaluating includes the processes for developing and implementing mechanisms for determining and influencing the effectiveness or efficiency of an organization or its endeavors. In rehabilitation organizations, this management function is encompassed in the program evaluation system or outcomes management system. Posavac and Carey (2003) defined program evaluation as

> a collection of methods, skills, and sensitivities necessary to determine whether a human service is needed and likely to be used, whether the service is sufficiently intensive to meet the unmet needs identified, whether the service is offered as planned, and whether the service actually does help people in need at a reasonable cost without unacceptable side effects. (p. 1)

The technical aspects of implementing a program evaluation system are frequently turned over to a professional program evaluator. However, a program evaluation system is so intrinsically tied in with the mission, goals, and objectives of a rehabilitation organization and its component programs that it would be incorrect to say that it is not within the purview of line management. Further, top administration set the direction and priorities for evaluation, and all levels of management use the data feedback produced by program evaluation.

Staffing

The process of staffing entails enabling the organization structure and goals, through the proper and effective selection, appraisal, and development of human resources, to fill the roles designed in the structure. Schmidt, Riggar, Crimando, and Bordieri (1992) detailed these staffing activities:

- Human resource planning: anticipating future business and environmental demands and attempting to meet the personnel needs dictated by those demands
- Job analysis: gathering, evaluating, and recording information about a given position, from a variety of sources
- Recruitment: identifying and attracting individuals from the labor market who are capable and desirous of filling employment vacancies
- Selection: choosing one person, in preference to others, for an announced job vacancy
- Orientation: introducing new employees to the organization and to their supervisors, jobs, and work groups
- Supervision: planning and directing the work activities of subordinate employees on a face-to-face, direct basis
- Training and development: providing employees with formal and informal learning experiences, in order that they might perform their current or future jobs more effectively, efficiently, or safely
- Performance appraisal: identifying and measuring human performance, for the purposes of making personnel decisions regarding an employee's retention, promotion, salary, and training requirements
- Individual planning and placement: integrated throughout the staffing process and involving such activities as assessment of individual potential, structured goal setting, career counseling, job rotation, and outplacement counseling, which might be performed as needed with or for an employee

From a practical standpoint, those activities earlier in the list tend to be more global and are performed by top administrators and midlevel managers; those at the end of the list are more specific to a work unit or employee and are performed by first-level supervisors, occasionally with staff assistance.

SUPERVISORY, MANAGERIAL, AND ADMINISTRATIVE CHARACTERISTICS

In the earlier version of this book (1997), Herbert provided characteristics and behaviors for supervisors, managers, and administrators. These are not addressed here, but readers are well advised to examine his work. A number of behavioral characteristics are identified in the recent literature as being important. The literature reviewed for this chapter is, for the most part, authoritative reportage and compilations of personal anecdotes, but few empirical studies on this topic have been produced. However, even the reportage and anecdotes have value, in that they provide bases for empirical studies.

Thompson (1992) listed these behavioral characteristics: allows employees to be involved in problem solving and decision making, recognizes and rewards good performance, provides support to employees, provides opportunities for growth and development, respects employees' dignity and uniqueness, encourages creativity, and allows employees to carry out their jobs with pride. Lisoski (1998) asserted that courage, character, and conviction are unique to the outstanding supervisor. He operationalized *courage* as displaying behaviors such as taking a risk based on faith in workers' abilities, taking individual responsibility for unpopular decisions, and protecting employees from unwarranted discipline from superiors. *Character* is having the values and ethical fiber to make tough decisions and to ensure that they are carried out; *conviction*, according to Lisoski, is displayed by a supervisor who "stand[s] firm when the going gets rough" (p. 11). Weiss (1998) suggested that promoting effective communication is the key to successful supervision, then gave specific instructions on how to do so. Being aware comes up several times: Seidenfeld (1998) stated that effective supervisors spend time with their employees and are aware of the performance and difficulties of each; Kaplan (2002) asserted that successful executives need to be aware of their own strengths and weaknesses. Although most authors would cite the power of praise as a motivational tool, McCormack (2000) averred that supervisors should be as careful with praise as they are with criticism. Sforza (1997) provided both positive and negative arguments on using fear as a motivator; Waddell and Waddell (1997) wrote against it. Acting fairly and consistently with employees was discussed in Seidenfeld (1998) and "Fairness breeds effective supervision" (2001). Seidenfeld (1998) also provided the seemingly paradoxical advice to practice genuine caring while maintaining distance. Finally, Macoby (1997) suggested that business success depends on building trust, that is, being trustworthy and trusting employees.

Consistent with Herbert's (1997) suggestion, there seems to be a paucity of recent empirical research linking specific supervisor behaviors and characteristics with organizational mission-critical outcomes. There is evidence that poor supervision in general is linked with employee withdrawal behavior and organizational turnover (cf. Barrett, Riggar, Flowers, Crimando, & Bailey, 1997). Tepper (2000) found that employees who perceived their supervisors as being more abusive were more likely to quit their jobs, and those who stayed had lower job commitment, job satisfaction, and life satisfaction. At the same time, they reported higher psychological distress and conflict between work and family. Stout (1984) found that higher job satisfaction was reported by employees who perceived their supervisors to exhibit consideration behaviors (i.e., displaying trust, respect, and warmth), and lower job stress was reported when employees believed their supervisors initiated structure (i.e., providing direction for group activities). As a result of a more recent analysis, Barrett and Crimando (1996) tentatively suggested that there is a negative correlation between initiating structure and job satisfaction, when supervisors do not at the same time exhibit specific empowering behaviors. Finally, Yoon and Thye (2000) found positive correlations between supervisory support and both organizational and coworker support.

As can be seen, the research concerns the links between supervisory behavior and contextual factors like job satisfaction, support, and psychological distress, and not employee or organizational performance. Indeed, it would be difficult to conclude causal relationships between supervisory behavioral characteristics and employee outcomes, because of the relative inability to use randomization and control for extraneous factors in a field setting.

SUPERVISORY AND ADMINISTRATIVE PREPARATION

The fact that so few rehabilitation administrators, managers, and supervisors attain their first supervisory jobs without formal training makes training no less important. The managerial role requires technical, interpersonal, and conceptual skills, in combinations that vary according to level of management and nature of the organization. Only some of these skills could be expected to be learned as a counselor.

Curriculum Needs

A chronological review of past issues of journals in rehabilitation reveals that the outcomes of training needs assessments of VR agency administrators are at once similar and distinct. There is a core of knowledge, skills, and abilities that, under various labels, come up repeatedly, but there is also a list that appears infrequently, possibly because of differing survey participants and changing political, economic, social, and technological environments. The earliest published assessment of training needs was competed by Hutchinson, Luck, and Hardy (1978). They found that skills building in managing people problems was the most pressing training need. A 1982 study by Matkin,

Sawyer, Lorenz, and Rubin contained the following training-need hierarchy: program planning and evaluation, fiscal management, public relations, general personnel management, production management, professional management, marketing, labor relations, research, and purchasing. Menz and Bordieri's (1986) survey of over 1,600 facility directors, assistant directors, and program managers suggested that these three groups shared the need for training in the following knowledge or skill areas: organizational planning; business operations, such as production efficiency and contract development; community image and fund raising; personnel administration and management; management techniques; access, control, and utilization of information systems; effective use of core workforce; administrative responsibilities; risk prevention and control; fiscal procedures; physical design and facility layout; and organizational continuity, consistency, and stability.

Mount and Schumacker (1991) listed seven primary content areas for graduate curriculum needs, as perceived by state and regional VR administrators: managing, developing, and supervising staff; problem solving; employee relations and communications; budgeting; employee performance evaluation; development of goals and objectives; management theory and practice; and program evaluation. The most recent study (Barrett, Flowers, Crimando, Riggar, & Bailey, 1997) reflects the stable, yet changing nature of training needs, alluded to previously. Barrett et al. reported the following training needs identified by 295 community rehabilitation program administrators: team building, communication skills, legal/ethical issues, Social Security work incentives, caseload management, stress management, advocacy, time management, program evaluation, effective staff supervision, managing community-based programs, leadership, quality control, public relations/marketing, performance appraisal, strategic planning, and management information systems.

Educational Opportunities

There are a number of resources available for rehabilitation professionals wishing to acquire the skills, knowledge, and abilities required to competently hold the position of administrator, manager, or supervisor. These include preservice and both formal and informal learn by doing (Stephens & Knapp, as cited in Herbert, 1997) programs:

- Preservice programs are provided at colleges and universities throughout the United States, sometimes in conjunction with, and sometimes separate from, master's level rehabilitation counselor training programs.

The first graduate training program in rehabilitation administration, started in 1957, was at Southern Illinois University at Carbondale (SIUC) (Barrett et al., 1997). Herbert (1997) pointed out that, although rehabilitation administration programs had been in existence for (now over) 40 years, the expansion of rehabilitation counseling programs over that period has not been accompanied by a similar expansion in administration programs. In fact, the number of such programs seems to be in decline. In 1988, Riggar, Crimando, Bordieri, and Phillips identified 10 rehabilitation administration programs. In contrast, the current membership directory of the National Council on Rehabilitation Education (2001–2002) lists four universities offering degrees, certificates, or diplomas in rehabilitation administration, management, or supervision: SIUC, Hofstra, Drake, and San Diego State. Further, the George Washington University and Virginia Commonwealth University offer degrees in rehabilitation leadership; the University of Wisconsin-Stout and University of Illinois offer an administration concentration as part of other degrees.

The current effort in the state VR system to provide an educational standard for those wishing to be employed as counselors has not been accompanied by the development of a similar standard for administrators and supervisors. Further, there is no accreditation for rehabilitation administration programs, indubitably because of the paucity of university programs. In fact, Herbert (1997) detailed the struggle between proponents and opponents of credentialing for rehabilitation administrators, but pointed out that there was still "no strong mandate by members of the National Rehabilitation Administration Association (now known as the National Association of Rehabilitation Leadership) to develop and implement such standards" (p. 257). In the absence of such a standard, those needing to choose among programs should compare university curricula in rehabilitation administration (which currently seem to range from two courses and an internship to comprehensive eight-course plus field experience programs) with the curricular needs outlined in the previous section, then determine which of the programs offers the best combination of comprehensiveness, academic rigor, reasonable cost, and accessible program delivery.

- Learn-by-doing, or, more generally, "learn-while-doing" experiences exist for those persons who either prefer not to, or cannot afford to, attend the protracted, generalized training (Herbert, 1997) offered in university programs. These range from informal on-the-job experiences, provided by supervisors acting as mentors or coaches (Riggar, Cri-

> mando, & Pusch, 1993; Viranyi, Crimando, Riggar, & Schmidt, 1992), to organizational opportunities like project or job rotation and shadowing, to formal in-service classes produced or purchased by the organization's human resource development unit. Administrative and management personnel who work in the state VR agency, or for a private nonprofit organization, may be able to avail themselves of continuing education opportunities through a Rehabilitation Continuing Education Program (RCEP) or Community Rehabilitation Program Rehabilitation Continuing Education Program. RCEPs are often in the best position to offer such programs (Riggar & Hansen, 1986). Certain administrators or future administrators in the public rehabilitation program may want to attend the certificate program maintained by the University of Oklahoma's National Executive Leadership Institute in Rehabilitation. Still others may wish to combine the best aspects of preservice and learn-while-doing programs, by attending concentrated master's degree programs in rehabilitation administration or leadership, such as the ones offered by SIUC and Virginia Commonwealth University.

The choice of preservice and learn-while-doing experiences is not an either–or proposition. The responsibility for attaining and maintaining competence as a rehabilitation administrator or supervisor does not end with obtaining a master's degree in rehabilitation administration. As Riggar et al. (1993) pointed out, "Learning never ends"; that is, the development of a competent supervisor, manager, or administrator is a continuous process. Those authors promote the development of learning cultures in rehabilitation organizations, in which each new experience can be treated as a learning event. This is the only way, they suggest, that an organization can "assur[e] its continued survival and success" (p. 38).

No discussion of training and education of rehabilitation administrators and supervisors is complete without at least a brief discussion of on-line learning, or e-learning (Rosenberg, 2001), as part of a broader distance education paradigm. In its broadest sense, distance education is the delivery of instruction in which the students are geographically separated from a central campus, and thus includes such delivery systems as courses in which instructors travel to an off-campus central site, correspondence courses, compressed video delivered to distributed classrooms, and the now-ubiquitous Internet courses. The 28th Institute on Rehabilitation Issues (28th Institute, 2002) listed the promises and perils of distance education. Reported advantages include convenience to those already working in the field, promotion of lifelong learning, and increased access to geographically isolated groups. Others, speaking about Internet courses per se, use terms like "anytime, anywhere instruction." Rosenberg (2001) lists 11 advantages of e-learning in the business world, including lowered training costs, enhanced business responsiveness, more timely and dependable content, universality (i.e., courses "[take] advantage of the universal Internet protocols and browsers" [p. 31]), and scalability (i.e., as long as the infrastructure is in place, courses can be offered to 10,000 persons as easily as they can be offered to 10).

These advantages notwithstanding, one must remain optimistically skeptical about on-line learning and distance education. Numerous studies suggest that there are no significant differences in outcomes between on-line and regular courses (e.g., Gagne & Shepherd, 2001; Johnson, 2002; Johnson, Aragon, Shaik, & Palma-Rivas, 2000). However, finding no significant differences is a function of poor research design, at least as often as, if not more often than, there not being any differences. The Institute for Higher Education Policy (1999) cited shortcomings in these studies: failure to control for extraneous variables, thus precluding cause and effect conclusions; failure to use randomization; poor reliability and validity of outcomes measurements; and inadequate control for feeling and attitudes of students and faculty. Furthermore, the 28th Institute (2002) warns about the possibility of the e-learning revolution leaving significant groups behind, such as persons with disabilities and cultural disadvantages.

Clearly, those wishing to offer on-line management and supervisory education and training should design courses that take advantage of the unique possibilities offered by computers and the Internet (cf. Rosenberg, 2001), while adhering to sound principles of instructional system design (Clark, 1995), adult learning (Knowles, 1990), instructional message design (Fleming & Levie, 1993), and universal program design (28th Institute, 2002). Customers (i.e., students, prospective students, and state VR agencies) should demand as much. Only then will the promise of online learning be fulfilled.

CONCLUSION

In this chapter, rehabilitation administration, management, and supervision have been introduced, with comprehensive, if not exhaustive, reviews of management functions, behavioral characteristics, and training needs. What is not included, for lack of space, is a discussion of the changing issues and factors that define the milieu in which management must operate. These include the legal and political ramifications of recent legislation (Riggar,

Flowers, & Crimando, 2002); the increasing necessity to manage cross-generational and cross-cultural workforces; new workplace stressors like the psychological funk ensuing after 9/11 and increased workplace violence (Barrett, Riggar, & Flowers, 1997); the general distrust of management, no doubt exacerbated by the ethical and fiduciary wrongdoings that have recently filled the newspapers; and ever-advancing technology, bringing with it concerns for computer security, electronic monitoring, and knowledge management. Each of these issues provides special challenges for the rehabilitation administrator, manager, and supervisor—challenges they must meet, in addition to fulfilling their regular functions of planning, organizing, leading, evaluating, and staffing.

APPENDIX **A**

Rehabilitation Acronyms

SELECTED ORGANIZATIONS

ACA	American Counseling Association

Subdivisions of the ACA

AAC	Association for Assessment in Counseling
AADA	Association for Adult Development and Aging
ACCA	American College Counseling Association
ACEG	Association for Counselors and Educators in Government
ACES	Association for Counselor Education and Supervision
AHEAD	Association for Humanistic Education and Development
AMCD	Association for Multicultural Counseling and Development
AMHCA	American Mental Health Counselors Association
ARCA	American Rehabilitation Counseling Association
ASCA	American School Counselor Association
ASERVIC	Association for Spiritual, Ethical and Religious Values in Counseling
ASGW	Association for Specialists in Group Work
IAAOC	International Association of Addiction and Offender Counselors
IAMFC	International Association of Marriage and Family Counselors

NCDA National Career Development Association
NECA National Employment Counseling Association

NRA National Rehabilitation Association

Subdivisions of the NRA

NAIL National Association for Independent Living
NAMCRC National Association of Multicultural Rehabilitation Concerns
NARI National Association of Rehabilitation Instructors
NARS National Association of Rehabilitation Secretaries
NASPPR National Association of Service Providers in Private Rehabilitation
NRAA National Rehabilitation Administration Association
NRAJPD National Rehabilitation Association of Job Placement Development
NRCA National Rehabilitation Counseling Association
VEWAA Vocational Evaluation and Work Adjustment Association

Other Organizations

AA Alcoholics Anonymous
AAMFT American Association of Marriage and Family Therapists
ACRM American Congress of Rehabilitation Medicine
ADARA American Deafness and Rehabilitation Association
APA American Psychological Association
Division 17 Rehabilitation Psychology
Division 22 Counseling Psychology
ARA American Rehabilitation Association
ARC Alliance for Rehabilitation Counseling
ARC Association for Retarded Citizens
ASHA American Speech-Hearing Association
BIA Brain Injury Association
CARP Canadian Association of Rehabilitation Personnel
CMSA Case Management Society of America
CSAVR Council of State Administrators of Vocational Rehabilitation
FRER Foundation for Rehabilitation Education and Research

IALCP	International Academy of Life Care Planners
IAPRS	International Association of Psychosocial Rehabilitation Services
NAMI	National Alliance of Mental Illness
NANWRW	National Association of Non-White Rehabilitation Workers
NARPPS	National Association of Rehabilitation Professionals in the Private Sector
NCIL	National Council of Independent Living
NCRE	National Council on Rehabilitation Education
NOD	National Organization on Disability
PVA	Paralyzed Veterans of America
RESNA	Rehabilitation Engineering Society of North America
WHO	World Health Organization

SELECTED JOURNALS

APM&R	*Archives of Physical Medicine and Rehabilitation* (ACRM)
AR	*American Rehabilitation* (RSA)
IJRR	*International Journal of Rehabilitation Research*
ITD	*Information Technology and Disabilities*
JARC	*Journal of Applied Rehabilitation Counseling* (NRCA)
JCD	*Journal of Counseling and Development* (ACA)
JJP	*Journal of Job Placement* (NRAJPD)
JR	*Journal of Rehabilitation* (NRA)
JRA	*Journal of Rehabilitation Administration* (NRAA)
JRRD	*Journal of Rehabilitation Research and Development* (DVA)
JVR	*Journal of Vocational Rehabilitation*
RCB	*Rehabilitation Counseling Bulletin* (ARCA)
RE	*Rehabilitation Education* (NCRE)
Rehab BRIEF	*Bringing Research Into Effective Focus* (NIDRR)
RP	*Rehabilitation Psychologist* (APA Division 17)
VEWA BULLETIN	*Vocational Evaluation and Work Adjustment Bulletin* (VEWAA)
VR&CPR	*Vocational Rehabilitation and Counseling Professional Review*

CERTIFICATION BODIES/CREDENTIALS

AASCB	American Association of State Counselor Licensure Boards
ACS	Approved Clinical Supervisor
CAC	Certified Addictions Counselor
CCM	Certified Case Manager
CCMC	Commission for Case Manager Certification
CCMHC	Certified Clinical Mental Health Counselor
CCRC	Certified Canadian Rehabilitation Counselor
CCWAVES	Commission on Certification of Work Adjustment and Vocational Evaluation Specialists
CDE	Certified Disability Examiner
CIRS	Certified Insurance Rehabilitation Specialists: now known as Certified Disability Management Specialist **(CDMS)**
CIRSC	Certification of Insurance Rehabilitation Specialists Commission: now known as Certification of Disability Management Specialists Commission **(CDMSC)**
COPA	Council on Postsecondary Accreditation
COTA	Certified Occupational Therapy Assistant
CRC	Certified Rehabilitation Counselor
CRCC	Commission for Rehabilitation Counselor Certification
CRC-MAC	Certified Rehabilitation Counselor—Master's in Addiction Counseling
CRRN	Certified Rehabilitation Registered Nurse
CVE	Certified Vocational Evaluator
FACP	Fellow of the American College of Physicians
FACS	Fellow of the American College of Surgeons
LPC	Licensed Professional Counselor
LPCC	Licensed Professional Clinical Counselor
LPMHC	Licensed Professional Mental Health Counselor
MAC	Master Addictions Counselor
NBCC	National Board for Counselor Certification
NCC	National Certified Counselor
NCCC	National Certified Career Counselor
OTR	Registered Occupational Therapist
PT	Physical Therapist
PTA	Physical Therapist Assistant
RPRC	Registered Professional Counselor—California

ACCREDITATION BODIES

CACREP	Commission on the Accreditation of Counseling and Related Educational Programs
CARF	Commission for Accreditation of Rehabilitation Facilities
CLCP	Certified Life Care Planner
CORE	Council on Rehabilitation Education
JCAHO	Joint Commission on the Accreditation of Healthcare Organizations

GOVERNMENTAL/LEGISLATIVE

ABA	Architectural Barriers Act
ADA	Americans with Disabilities Act
ADAAG	Americans with Disabilities Act Accessibility Guidelines
ATBCB	Architectural and Transportation Barriers Compliance Board
CAP	Client Assistance Projects
CDC	Center for Disease Control
CIL	Center for Independent Living
CRA	Civil Rights Act
DBTAC	Disability Business and Technical Assistance Centers
DOE	Department of Education
DOJ	Department of Justice
DOL	Department of Labor
DOT	Department of Transportation
DOT	*Dictionary of Occupational Titles*
DVA	Department of Veterans Affairs
DVR	Division/Department of Vocational Rehabilitation
EEOC	Equal Employment Opportunity Commission
FCC	Federal Communications Commission
GAO	General Accounting Office
GOE	Guide to Occupational Exploration
HEW	Department of Health, Education and Welfare
HHS	Department of Health and Human Services
HUD	Department of Housing and Urban Development
IDEA	Individuals with Disabilities Education Act
IEP	Individual Evaluation/Education Plan
IL	Independent Living

ILR	Independent Living Rehabilitation
ILRU	Independent Living Research Utilization
IWRP	Individual Written Rehabilitation Plan
JAN	Job Accommodations Network
NARIC	National Rehabilitation Information Center
NCD	National Council on Disability
NCHRTM	National Clearinghouse on Rehabilitation Training Materials
NCMRR	National Center for Medical Rehabilitation Research
NIDRR	National Institute on Disability and Rehabilitation Research
NIH	National Institutes of Health
NIMH	National Institute of Mental Health
NOD	National Organization on Disability
OPM	Office of Personnel Management
OSEP	Office of Special Education Programs
OSERS	Office of Special Education and Rehabilitation Services
OSHA	Occupational Health and Safety Administration
PCEPD	President's Commission on the Environment of Persons with Disabilities
PWI	Projects with Industry
QRP	Qualified Rehabilitation Professional
RCEP	Regional Continuing Education Program
R&D	Research and Development
RSA	Rehabilitation Services Administration
RTC	Research and Training Center
SSA	Social Security Administration
SSDI	Social Security Disability Insurance
SSI	Supplemental Security Income
UAF	University Affiliated Facility
VA	Veterans Administration
VBA	Veterans' Benefits Administration
VHA	Veterans' Health Administration
VR&C	Vocational Rehabilitation and Counseling
WID	World Institute on Disability

CANADIAN ACRONYMS

ACW	Accredited Rehabilitation Workers
CARP	Canadian Association of Rehabilitation Professionals

CCA	Canadian Counselling Association
CCC	Canadian Certified Counsellor
CCRC	Canadian Certified Rehabilitation Counsellor
EAPD	Employment Assistance for People with Disabilities
EPF	Federal–Provincial Arrangements and Established Programs Financing Act
HRC	Human Rights Code
ILRC	Independent Living Resource Centres
RRP	Registered Rehabilitation Professional
VRDP	Vocational Rehabilitation of Disabled Persons Act

MISCELLANEOUS

ATI	Attitude–treatment interaction
ATP	Assistive Technology Professional
CAI	Computer-assisted instruction
CEU	Continuing education unit
CLM	Caseload management
DD	Developmental disability
DSM-IV	Diagnostic and Statistical Manual—4th ed.
EAP	Employee Assistance Program
EASI	Equal Access to Software and Information
ICD	International Center for Disability
ITV	Interactive television
LDL	Long-distance learning
LTD	Long-term disability
OJE	On-the-job evaluation
OJT	On-the-job training
PDR	*Physician's Desk Reference*
RCE	Rehabilitation counselor education
RCT	Rehabilitation counselor training
RFP	Request for proposals
RTW	Return to work
SGA	Substantial gainful activity
TDD	Telecommunication Devices for the Deaf
TTY	Teletypewriters
VDARE	Vocational Diagnosis and Assessment of Residual Employability
VE	Vocational Experts

APPENDIX **B**

Scope of Practice for Rehabilitation Counseling

I. ASSUMPTION

1. The Scope of Practice Statement identifies knowledge and skills required for the provision of effective rehabilitation counseling services to persons with physical, mental, developmental, cognitive, and emotional disabilities as embodied in the standards of the profession's credentialing organizations.
2. The several rehabilitation disciplines and related processes (e.g., vocational evaluation, job development and job placement, work adjustment, case management) are tied to the central field of rehabilitation counseling. The field of rehabilitation counseling is a specialty within the rehabilitation profession, with counseling at its core, and is differentiated from other related counseling fields.
3. The professional scope of rehabilitation counseling practice is also differentiated from an individual scope of practice, which may overlap, but is more specialized than the professional scope. An individual scope of practice is based on one's own knowledge of the abilities and skills that have been gained through a program of education and professional experience. A person is ethically bound to limit his/her practice to that individual scope of practice.

II. UNDERLYING VALUES

1. Facilitation of independence, integration, and inclusion of people with disabilities in employment and the community.
2. Belief in the dignity and worth of all people.
3. Commitment to a sense of equal justice based on a model of accommodation to provide and equalize the opportunities to participate in all rights and privileges available to all people; and a commitment to supporting persons with disabilities in advocacy activities to enable them to achieve this status and empower themselves.
4. Emphasis on the holistic nature of human function, which is procedurally facilitated by the utilization of such techniques as:

   - interdisciplinary teamwork;
   - counseling to assist in maintaining a holistic perspective;
   - a commitment to counseling individuals within the context of their family systems and communities.

5. Recognition of the importance of focusing on the assets of the person.
6. Commitment to models of service delivery that emphasize integrated, comprehensive services which are mutually planned by the consumer and the rehabilitation counselor.

III. SCOPE OF PRACTICE STATEMENT

Rehabilitation counseling is a systematic process that assists persons with physical, mental, developmental, cognitive, and emotional disabilities to achieve their personal, career, and independent-living goals in the most integrated setting possible, through the application of the counseling process. The counseling process involves communication, goal setting, and beneficial growth or change through self-advocacy, psychological, vocational, social, and behavioral interventions. The specific techniques and modalities used within this rehabilitation counseling process may include, but are not limited to:

assessment and appraisal;

diagnosis and treatment planning;

career (vocational) counseling;

individual and group counseling treatment interventions focused on facilitating adjustments to the medical and psychosocial impact of disability;

case management, referral, and service coordination;

program evaluation and research;

interventions to remove environmental, employment, and attitudinal barriers;

consultation services among multiple parties and regulatory systems;

job analysis, job development, and placement services, including assistance with employment and job accommodations; and

the provision of consultation about, and access to, rehabilitation technology.

IV. SELECTED DEFINITIONS

The following definitions are provided to increase the understanding of certain key terms and concepts used in the Scope of Practice Statement for Rehabilitation Counseling.

Appraisal: Selecting, administering, scoring, and interpreting instruments designed to assess an individual's attitudes, abilities, achievements, interests, personal characteristics, disabilities, and mental, emotional, or behavioral disorders, as well as the use of methods and techniques for understanding human behavior in relation to coping with, adapting to, or changing life situations.

Diagnosis and Treatment Planning: Assessing, analyzing, and providing diagnostic descriptions of mental, emotional, or behavioral conditions or disabilities; exploring possible solutions; and developing and implementing a treatment plan for mental, emotional, and psychosocial adjustment or development. Diagnosis and treatment planning shall not be construed to permit the performance of any act that rehabilitation counselors are not educated and trained to perform.

Counseling Treatment Intervention: The application of cognitive, affective, behavioral, and systemic counseling strategies, which include developmental, wellness, pathologic, and multicultural principles of human behavior. Such interventions are specifically implemented in the context of a professional counseling relationship and may include, but are not limited to: appraisal; individual, group, marriage, and family counseling and psychotherapy; the diagnostic description and treatment of persons with mental, emotional, and behavioral disorders or disabilities; guidance and consulting to facilitate normal growth and development, including educational and career development; the utilization of functional assessments and career counseling for persons requesting assistance in adjusting to a disability or handicapping condition; referrals; consulting; and research.

Referral: Evaluating and identifying the needs of a counselee to determine the advisability of referrals to other specialists, advising the counselee of such judgments, and communicating as requested or deemed appropriate to such referral sources.

Case Management: A systematic process merging counseling and managerial concepts and skills, through the application of techniques derived from intuitive and researched methods, thereby advancing efficient and effective decision making for functional control of self, client, setting, and other relevant factors for anchoring a proactive practice. In case management, the counselor's role is focused on interviewing, counseling, planning rehabilitation programs, coordinating services, interacting with significant others, placing clients and following up with them, monitoring a client's progress, and solving problems.

Program Evaluation: The effort to determine what changes occur as a result of a planned program, by comparing actual changes (results) with desired changes (stated goals), and by identifying the degree to which the activity (planned program) is responsible for those changes.

Research: A systematic effort to collect, analyze, and interpret quantitative or qualitative data that describe how social characteristics, behavior, emotions, cognition, disabilities, mental disorders, and interpersonal transactions among individuals and organizations interact.

Consultation: The application of scientific principles and procedures in counseling and human development to provide assistance in understanding and solving current or potential problems that the consultee may have in relation to a third party, be it an individual, group, or organization.

APPENDIX **C**

Code of Professional Ethics for Rehabilitation Counselors

Adopted in June 2001 by the
Commission on Rehabilitation Counselor Certification
for its Certified Rehabilitation Counselors.
This Code is effective as of January 1, 2002.

Developed and Administered by the
Commission on Rehabilitation Counselor Certification
(CRCC®)
1835 Rohlwing Road, Suite E
Rolling Meadows, Illinois 60008
(847) 394-2104
http://www.crccertification.com

PREAMBLE

Rehabilitation counselors are committed to facilitating the personal, social, and economic independence of individuals with disabilities. In fulfilling this commitment, rehabilitation counselors work with people, programs, institutions, and service delivery systems. Rehabilitation counselors provide services within the Scope of Practice for Rehabilitation Counseling (see the Scope of Practice document) and recognize that both action and inaction can be facilitating or debilitating. It is essential that rehabilitation counselors demonstrate adherence to ethical standards and ensure that the standards are enforced vigorously. The Code of Professional Ethics for Rehabilitation Counselors, henceforth referred to as the Code, is designed to facilitate these goals.

The fundamental spirit of caring and respect with which the Code is written is based upon five principles of ethical behavior.[1] These include autonomy, beneficence, nonmaleficence, justice, and fidelity, as defined below:

Autonomy: To honor the right to make individual decisions.
Beneficence: To do good to others. Nonmaleficence: To do no harm to others.
Justice: To be fair and give equally to others.
Fidelity: To be loyal, honest, and keep promises.

The primary obligation of rehabilitation counselors is to their clients, defined in the Code as individuals with disabilities who are receiving services from rehabilitation counselors. Regardless of whether direct client contact occurs or whether indirect services are provided, rehabilitation counselors are obligated to adhere to the Code. At times, rehabilitation counseling services may be provided to individuals other than those with disabilities, such as a student population. In all instances, the primary obligation remains with the client and adherence to the Code is required.

The basic objective of the Code is to promote public welfare by specifying ethical behavior expected of rehabilitation counselors. The Enforceable Standards within the Code are the exacting standards intended to provide guidance in specific circumstances and will serve as the basis for processing ethical complaints initiated against certificants.

Rehabilitation counselors who violate the Code are subject to disciplinary action. Since the use of the Certified Rehabilitation Counselor (CRC®) designation is a privilege granted by the Commission on Rehabilitation Coun-

---

[1]Beauchamp, T. L., & Childress, J. F. (1994), 4th Ed. *Principles of biomedical ethics.* Oxford: Oxford University Press. Kitchener, K. S. (1984). Ethics in counseling psychology: Distinctions and directions. *Counseling Psychologists, 12*(3), 43–55.

selor Certification (CRCC®), CRCC reserves unto itself the power to suspend or to revoke the privilege or to approve other penalties for a violation. Disciplinary penalties are imposed as warranted by the severity of the offense and its attendant circumstances. All disciplinary actions are undertaken in accordance with published procedures and penalties designed to assure the proper enforcement of the Code within the framework of due process and equal protection under the law.

ENFORCEABLE STANDARDS OF ETHICAL PRACTICE

SECTION A: THE COUNSELING RELATIONSHIP

A.1. CLIENT WELFARE

a. **DEFINITION OF CLIENT.** The primary obligation of rehabilitation counselors will be to their clients, defined as individuals with disabilities who are receiving services from rehabilitation counselors.

b. **REHABILITATION AND COUNSELING PLANS.** Rehabilitation counselors will work jointly with their clients in devising and revising integrated, individual rehabilitation and counseling plans that contain realistic and mutually agreed upon goals and are consistent with abilities and circumstances of clients.

c. **CAREER AND EMPLOYMENT NEEDS.** Rehabilitation counselors will work with their clients in considering employment that is consistent with the overall abilities, vocational limitations, physical restrictions, psychological limitations, general temperament, interest and aptitude patterns, social skills, education, general qualifications, and cultural and other relevant characteristics and needs of clients. Rehabilitation counselors will neither place nor participate in placing clients in positions that will result in damaging the interest and the welfare of clients, employers, or the public.

d. **AUTONOMY.** Rehabilitation counselors will respect the autonomy of the client if actions such as involuntary commitment or initiation of guardianship are taken that diminish client autonomy. The assumption of responsibility for decision-making on behalf of the client will be taken only after careful deliberation. The rehabilitation counselor will advocate for client resumption of responsibility as quickly as possible.

A.2. RESPECTING DIVERSITY

a. **RESPECTING CULTURE.** Rehabilitation counselors will demonstrate respect for clients' cultural backgrounds.

b. **INTERVENTIONS.** Rehabilitation counselors will develop and adapt interventions and services to incorporate consideration of clients' cultural perspectives and recognition of barriers external to clients that may interfere with achieving effective rehabilitation outcomes.

c. **NON-DISCRIMINATION.** Rehabilitation counselors will not condone or engage in discrimination based on age, color, culture, disability, ethnic group, gender, race, religion, sexual orientation, marital status, or socioeconomic status.

A.3. CLIENT RIGHTS

a. **DISCLOSURE TO CLIENTS.** When counseling is initiated, and throughout the counseling process as necessary, rehabilitation counselors will inform clients, preferably through both written and oral means, of their credentials, the purposes, goals, techniques, procedures, limitations, potential risks, and benefits of services to be performed, and other pertinent information. Rehabilitation counselors will take steps to ensure that clients understand the implications of diagnosis, the intended use of tests and reports, fees, and billing arrangements. Clients have the right to (1) expect confidentiality and will be provided with an explanation of its limitations, including disclosure to supervisors and/or treatment team professionals; (2) obtain clear information about their case records; (3) actively participate in the development and implementation of rehabilitation counseling plans; and (4) refuse any recommended services and be advised of the consequences of such refusal.

b. **THIRD PARTY REFERRAL.** Rehabilitation counselors who have direct contact with a client at the request of a third party will define the nature of their relationships and role to all rightful, legal parties with whom they have direct contact. Direct contact is defined as any written, oral, or electronic communication. Legal parties may include clients, legal guardians, referring third parties, and attorneys actively involved in a matter directly related to rehabilitation services.

c. **INDIRECT SERVICE PROVISION.** Rehabilitation counselors who are employed by third parties as case consultants or expert witnesses, and who engage in communication with the individual with a disability, will fully disclose to the individual with a disability and/or his or her designee their role and limits of their relationship. Communication includes all forms of written or oral interactions regardless of the type of communication tool used. When there is no pretense or intent to provide rehabilitation counseling services directly to the individual with a disability, and where there will be no communication, disclosure by the rehabilitation counselor is not required. When serving as case consultants or expert witnesses, rehabilitation counselors will provide unbiased, objective opinions. Rehabilitation counselors acting as expert witnesses will generate written documentation, either in the form of case notes or a report, as to their involvement and/or conclusions.

d. **FREEDOM OF CHOICE.** To the extent possible, rehabilitation counselors will offer clients the freedom to choose whether to enter into a counseling relationship and to determine which professional(s) will provide counseling. Restrictions that limit choices of clients will be fully explained. Rehabilitation counselors will honor the rights of clients to consent to participate and the right to make decisions with regard to rehabilitation services. Rehabilitation counselors will inform clients or the clients' legal guardians of factors that may affect decisions to participate in rehabilitation services, and they will obtain written consent or will acknowledge consent in writing after clients or legal guardians are fully informed of such factors.

e. **INABILITY TO GIVE CONSENT.** When counseling minors or persons unable to give voluntary informed consent, rehabilitation counselors will obtain written informed consent from legally responsible parties. Where no legally responsible parties exist, rehabilitation counselors will act in the best interest of clients.

f. **INVOLVEMENT OF SIGNIFICANT OTHERS.** Rehabilitation counselors will attempt to enlist family understanding and involvement of family and/or significant others as a positive resource if (or when) appropriate. The client or legal guardian's permission will be secured prior to any involvement of family and/or significant others.

A.4. PERSONAL NEEDS AND VALUES

In the counseling relationship, rehabilitation counselors will be aware of the intimacy and responsibilities inherent in the counseling relationship, maintain respect for clients, and avoid actions that seek to meet their personal needs at the expense of clients.

A.5. SEXUAL INTIMACIES WITH CLIENTS

a. **CURRENT CLIENTS.** Rehabilitation counselors will not have any type of sexual intimacies with clients and will not counsel persons with whom they have had a sexual relationship.

b. **FORMER CLIENTS.** Rehabilitation counselors will not engage in sexual intimacies with former clients within a minimum of 5 years after terminating the counseling relationship. Rehabilitation counselors who engage in such relationship after 5 years following termination will have the responsibility to examine and document thoroughly that such relations do not have an exploitative nature, based on factors such as duration of counseling, amount of time since counseling, termination circumstances, client's personal history and mental status, adverse impact on the client, and actions by the counselor suggesting a plan to initiate a sexual relationship with the client after termination. Rehabilitation counselors will seek peer consultation prior to engaging in a sexual relationship with a former client.

A.6. NON-PROFESSIONAL RELATIONSHIPS WITH CLIENTS

a. **POTENTIAL FOR HARM.** Rehabilitation counselors will be aware of their influential positions with respect to clients, and will avoid exploiting the trust and dependency of clients. Rehabilitation counselors will make every effort to avoid non-professional relationships with clients that could impair professional judgment or increase the risk of harm to clients. (Examples of such relationships include, but are not limited to, familial, social, financial, business, close personal relationships with clients, or volunteer or paid work within an office in which the client is actively receiving services.) When a non-professional relationship cannot be avoided, rehabilitation counselors will take appropriate professional precautions such as informed consent, consultation, supervision, and documentation to ensure that judgment is not impaired and no exploitation occurs.

b. **SUPERIOR/SUBORDINATE RELATIONSHIPS.** Rehabilitation counselors will not accept as clients, superiors or subordinates with whom they have administrative, supervisory, or evaluative relationships.

A.7. MULTIPLE CLIENTS

When rehabilitation counselors agree to provide counseling services to two or more persons who have a relationship (such as husband and wife, or parents and children), rehabilitation counselors will clarify at the outset, which person or persons are clients and the nature of the relationships they will have with each involved person. If it becomes apparent that rehabilitation counselors may be called upon to perform potentially conflicting roles, they will clarify, adjust, or withdraw from such roles appropriately.

A.8. GROUP WORK

a. **SCREENING.** Rehabilitation counselors will screen prospective group counseling/therapy participants. To the extent possible, rehabilitation counselors will select members whose needs and goals are compatible with goals of the group, who will not impede the group process, and whose well being will not be jeopardized by the group experience.

b. **PROTECTING CLIENTS.** In a group setting, rehabilitation counselors will take reasonable precautions to protect clients from physical or psychological trauma.

A.9. TERMINATION AND REFERRAL

a. **ABANDONMENT PROHIBITED.** Rehabilitation counselors will not abandon or neglect clients in counseling. Rehabilitation counselors will assist in making appropriate arrangements for the continuation of treatment, when necessary, during interruptions such as vacations, and following termination.

b. **INABILITY TO ASSIST CLIENTS.** If rehabilitation counselors determine an inability to be of professional assistance to clients, they will avoid entering or immediately terminate a counseling relationship.

c. **APPROPRIATE TERMINATION.** Rehabilitation counselors will terminate a counseling relationship, securing client agreement when possible, when it is reasonably clear that the client is no longer benefiting, when services are no longer required, when counseling no longer serves the client's needs or interests, or when there is failure to pay fees according to Section J of this document.

d. **REFERRAL UPON TERMINATION.** Rehabilitation counselors will be knowledgeable about referral resources and suggest appropriate alternatives. If clients decline the suggested referral, rehabilitation counselors have the right to discontinue the relationship.

A.10. COMPUTER TECHNOLOGY

a. **USE OF COMPUTERS.** When computer applications are used in counseling services, rehabilitation counselors will ensure that (1) the client is intellectually, emotionally, and physically capable of using the computer application; (2) the computer application is appropriate for the needs of the client; (3) the client understands the purpose and operation of the computer applications; and (4) a follow-up of client use of a computer application is provided to correct possible misconceptions, discover inappropriate use, and assess subsequent needs.

b. **EXPLANATION OF LIMITATIONS.** Rehabilitation counselors will ensure that clients are provided information as a part of the counseling relationship that adequately explains the limitations of computer technology.

c. **ACCESS TO COMPUTER APPLICATIONS.** Rehabilitation counselors will provide reasonable access to computer applications in counseling services.

SECTION B: CONFIDENTIALITY

B.1. RIGHT TO PRIVACY

a. **RESPECT FOR PRIVACY.** Rehabilitation counselors will respect clients' rights to privacy and will avoid illegal and unwarranted disclosures of confidential information.

b. **CLIENT WAIVER.** Rehabilitation counselors will respect the right of the client or his/her legally recognized representative to waive the right to privacy.

c. **EXCEPTIONS.** When disclosure is required to prevent clear and imminent danger to the client or others, or when legal requirements demand that confidential information be revealed, the general requirement that rehabilitation counselors keep information confidential will not apply. Rehabilitation counselors will consult with other professionals when in doubt as to the validity of an exception.

d. **CONTAGIOUS, FATAL DISEASES.** Rehabilitation counselors will become aware of the legal requirements for disclosure of contagious and fatal diseases in their jurisdiction. In jurisdictions where allowable, a rehabilitation counselor who receives information will confirm that a client has a disease known to be communicable and/or fatal. If allowable by law, the rehabilitation counselor will disclose this information to a third party, who by his or her relationship with the client is at high risk of contracting the disease. Prior to disclosure, the rehabilitation counselor will ascertain that the client has not already informed the third party about his or her disease and that the client is not intending to inform the third party in the immediate future.

e. **COURT-ORDERED DISCLOSURE.** When court ordered to release confidential information without a client's permission, rehabilitation counselors will request to the court that the disclosure not be required due to potential harm to the client or counseling relationship.

f. **MINIMAL DISCLOSURE.** When circumstances require the disclosure of confidential information, rehabilitation counselors will endeavor to reveal only essential information. To the extent possible, clients will be informed before confidential information is disclosed.

g. **EXPLANATION OF LIMITATIONS.** When counseling is initiated and throughout the counseling process as necessary, rehabilitation counselors will inform clients of the limitations of confidentiality and will identify foreseeable situations in which confidentiality must be breached.

h. **WORK ENVIRONMENT.** Rehabilitation counselors will make every effort to ensure that a confidential work environment exists and that subordinates including employees, supervisees, clerical assistants, and volunteers maintain the privacy and confidentiality of clients.

i. **TREATMENT TEAMS.** If client treatment will involve the sharing of client information among treatment team members, the client will be advised of this fact and will be informed of the team's existence and composition.

j. **CLIENT ASSISTANTS.** When a client is accompanied by an individual providing assistance to the client (e.g., interpreter, personal care assistant, etc.), rehabilitation counselors will ensure that the assistant is apprised of the need to maintain confidentiality.

B.2. GROUPS AND FAMILIES

a. **GROUP WORK.** In group work, rehabilitation counselors will clearly define confidentiality and the parameters for the specific group being entered, explain its importance, and discuss the difficulties related to confidentiality involved in group work. The fact that confidentiality cannot be guaranteed will be clearly communicated to group members.

b. **FAMILY COUNSELING.** In family counseling, unless otherwise directed by law, information about one family member will not be disclosed to another member without permission. Rehabilitation counselors will protect the privacy rights of each family member.

B.3. RECORDS

a. **REQUIREMENT OF RECORDS.** Rehabilitation counselors will maintain records necessary for rendering professional services to their clients and as required by laws, regulations, or agency or institution procedures.

b. **CONFIDENTIALITY OF RECORDS.** Rehabilitation counselors will be responsible for securing the safety and confidentiality of any counseling records they create, maintain, transfer, or destroy whether the records are written, taped, computerized, or stored in any other medium.

c. **PERMISSION TO RECORD OR OBSERVE.** Rehabilitation counselors will obtain and document written or recorded permission from clients prior to electronically recording or observing sessions. When counseling clients who are minors or individuals who are unable to give voluntary, informed consent, written or recorded permission of guardians must be obtained.

d. **CLIENT ACCESS.** Rehabilitation counselors will recognize that counseling records are kept for the benefit of clients, and therefore provide access to records and copies of records when requested by clients, unless prohibited by law. In instances where the records contain information that may be sensitive or detrimental to the client, the rehabilitation counselor has a responsibility to adequately interpret such information to the client. In situations involving multiple clients, access to records will be limited to those parts of records that do not include confidential information related to another client.

e. **DISCLOSURE OR TRANSFER.** Rehabilitation counselors will obtain written permission from clients to disclose or transfer records to legitimate third parties unless exceptions to confidentiality exist as listed in Section B.1.

B.4. CONSULTATION

a. **RESPECT FOR PRIVACY.** Information obtained in a consulting relationship will be discussed for professional purposes only with persons clearly concerned with the case. Written and oral reports will present data germane to the purposes of the consultation, and every effort will be made to protect client identity and to avoid undue invasion of privacy.

b. **COOPERATING AGENCIES.** Before sharing information, rehabilitation counselors will make efforts to ensure that there are defined policies in other agencies serving the counselor's clients that effectively protect the confidentiality of information.

B.5. ALTERNATIVE COMMUNICATION

Rehabilitation counselors will make every effort to ensure that methods of exchanging information that utilize alternative means of communication (i.e., facsimile, cellular telephone, computer, or videoconferencing) will be conducted in such a manner that ensures protection of client confidentiality. If confidentiality cannot be ensured, client or guardian permission must be obtained.

SECTION C: ADVOCACY AND ACCESSIBILITY

C.1. ADVOCACY

a. **ATTITUDINAL BARRIERS.** Rehabilitation counselors will strive to eliminate attitudinal barriers, including stereotyping and discrimination, toward individuals with disabilities and to increase their own awareness and sensitivity to such individuals.

b. **ADVOCACY WITH COOPERATING AGENCIES.** Rehabilitation counselors will remain aware of actions taken by cooperating agencies on behalf of their clients and will act as advocates of such clients to ensure effective service delivery.

c. **EMPOWERMENT.** Rehabilitation counselors will provide the client with appropriate information and will support their efforts at self-advocacy both on an individual and an organizational level.

C.2. ACCESSIBILITY

a. **COUNSELING PRACTICE.** Rehabilitation counselors will demonstrate, in their practice, an appreciation of the need to provide necessary accommodations, including accessible facilities and services, to individuals with disabilities.

b. **BARRIERS TO ACCESS.** Rehabilitation counselors will identify physical, communication, and transportation barriers to clients and will communicate information on barriers to public and private authorities to facilitate removal of barriers to access.

c. **REFERRAL ACCESSIBILITY.** Rehabilitation counselors, as advocates for individuals with disabilities, will ensure, prior to referring clients to programs, facilities, or employment settings, that they are appropriately accessible.

SECTION D: PROFESSIONAL RESPONSIBILITY

D.1. PROFESSIONAL COMPETENCE

a. **BOUNDARIES OF COMPETENCE.** Rehabilitation counselors will practice only within the boundaries of their competence, based on their education, training, supervised experience, state and national professional credentials, and appropriate professional experience. Rehabilitation counselors will demonstrate a commitment to gain knowledge, personal awareness, sensitivity, and skills pertinent to working with a diverse client population. Rehabilitation counselors will not misrepresent their role or competence to clients.

b. **REFERRAL.** Rehabilitation counselors will refer clients to other specialists as the needs of the clients dictate.

c. **NEW SPECIALTY AREAS OF PRACTICE.** Rehabilitation counselors will practice in specialty areas new to them only after appropriate education, training, and supervised experience. While developing skills in new specialty areas, rehabilitation counselors will take steps to ensure the competence of their work and to protect clients from possible harm.

d. **RESOURCES.** Rehabilitation counselors will ensure that the resources used or accessed in counseling are credible and valid (e.g., web link, books used in Bibliotherapy, etc.).

e. **QUALIFIED FOR EMPLOYMENT.** Rehabilitation counselors will accept employment only for positions for which they are qualified by education, training, supervised experience, state and national professional credentials, and appropriate professional experience. Rehabilitation counselors will hire only individuals who are qualified and competent for professional rehabilitation counseling positions.

f. **MONITOR EFFECTIVENESS.** Rehabilitation counselors will take reasonable steps to seek peer supervision to evaluate their efficacy as rehabilitation counselors.

g. **ETHICAL ISSUES CONSULTATION.** Rehabilitation counselors will take reasonable steps to consult with other rehabilitation counselors or related professionals when they have questions regarding their ethical obligations or professional practice.

h. **CONTINUING EDUCATION.** Rehabilitation counselors will engage in continuing education to maintain a reasonable level of awareness of current scientific and professional information in their fields of activity. They will take steps to maintain competence in the skills they use, will be open to new techniques, and will develop and maintain competence for practice with the diverse and/or special populations with whom they work.

i. **IMPAIRMENT.** Rehabilitation counselors will refrain from offering or rendering professional services when their physical, mental, or emotional problems are likely to harm the client or others. They will seek assistance for problems, and, if necessary, will limit, suspend, or terminate their professional responsibilities.

D.2. LEGAL STANDARDS

a. **LEGAL VERSUS ETHICAL.** Rehabilitation counselors will obey the laws and statutes of the legal jurisdiction in which they practice unless there is a conflict with the Code, in which case they should seek immediate consultation and advice.

b. **LEGAL LIMITATIONS.** Rehabilitation counselors will be familiar with and observe the legal limitations of the services they offer to clients. They will discuss these limitations as well as all benefits available to clients they serve in order to facilitate open, honest communication and avoid unrealistic expectations.

D.3. ADVERTISING AND SOLICITING CLIENTS

a. **ACCURATE ADVERTISING.** Advertising by rehabilitation counselors shall not be restricted. Rehabilitation counselors will advertise or will represent their services to the public by identifying their credentials in an accurate manner that is not false, misleading, deceptive, or fraudulent. Rehabilitation counselors will only advertise the highest degree earned which is in counseling or a closely related field from a college or university that was accredited when the degree was awarded by one of the regional accrediting bodies recognized by the Council on Higher Education Accreditation.

b. **TESTIMONIALS.** Rehabilitation counselors who use testimonials will not solicit them from clients or other persons who, because of their particular circumstances, may be vulnerable to undue influence. Full disclosure of uses and the informed consent of the client or guardian will be obtained. Use of testimonials will be for a specified and agreed upon period of time.

c. **STATEMENTS BY OTHERS.** Rehabilitation counselors will make reasonable efforts to ensure that statements made by others about them or the profession of rehabilitation counseling are accurate.

d. **RECRUITING THROUGH EMPLOYMENT.** Employed rehabilitation counselors will not use their institutional affiliations or relationship with their employers to recruit clients, supervisees, or consultees for their separate private practices.

e. **PRODUCTS AND TRAINING ADVERTISEMENTS.** Rehabilitation counselors who develop products related to their profession or conduct workshops or training events will ensure that the advertisements concerning these products or events are accurate and disclose adequate information for consumers to make informed choices.

f. **PROMOTING TO THOSE SERVED.** Rehabilitation counselors will not use counseling, teaching, training, or supervisory relationships to promote their products or training events in a manner that is deceptive or would exert undue influence on individuals who may be vulnerable. Rehabilitation counselors may adopt textbooks they have authored for instructional purposes.

D.4. CREDENTIALS

a. **CREDENTIALS CLAIMED.** Rehabilitation counselors will claim or will imply only professional credentials possessed and are responsible for correcting any known misrepresentations of their credentials by others. Professional credentials include graduate degrees in counseling or closely related fields, accreditation of graduate programs, national voluntary certifications, government-issued certifications or licenses, or any other credential that might indicate to the public specialized knowledge or expertise in counseling.

b. **CREDENTIAL GUIDELINES.** Rehabilitation counselors will follow the guidelines for use of credentials that have been established by the entities that issue the credentials.

c. **MISREPRESENTATION OF CREDENTIALS.** Rehabilitation counselors will not attribute more to their credentials than the credentials represent, and will not imply that other rehabilitation counselors are not qualified because they do not possess certain credentials.

d. **DOCTORAL DEGREES FROM OTHER FIELDS.** Rehabilitation counselors who hold a master's degree in counseling or a closely related field, but hold a doctoral degree from other than counseling or a closely related field, will not use the title "Dr." in their practices and will not announce to the public in relation to their practice or status as a rehabilitation counselor that they hold a doctorate.

D.5. CRC CREDENTIAL

a. **ACTING ON BEHALF OF CRCC.** Certified Rehabilitation Counselors will not write, speak, nor act in ways that lead others to believe the counselor is officially representing CRCC unless the Commission has granted permission in writing.

b. **SUPPORT OF CANDIDATES.** Certified Rehabilitation Counselors will not initiate or support the candidacy of an individual for certification by CRCC if the individual is known to engage in professional practices that violate the Code of Professional Ethics for Rehabilitation Counselors.

D.6. PUBLIC RESPONSIBILITY

a. **SEXUAL HARASSMENT.** Rehabilitation counselors will not engage in sexual harassment. Sexual harassment is defined as sexual solicitation, physical advances, or verbal or nonverbal conduct that is sexual in nature, that occurs in connection with professional activities or roles, and that either (1) the rehabilitation counselor knows or is told the act is unwelcome, offensive, or creates a hostile workplace environment; or (2) is sufficiently severe or intense to be perceived as harassment to a reasonable person within the context in which it occurs. Sexual harassment may consist of a single intense or severe act or multiple persistent or pervasive acts.

b. **REPORTS TO THIRD PARTIES.** Rehabilitation counselors will be accurate, timely, and objective in reporting their professional activities and opinions to appropriate third parties including courts, health insurance companies, those who are the recipients of evaluation reports, and others.

c. **MEDIA PRESENTATIONS.** When rehabilitation counselors provide advice or comment by means of public lectures, demonstrations, radio or television programs, prerecorded tapes, printed articles, mailed material, or other media, they will take reasonable precautions to ensure that (1) the statements are based on appropriate professional counseling literature and practice; (2) the statements are otherwise consistent with the Code of Professional Ethics for Rehabilitation Counselors; and (3) the recipients of the information are not encouraged to infer that a professional rehabilitation counseling relationship has been established.

d. **CONFLICTS OF INTEREST.** Rehabilitation counselors will not use their professional positions to seek or receive unjustified personal gains, sexual favors, unfair advantage, or unearned goods or services.

e. **DISHONESTY.** Rehabilitation counselors will not engage in any act or omission of a dishonest, deceitful or fraudulent nature in the conduct of their professional activities.

D.7. RESPONSIBILITY TO OTHER PROFESSIONALS

a. **DISPARAGING COMMENTS.** Rehabilitation counselors will not discuss in a disparaging way the competency of other professionals or agencies, or the findings made, the methods used, or the quality of rehabilitation plans.

b. **PERSONAL PUBLIC STATEMENTS.** When making personal statements in a public context, rehabilitation counselors will clarify that they are speaking from their personal perspectives and that they are not speaking on behalf of all rehabilitation counselors or the profession.

c. **CLIENTS SERVED BY OTHERS.** When rehabilitation counselors learn that their clients have an ongoing professional relationship with another rehabilitation or treating professional, they will request release from clients to inform the other professionals and strive to establish positive and collaborative professional relationships. File reviews, second-opinion services, and other indirect services are not considered ongoing professional services.

SECTION E: RELATIONSHIPS WITH OTHER PROFESSIONALS

E.1. RELATIONSHIPS WITH EMPLOYERS AND EMPLOYEES

a. **NEGATIVE CONDITIONS.** Rehabilitation counselors will alert their employers to conditions that may be potentially disruptive or damaging to the counselor's professional responsibilities or that may limit their effectiveness.

b. **EVALUATION.** Rehabilitation counselors will submit regularly to professional review and evaluation by their supervisor or the appropriate representative of the employer.

c. **DISCRIMINATION.** Rehabilitation counselors, as either employers or employees, will engage in fair practices with regard to hiring, promotion, or training.

d. **EXPLOITATIVE RELATIONSHIPS.** Rehabilitation counselors will not engage in exploitative relationships with individuals over whom they have supervisory, evaluative, or instructional control or authority.

e. **EMPLOYER POLICIES.** In those instances where rehabilitation counselors are critical of policies, they will attempt to affect change through constructive action within the organization. Where such change cannot be affected, rehabilitation counselors will take appropriate further action. Such action may include referral to appropriate certification, accreditation, or state licensure organizations or termination of employment.

E.2. CONSULTATION

a. **CONSULTATION AS AN OPTION.** Rehabilitation counselors may choose to consult with professionally competent persons about their clients. In choosing consultants, rehabilitation counselors will avoid placing the consultant in a conflict of interest situation that will preclude the consultant from being a proper party to the counselor's efforts to help the client. If rehabilitation counselors are engaged in a work setting that compromises this consultation standard, they will consult with other professionals whenever possible to consider justifiable alternatives.

b. **CONSULTANT COMPETENCY.** Rehabilitation counselors will be reasonably certain that they have, or the organization represented has, the necessary competencies and resources for giving the kind of consulting services needed and that appropriate referral resources are available.

E.3. AGENCY AND TEAM RELATIONSHIPS

a. **CLIENT AS A TEAM MEMBER.** Rehabilitation counselors will ensure that clients and/or their legally recognized representative are afforded the opportunity for full participation in their own treatment team.

b. **COMMUNICATION.** Rehabilitation counselors will ensure that there is fair mutual understanding of the rehabilitation plan by all agencies cooperating in the rehabilitation of clients and that any rehabilitation plan is developed with such mutual understanding.

c. **DISSENT.** Rehabilitation counselors will abide by and help to implement team decisions in formulating rehabilitation plans and procedures, even when not personally agreeing with such decisions, unless these decisions breach the Code.

d. **REPORTS.** Rehabilitation counselors will attempt to secure from other specialists appropriate reports and evaluations, when such reports are essential for rehabilitation planning and/or service delivery.

SECTION F: EVALUATION, ASSESSMENT, AND INTERPRETATION

F.1. INFORMED CONSENT

a. **EXPLANATION TO CLIENTS.** Prior to assessment, rehabilitation counselors will explain the nature and purposes of assessment and the specific use of results in language the client (or other legally authorized person on behalf of the client) can understand. Regardless of whether scoring and interpretation are completed by rehabilitation counselors, by assistants, or by computer or other outside services, rehabilitation counselors will take reasonable steps to ensure that appropriate explanations are given to the client.

b. **RECIPIENTS OF RESULTS.** The client's welfare, explicit understanding, and prior agreement will determine the recipients of test results. Rehabilitation counselors will include accurate and appropriate interpretations with any release of test results.

F.2. RELEASE OF INFORMATION TO COMPETENT PROFESSIONALS

a. **MISUSE OF RESULTS.** Rehabilitation counselors will not misuse assessment results, including test results and interpretations, and will take reasonable steps to prevent the misuse of such by others.

b. **RELEASE OF RAW DATA.** Rehabilitation counselors will ordinarily release data (e.g., protocols, counseling or interview notes, or questionnaires) in which the client is identified only with the consent of the client or the client's legal representative. Such data will be released only to persons recognized by rehabilitation counselors as competent to interpret the data.

F.3. RESEARCH AND TRAINING

a. **DATA DISGUISE REQUIRED.** Use of data derived from counseling relationships for purposes of training, research, or publication will be confined to content that is disguised to ensure the anonymity of the individuals involved.

b. **AGREEMENT FOR IDENTIFICATION.** Identification of a client in a presentation or publication will be permissible only when the client has agreed in writing to its presentation or publication.

F.4. PROPER DIAGNOSIS OF MENTAL DISORDERS

a. **PROPER DIAGNOSIS.** Rehabilitation counselors qualified to provide proper diagnosis of mental disorders will take special care when doing so. Assessment techniques (including personal interview) used to determine client care (e.g., locus of treatment, type of treatment, or recommended follow-up) will be carefully selected and appropriately used.

b. **CULTURAL SENSITIVITY.** Disability, socioeconomic, and cultural experience of clients will be considered when diagnosing mental disorders.

F.5. COMPETENCE TO USE AND INTERPRET TESTS

a. **LIMITS OF COMPETENCE.** Rehabilitation counselors will recognize the limits of their competence and perform only those testing and assessment services for which they have been trained. They will be familiar with reliability, validity, related standardization, error of measurement, and proper application of any technique utilized. Rehabilitation counselors using computer-based test interpretations will be trained in the construct being measured and the specific instrument being used prior to using this type of computer application. Rehabilitation counselors will take reasonable measures to ensure the proper use of psychological assessment techniques by persons under their supervision.

b. **APPROPRIATE USE.** Rehabilitation counselors will be responsible for the appropriate application, scoring, interpretation, and use of assessment instruments, whether they score and interpret such tests themselves or use computerized or other services.

c. **DECISIONS BASED ON RESULTS.** Rehabilitation counselors will be responsible for decisions involving individuals or policies that are based on assessment results and will have a thorough understanding of educational and psychological measurement, including validation criteria, test research, and guidelines for test development and use.

d. **ACCURATE INFORMATION.** Rehabilitation counselors will provide accurate information and avoid false claims or misconceptions when making statements about assessment instruments or techniques. Special efforts will be made to avoid utilizing test results to make inappropriate diagnoses or inferences.

F.6. TEST SELECTION

a. **APPROPRIATENESS OF INSTRUMENTS.** Rehabilitation counselors will carefully consider the validity, reliability, psychometric limitations, and appropriateness of instruments when selecting tests for use in a given situation or with a particular client.

b. **REFERRAL INFORMATION.** If a client is referred to a third party provider for testing, the rehabilitation counselor will provide specific referral questions and sufficient objective data about the client so as to ensure that appropriate test instruments are utilized.

c. **CULTURALLY DIVERSE POPULATIONS.** Rehabilitation counselors will be cautious when selecting tests for disability or culturally diverse populations to avoid inappropriateness of testing that may be outside of socialized behavioral or cognitive patterns or functional abilities.

d. **NORM DIVERGENCE.** Rehabilitation counselors will be cautious in using assessment techniques, making evaluations, and interpreting the performance of populations not represented in the norm group on which an instrument was standardized and will disclose such information.

F.7. CONDITIONS OF TEST ADMINISTRATION

a. **ADMINISTRATION CONDITIONS.** Rehabilitation counselors will administer tests under the same conditions that were established in the test standardization. When tests are not administered under standard conditions, as may be necessary to accommodate modifications for clients with disabilities or when unusual behavior or irregularities occur during the testing session, those conditions will be noted in interpretation.

b. **COMPUTER ADMINISTRATION.** When a computer or other electronic methods are used for test administration, rehabilitation counselors will be responsible for ensuring that programs function properly to provide clients with accurate results.

c. **UNSUPERVISED TEST-TAKING.** Rehabilitation counselors will not permit unsupervised or inadequately supervised use of tests or assessments unless the tests or assessments are designed, intended, and validated for self-administration and/or scoring.

F.8. TEST SCORING AND INTERPRETATION

a. **REPORTING RESERVATIONS.** In reporting assessment results, rehabilitation counselors will indicate any reservations that exist regarding validity or reliability because of the circumstances of the assessment or the inappropriateness of the norms for the person tested.

b. **DIVERSITY IN TESTING.** Rehabilitation counselors will place test results and their interpretations in proper perspective considering other relevant factors including age, color, culture, disability, ethnic group, gender, race, religion, sexual orientation, marital status, and socioeconomic status.

c. **RESEARCH INSTRUMENTS.** Rehabilitation counselors will exercise caution when interpreting the results of research instruments possessing insufficient technical data to support respondent results. The specific purposes for the use of such instruments will be stated explicitly to the examinee.

d. **TESTING SERVICES.** Rehabilitation counselors who provide test scoring and test interpretation services to support the assessment process will confirm the validity of such interpretations. The interpretation of assessment data will be related to the particular goals of evaluation. Rehabilitation counselors will accurately describe the purpose, norms, validity, reliability, and applications of the procedures and any special qualifications applicable to their use.

e. **AUTOMATED TESTING SERVICES.** The public offering of an automated test interpretation service will be considered a professional-to-professional consultation. The formal responsibility of the consultant will be to the consultee, but the ultimate and overriding responsibility will be to the client.

F.9. TEST SECURITY

Rehabilitation counselors will maintain the integrity and security of tests and other assessment techniques consistent with legal and contractual obligations. Rehabilitation counselors will not appropriate, reproduce, or modify published tests or parts thereof without acknowledgment and permission from the publisher.

F.10. OBSOLETE TESTS AND OUTDATED TEST RESULTS

Rehabilitation counselors will not use data or test results that are obsolete or outdated for the current purpose. Rehabilitation counselors will make every effort to prevent the misuse of obsolete measures and test data by others.

F.11. TEST CONSTRUCTION

Rehabilitation counselors will use established scientific procedures, relevant standards, and current professional knowledge for test design in the development, publication, and utilization of educational and psychological assessment techniques.

F.12. FORENSIC EVALUATION

When providing forensic evaluations, the primary obligation of rehabilitation counselors will be to produce objective findings that can be substantiated based on information and techniques appropriate to the evaluation, which may include examination of the individual with a disability and/or review of records. Rehabilitation counselors will define the limits of their reports or testimony, especially when an examination of the individual with a disability has not been conducted.

SECTION G: TEACHING, TRAINING, AND SUPERVISION

G.1. REHABILITATION COUNSELOR EDUCATORS AND TRAINERS

a. **RELATIONSHIP BOUNDARIES WITH STUDENTS AND SUPERVISEES.** Rehabilitation counselors will clearly define and maintain ethical, professional, and social relationship boundaries with their students and supervisees. They will be aware of the differential in power that exists and the student or supervisee's possible incomprehension of that power differential. Rehabilitation counselors will explain to students and supervisees the potential for the relationship to become exploitive.

b. **SEXUAL RELATIONSHIPS.** Rehabilitation counselors will not engage in sexual relationships with students or supervisees and will not subject them to sexual harassment.

c. **SUPERVISION PREPARATION.** Rehabilitation counselors will supervise only within the boundaries of their competence, based on their education, training, supervised experience, state and national professional credentials, and appropriate professional experience. Rehabilitation counselors who are doctoral students serving as practicum or internship supervisors will be adequately prepared and supervised by the training program.

d. **RESPONSIBILITY FOR SERVICES TO CLIENTS.** Rehabilitation counselors who supervise the rehabilitation counseling services of others will perform direct supervision sufficient to ensure that rehabilitation counseling services provided to clients are adequate and do not cause harm to the client.

e. **ENDORSEMENT.** Rehabilitation counselors will not endorse students or supervisees for certification, licensure, employment, or completion of an academic or training program if they believe students or supervisees are not qualified for the endorsement. Rehabilitation counselors will take reasonable steps to assist students or supervisees who are not qualified for endorsement to become qualified.

G.2. REHABILITATION COUNSELOR EDUCATION AND TRAINING PROGRAMS

a. **ORIENTATION.** Prior to admission, rehabilitation counselor educators will orient prospective students to the counselor education or training program's expectations, including but not limited to the following: (1) the type and level of skill acquisition required for successful completion of the training, (2) subject matter to be covered, (3) basis for evaluation, (4) training components that encourage self-growth or self-disclosure as part of the training process, (5) the type of supervision settings and requirements of the sites for required clinical field experiences, (6) student evaluation and dismissal policies and procedures, and (7) up-to-date employment prospects for graduates.

b. **EVALUATION.** Rehabilitation counselor educators will clearly state, in advance of training, to students and internship supervisees, the levels of competency expected, appraisal methods, and timing of evaluations for both didactic and experiential components. Rehabilitation counselor educators will provide students and internship supervisees with periodic performance appraisal and evaluation feedback throughout the training program.

c. **TEACHING ETHICS.** Rehabilitation counselor educators will teach students and internship supervisees the ethical responsibilities and standards of the profession and the students' and supervisees' professional ethical responsibilities.

d. **PEER RELATIONSHIPS.** When students are assigned to lead counseling groups or provide clinical supervision for their peers, rehabilitation counselor educators will take steps to ensure that students placed in these roles do not have personal or adverse relationships with peers and that they understand they have the same ethical obligations as counselor educators, trainers, and supervisors. Rehabilitation counselor educators will make every effort to ensure that the rights of peers are not compromised when students are assigned to lead counseling groups or provide clinical supervision.

e. **VARIED THEORETICAL POSITIONS.** Rehabilitation counselor educators will present varied theoretical positions so that students may make comparisons and have opportunities to develop their own positions. Rehabilitation counselor educators will provide information concerning the scientific bases of professional practice.

f. **FIELD PLACEMENTS.** Rehabilitation counselor educators will develop clear policies within their training program regarding field placement and other clinical experiences. Rehabilitation counselor educators will provide clearly stated roles and responsibilities for the student and the site supervisor. Rehabilitation counselor educators will confirm that site supervisors will be qualified to provide supervision and are informed of their professional and ethical responsibilities in this role. Rehabilitation counselor educators will not accept any form of professional services, fees, commissions, reimbursement, or remuneration from a site for student placement.

g. **DIVERSITY IN PROGRAMS.** Rehabilitation counselor educators will respond to their institution and program's recruitment and retention needs for training program administrators, faculty, and students with diverse backgrounds and special needs.

G.3. STUDENTS AND SUPERVISEES

a. **LIMITATIONS.** Rehabilitation counselors, through ongoing evaluation and appraisal, will be aware of the academic and personal limitations of students and supervisees that might impede performance. Rehabilitation counselors will assist students and supervisees in securing remedial assistance when needed, and will dismiss students or supervisees who are unable to provide competent service due to academic or personal limitations. Rehabilitation counselors will seek professional consultation and document their decision to dismiss or to refer students or supervisees for assistance. Rehabilitation counselors will advise students and supervisees of appeals processes as appropriate.

b. **SELF-GROWTH EXPERIENCES.** Rehabilitation counselor educators, when designing training groups or other experiences conducted by the rehabilitation counselor educators themselves, will inform students of the potential risks of self-disclosure. Rehabilitation counselor educators will respect the privacy of students by not requiring self-disclosure that could reasonably be expected to be harmful and student evaluation criteria will not include the level of the student's self-disclosure.

c. **COUNSELING FOR STUDENTS AND SUPERVISEES.** If students or supervisees request counseling, supervisors or rehabilitation counselor educators will provide them with acceptable referrals. Supervisors or rehabilitation counselor educators will not serve as rehabilitation counselors to students or supervisees over whom they hold administrative, teaching, or evaluative roles unless this is a brief role associated with a training experience.

d. **CLIENTS OF STUDENTS AND SUPERVISEES.** Rehabilitation counselors will make every effort to ensure that clients are aware of the services rendered and the qualifications of the students and supervisees rendering those services. Clients will receive professional disclosure information and will be informed of the limits of confidentiality. Client permission will be obtained in order for the students and supervisees to use any information concerning the counseling relationship in the training process.

e. **PROFESSIONAL DEVELOPMENT.** Rehabilitation counselors who employ or supervise individuals will provide appropriate working conditions, timely evaluations, constructive consultations, and suitable opportunities for experience and training.

SECTION H: RESEARCH AND PUBLICATION

H.1. RESEARCH RESPONSIBILITIES

a. **USE OF HUMAN PARTICIPANTS.** Rehabilitation counselors will plan, design, conduct, and report research in a manner that reflects cultural sensitivity, is culturally appropriate, and is consistent with pertinent ethical principles, federal and state/provincial laws, host institutional regulations, and scientific standards governing research with human participants.

b. **DEVIATION FROM STANDARD PRACTICES.** Rehabilitation counselors will seek consultation and observe stringent safeguards to protect the rights of research participants when a research problem suggests a deviation from standard acceptable practices.

c. **PRECAUTIONS TO AVOID INJURY.** Rehabilitation counselors who conduct research with human participants will be responsible for the participants' welfare throughout the research and will take reasonable precautions to avoid causing injurious psychological, physical, or social effects to their participants.

d. **PRINCIPAL RESEARCHER RESPONSIBILITY.** While ultimate responsibility for ethical research practice lies with the principal researcher, rehabilitation counselors involved in the research activities will share ethical obligations and bear full responsibility for their own actions.

e. **MINIMAL INTERFERENCE.** Rehabilitation counselors will take precautions to avoid causing disruptions in participants' lives due to participation in research.

f. **DIVERSITY.** Rehabilitation counselors will be sensitive to diversity and research issues with culturally diverse populations and they will seek consultation when appropriate.

H.2. INFORMED CONSENT

a. **TOPICS DISCLOSED.** In obtaining informed consent for research, rehabilitation counselors will use language that is understandable to research participants and that (1) accurately explains the purpose and procedures to be followed; (2) identifies any procedures that are experimental or relatively untried; (3) describes the attendant discomforts and risks; (4) describes the benefits or changes in individuals or organizations that might reasonably be expected; (5) discloses appropriate alternative procedures that would be advantageous for participants; (6) offers to answer any inquiries concerning the procedures; (7) describes any limitations of confidentiality; and (8) instructs that participants are free to withdraw their consent and to discontinue participation in the project at any time.

b. **DECEPTION.** Rehabilitation counselors will not conduct research involving deception unless alternative procedures are not feasible and the prospective value of the research justifies the deception. When the methodological requirements of a study necessitate concealment or deception, the investigator will be required to explain clearly the reasons for this action as soon as possible.

c. **VOLUNTARY PARTICIPATION.** Participation in research is typically voluntary and without any penalty for refusal to participate. Involuntary participation will be appropriate only when it can be demonstrated that participation will have no harmful effects on participants and is essential to the investigation.

d. CONFIDENTIALITY OF INFORMATION. Information obtained about research participants during the course of an investigation will be confidential. When the possibility exists that others may obtain access to such information, ethical research practice requires that the possibility, together with the plans for protecting confidentiality, will be explained to participants as a part of the procedure for obtaining informed consent.

e. PERSONS INCAPABLE OF GIVING INFORMED CONSENT. When a person is incapable of giving informed consent, rehabilitation counselors will provide an appropriate explanation, obtain agreement for participation, and obtain appropriate consent from a legally authorized person.

f. COMMITMENTS TO PARTICIPANTS. Rehabilitation counselors will take reasonable measures to honor all commitments to research participants.

g. EXPLANATIONS AFTER DATA COLLECTION. After data are collected, rehabilitation counselors will provide participants with full clarification of the nature of the study to remove any misconceptions. Where scientific or human values justify delaying or withholding information, rehabilitation counselors will take reasonable measures to avoid causing harm.

h. AGREEMENTS TO COOPERATE. Rehabilitation counselors who agree to cooperate with another individual in research or publication will incur an obligation to cooperate as agreed.

i. INFORMED CONSENT FOR SPONSORS. In the pursuit of research, rehabilitation counselors will give sponsors, institutions, and publication channels the same opportunity for giving informed consent that they accord to individual research participants. Rehabilitation counselors will be aware of their obligation to future researchers and will ensure that host institutions are given feedback information and proper acknowledgment.

H.3. REPORTING RESULTS

a. INFORMATION AFFECTING OUTCOME. When reporting research results, rehabilitation counselors will explicitly mention all variables and conditions known to the investigator that may have affected the outcome of a study or the interpretation of data.

b. **ACCURATE RESULTS.** Rehabilitation counselors will plan, conduct, and report research accurately and in a manner that minimizes the possibility that results will be misleading. They will provide thorough discussions of the limitations of their data and alternative hypotheses. Rehabilitation counselors will not engage in fraudulent research, distort data, misrepresent data, or deliberately bias their results.

c. **OBLIGATION TO REPORT UNFAVORABLE RESULTS.** Rehabilitation counselors will make available the results of any research judged to be of professional value even if the results reflect unfavorably on institutions, programs, services, prevailing opinions, or vested interests.

d. **IDENTITY OF PARTICIPANTS.** Rehabilitation counselors who supply data, aid in the research of another person, report research results, or make original data available will take due care to disguise the identity of respective participants in the absence of specific authorization from the participants to do otherwise.

e. **REPLICATION STUDIES.** Rehabilitation counselors will be obligated to make sufficient original research data available to qualified professionals who may wish to replicate the study.

H.4. PUBLICATION

a. **RECOGNITION OF OTHERS.** When conducting and reporting research, rehabilitation counselors will be familiar with and give recognition to previous work on the topic, observe copyright laws, and give full credit to those to whom credit is due.

b. **CONTRIBUTORS.** Rehabilitation counselors will give credit through joint authorship, acknowledgment, footnote statements, or other appropriate means to those who have contributed significantly to research or concept development in accordance with such contributions. The principal contributor will be listed first and minor technical or professional contributions are acknowledged in notes or introductory statements.

c. **STUDENT RESEARCH.** For an article that is substantially based on a student's dissertation or thesis, the student will be listed as the principal author.

d. **DUPLICATE SUBMISSION.** Rehabilitation counselors will submit manuscripts for consideration to only one journal at a time. Manuscripts that are published in whole or in substantial part in another journal or published work will not be submitted for publication without acknowledgment and permission from the previous publication.

e. **PROFESSIONAL REVIEW.** Rehabilitation counselors who review material submitted for publication, research, or other scholarly purposes will respect the confidentiality and proprietary rights of those who submitted it.

SECTION I: ELECTRONIC COMMUNICATION AND EMERGING APPLICATIONS

I.1. COMMUNICATION

a. **COMMUNICATION TOOLS.** Rehabilitation counselors will be held to the same level of expected behavior as defined by the Code of Professional Ethics for Rehabilitation Counselors regardless of the form of communication they choose to use (i.e., cellular phones, electronic mail, facsimile, video, audio-visual).

b. **IMPOSTERS.** In situations where it is difficult to verify the identity of the rehabilitation counselor, the client, or the client's guardian, rehabilitation counselors will take steps to address imposter concerns, such as using code words, numbers, or graphics.

c. **CONFIDENTIALITY.** Rehabilitation counselors will ensure that clients are provided sufficient information to adequately address and explain the limits of: (1) computer technology in the counseling process in general; and (2) the difficulties of ensuring complete client confidentiality of information transmitted through electronic communication over the Internet through on-line counseling.

I.2. COUNSELING RELATIONSHIP

a. **ETHICAL/LEGAL REVIEW.** Rehabilitation counselors will review pertinent legal and ethical codes for possible violations emanating from the practice of distance counseling and supervision. Distance counseling is defined as any counseling that occurs at a distance through electronic means, such as web-counseling, tele-counseling, or video-counseling.

b. **SECURITY.** Rehabilitation counselors will use encryption methods whenever possible. If encryption is not made available to clients, clients must be informed of the potential hazards of unsecured communication on the Internet. Hazards may include authorized or unauthorized monitoring of transmissions and/or records of sessions.

c. **RECORDS PRESERVATION.** Rehabilitation counselors will inform clients whether the records are being preserved, how they are being preserved, and how long the records are being maintained.

d. **SELF-DESCRIPTION.** Rehabilitation counselors will provide information about themselves as would be available if the counseling were to take place face-to-face (e.g., possibly ethnicity or gender).

e. **CONSUMER PROTECTION.** Rehabilitation counselors will provide information to the client regarding all appropriate certification bodies and licensure boards to facilitate consumer protection, such as links to websites.

f. **CRISIS CONTACT.** Rehabilitation counselors will provide the name of at least one agency or counselor-on-call for purposes of crisis intervention within the client's geographical region.

g. **UNAVAILABILITY.** Rehabilitation counselors will provide clients with instructions for contacting them when they are unavailable through electronic means.

h. **INAPPROPRIATE USE.** Rehabilitation counselors will mention at their websites or in their initial contacts with potential clients those presenting problems they believe to be inappropriate for distance counseling.

i. **TECHNICAL FAILURE.** Rehabilitation counselors will explain to clients the possibility of technology failure and will provide an alternative means of communication.

j. **POTENTIAL MISUNDERSTANDINGS.** Rehabilitation counselors will explain to clients how to prevent and address potential misunderstandings arising from the lack of visual cues and voice intonations from the counselor or client.

SECTION J: BUSINESS PRACTICES

J.1. BILLING

Rehabilitation counselors will establish and maintain billing records that accurately reflect the services provided and the time engaged in the activity, and that clearly identify who provided the service.

J.2. TERMINATION

Rehabilitation counselors in fee for service relationships may terminate services with clients due to nonpayment of fees under the following conditions: a) the client was informed of payment responsibilities and the effects of nonpayment or the termination of payment by a third party, and b) the client does not pose an imminent danger to self or others. As appropriate, rehabilitation counselors will refer clients to another qualified professional to address issues unresolved at the time of termination.

J.3. CLIENT RECORDS

a. **ACCURATE DOCUMENTATION.** Rehabilitation counselors will establish and will maintain documentation that accurately reflects the services provided and that identifies who provided the service. If case notes need to be altered, it will be done so in a manner that preserves the original note and will be accompanied by the date of change, information that identifies who made the change, and the rationale for the change.

b. **SUFFICIENT DOCUMENTATION.** Rehabilitation counselors will provide sufficient documentation in a timely manner (e.g., case notes, reports, plans).

c. **PRIVACY.** Documentation generated by rehabilitation counselors will protect the privacy of clients to the extent that it is possible and appropriate, and will include only relevant information.

d. **MAINTENANCE.** Rehabilitation counselors will maintain records necessary for rendering professional services to their clients and as required by applicable laws, regulations, or agency/institution procedures. Subsequent to file closure, records will be maintained for the number of years consistent with jurisdictional requirements or for a longer period during which maintenance of such records is necessary or helpful to provide reasonably anticipated future services to the client. After that time, records will be destroyed in a manner assuring preservation of confidentiality.

J.4. FEES AND BARTERING

a. **ADVANCE UNDERSTANDING.** Rehabilitation counselors will clearly explain to clients, prior to entering the counseling relationship, all financial arrangements related to professional services including the use of collection agencies or legal measures for nonpayment.

b. **ESTABLISHING FEES.** In establishing fees for professional rehabilitation counseling services, rehabilitation counselors will consider the financial status and locality of clients. In the event that the established fee structure is inappropriate for a client, assistance will be provided in attempting to find comparable services of acceptable cost.

c. **BARTERING DISCOURAGED.** Rehabilitation counselors will ordinarily refrain from accepting goods or services from clients in return for rehabilitation counseling services because such arrangements create inherent potential for conflicts, exploitation, and distortion of the professional relationship. Rehabilitation counselors will participate in bartering only if the relationship is not exploitative, if the client requests it, if a clear written contract is established, and if such arrangements are an accepted practice in the client's community or culture.

J.5. FEES FOR REFERRAL

a. **ACCEPTING FEES FROM AGENCY CLIENTS.** Rehabilitation counselors will not accept a private fee or other remuneration for rendering services to persons who are entitled to such services through the rehabilitation counselor's employing agency or institution. However, the policies of a particular agency may make explicit provisions for agency clients to receive rehabilitation counseling services from members of its staff in private practice. In such instances, the clients will be informed of other options open to them should they seek private rehabilitation counseling services.

b. **REFERRAL FEES.** Rehabilitation counselors will neither give nor receive commissions, rebates or any other form of remuneration when referring clients for professional services.

SECTION K: RESOLVING ETHICAL ISSUES

K.1. KNOWLEDGE OF STANDARDS

Rehabilitation counselors are responsible for learning the Code and should seek clarification of any standard that is not understood. Lack of knowledge or misunderstanding of an ethical responsibility will not be used as a defense against a charge of unethical conduct.

K.2. SUSPECTED VIOLATIONS

a. **CONSULTATION.** When uncertain as to whether a particular situation or course of action may be in violation of the Code of Professional Ethics for Rehabilitation Counselors, rehabilitation counselors will consult with other rehabilitation counselors who are knowledgeable about ethics, with colleagues, and/or with appropriate authorities, such as CRCC, state licensure boards, or legal counsel.

b. **ORGANIZATION CONFLICTS.** If the demands of an organization with which rehabilitation counselors are affiliated pose a conflict with the Code of Professional Ethics for Rehabilitation Counselors, rehabilitation counselors will specify the nature of such conflicts and express to their supervisors or other responsible officials their commitment to the Code of Professional Ethics for Rehabilitation Counselors. When possible, rehabilitation counselors will work toward change within the organization to allow full adherence to the Code of Professional Ethics for Rehabilitation Counselors.

c. **INFORMAL RESOLUTION.** When rehabilitation counselors have reasonable cause to believe that another rehabilitation counselor is violating an ethical standard, they will attempt to resolve the issue informally with the other rehabilitation counselor if feasible, providing that such action does not violate confidentiality rights that may be involved.

d. **REPORTING SUSPECTED VIOLATIONS.** When an informal resolution is not appropriate or feasible, rehabilitation counselors, upon reasonable cause, will take action such as reporting the suspected ethical violation to state or national ethics committees or CRCC, unless this action conflicts with confidentiality rights that cannot be resolved.

e. **UNWARRANTED COMPLAINTS.** Rehabilitation counselors will not initiate, participate in, or encourage the filing of ethics complaints that are unwarranted or intended to harm a rehabilitation counselor rather than to protect clients or the public.

K.3. COOPERATION WITH ETHICS COMMITTEES

Rehabilitation counselors will assist in the process of enforcing the Code of Professional Ethics for Rehabilitation Counselors. Rehabilitation counselors will cooperate with investigations, proceedings, and requirements of the CRCC Ethics Committee or ethics committees of other duly constituted associations or boards having jurisdiction over those charged with a violation.

Acknowledgments—CRCC recognizes the American Counseling Association for permitting the Commission to adopt, in part, the ACA Code of Ethics and Standards of Practice.

References

Access Board (n.d.). *The Architectural Barriers Act (ABA) of 1968*. Retrieved October 25, 2002, from http://www.access-board.gov/about/ABA.htm

Ackoff, R. L. (1970). *A concept of corporate planning*. New York: Wiley Interscience.

Adair, J. G., Paivo, A., & Ritchie, P. (1996). Psychology in Canada. *Annual Review of Psychology, 47*, 341–370.

Adkins, C. L. (2001). *Case management salary survey*. Retrieved January 2, 2002, from www.advanceforpac.com/ppsalarysurvey.html.

Albrecht, G. L. (1992). *The disability business: Rehabilitation in America*. Newbury Park, CA: Sage.

Albrecht, G. L. (Ed.). (1981). *Cross national rehabilitation policies: A sociological perspective*. Beverly Hills: Sage.

Al-Darmaki, F., & Kivligham, D. M. (1993). Congruence in client-counselor expectations for relationship and the working alliance. *Journal of Counseling Psychology, 40*, 379–384.

Allen, B. P., & Adams, J. Q. (1992). The concept "race": Let's go back to the beginning. *Journal of Social Behavior and Personality, 7,* 163–168.

Allen, H. A., Stebnicki, M. A., & Lynch, R. T. (1995). Training clinical supervisors in rehabilitation: A conceptual model for training doctoral-level supervisors. *Rehabilitation Counseling Bulletin, 38*, 307–317.

Altman, B. M. (2001). Disability definitions, models, classification schemes, and applications. In G. Albrecht, K. Seelman, & M. Bury (Eds.), *Handbook of disability studies* (pp. 97–123). Thousand Oaks, CA: Sage.

American Educational Research Association, American Psychological Association, & National Council on Measurement in Education. (1999). *Standards for educational and psychological testing*. Washington, DC: American Educational Research Association.

American Psychiatric Association. (2000). *Diagnostic and statistical manual of mental disorders* (4th ed., text revision). Washington, DC: Author.

American Psychological Association. (1986). *Guidelines for computer-based tests and their interpretation.* Washington, DC: Author.

American Psychological Association. (2001). *Publication manual of the American Psychological Association* (5th ed.). Washington, DC: Author.

American Psychological Association. (2002). *Guidelines on multicultural education, training, research, practice, and organizational change for psychologists.* Washington, DC: Author.

Americans with Disabilities Act of 1990, 42 U.S.C.A. Sec. § 12101.

Anastasi, A. (1992). Tests and assessment. What counselors should know about the use and interpretation of psychological tests. *Journal of Counseling and Development, 70,* 610–615.

Arokiasamy, C. V. (1993). A theory for rehabilitation: *Rehabilitation Education, 7,* 77–98.

Arredondo, P., Toporek, R., Brown, S., Jones, J., Locke, D. Sanchez, J., et al. (1996). Operationalization of multicultural counseling competencies. *Journal of Multicultural Counseling and Development, 24*(1), 42–78.

Arthur, D. (1991). *Recruiting, interviewing, selecting, and orienting new employees* (2nd ed.). New York: AMACOM.

Ashley, M., et al. (1994). Post acute rehabilitation outcome: relationship to case management techniques and strategy. *Journal of Insurance Medicine, 26*(3), 348–354.

Atkins, B. J., & Wright, G. N. (1980). Three views: Vocational rehabilitation of Blacks. The statement, the response, the comment. *Journal of Rehabilitation, 46*(2), 40–49.

Atkinson, D. R., Morten, G., & Sue, D. W. (1993). *Counseling American minorities: A cross-cultural perspective* (4th ed.). Dubuque, IA: William C. Brown.

Atkinson, D. R., Thompson, C. E., & Grant, S. K. (1993). A three-dimensional model for counseling racial/ethnic minorities. *The Counseling Psychologist, 21,* 257–277.

Bailey, J. M. (1997). Gender identity. In R. C. Savin-Williams & K. M. Cohen (Eds.), *The lives of lesbians, gays, and bisexuals: Children to adults* (pp. 71–93). Forth Worth, TX: Harcourt Brace.

Bandura, A. (1982). Self-efficacy mechanism in human agency. *American Psychologist, 37,* 122–147.

Banja, J. (1990). Rehabilitation and empowerment. *Archives of Physical Medicine and Rehabilitation, 7*(1), 614–615

Banting, K. G. (1987). *The Welfare State and Canadian Federalism* (2nd ed.). Kingston, ON: McGill-Queen's University Press.

Barnartt, S., Schriner, K., & Scotch, R. (2001). Advocacy and political action. In G. Albrecht, K. Seelman, & M. Bury (Eds.), *Handbook of disability studies* (pp. 430–450). Thousand Oaks, CA: Sage.

Barrett, K., & Crimando, W. (1996). Empowering rehabilitation organizations: An analysis. *Journal of Rehabilitation Administration, 20,* 63–74.

Barrett, K., Flowers, C., Crimando, W., Riggar, T. F., & Bailey, T. (1997). Training never ends: Human resource development of rehabilitation administrators. *Journal of Rehabilitation Administration, 21,* 3–17.

Barrett, K., Riggar, T. F., & Flowers, C. (1997). Violence in the workplace: Preparing for the age of rage. *Journal of Rehabilitation Administration, 21,* 171–188.

Barrett, K., Riggar, T. F., Flowers, C., Crimando, W., & Bailey, T. (1997). The turnover dilemma: A disease with solutions. *Journal of Rehabilitation, 63*(2), 36–42.

Bass, B. M., & Avoglio, B. J. (1994). *Improving organizational effectiveness through transformational leadership.* Thousand Oaks, CA: Sage.

Bauman, H. D. L., & Drake, J. (1997). Silence is not without voice: Including deaf culture within the multicultural curricula. In L. J. Davis (Ed.), *Disability studies reader* (pp. 307–314). New York: Routledge.

Baumann, N. (1986). Keeping business advisory councils active and involved: The Aging in America model. *Journal of Job Placement, 2,* 16–17.

Beauchamp, T. L., & Childress, J. F. (1994). *Principles of biomedical ethics* (4th ed.). New York: Oxford University Press.

Bellini, J., & Rumrill, P. (2002). Contemporary insights in the philosophy of science: Implications for rehabilitation counseling research. *Rehabilitation Education, 16,* 115–134.

Benshoff, J. J. (1990). The role of rehabilitation and the issues of employment in the 1990s. In L. Perlman & C. Hansen (Eds.), *Employment and disability: Trends and issues for the 1990s* (pp. 50–59). Alexandria, VA: National Rehabilitation Association.

Benton, M. K., & Schroeder, H. E. (1990). Social skills training with schizophrenia: A meta-analysis evaluation. *Journal of Consulting and Clinical Psychology, 58,* 741–747.

Berkowitz, E. D. (1985). Social influences on rehabilitation: Introductory remarks. In L. Perlman & G. Austin (Eds.), *Social influences in rehabilitation planning: Blueprint for the 21st century* (pp. 11–18). Alexandria, VA: National Rehabilitation Association.

Berkowitz, E. D. (1987). *Disabled policy: America's programs for the handicapped.* New York: Cambridge University Press.

Berkowitz, E. D. (1992). Disabled policy: A personal postscript. *Journal of Disability Policy Studies, 3*(1), 1–16.

Berkowitz, M. (1987). *Disabled policy: America's programs for the handicapped.* London, England: Cambridge University Press.

Berkowitz, M. (1996, October). *Federal programs for persons with disabilities.* Paper presented at the Conference on Employment and Return to Work for People with Disabilities, Social Security Administration and National Institute on Disability and Rehabilitation Research, Washington, DC.

Berkowitz, M., & Hill, M. A. (Eds.). (1986). *Disability and the labor market: Economic problems, policies, and programs.* Ithica, NY: Cornell University.

Berkowitz, M., Englander, V., Rubin, J., & Worrall, J. D. (1975). *An evaluation of policy-related research.* New York: Praeger.

Berkowitz, M., Englander, V., Rubin, J., & Worrall, J. D. (1976). A summary of "An evaluation of policy-related research." *Rehabilitation Counseling Bulletin, 20,* 29–45.

Bernard, J. M. (1992). Training master's level counseling students in the fundamentals of clinical supervision. *The Clinical Supervisor, 10,* 133–143.

Bernard, J. M., & Goodyear, R. K. (1998). *Fundamentals of clinical supervision* (2nd ed.). Needham Heights, MA: Allyn and Bacon.

Berven, N. L. (1979). The roles and functions of the rehabilitation counselor revisited. *Rehabilitation Counseling Bulletin, 23,* 84–88.

Berven, N. L. (1980). Psychometric assessment in rehabilitation. In B. Bolton & D. W. Cook (Eds.), *Rehabilitation client assessment* (pp. 46–64). Baltimore: University Park Press.

Berven, N. L. (1994, April). Ten priority research topics to facilitate assessment in rehabilitation settings. Paper presented at the Form on Rehabilitation Research and Practice, held at the meeting of the American Counseling Association, Minneapolis, MN.

Berven, N. L. (2001). Assessment interviewing. In B. F. Bolton (Ed.), *Handbook of measurement and evaluation in rehabilitation* (3rd ed., pp. 197–213). Gaithersburg, MD: Aspen.

Betan, E. J., & Stanton, A. L. (1999). Fostering ethical willingness: Integrating emotional and contextual awareness with rational analysis. *Professional Psychology: Research and Practice, 30*, 295–301.

Bickenbach, J. E. (1993). *Physical disability and social policy*. Toronto: University of Toronto.

Bickenbach, J. E. (2001). Disability human rights, law, and policy. In G. Albrecht, K. Seelman, & M. Bury (Eds.), *Handbook of disability studies* (pp. 565–585). Thousand Oaks, CA: Sage.

Bieschke, K. J., & Herbert, J. T. (2000). The supervision practicum. *Rehabilitation Education, 12,* 155–162.

Billingsley, W., Knauss, J., & Oehlers, L. (2002). Introduction: Vocational rehabilitation meets the third wave. In D. Dew, M. McGuire-Kuletz, & G. Alan (Eds.), *Using the Internet as a resource to the work of the state VR counselor* (pp. 1–6). Washington, DC: The George Washington University.

Bishop, M., & Feist-Price, S. (2002). Quality of life assessment in the rehabilitation counseling relationship: Strategies and measures. *Journal of Applied Rehabilitation Counseling, 33*(1), 35–41.

Black, H. (1990). *Black's Law Dictionary* (6th ed.). St. Paul, MN: West Publishing.

Blackwell, T. L., Strohmer, D. C., Belcas, E. M., & Burton, K. A. (2002). Ethics in rehabilitation counselor supervision. *Rehabilitation Counseling Bulletin, 45,* 240–247.

Bloom, J., Gerstein, L., Tarvydas, V., Conaster, J., Davis, E., Kater, D., et al. (1990). Model legislation for licensed professional counselors. *Journal of Counseling and Development, 68*, 511–523.

Bolton, B. (1978). Methodological issues in the assessment of rehabilitation counselor performance. *Rehabilitation Counseling Bulletin, 21*, 140–153.

Bolton, B. (1979). *Rehabilitation counseling research.* Baltimore: University Park Press.

Borders, L. D. (1991). A systematic approach to peer group supervision. *Journal of Counseling & Development, 69*, 248–252.

Bordin, E. S. (1983). A working alliance model of supervision. *Counseling Psychologist, 11*, 35–42.

Boschen, K. A. (1989). Early intervention in vocational rehabilitation. *Rehabilitation Counseling Bulletin, 32*, 254–265.

Boschen, K. A., & Krane, N. (1992). A history of independent living in Canada. *Canadian Journal of Rehabilitation*, *6*(2), 79–88.

Bowe, F. (1980). *Rehabilitating America: Toward independence for disabled and elderly people.* New York: Harper and Row.

Bowe, F. (1984). *U.S. Census and disabled adults*. Hot Springs, AR: University of Arkansas, Arkansas Services, Arkansas Rehabilitation Research and Training Center.

Bowe, F. G. (1993). Statistics, politics, and employment of people with disabilities. *Journal of Disability Policy Studies, 4*(2), 83–91.

Brodwin, M., & Brodwin, S. (1992). Rehabilitation: A case study approach. In M. Brodwin, F. Tellez, & S. Brodwin (Eds.), *Medical, psychological and vocational aspects of disability* (pp. 1–19). Athens, GA: Elliott & Fitzpatrick.

Brooks, D. J., Barrett, D., & Oehlers, L. (2002). The how chapter: Computer competency and information literacy. In D. Dew, M. McGuire-Kuletz, & G. Alan (Eds.), *Using the Internet as a resource to the work of the state VR counselor* (pp. 30–64). Washington, DC: The George Washington University.

Browder, D. (1991). *Assessment of individuals with severe disabilities: An applied behavior approach to life skills assessment* (2nd ed.). Baltimore: Paul H. Brookes.

Brown, C., McDaniel, R., Couch, R., & McClanahan, M. (1994). *Vocational evaluation systems and software: A consumer's guide.* Menomonie: University of Wisconsin-Stout, Stout Vocational Rehabilitation Institute.

Brown, D. (1988). Empowerment through advocacy. In D. J. Kurpius & D. Borwn (Eds.), *Handbook of consultation: An intervention for advocacy and outreach* (pp. 8–17). Alexandria, VA: Association for Counselor Education and Supervision.

Brown, D., Pryzwansky, W. B., & Schulte, A. C. (1995). *Psychological consultation: Introduction to theory and practice* (3rd ed.). Boston: Allyn & Bacon.

Brown, M., Gordon, W. A., & Diller, L. (1983). Functional assessment and outcome measurement: An integrative review. In E. L. Pan, T. E. Backer, & C. L. Vash (Eds.), *Annual review of rehabilitation: Vol. 3* (pp. 93–120). New York: Springer.

Browne, G., Roberts, J., Watt, S., Gafni, A., Stockwell, M., & Alcock, S. (1994). Community rehabilitation: Strategies, outcomes, expenditures. *Canadian Journal of Rehabilitation, 8*(1), 9–22.

Bruyere, S. M. (2001). Civil rights and employment issues of disability policy. *Journal of Disability Policy Studies, 11*(1), 18–36.

Bunderson, C. V., Inouye, D. K., & Olsen, J. B. (1989). The four generations of computerized educational measurement. In R. L. Linn (Ed.), *Educational measurement* (3rd ed., pp. 367–407). New York: Macmillan.

Burkhead, E. J., & Sampson, J. P., Jr. (1985). Computer-assisted assessment in support of the rehabilitation process. *Rehabilitation Counseling Bulletin, 28,* 262–274.

Byon, K. H., Chan, F., & Thomas, K. R. (1999). Korean international students' expectations about counseling. *Journal of College Counseling, 2,* 99–109.

California Workers' Compensation Institute. (1991). *Vocational rehabilitation: The California experience 1975–1989.* San Francisco: Author.

Campbell, F. (2001). Human rights issues and employee benefit plans. *Employee Benefits Journal, 26*(1), 41–48.

Campbell, M. K., DeVellis, B. M., Strecher, V. J., Ammerman, A. S., De Vellis, R. E., & Sandler, R. S. (1994). Improving dietary behavior: The effectiveness of tailored messages in primary care settings. *American Journal of Public Health, 84,* 783–787.

Canadian Association of Rehabilitation Professionals. (2000). *Registered Rehabilitation Professional (RRP) Application Guide*. Toronto, ON: Author.

Canadian Association of Rehabilitation Professionals, Ontario. (1999). *Practice Guidelines for Rehabilitation Counsellors in Ontario*. Toronto, ON: Author.

Canadian Counseling Association (2001). *Canadian Counsellor Certification.* Ottawa: Author.

Carter, R. T. (1995). *The influence of race and racial identity in psychotherapy: Toward a racially inclusive model.* New York: Wiley-Interscience.

Case Management Society of America. (1994). CMSA proposes standards of practice. *The Case Manager*, 69–70.

Cassell, J. L., & Mulkey, S. W. (1985). *Rehabilitation caseload management: Concepts and practice.* Austin, TX: Pro-Ed.

Cassell, J. L., & Mulkey, S. W. (1992). Caseload management in the rehabilitation curriculum. *Rehabilitation Education, 6,* 151–158.

Cassell, J. L., Mulkey, S. W., & Engen, C. (1997). Systematic practice: Case and caseload management. In D. R. Maki & T. F. Riggar (Eds.), *Rehabilitation counseling: Profession and practice* (pp. 214–233). New York: Springer Publishing.

Chan, A. (1979). The role of advocacy in rehabilitation counseling: Implications and recommendations for training. *AMICUS,* 253–261.

Chan, A., Brophy, M. C., & Fisher, J. C. (1981). Advocate counseling and institutional racism. In National Institutes of Mental Health, *Institutional racism and community competence* (ADM 81-907) (pp. 194–205). Washington, DC: U.S. Department of Health and Human Services.

Chan, F., & Leahy, M. (1999). *Healthcare and disability case management.* Lake Zurich, IL: Vocational Consultants Press.

Chan, F., & Rubin, S. E. (1999). *Developing a multidimensional program evaluation system in rehabilitation.* (A field-initiated project proposal submitted to the National Institute on Disability and Rehabilitation Research.) Rolling Meadows, IL: Foundation for Rehabilitation Education and Research.

Chan, F., & Rubin, S. (2002). *Developing a multidimensional program evaluation system in rehabilitation: A final report submitted to the National Institute on Disability and Rehabilitation Research.* Rolling Meadows, IL: Foundation for Rehabilitation Education and Research.

Chan, F., Lui, J., Rosenthal, D., Pruett, S., & Ferrin, J. M. (2002). Managed care and rehabilitation counseling. *Journal of Rehabilitation Administration, 26*(2), 85–97.

Chan, F., McMahon, B. T., Shaw, L., & Lee, G. (in press). Psychometric validation of the Expectations About Rehabilitation Counseling Scale. *Journal of Rehabilitation Research.*

Chan, F., Rubin, S. E., Kubota, C., Lee, G., & Chronister, J. (in press). Counselors' and consumers' derived criteria for assessing the effectiveness of rehabilitations services. *Journal of Rehabilitation Research.*

Chan, F., Rubin, S. E., Lee, G., & Pruett, S. (2002). Empirically derived life skill factors for program evaluation in rehabilitation. *Professional Rehabilitation.*

Chan, F., Shaw, L. R., McMahon, B. T., Koch, L., & Strauser, D. (1997). A model for enhancing rehabilitation counselor-consumer working relationships. *Rehabilitation Counseling Bulletin, 41,* 122–137.

Chesler, M. A., Bryant, B. I., & Crowfoot, J. E. (1976). Consultation in schools: Inevitable conflict, partisanship, and advocacy. *Professional Psychology, 7*(4), 637–645.

Choppa, A. J., Shafer, K., Reid, K. M., & Siefker, J. M. (1996). Vocational rehabilitation counselors as case managers. *The Case Manager, 7,* 45–50.

Choudry, S. (2000). Bill 11, the Canada health act and the social union: The need for institutions. *Osgoode Hall Law Journal, 38,* 39–99.

Chouinard, V. (2001). Legal peripheries: Struggles over disabled Canadians' places in law, society and space. *The Canadian Geographer, 45*(1), 187–192.

Clark, D. (1995). Big dog's ISD page [Online]. Retrieved December 4, 2002, from http://www.nwlink.com/%7Edonclark/hrd/sat.html.

Clawson, P. D., & Skinner, A. L. (2002). Accessibility of the ten most frequently used Internet career sites. *Journal of Applied Rehabilitation Counseling, 33*(2), 3–7.

Clendenin, D., & Nagourney, A. (1999). *Out for good: The struggle to build a gay rights movement in America.* New York: Simon & Schuster.

Cohen, E. D. (1990). Confidentiality, counseling, and clients who have AIDS: Ethical foundations of a model rule. *Journal of Counseling and Development, 68*, 282–286.

Cokley, K. O. (2002). Testing Cross's revised racial identity model: An examination of the relationship between racial identity and internalized racialism. *Journal of Counseling Psychology, 49,* 476–483.

Coleman, H. L. K., & Hau, J. M. (2003). Multicultural counseling competency and portfolios. In D. B. Pope-Davis, H. L. K. Coleman, W. M. Liu, & R. L. Toporek (Eds.), *Handbook of multicultural competencies in counseling and psychology* (pp. 168–182). Thousand Oaks, CA: Sage.

Collignon, F., Barker, L., & Vencill, M. (1992). The growth and structure of the proprietary rehabilitation sector. *American Rehabilitation, 18*, 7–10, 43.

Collison, B. B., Osborne, J. L., Gray, L. A., House, R. M., Firth, J., & Lou, M. (1998). Preparing counselors for social action. In C. C. Lee & G. R. Walz (Eds.), *Social action: A mandate for counselors* (pp. 263–278). Alexandria, VA: American Counseling Association.

Commission on Certification of Work Adjustment and Vocational Evaluation Specialists. (1999). *Standards and Procedures for Certification in Vocational Evaluation.* Rolling Meadows, IL: Author.

Commission on Rehabilitation Counselor Certification. (1990). *CCRC Certification Guide.* Rolling Meadows, IL: Author.

Commission on Rehabilitation Counselor Certification. (1994). *CRCC certification guide.* Rolling Meadows, IL: Author.

Commission on Rehabilitation Counselor Certification. (1999). *Certified rehabilitation counselor–clinical supervisor: An adjunct designation for specialized practice within rehabilitation counseling.* Rolling Meadows, IL: Author.

Commission on Rehabilitation Counselor Certification. (2001). *Code of professional ethics for rehabilitation counselors.* Rolling Meadows, IL: Author.

Commission on Rehabilitation Counselor Certification. (2002). *Professional code of ethics for rehabilitation counselors.* Rolling Meadows, IL: Author.

Cook, D., & Bolton, B. (1992). Rehabilitation counselor education and case performance: An independent replication. *Rehabilitation Counseling Bulletin, 36*, 37–43.

Cook, J. S., & Fritts, G. G. (1994). Planning process determines results. *Health Care Strategic Management, 12*(12), 19–21.

Coombs, N. (1998). Bridging the disability gap with distance learning. *Technology and Disability, 8*, 149–152.

Corey, G., Corey, M. S., & Callanan, P. (2003). *Issues and ethics in the helping professions* (6th ed.). Pacific Grove, CA: Brooks/Cole.

Corrigan, P. W., McCracken, S. G., & Holmes, E. P. (2001) Motivational interviews as goal assessment for persons with psychiatric disability. *Community Mental Health Journal, 37*(2), 113–122.

Corrigan, P. W., Rao, D., & Lam, C. (1999). Psychiatric rehabilitation. In F. Chan & M. Leahy (Eds.), *Health care and disability case management* (pp. 527–564). Lake Zurich, IL: Vocational Consultants Press.

Cottone, R. R. (1987). A systematic theory of vocational rehabilitation. *Rehabilitation Counseling Bulletin, 30,* 167–176.

Cottone, R. R., & Claus, R. E. (2000). Ethical decision making models: A review of the literature. *Journal of Counseling and Development, 78,* 275–283.

Cottone, R., & Cottone, L. (1986). A systematic analysis of vocational evaluation in the state-federal rehabilitation system. *Vocational Evaluation and Work Adjustment Bulletin, 19*(2), 47–54.

Cottone, R., & Emener, W. (1990). The psychomedical paradigm of vocational rehabilitation and its alternatives. *Rehabilitation Counseling Bulletin, 34,* 91–102.

Cottone, R. R., Tarvydas, V., & House, G. (1994). The effect of number and type of consulted relationships on the ethical decision making of graduate students in counseling. *Counseling and Values, 39,* 56–68.

Coudroglou, A., & Poole, D. L. (1984). *Disability, work, and social policy.* New York:

Council for Higher Education Accreditation. (2002). Accreditation and assuring quality in distance learning. *CHEA Monograph Series 2002, 1.*

Council on Rehabilitation Education. (2002). *CORE standards revised draft.* http://www.core-rehab.org/CoreStandardsReview.html

Council on Rehabilitation Education (CORE). (1991). *CORE Policy and Procedures Manual.* Champaign-Urbana, IL: Author.

Council on Rehabilitation Education (CORE). (1997). *Accreditation manual.* Retrieved October 2002, from http://www.core-rehab.org

Covey, S. R. (1989). *The seven habits of highly effective people: Restoring the character ethic.* New York: Simon & Schuster.

Cox, T. (Ed.). (1993). *Cultural diversity in organizations: Theory, research, & practice.* San Francisco: Berrett-Koehler.

Craig, G. J. (1992). *Human development* (6th ed.). Englewood Cliffs, NJ: Prentice-Hall.

Crewe, N. M. (2001). Assessment of independence. In B. F. Bolton (Ed.), *Handbook of measurement and evaluation in rehabilitation* (3rd ed., pp. 215–232). Gaithersburg, MD: Aspen.

Crewe, N. M., & Dijkers, M. (1995). Functional assessment. In L. A. Cushman & M. J. Scherer (Eds.), *Psychological assessment in medical rehabilitation* (pp. 101–144). Washington, DC: American Psychological Association.

Crichton, A., & Jongbloed, L. (1998). *Disability and social policy in Canada.* North York, ON: Catpus Press.

Crimando, W., & Riggar, T. F. (Eds.). (1991). *Utilizing community resources.* Delray Beach, FL: St. Lucie Press.

Crimando, W., Hansen, G., & Riggar, T. F. (1986). Personnel turnover: The plague of rehabilitation facilities. *Journal of Applied Rehabilitation Counseling, 17*(2), 17–20.

Crimando, W., Riggar, T. F., Bordieri, J. E., Benshoff, J. J., & Hanley-Maxwell, C. (1989). Managing change: A P.O.L.E.S. perspective. *Journal of Rehabilitation Administration, 13,* 143–150.

Cronbach, L. J. (1990). *Essentials of psychological testing* (5th ed.). New York: HarperCollins.

Cronin, M. (1996). Life skills curricula for students with learning disabilities: A review of the literature. *Journal of Learning Disabilities, 29*(1), 53–68.

Cross, W. E., Jr. (1995). The psychology of nigrescence: Revising the Cross model. In J. G. Ponterotto, J. M. Casas, L. A. Suzuki, & C. M. Alexander (Eds.), *Handbook of multicultural counseling* (pp. 93–122). Thousand Oaks, CA: Sage.

Currier, K. F., Chan, F., Berven, N. L., Habeck, R. V., & Taylor, D. W. (2001). Functions and knowledge domains for disability management practice: A Delphi study. *Rehabilitation Counseling Bulletin, 44*, 133–143.

Czerlinsky, T., Jensen, R., & Pell, K. L. (1987). Construct validity of the Vocational Decision-Making Interview (VDMI). *Rehabilitation Counseling Bulletin, 31,* 28–33.

D'Andrea, M., & Daniels, J. (1997, December). RESPECTFUL counseling: A new way of thinking about diversity counseling. *Counseling Today*, *40*(6), 30, 31, 34.

D'Andrea, M., & Daniels, J. (2001). RESPECTFUL counseling: An integrative model for counselors. In D. Pope-Davis & H. Coleman (Eds.), *The interface of class, culture and gender in counseling* (pp. 417–466). Thousand Oaks, CA: Sage.

D'Andrea, M., & Daniels, J. (in press). *Multicultural counseling: Empowerment strategies for a diverse society*. Pacific Grove, CA: Brooks/Cole.

Daniels, J. A., & Larson, L. M. (2001). The impact of performance feedback on counseling self-efficacy and counselor anxiety. *Counselor Education & Supervision, 41*, 120–130.

Davis, L. J. (1997). Constructing normalcy: The bell curve, the novel, and the invention of the disabled body in the nineteenth century. In L. J. Davis (Ed.), *Disability studies reader* (pp. 307–314). New York: Routledge.

Dawis, R. (1996).The theory of work adjustment and person-environment correspondence counseling. In D. Brown, L. Brooks, & Associates (Eds.), *Career choice and development* (3rd ed., pp. 75–120). San Francisco: Jossey-Bass.

DeJong, G., & Batavia, A. (1990). The Americans with Disabilities Act and the current state of U.S. disability policy. *Journal of Disability Policy Studies, 1*(3), 65–75.

Dembo, T., Leviton, G. L., & Wright, B. A. (1975). Adjustment to misfortune: A problem of social-psychological rehabilitation. *Rehabilitation Psychology, 2,* 1–100.

Dennis, R., Williams, W., Giangreco, M., & Cloninger, C. (1993). Quality of life as context for planning and evaluation of services for people with disabilities. *Exceptional Children, 59*(6), 499–512.

Deutsch, P. M. (1990). *A guide to rehabilitation testimony: The expert's role as an educator.* Orlando, FL: Paul M. Deutsch Press.

Deutsch, P. M. (1995). Life care planning. In A. E. Dell Orto & R. P. Marinelli (Eds.), *Encyclopedia of disability and rehabilitation* (pp. 436–442). New York: Simon & Schuster/MacMillan.

DeVinney, D., McReynolds, C., Currier, K., Mirch, M. C., & Chan, F. (1999). Vocational issues in disability case management. In F. Chan & M. J. Leahy (Eds.), *Health care and disability management* (pp. 183–212). Lake Zurich, IL: Vocational Consultants Press.

Dew, D. W., & Alan, G. M. (Eds.). (2002). *Distance education: Opportunities and issues for public vocational rehabilitation programs*. 28th Institute on Rehabilitation Issues. Washington, DC: George Washington University.

DiClemente, C. C. (1986). Self-efficacy and the addictive behaviors. *Journal of Social and Clinical Psychology, 4,* 302–315.

Dickinson, H. D., & Bolaria, B. S. (2002). The Canadian health care system: Evolution and current status. In B. S. Bolaria & H. D. Dickinson (Eds.), *Health, illness, and health care in Canada* (pp. 20–36). Scarborough, ON: Nelson Thomson Learning.

DiMichael, S. G. (1967). New directions and expectations in rehabilitation counseling. *Journal of Rehabilitation, 33*, 38–39.

Dixon, T. P., Goll, S., & Stanton, K. M. (1988). Case management issues and practices in head injury rehabilitation. *Rehabilitation Counseling Bulletin, 31*, 325–343.

Donnell, C. M., Lustig, D., & Strauser, D. R. (2002). The working alliance: Rehabilitation outcomes for persons with severe mental illness (2002 APA Annual Convention, Division 22 Poster Abstract). *Rehabilitation Psychology, 47,* 367.

Dowd, L. R. (1993). *Glossary of terminology for vocational assessment, evaluation, and work adjustment.* Menomonie: University of Wisconsin–Stout, Stout Vocational Rehabilitation Institute.

Drasgow, F., & Olson-Buchanan, J. B. (Eds.). (1999). *Innovations in computerized assessment.* Mahwah, NJ: Erlbaum.

Drummond, D. C., & Glautier, S. (1994). A controlled trial of cue exposure treatment in alcohol dependence. *Journal of Consulting and Clinical Psychology, 62*, 809–817.

Drury, D. (1991). Disability management in small firms. *Rehabilitation Counseling Bulletin, 34,* 243–256.

Dunn, P. L. (2001). Trends and issues in proprietary rehabilitation. In P. D. Rumrill, Jr., J. L. Bellini, & L. C. Koch (Eds.), *Emerging issues in rehabilitation counseling* (pp. 173–201). Springfield, IL: Charles C Thomas.

Ebener, D., Berven, N., & Wright, G. (1993). Self-perceived abilities of rehabilitation educators to teach competencies for rehabilitation practice. *Rehabilitation Counseling Bulletin, 37,* 6–14.

Edwards, P. (1999). Work activities of middle managers in rehabilitation facilities. *Journal of Rehabilitation Administration, 22,* 179–189.

Eisenberg, L. (1996). Foreword. In J. E. Mezzich, A. Kleinman, H. Fabrega, Jr., & D. L. Parron (Eds.), *Culture and psychiatric diagnosis: A DSM-IV perspective* (pp. xiii–xv). Washington, DC: American Psychiatric Association.

Eisenberg, M. G., Griggins, C., & Duval, R. J. (Eds.). (1982). *Disabled people as second class citizens.* New York: Springer.

Ekstrom, R. B., & Smith, D. K. (2002). *Assessing individuals with disabilities in educational, employment, and counseling settings.* Washington, DC: American Psychological Association.

Eldredge, G. M., McNamara, S., Stensrud, R., Gilbride, D., Hendren, G., Siegfried, T., et al. (1999). Distance education: A look at five programs. *Rehabilitation Education, 13*, 231–248.

Elliott, J., & Santner, D. (n.d.). *How to set up a tickler system that works.* Unpublished manuscript.

Embretson, S. E. (1992). Computerized adaptive testing: Its potential substantive contributions to psychological research and assessment. *Current Directions in Psychological Science, 1,* 129–131.

Emener, W. G., & Rubin, S. E. (1980). Rehabilitation counselor roles and functions and sources of role strain. *Journal of Applied Rehabilitation Counseling, 11*, 57–69.

English, W. R., Oberle, J. B., & Byrne, A. R. (1979). Rehabilitation counselor supervision: A national perspective [Special issue]. *Rehabilitation Counseling Bulletin, 22*, 7–123.

Eriksen, K. (1997). *Making an impact: A handbook on counseling advocacy.* Washington, DC: Taylor & Francis/Accelerated Development.

Eriksen, K. (1999). Counseling advocacy: A qualitative analysis of leaders' perceptions, organizational activities, and advocacy documents. *Journal of Mental Health Counseling, 21*(1), 33–49.

Eriksen, L., Bjornstad, S., & Gotestam, K. G. (1986). Social skills training in groups for alcoholic: One-year treatment outcomes for group and individuals. *Addictive Behavior, 11,* 309–329.

Erikson, E. (1968). *Identity: Youth and crisis.* New York: Norton.

Esser, T. J. (1975). *Client rating instruments for use in vocational rehabilitation agencies.* Menomonie: University of Wisconsin-Stout, Stout Vocational Rehabilitation Institute.

Esser, T. J. (1980). *Gathering information for evaluation planning.* Menomonie: University of Wisconsin-Stout, Stout Vocational Rehabilitation Institute.

Evenson, T. L., & Holloway, L. L. (2002). What is professionalism? In J. Andrews & C. Faubion (Eds.), *Rehabilitation services: An introduction for the human services professional* (pp. 238–278). Osage Beach, MO: Aspen Professional Services.

Fairness breeds effective supervision. (2001, October 15). *Leadership for the front lines,* p. 8.

Federal/Provincial/Territorial Ministers Responsible for Social Services. (1997). *In unison: A Canadian approach to disability issues.* Hull, PQ: Human Resources Development Canada.

Feist-Price, S. (1995). African Americans with disabilities and equity in vocational rehabilitation services: One state's review. *Rehabilitation Counseling Bulletin, 39,* 119–129.

Felce, D., & Perry, J. (1995). Quality of life: Its definition and measurement. *Research in Developmental Disabilities, 16*(1), 51–74.

Feldman, D. (1981). The multiple socialization of organization members. *Academy of Management Review, 6,* 309–318.

Field, T. F. (1993). *Strategies for the rehabilitation consultant: Transferability, loss of employment, lost earning capacity, and damages.* Athens, GA: Elliot & Fitzpatrick.

Field, T. F., & Sink, J. M. (1981). *The vocational expert.* Athens, GA: VSB.

Flanagan, J. (1978). A research approach to improving our quality of life. *American Psychologist, 33*(2), 138–147.

Fleming, M., & Levie, W. H. (1993). *Instructional message design: Principles from the behavioral sciences.* Englewood Cliffs, NJ: Educational Technology.

Flowers, C., Griffin-Dixon, C., & Trevino, B. (1997). Cultural pluralism: Contexts of practice. In D. R. Maki & T. F. Riggar (Eds.), *Rehabilitation counseling: Profession and practice* (pp. 124–136). New York: Springer Publishing Company.

Follette, W. C., & Houts, A. C. (1996). Models of scientific progress and the role of theory in taxonomy development: A case study of the DSM. *Journal of Consulting and Clinical Psychology, 64,* 1120–1132.

Francouer, R. T. (1983). Teaching decision making in biomedical ethics for the allied health student. *Journal of Allied Health, 12,* 202–209.

Freemantle, D. (2002). *How to choose.* Upper Saddle River, NJ: Prentice Hall Business.

Freiberg, P. (1991). Surprise—most bosses are incompetent. *APA Monitor, 22*(1), 23.

Freire, P. (1989). *Pedagogy of the oppressed.* New York: Continuum.

Fry, F. (1998). Canada moves toward a fuller funding for its pension plan. *Social Security Bulletin, 61*(1), 63–64.

Fuhrer, M. J. (1987). Overview of outcome analysis in rehabilitation. In M. J. Fuhrer (Ed.), *Rehabilitation outcomes: Analysis and measurement* (pp. 1–15). Baltimore: Paul H. Brookes.

Fulmer, R. M. (1988). *The new management.* New York: Macmillan.

Gagne, M., & Shepherd, M. (2001). Distance learning in accounting: A comparison between a distance and traditional graduate accounting class. *T.H.E. Journal, 28*(9), 58–65.

Gaines, T. F. (1979). Caseload management revisited. *Journal of Rehabilitation Administration, 110,* 112–118.

Galassi, J. P., & Perot, A. R. (1992). What you should know about behavioral assessment. *Journal of Counseling and Development, 70,* 624–631.

Gann, C., & Moreland, T. (1992). Introduction to insurance and workers' compensation. In J. M. Siefker (Ed.), *Vocational evaluation in private sector rehabilitation* (pp. 67–98). Menomonie, WI: Materials Development Center.

Garb, H. N. (1998). *Studying the clinician: Judgment research and psychological assessment.* Washington, DC: American Psychological Association.

Garb, H. N., Klein, D. F., & Grove, W. M. (2002). Comparison of medical and psychological tests. *American Psychologist, 57,* 137–138.

Garcia, J., Cartwright, B., Winston, S. M., & Borzuchowska, B. (in press). Model for integrating culture into ethical decision-making in counseling. *Journal of Counseling and Development.*

Gatens-Robinson, E., & Rubin, S. E. (1995). Societal values and ethical commitments that influence rehabilitation service delivery behavior. In S. E. Rubin & R. T. Roessler (Eds.), *Foundations of the vocational rehabilitation process* (pp. 157–174). Austin, TX: Pro-Ed.

General Accounting Office. (1993). *Vocational Rehabilitation: Evidence for federal program's effectiveness is mixed* (GAO/PEMD-93-19). Washington, DC: Author.

Gephart, R. P. (2002). Introduction to the brave new workplace: Organizational behavior in the electronic age. *Journal of Organizational Behavior, 23,* 327–344.

Gibson, T. F., & Mazur, D. A. (1995). Preparing for the strategic planning process helps ensure implementation success. *Health Care Strategic Management, 13*(1), 14–17.

Gilbride, D. (1993). Rehabilitation education in the private sector. In L. Perlman & C. Hansen (Eds.), *Private sector rehabilitation insurance: Trends and issues for the 21st century* (pp. 22–26). Alexandria, VA: National Rehabilitation Association.

Gilbride, D. (2000). Going to work: Placement trends in public rehabilitation. *Journal of Vocational Rehabilitation, 14,* 89–94.

Gilbride, D., & Burr, F. (1993). Self-directed labor market survey: An empowering approach. *Journal of Job Placement, 9*(2), 13–17.

Gilbride, D., & Stensrud, R. (1992). Demand-side job development: A model for the 1990s. *Journal of Rehabilitation, 58,* 34–39.

Gilbride, D., & Stensrud, R. (1993). Challenges and opportunities for rehabilitation counselors in the Americans with Disabilities Act era. *NARPPS Journal, 8,* 67–74.

Gilbride, D., & Stensrud, R. (1999). Demand-side job development and system change. *Rehabilitation Counseling Bulletin, 42,* 329–342.

Gilbride, D., Connolly, M., & Stensrud, R. (1990). Rehabilitation education for the private-for-profit sector. *Rehabilitation Education, 4,* 155–162.

Gilbride, D., Stensrud, R., & Johnson, M. (1994). Current models of job placement and employer development: Research, competencies and educational considerations. *Rehabilitation Education, 7,* 215–239.

Gilbride, D., Stensrud, R., Vandergoot, D., & Golden, K. (2003). Identification of the characteristics of employers who are open to hiring and accommodating people with disabilities. *Rehabilitation Counseling Bulletin, 46,* 130–137.

Gilligan, C. (1982). *In a different voice: Psychological theory and women's development.* Cambridge, MA: Harvard University Press.

Gleeson, B. (1999). *Geographics of disability.* New York: Rutledge.

Glosofs, H., Benshoff, J., Hosie, T., & Maki, D. (1995). The 1994 model legislation for licensed professional counselors. *Journal of Counseling and Development, 74,* 209–220.

Glueckauf, R. L., Fritz, S. P., Ecklund-Johnson, E. P., Liss, H. J., Dages, P., & Carney, P. (2002). Videoconferencing-based family counseling for rural teenagers with epilepsy: Phase 1 findings. *Rehabilitation Psychology, 47*(1), 49–72.

Goffman, E. (1963). *Stigma: Notes on the management of spoiled identity.* Englewood Cliffs, NJ: Prentice-Hall.

Goldman, B. A., & Mitchell, D. F. (2002). *Directory of unpublished experimental mental measures: Vol. 8.* Washington, DC: American Psychological Association.

Goldman, L. (1971). *Using tests in counseling* (2nd ed.). Pacific Palisades, CA: Goodyear.

Goodinson, S., & Singleton, J. (1989). Quality of life: A critical review of current concepts, measures and their clinical implications. *International Journal of Nursing Students, 26*(4), 327–341.

Gray, L. A., Ladany, N., Walker, J. A., & Ancis, J. R. (2001). Psychotherapy trainees' experience of counterproductive events in supervision. *Journal of Counseling Psychology, 48,* 371–383.

Grech, E. (2002). Case management: A critical analysis of the literature. *International Journal of Psychosocial Rehabilitation, 6,* 89–98.

Greenwood, R. (1992). Systematic caseload management. In R. T. Roessler & S. E. Rubin (Eds.), *Case management and rehabilitation counseling* (2nd ed., pp. 143–154). Austin, TX: Pro-Ed.

Grob, G. N. (1973). *Mental institutions in America: Social policy to 1875.* New York: The Free Press.

Groth-Marnat, G. (1997). *Handbook of psychological assessment* (3rd ed.). New York: Wiley.

Growick, B. (1993). Rehabilitation in workers' compensation: A growth potential. In L. G. Perlman & C. E. Hansen (Eds.), *Private sector rehabilitation: Insurance, trends & issues for the 21st century: A report on the 17th Mary E. Switzer Seminar* (pp. 68–70). Alexandria, VA: National Rehabilitation Association.

Gruber, J., & Trickett, E. J. (1987). Can we empower others? The paradox of empowerment in the governing of alternative public schools. *American Journal of Community Psychology, 15*(3), 355–371.

Guest, C. L., Jr., & Dooley, K. (1999). Supervisor malpractice: Liability to the supervisee in clinical supervision. *Counselor Education and Supervision, 38,* 269–279.

Gunn, L. D., & Gunn, T. R. (1999). A defense attorney's perspective on life care planning. In R. O. Weed (Ed.), *Life Care Planning and Case Management Handbook.* Boca Raton, FL: CRC Press.

Gutteridge, T., Leibowitz, Z., & Shore, J. (1993). Career development in the United States: Rethinking careers in the flattened organization. In T. Gutteridge, Z. Leibowitz, & J. Shore (Eds.), *Organizational career development: Benchmarks for building a world-class workforce* (pp. 11–34). San Francisco: Jossey-Bass.

Habeck, R. V., & Kirchner, K. (1999). Case management issues within employer-based disability management. In F. Chan & M. J. Leahy (Eds.), *Health care and disability management* (pp. 239–264). Lake Zurich, IL: Vocational Consultants Press.

Habeck, R. V., Hunt, H. A., & VanTol, B. (1998). Workplace factors associated with preventing and managing work disability. *Rehabilitation Counseling Bulletin, 42,* 98–143.

Habeck, R. V., Leahy, M. J., Hunt, H. A., Chan, F., & Welch, E. M. (1991). Employer factors related to workers' compensation claims and disability management. *Rehabilitation Counseling Bulletin, 34,* 210–225.

Habeck, R. V., Scully, S. M., VanTol, B., & Hunt, H. A. (1998). Successful employer strategies for preventing and managing disability. *Rehabilitation Counseling Bulletin, 42,* 144–161.

Hahn, H. (1985). Changing perception of disability and the future of rehabilitation. In L. Perlman & G. Austin (Eds.), *Social influences in rehabilitation planning: Blueprint for the 21st century* (pp. 53–64). Alexandria, VA: National Rehabilitation Association.

Hahn, H. (1988). The politics of physical differences: Disability and discrimination. *Journal of Social Issues, 44,* 39–47.

Hahn, H. (1993). The political implications of disability definitions and data. *Journal of Disability Policy Studies, 4*(1), 41–52.

Hahn, H. (1997). Advertising the acceptable employment image: Disability and capitalism. In L. J. Davis (Ed.), *The disabilities studies reader* (pp. 172–186). New York: Routledge.

Half, R. (1985). *On hiring.* New York: Crown.

Hall, J. H., & Warren, S. L. (Eds.). (1956). *Rehabilitation counselor preparation.* Washington, DC: National Rehabilitation Association and the National Vocational Guidance Association.

Halpern, A. S., & Fuhrer, M. J. (Eds.). (1984). *Functional assessment in rehabilitation.* Baltimore: Paul H. Brookes.

Handelsman, M. M., & Uhelemann, M. R. (1998). Be careful what you wish for: Issues in the statutatory regulation of counsellors. *Canadian Journal of Counselling, 32*(4), 315–331.

Hannah, M. E., & Midlarsky, E. (1987). Differential impact of labels and behavioral descriptions on attitudes toward people with disabilities. *Rehabilitation Psychology, 32,* 227–238.

Hanson, M. A., Matheson, L. N., & Borman, W. C. (2001). The O*NET occupational information system. In B. F. Bolton (Ed.), *Handbook of measurement and evaluation in rehabilitation* (3rd ed., pp. 281–309). Gaithersburg, MD: Aspen.

Harrison, D. K., & Lee, C. C. (1979). Rehabilitation counselor competencies. *Journal of Applied Rehabilitation Counseling, 10,* 135–141.

Harrison, D. K., Garnett, J. M., & Watson, A. L. (1981). *Client assessment measures in rehabilitation* (Michigan Studies in Rehabilitation Utilization Series: 5). Ann Arbor: University of Michigan Rehabilitation Research Institute.

Haverkamp, B. E. (1993). Confirmatory bias in hypothesis testing for client-identified and counselor self-generated hypotheses. *Journal of Counseling Psychology, 40,* 303–315.

Havighurst, R. J. (1953). *Human development and education.* New York: Longman.

Havranek, J., Grimes, J. W., Field, T. F., & Sink, J. M. (1994). *Vocational assessment: Evaluating employment potential.* Athens, GA: Elliot & Fitzpatrick.

Helms, J. E. (1995). An update of Helm's White and people of color racial identity models. In J. G. Ponterotto, J. M. Casas, L. A. Suzuki, & C. M. Alexander (Eds.), *Handbook of multicultural counseling* (pp. 181–191). Thousand Oaks, CA: Sage.

Helms, J. E., & Cook, D. A. (1999). *Using race and culture in counseling and psychotherapy: Theory and process.* Boston: Allyn and Bacon.

Henke, R. O., Connolly, S. G., & Cox, J. S. (1975). Caseload management: The key to effectiveness. *Journal of Applied Rehabilitation Counseling, 6*(4), 217–227.

Herbert, J. T. (1995). Clinical supervision. In A. E. Del Orto & R. P. Marinelli (Eds.), *Encyclopedia of disability and rehabilitation* (pp. 178–190). New York: Macmillan.

Herbert, J. T. (1997). Quality assurance: Administration and supervision. In D. R. Maki & T. F. Riggar (Eds.), *Rehabilitation counseling: Profession and practice* (pp. 247–258). New York: Springer Publishing.

Herbert, J. T. (in press). Clinical supervision in rehabilitation settings. In F. Chan, K. R. Thomas, & N. Berven (Eds.), *Counseling theories and techniques for rehabilitation health professionals.*

Herbert, J. T., & Bieschke, K. J. (2000). A didactic course in clinical supervision. *Rehabilitation Education, 14,* 187–198.

Herbert, J. T., & Richardson, B. K. (1995). Introduction to the special issue on rehabilitation counselor supervision [Special issue]. *Rehabilitation Counseling Bulletin, 36,* 278–281.

Herbert, J. T., & Ward, T. J. (1989). Rehabilitation counselor supervision: A national survey of graduate training practica. *Rehabilitation Education, 3,* 163–175.

Herbert, J. T., Ward, T. J., & Hemlick, L. M. (1995). Confirmatory factor analysis of the Supervisory Style Inventory and Revised Supervision Questionnaire. *Rehabilitation Counseling Bulletin, 38,* 334–349.

Hergenhahn, B. R. (2001). *An introduction to the history of psychology* (4th ed.). Belmont, CA: Wadsworth.

Hershenson, D. (1996). A theoretical model for rehabilitation counseling. *Rehabilitation Counseling Bulletin, 33,* 268–278.

Higgins, P. C. (1992). *Making disability: Exploring the social transformation of human variation.* Springfield, IL: Charles C Thomas.

Himmelstein, D. U., & Woolhandler, S. (1998). Canada's national health program. In R. Chernomas & A. Sepehri (Eds.), *How to Choose? A Comparison of U.S. and Canadian Health Care Systems* (pp. 145–152). Amityville, NY: Baywood Publishing.

Holleman, M. P. (1991). *From darkness into light: The founding of the Canadian Paraplegic Association.* Toronto: The Canadian Paraplegic Association.

Holmes, G. E. (1993). The historical roots of the empowerment dilemma in vocational rehabilitation. *Journal of Disability Policy Studies, 4,* 1–20.

Holmes, G. E., Hall, L., & Karst, R. H. (1989). Litigation avoidance through conflict resolution: Issues for state rehabilitation agencies. *American Rehabilitation, 15*(3), 12–15.

Holzbauer, J. J., & Berven, N. L. (1999). Issues in vocational evaluation and testing related to the Americans with Disabilities Act. *Vocational Evaluation and Work Adjustment Bulletin, 32,* 83–96.

Hosack, K. (1998). The value of case management in catastrophic injury rehabilitation and long-term management. *The Journal of Care Management, 4,* 58–67.

Howe, R. S. (1999). Case management in managed care: Past, present and future. *The Case Manager, 10,* 37–40.

Hunsley, J. (2002). Psychological testing and psychological assessment: A closer examination. *American Psychologist, 57,* 139–140.

Hutchinson, J. D., Luck, R. S., & Hardy, R. E. (1978). Training needs of a group of vocational rehabilitation agency administrators. *Journal of Rehabilitation Administration, 2,* 156–159, 178.

Hutchinson, P., Dunn, P., Lord, J., & Pedlar, A. (1996). *Impact of independent living resource centres in Canada.* St. Catharines, ON: Brock University.

Institute for Higher Education Policy. (1999, April). *What's the difference? A review of contemporary research on the effectiveness of distance learning in higher education.* Retrieved December 4, 2002, from http://www.nea.org/abouthe/diseddif.pdf

Ison, T. G. (1996). A historical perspective on contemporary challenges in workers' compensation. *Osgoode Hall Law Journal, 34,* 806–833.

Ivey, A., D'Andrea, M., Ivey, M., & Simek-Morgan, L. (2002). *Counseling and psychotherapy: A multicultural perspective* (5th ed.). Boston: Allyn & Bacon.

Jacobs, H. E., Wissusik, D., Collier, R., Stackman, D., & Burkeman, D. (1992). Correlations between psychiatric disabilities and vocational outcome. *Hospital and Community Psychiatry, 43,* 365–369.

Jaet, D. N., & McMahon, B. T. (1999). Implications of disability legislation for case managers. In F. Chan & M. J. Leahy (Eds.), *Health care & disability case management.* Lake Zurich, IL: Vocational Consultants Press.

Jaques, M. E. (1959). *Critical counseling behavior in rehabilitation settings.* Iowa City: State University of Iowa, College of Education.

Jaques, M. E. (1970). *Rehabilitation counseling: Scope and services.* Boston: Houghton Mifflin.

Jenkins, W., Patterson, J. B., & Szymanski, E. M. (1992). Philosophical, historic, and legislative aspects of the rehabilitation counseling profession. In R. M. Parker & E. M. Szymanski (Eds.), *Rehabilitation counseling: Basics and beyond* (2nd ed., pp. 1–41). Austin, TX: Pro-Ed.

Johnson, M. (2002). Introductory biology online: Assessing outcomes of two student populations. *Journal of College Science Teaching, 31,* 312–317.

Johnson, S. D., Aragon, S. R., Shaik, N., & Palma-Rivas, N. (2000). Comparative analysis of learner satisfaction and learning outcomes in online and face-to-face learning environments. *Journal of Interactive Learning Research, 11*(1), 29–49.

Jones, J. M. (1997). *Prejudice and racism* (2nd ed.). New York: McGraw-Hill.

Jones, R. J. E. (1994). *Their rightful place: Society and disability.* Toronto, ON: Canadian Academy of the Arts.

Kahneman, D., Slovic, P., & Tversky, A. (1982). *Judgment under uncertainty: Heuristics and biases.* New York: Cambridge University Press.

Kaplan, I., & Hammond, N. (1982). Projects with Industry: The concept and the realization. *American Rehabilitation, 8,* 3–7.

Kaplan, R. E. (2002). Know your strengths. *Harvard Business Review, 80*(3), 20–22.

Kaplan, R. M., & Saccuzzo, D. P. (1997). *Psychological testing. Principles, applications, and issues* (4th ed.). Pacific Grove, CA: Brooks/Cole.

Keith-Spiegel, P., & Koocher, G. P. (1998). *Ethics in psychology* (2nd ed.). New York: Random House.

Kelly, E. W. (1995). *Spirituality and religion in counseling and psychotherapy: Diversity in theory and practice.* Alexandria, VA: American Counseling Association.

Kenny, G. (1994). Multicultural investigation of counseling expectations and preferences. *Journal of College Student Psychotherapy, 9,* 21–39.

Key, S. (2002). Perceived managerial discretion: An analysis of individual ethical intentions. *Journal of Managerial Issues, 14*(2), 218–233.

Kiernan, W., Sanchez, R., & Schalock, R. (1989). Economics, industry, and disability in the future. In W. Kiernan & R. Schalock (Eds.), *Economics, industry, and disability* (pp. 365–374). Baltimore: Paul H. Brookes.

Kiesler, D. J. (1999). *Beyond the disease model of mental disorders.* Westport, CT: Praeger.

Kim, D. (1999). *Introduction to systems thinking.* Williston, VT: Pegasus Communications.

Kinney, C. F. (1996). Organizing work as a system. *Today's management methods*, p. 41, 14p. Retrieved November 25, 2002, from EBSCO database.

Kirk, S. A., & Kutchins, H. (1992). *The selling of the DSM: The rhetoric of science in psychiatry.* New York: Aldine Degruyter.

Kitchener, K. S. (1984). Intuition, critical evaluation and ethical principles: The foundation for ethical decisions in counseling psychology. *The Counseling Psychologist, 12*(3), 43–55.

Kleinfield, S. (1979). *The hidden minority: A profile of handicapped Americans.* Boston: Atlantic Monthly Press.

Knowles, M. (1990). *The adult learner: A neglected species* (4th ed.). Houston: Gulf Publishing.

Knowles, M. S. (1990). Adult learning: Theory and practice. In L. Nadler & Z. Nadler (Eds.), *Handbook of human resource development* (2nd ed., pp. 6.1–6.23). New York: John Wiley & Sons.

Koch, L. C., & Rumrill, P. D. (1997). Rehabilitation counseling outside the state agency: Settings, roles, and functions for the new millennium. *Journal of Applied Rehabilitation Counseling, 28,* 9–14.

Kohlberg, L. (1981). *The philosophy of moral development.* San Francisco, CA: Harper & Row.

Kosciulek, J. (1993). Advances in trait-and-factor theory: A person × environment fit approach to rehabilitation counseling. *Journal of Applied Rehabilitation Counseling, 24*(2), 11–14.

Kosciulek, J. F. (1999). The consumer-directed theory of empowerment. *Rehabilitation Counseling Bulletin, 42,* 196–213.

Kosciulek, J. F., & Merz, M. A. (2001). Structural analysis of the consumer-directed theory of empowerment. *Rehabilitation Counseling Bulletin, 44,* 209–216.

Kozlowska, K., Nunn, K., & Cousins, P. (1997). Adverse experiences in psychiatric training. Part 2. *Australian and New Zealand Journal of Psychiatry, 31,* 641–652.

Kreider, J. (1996). All lines case management coverage. *The Case Manager, 7,* 47–52.

Kuehn, M. D. (1991). An agenda for professional practice in the 1990s. *Journal of Applied Rehabilitation Counseling, 22*(3), 6–15.

Kuehn, M. D., Crystal, R. M., & Ursprung, A. (1988). Challenges for rehabilitation counselor education. In S. Rubin & N. Rubin (Eds.), *Contemporary challenges to the rehabilitation counseling profession* (pp. 273–302). Baltimore: Paul H. Brookes.

Kunkel, M. A. (1990) Expectations about counseling in relation to acculturation in Mexican-American and Anglo-American student samples. *Journal of Counseling Psychology, 37,* 286–292.

Kurpius, D. J., Fuqua, D. R., & Rozecki, T. (1993). The consulting process: A multidimensional approach. *Journal of Counseling and Development, 71,* 601–606.

LaBuda, J. (1995, Fall). Counselors counsel; Clients sue. *CRC: The Counselor,* 6–7.

Lakein, A. (1973). *How to get control of your time and your life.* New York: Signet.

Langton, A. (2000). *Integrating rehabilitation technology: The TECH point process.* Columbia, SC: The Langton Group.

Larson, L. M. (1998). The social cognitive model of counselor training. *The Counseling Psychologist, 26,* 219–273.

Larson, L. M., & Daniels, J. A. (1998). Review of the counseling self-efficacy literature. *The Counseling Psychologist, 26,* 179–218.

Lauterbach, J. R. (1982, April 5). Coaching the disabled back to work. *Industry Week,* 52–55.

Leahy, M. J. (1994). *Validation of essential knowledge dimensions for case management (Technical report).* Rolling Meadows, IL: Foundation for Rehabilitation Certification, Education and Research.

Leahy, M. J. (1999). Practitioner accountability: Professionalism, credentials, and regulation. *Report of the 20th Mary Switzer Memorial Seminar.* Washington, DC: National Rehabilitation Association.

Leahy, M. J., Chan, F., & Magrega, D. J. (1997). Knowledge importance and training needs in rehabilitation counselling: Perceptions of Canadian certified rehabilitation counsellors. *Canadian Journal of Rehabilitation, 10*(3), 215–229.

Leahy, M. J., Chan, F., & Saunders, J. (2001). *An analysis of job functions and knowledge requirements of Certified Rehabilitation Counselors in the 21st century.* Chicago: Foundation for Rehabilitation Education and Research.

Leahy, M. J., Chan, F., & Shaw, L. R. (1999). Essential knowledge underlying case management practice. In F. Chan & M. J. Leahy (Eds.), *Health care and disability management* (pp. 61–88). Lake Zurich, IL: Vocational Consultants Press.

Leahy, M. J., & Holt, E. (1993). Certification in rehabilitation counseling: History and process. *Rehabilitation Counseling Bulletin, 37*(2), 71–80.

Leahy, M. J., Shapson, P. R., & Wright, G. N. (1987). Rehabilitation practitioners competencies by role and setting. *Rehabilitation Counseling Bulletin, 31,* 119–131.

Leahy, M. J., & Szymanski, E. M. (1995). Rehabilitation counseling: Evolution and current status. *Journal of Counseling and Development, 74,* 163–166.

Leahy, M. J., Szymanski, E. M., & Linkowski, D. C. (1993). Knowledge importance in rehabilitation counseling. *Rehabilitation Counseling Bulletin, 37,* 130–145.

Leahy, M. J., & Tarvydas, V. T. (2001). Transforming our professional organizations: A first step toward unification of the rehabilitation counseling profession. *Journal of Applied Rehabilitation Counseling, 32,* 3–8.

Lerner (1972). *Therapy in the ghetto: Political impotence and personal disintegration.* Baltimore: Johns Hopkins University.

Levers, L. L., & Maki, D.R. (1995). African indigenous healing and cosmology: Toward a philosophy of ethnorehabilitation. *Rehabilitation Education, 9*(2–3), 127–145.

Lewis, J., Lewis, M., Daniels, J., & D'Andrea, M. (2003). *Community counseling: Empowerment strategies for a diverse society.* Pacific Grove, CA: Brooks/Cole.

Lewis, J. A., & Lewis, M. D. (1983). *Community counseling: A human services approach.* New York: John Wiley.

Lewis, J. A., Hayes, B. A., & Bradley, L. J. (Eds.). (1992). *Counseling women over the life span.* Denver, CO: Love Publishing.

Lewis, W. (1998). A supervision model for public agencies. *Clinical Supervisor, 6*(2), 85–91.

Liachowitz, C. H. (1988). *Disability as a social construct: Legislative roots.* Philadelphia: University of Pennsylvania Press.

Linkowski, D. L., & Szymanski, E. M. (1993). Accreditation in rehabilitation counseling: Historical and current content and process. *Rehabilitation Counseling Bulletin, 37,* 81–91.

Lisoski, E. (1998). Courage, character and conviction—The three "c's" of outstanding supervision. *Supervision, 59*(9), 7–9.

Liss, H. J., Glueckauf, R. L., & Ecklund-Johnson, E. P. (2002). Research on telehealth and chronic medical conditions: Critical review, key issues, and future directions. *Rehabilitation Psychology, 47*(1), 8–30.

Liu, W. M., & Pope-Davis, D. B. (in press). Moving from diversity to multiculturalism: Exploring power and the implications for psychology. In D. B. Pope-Davis, H. L. K. Coleman, W. M. Liu, & R. L. Toporek (Eds.), *The handbook of multicultural competencies.* Thousand Oaks: Sage.

Livneh, H. (1995). The tripartite model of rehabilitation intervention: Basics, goals and rehabilitation strategies. *Journal of Applied Rehabilitation Counseling, 26*(1), 25–29.

Livneh, H. (2000). Psychosocial adaptation to spinal cord injury: The role of coping strategies. *Journal of Applied Rehabilitation Counseling, 31*(2), 3–10.

Loevinger, J. (1976). *Ego development.* San Francisco, CA: Jossey-Bass.

Lofquist, L. H., & Dawis, R. V. (1969). *Adjustment to work: A psychological view of man's problems in a work-oriented society.* New York: Appleton-Century-Crofts.

Lofquist, L., & Dawis, R. (2002). Person-environment-correspondence theory. In D. Brown (Ed.), *Career choice and development* (4th ed.). San Francisco: Jossey-Bass.

Lopez, S. R. (1989). Patient variable biases in clinical judgment: Conceptual overview and methodological implications. *Psychological Bulletin, 106,* 184–203.

Lui, J. (1993). Trends and innovation in private sector rehabilitation for the 21st century. In L. Perlman & C. Hansen (Eds.), *Private sector rehabilitation insurance: Trends and issues for the 21st century* (pp. 47–50). Alexandria, VA: National Rehabilitation Association.

Lui, J., Chan, F., Kwok, J. M., & Thorson, R. (1999). Managed care concepts in the delivery of case management services. In F. Chan & M. J. Leahy (Eds.), *Health care and disability management* (pp. 91–119). Lake Zurich, IL: Vocational Consultants Press.

Luthans, F. (2002). The need for and meaning of positive organizational behavior. *Journal of Organizational Behavior, 23*, 696–706.

Luther, D. B. (1995). Put strategic planning to work. *Association Management, 47*(1), 73–76.

Lynch, R. K. (1983). The vocational expert. *Rehabilitation Counseling Bulletin, 27,* 18–25.

Lynch, R., Habeck, R., & Sebastian, M. (1997). Professional practice: Consultation. In D. Maki & T. F. Riggar (Eds.), *Rehabilitation counseling: Profession and practice* (pp. 183–196). New York: Springer Publishing Co.

Lynch, R. K., & Lynch, R. T. (1998). Rehabilitation counseling in the private sector. In R. M. Parker & E. M. Szymanski (Eds.), *Rehabilitation counseling: Basics and beyond* (3rd ed., pp. 71–105). Austin, TX: Pro-Ed.

Lynch, R., & Martin, T. (1982). Rehabilitation counseling: A training needs survey. *Journal of Rehabilitation, 48,* 51–52, 73.

Lynch, R. K., Lynch, R. T., & Beck, R. (1992). Rehabilitation counseling in the private sector. In R. M. Parker & E. M. Szymanski (Eds.), *Rehabilitation counseling. Basics and beyond* (pp. 73–102). Austin, TX: Pro-Ed.

Lynk, M. (1998). A hardy transplant: The duty to accommodate and disability rights in Canadian labour law. *Labor Law Journal, 48,* 962.

Mabe, A. R., & Rollin, S. A. (1986). The role of a code of ethical standards in counseling. *Journal of Counseling and Development, 64*, 294–297.

Macoby, M. (1997). Building trust is an art. *Research Technology Management, 40*(5), 56–57.

Maki, D. R. (1986). Foundations of applied rehabilitation counseling. In T. F. Riggar, D. Maki, & A. Wolf (Eds.), *Applied rehabilitation counseling* (pp. 3–11). New York: Springer Publishing.

Maki, D. R., & Delworth, U. (1995). Clinical supervision: A definition and model for the rehabilitation counseling profession. *Rehabilitation Counseling Bulletin, 38*, 282–293.

Maki, D. R., McCracken, N., Pape, D. A., & Scofield, M. E. (1979). A systems approach to vocational assessment. *Journal of Rehabilitation, 45*(1), 48–51.

Maki, D., & Murray, G. (1995). Philosophy of rehabilitation. In A. Dell Orto & R. Marenelli (Eds.), *Encyclopedia of disability and rehabilitation* (pp. 555–561). New York: Macmillan.

Maki, D. R., & Riggar, T. F. (Eds.). (1997a). *Rehabilitation counseling: Profession and practice.* New York: Springer Publishing.

Maki, D. R., & Riggar, T. F. (1997b). Rehabilitation counseling. Concepts and paradigms. In D. R. Maki & T. F. Riggar (Eds.), *Rehabilitation counseling: Profession and practice* (pp. 3–31). New York: Springer Publisher.

Malkmus, D. D. (1993). Facility-based case management: Accountability for outcome, costs and value. In C. J. Durgin & N. D. Schmidt (Eds.), *Staff development and clinical intervention in brain injury rehabilitation* (pp. 303–334). Gaithersburg, MD: Aspen.

Mannock, T. J., Levesque, D. A., & Prochaska, J. M. (2002). Assessing readiness of clients with disabilities to engage in job seeking behaviors. *Journal of Rehabilitation, 68*(3), 16–23.

Marcus, B. H., Emmons, K. M., Simkin-Silverman, L. R., Linnan, L. A., Taylor, E. R., Bock, B. C., et al. (1998). Evaluation of motivationally tailored vs. standard self-help physical activity interventions at the workplace. *American Journal of Health Promotion, 12,* 246–253.

Marini, I., & Reid, C. (2001). A survey of rehabilitation professionals as alternative provider contractors with Social Security: Problems and solutions. *Journal of Rehabilitation, 67*(2), 36–41.

Marini, I., & Stebnicki, M. (1999). Social Security Administration's alternative provider program: What can rehabilitation administrators expect? *Journal of Rehabilitation Administration, 23*(1), 31–43.

Marshall, K. T., & Oliver, R. M. (1995). *Decision making and forecasting.* New York: McGraw-Hill.

Matkin, R. (1983). The roles and functions of rehabilitation specialists in the private sector. *Journal of Applied Rehabilitation Counseling, 14,* 14–27.

Matkin, R. (1987). Content areas and recommended training sites of insurance rehabilitation specialists. *Rehabilitation Education, 1,* 233–246.

Matkin, R. E. (1982). Preparing rehabilitation counselors to perform supervisory and administrative responsibilities. *Journal of Applied Rehabilitation Counseling, 49,* 25–28, 67.

Matkin, R. E. (1983). Credentialing and the rehabilitation profession. *Journal of Rehabilitation, 49,* 25–28, 67.

Matkin, R. E. (1985). *Insurance rehabilitation.* Austin, TX: Pro-Ed.

Matkin, R. E., Sawyer, H. W., Lorenz, J. R., & Rubin, S. E. (1982). Rehabilitation administrators and supervisors: Their work assignments, training needs, and suggestions for preparation. *Journal of Rehabilitation Administration, 6,* 170–183.

McArthur, C. (1954). Analyzing the clinical process. *Journal of Counseling Psychology, 1,* 203–208.

McCarthy, H. (1993). Learning with Beatrice A. Wright: A breath of fresh air that uncovers the unique virtues and human flaws in us all. *Rehabilitation Education, 10,* 149–166.

McClure, B. A., & Russo, T. R. (1996). The politics of counseling: Looking back and forward. *Counseling & Values, 40*(3), 162–174.

McCormack, M. (2000). The dangers of praise. *New Zealand Management, 47*(9), 17.

McCourt, A. E. (1993). *The specialty practice of rehabilitation nursing: A core curriculum* (3rd ed.). Skokie, IL: Rehabilitation Nursing Foundation.

McKenna, I. B. (1998). Legal rights for persons with disabilities in Canada: Can the impasse be resolved? *Ottawa Law Review, 29,* 153–197.

McMahon, B. T., Shaw, L. R., & Mahaffey, D. P. (1988). Career opportunities and professional preparation in had injury rehabilitation. *Rehabilitation Counseling Bulletin, 31,* 344–354.

McWhirter, E. H. (1994). *Counseling for empowerment.* Alexandria, VA: American Counseling Association.

McWhirter, E. H. (1997). Empowerment, social activism, and counseling. *Counseling and Human Development, 29*(8), 1–14.

Meara, N. M., Schmidt, L. D., & Day, J. D. (1996). Principles and virtue: A foundation for ethical decisions, policies, and character. *The Counseling Psychologist, 24*(1), 4–77.

Meili, P. (1993, April/May). The rehabilitation market. *Rehabilitation Management,* 96–102.

Melvyn, J. L. (1980). Interdisciplinary and multidisciplinary activities and the ACRM. *Archives of Physical Medicine and Rehabilitation, 61*, 379–380.

Menz, F. E., & Bordieri, J. E. (1986). Rehabilitation facility administrator training needs: Priorities and patterns for the 1980's. *Journal of Rehabilitation Administration, 10,* 89–98.

Meyer, G. J., Finn, S. E., Eyde, L. D., Kay, G. G., Moreland, K. L., Dies, R. R., et al. (2001). Psychological testing and psychological assessment. A review of evidence. *American Psychologist, 56,* 128–165.

Meyer, J., & Donaho, M. (1979). *Get the right person for the job.* Englewood Cliffs, NJ: Prentice-Hall.

Miller, L. A., Moriarty, J. B., Noble, J. H., Oestrich, R. P., Wright, G., & Collington, F. C. (1976). Reviews of "An evaluation of policy-related rehabilitation research." *Rehabilitation Counseling Bulletin, 20,* 46–61.

Miller, W. R., & Rollnick, S. (1991). *Motivational interview.* New York: Guilford.

Millington, M., Asner, K., Linkowski, D., & Der-Stepanian, J. (1996) Employers and job development: The business perspective. In R. Parker & E. Szymanski (Eds.), *Rehabilitation counseling: Basics and beyond* (pp. 277–308). Austin, TX: Pro-Ed.

Mittra, S. S. (1986). *Decision support systems.* New York: Wiley.

Montgomery, M. J., Hendricks, B. C., & Bradley, L. J. (2001). Using systems perspectives in supervision. *Family Journal, 9,* p. 305, 9p. Retrieved November 25, 2002, from EBSCO database.

Moore, C., & Feist-Price, S. (1999). Societal attitudes and the civil rights of persons with disabilities. *Journal of Applied Rehabilitation Counseling, 30*(2), 19–24.

Moore, C. L. (2001). Disparities in job placement outcomes among deaf, late-deafened, and hard of hearing consumers. *Rehabilitation Counseling Bulletin, 44*(3), 144.

Morelock, K., Roessler, R., & Bolton, B. (1987). The employability maturity interview: Reliability and construct validity. *Vocational Evaluation and Work Adjustment Bulletin, 20,* 3–59.

Morgan, G. (1997). *Images of organization* (2nd ed.). Thousand Oaks, CA: Sage.

Moriarty, J. B., Walls, R. T., & McLaughlin, D. E. (1987). The Preliminary Diagnostic Questionnaire (PDQ): Functional assessment of employability. *Rehabilitation Psychology, 32,* 5–15.

Morris, K. (1973). Welfare reform 1973: The social services dimension. *Science, 81*, 515–522.

Morrow, K. A., & Deidan, C. T. (1992). Bias in the counseling process: How to recognize it and avoid it. *Journal of Counseling and Development, 70,* 571–577.

Moskowitz, S. A., & Rupert, P. A. (1983). Conflict resolution within the supervisory relationship. *Professional Psychology: Research and Practice, 14*, 632–641.

Mount, R. E., & Schumacker, R. E. (1991). Rehabilitation administrator perceptions of graduate curriculum needs: A guide to curriculum development. *Rehabilitation Education, 5*, 53–58.

Moxley, D. P. (1989). *The practice of case management.* Newberry Park, CA: Sage.

Mullahy, C. (1998). *The case manager's handbook* (2nd ed.). Gaithersburg, MD: Aspen.

Mullahy, C. M. (1995). *The case manager's handbook.* Gaithersburg, MD: Aspen.

Muratori, M. C. (2001). Examining supervisor impairment from the counselor trainee's perspective. *Counselor Education & Supervision, 41*, 41–56.

Murphy, L. L., Plake, B. S., Impara, J. C., & Spies, R. A. (Eds.). (2002). *Tests in print VI. An index to tests, test reviews, and the literature on specific tests.* Lincoln: University of Nebraska Press.

Murphy, O., & Williams, J. (1999). *Assessment of rehabilitative and quality of life issues in litigation.* Boca Raton: CRC Press.

Murphy, S. T. (1975). Problems in research utilization: A review. *Rehabilitation Counseling Bulletin, 19*, 364–376.

Musco, T. D., et al. (1995, November). *A survey of disability income and medical rehabilitation/case management programs.* Washington, DC: Health Insurance Association of America.

Muthard, J., & Salomone, P. (1969). Roles and functions of the rehabilitation counselor. *Rehabilitation Counseling Bulletin, 13,* (whole issue).

Muthard, J. E., & Salomone, P. (1969). The roles and functions of the rehabilitation counselor. *Rehabilitation Counseling Bulletin, 13*, 81–168.

Nagi, S. Z. (1969). *Disability and rehabilitation: Legal, clinical, and self-concepts and measurements.* Columbus: Ohio State University.

Nathanson, R. (1979). Counseling persons with disabilities: Are the feelings, thoughts, and behaviors of helping professionals helpful? *Personnel and Guidance Journal, 58,* 233–237.

National Board of Certified Counselors. (2002). *The ACS credential.* http://www.cceglobal.org/acs.htm: Author.

National Council on Disability. (n.d.). *The Americans with Disabilities Act Policy Brief: Righting the ADA.* Retrieved October 30, 2002, from http://www.ncd.gov/newsroom/publications/carefullyconstructedlaw.htm

National Council on Rehabilitation Education. (2001–2002). *Membership directory.*

National Council on Rehabilitation Education. (2002) Online. Retrieved October 2002, from http://www.rehabeducators.org/schools.htm

National Head Injury Foundation Insurance Committee. (1988, September). *A review of gaps and problems in insurance coverages and their relationship to traumatic brain injury.*

National Institute on Consumer-Directed Long-Term Services. (1996). *Principles of consumer-directed home and community-based services.* Washington, DC: Author.

Neely, C. (1974). Rehabilitation counselor attitudes: A study to compare the attitudes of general and special counselors. *Journal of Applied Rehabilitation Counseling, 5,* 153–158.

Nelson, M. L., & Friedlander, M. L. (2001). A close look at conflictual supervisory relationships: The trainee's perspective. *Journal of Counseling Psychology, 48*, 384–395.

Nester, M. A. (1993). Psychometric testing and reasonable accommodation for persons with disabilities. *Rehabilitation Psychology, 38,* 75–83.

Newman, J., & Lovell, M. (1993). A description of a supervisory group for group counselors. *Counselor Education and Supervision, 33*, 22–31.

Nezu, A. M., & Nezu, C. M. (1993). Identifying and selecting target problems for clinical interventions: A problem-solving model. *Psychological Assessment, 5,* 254–263.

Nordlund, W. J. (1991). The Federal Employees' Compensation Act. *Monthly Labor Review, 114*(9), 3–14.

Nosek, M. A. (1998). Independent living. In R. M. Parker & E. M. Szymanski (Eds.), *Rehabilitation counseling: Basics and beyond* (3rd ed., pp. 107–141). Austin, TX: Pro-Ed.

Obermann, C. E. (1965). *A history of vocational rehabilitation in America.* Minneapolis, MN: T. S. Dennison.

Oehlers, L., & Billingsley, W. (2002). Some final interim thoughts. In D. Dew, M. McGuire-Kuletz, & G. Alan (Eds.), *Using the Internet as a resource to the work of the state VR counselor* (pp. 102–125). Washington, DC: The George Washington University Press.

Olk, M. E., & Friedlander, M. L. (1992). Trainees' experiences of role conflict and role ambiguity in supervisory relationships. *Journal of Counseling Psychology, 39,* 389–397.

Olkin, R. (1999). *What psychotherapists should know about disability.* New York: Guilford Press.

Olkin, R. (2002). Could you hold the door for me? Including disability in diversity. *Cultural Diversity and Ethnic Minority Psychology, 8,* 130–137.

Oncken, W., Jr., & Wass, D. L. (1974). Management time: Who's got the monkey? *Harvard Business Review, 52*(6), 75–80.

Parker, R. L., & Szymanski, E. M. (Eds.). (1987). *Rehabilitation counseling: Basics and beyond.* Austin, TX: Pro-Ed.

Parker, R. L., & Szymanski, E. M. (Eds.). (1992). *Rehabilitation counseling: Basics and beyond* (2nd ed.). Austin, TX: Pro-Ed.

Parker, R. L., & Szymanski, E. M. (Eds.). (1998). *Rehabilitation counseling: Basics and beyond* (3rd ed.). Austin, TX: Pro-Ed.

Parker, R. M. (2001). Aptitude testing. In B. F. Bolton (Ed.), *Handbook of measurement and evaluation in rehabilitation* (3rd ed., pp. 103–124). Gaithersburg, MD: Aspen.

Parker, R. M., & Hansen, C. E. (1981). *Rehabilitation counseling: Foundations, consumers, and service delivery.* Boston: Allyn and Bacon.

Parker, R. M., & Schaller, J. L. (1996). Issues in vocational assessment and disability. In E. M. Szymanski & R. M. Parker (Eds.), *Work and disability. Issues and strategies in career development and job placement* (pp. 127–164). Austin, TX: Pro-Ed.

Parker, R. M., Szymanski, E. M., & Hanley-Maxwell, C. (1989). Ecological assessment in supported employment. *Journal of Applied Rehabilitation Counseling, 20*(3), 26–33.

Parker, R., & Szymanski, E. (1992). *Rehabilitation counseling: Basics and beyond* (2nd ed.). Austin, TX: Pro-Ed.

Parker, R. M., & Szymanski, E. M. (1998). *Rehabilitation counseling: Basics and beyond.* Austin, TX: Pro-Ed.

Parker, W. C. (2002). Monkey Management. Retrieved October 2002, from http:workstar.net/library/monkey.htm.

Parsons, J. T., Huszti, H. C., Crudder, S. O., Rich, L., & Mendoza, J. (2000). Maintenance of safer sexual behaviors: Evaluation of a theory-based intervention for HIV seropositive men with haemophilia and their female partners. *Haemophilia, 6,* 181–190.

Patterson, C. H. (1957). Counselor or coordinator. *Journal of Rehabilitation, 23,* 13–15.

Patterson, C. H. (1966). The rehabilitation counselor: A projection. *Journal of Rehabilitation, 32,* 31, 49.

Patterson, C. H. (1967). Specialization in rehabilitation counseling. *Rehabilitation Counseling Bulletin, 10,* 147–154.

Patterson, J. B. (1998). Ethics and ethical decision making in rehabilitation counseling. In R. M. Parker & E. M. Szymanski (Eds.), *Rehabilitation counseling: Basics and beyond* (3rd ed., pp. 181–223). Austin, TX: Pro-Ed.

Patterson, J. B. (2000). Using the Internet to facilitate the rehabilitation process. *Journal of Rehabilitation, 66*(1), 4–10.

Patterson, J. B. (2001). Assessing work behavior. In B. F. Bolton (Ed.), *Handbook of measurement and evaluation in rehabilitation* (3rd ed., pp. 255–279). Gaithersburg, MD: Aspen.

Patterson, J. B. (2002). Internet applications and beliefs of state agency personnel. *Journal of Rehabilitation, 68*(2), 33–38.

Patterson, J., Knauss, J., Lawton, D., Raybould, R. & Oehlers, L. (2002). The why chapter or: Do you realize the size of my caseload? In D. Dew, M. McGuire-Kuletz, & G. Alan (Eds.), *Using the Internet as a resource to the work of the state VR counselor* (pp. 7–29). Washington, DC: The George Washington University Press.

Patterson, J. B., Allen, T. B., Parnell, L., Crawford, R., & Beardall, R. L. (2000). Equitable treatment in the rehabilitation process: Implications for future investigations related to ethnicity. *The Journal of Rehabilitation*, *66*(2), 14.

Pepinsky, H. B., & Pepinsky, N. (1954). *Counseling theory and practice.* New York: Ronald Press.

Percy, S. L. (1989). *Disability, civil rights, and public policy: The politics of implementation.* Tuscaloosa: University of Alabama Press.

Perry, W. G. (1970). *Forms of intellectual and ethical development in the college years: A scheme.* New York: Holt, Rinehart, and Winston.

Peterson, D. (2000). Clinical problem solving micro-case management: Computer assisted instruction for information gathering strategies in rehabilitation counseling. *Rehabilitation Counseling Bulletin, 43*(2), 84–96.

Peterson, D. B. (2002). *International classification of functioning, disability, and health (IFC): A primer for rehabilitation psychologists.* New York University: Unpublished manuscript.

Peterson, D. B., & Growick, B. (2000). The Work Incentive Improvement Act of 1999. *Rehabilitation Psychology Newsletter (Division 22 of the APA), 27*(2).

Petrocelli, J. V. (2002). Processes and stages of change: Counseling with the transtheoretical model of change. *Journal of Counseling and Development, 80,* 22–30.

Piaget, J. (1977). *The development of thought: Equilibrium of cognitive structure.* New York: Viking.

Pinderhughes, E. B. (1983). Empowerment for our clients and our selves. *Social Casework, 64*(6), 331–338.

Plake, B. S., Impara, J. C., & Spies, R. A. (Ed.). (2003). *The fifteenth mental measurements yearbook.* Lincoln: University of Nebraska Press.

Pope, A., & Tarlov, A. (1991). *Disability in America: Toward a national agenda for prevention.* Washington, DC: Institute of Medicine, National Academy Press.

Pope-Davis, D. B., Liu, W. M., Toporek, R., & Brittan, C. (2001). How do we identify cultural competence in counseling: Review, introspection, and recommendations for future research. *Cultural Diversity and Ethnic Minority Psychology, 7,* 121–138.

Pope-Davis, D. B., Toporek, R. L., Ortega-Villalobos, L., Ligiero, D. P., Brittan-Powell, C. S., Liu, W. M., et al. (2002). A qualitative study of clients' perspectives of multicultural counseling competence. *The Counseling Psychologist, 30,* 355–393.

Posavac, E. J., & Carey, R. G. (2003). *Program evaluation: Methods and case studies* (6th ed.). Upper Saddle River, NJ: Prentice-Hall.

Powell, S. K., & Wekell, P. M. (1996). *Nursing case management.* Philadelphia: Lippincott.

Power, P. W. (2000). *A guide to vocational assessment* (3rd ed.). Austin, TX: Pro-Ed.

Pransky, G., & Himmelstein, J. (1996a). Outcome research: Implications for occupational health. *Journal of Industrial Medicine, 29,* 573–583.

Pransky, G., & Himmelstein, J. (1996b). *Evaluating outcomes of workers' compensation medical care.* Occupational Health Program and the New England Center for Occupational Musculoskeletal Disorders (NECOMD), University of Massachusetts Medical Center, Worchester, MA.

Prestin, E. I., & Havranek, J. E. (1998). The future of private sector rehabilitation: A survey of perceptions of members of the National Association of Rehabilitation Professionals. *The Rehabilitation Professional, 6,* 30–39.

Prilleltensky, I. (1997). Values, assumptions, and practices: Assessing the moral implications of psychological discourse and action. *American Psychologist, 52,* 517–535.

Prochaska, J. O. (1994). Strong and weak principles for progressing from precontemplation to action on the basis of twelve problem behaviors. *Health Psychology, 13*(1), 47–51.

Prochaska, J. O., & DiClemente, C. C. (1983). Stages and processes of self-change of smoking: Toward an integrative model of change. *Journal of Consulting and Clinical Psychology, 51*(3), 390–395.

Prochaska, J. O., DiClemente, C. C., & Norcross, J. C. (1992). In search of how people change: Applications to addictive behaviors. *American Psychologist, 47,* 1102–1114.

Prochaska, J. O., DiClemente, C. C., Velicer, W. F., & Rossi, J. S. (1993). Standardized, individualized interactive and personalized self-help interventions for stages of smoking cessation. *Health Psychology, 12,* 399–405.

Puskin, D. (May 1, 2003). Welcome: So what is telehealth? http://telehealth.hrsa.gov/welcome.htm

Ramm, D. R. (1998). Consider the scientific study of morality. *American Psychologist, 53,* 323–324.

Rasch, J. D. (1979). The case for an independent association of rehabilitation counselors. *Journal of Applied Rehabilitation Counseling, 10,* 171–176.

Reagles, K. W. (1981). Perspectives on the proposed merger of rehabilitation organizations. *Journal of Applied Rehabilitation Counseling, 12,* 75–79.

Reeves, T. (1994). *Managing effectively: Developing yourself through experience.* Oxford, England: The Institute of Management, Butterworth Heinemann.

Reid, C. A., Deutsch, P. M., & Kitchen, J. (2001). Life care planning: An emerging rehabilitation intervention. In P. D. Rumrill, J. L. Bellini, & L. C. Koch (Eds.), *Emerging issues in rehabilitation counseling: Perspectives on the new millennium* (pp. 59–88), Springfield, IL: Charles C Thomas.

Reid, C. A., Deutsch, P. M., Kitchen, J., & Aznavoorian, K. (1999). Life Care Planning. In F. Chan & M. J. Leahy (Eds.), *Health care and disability management* (pp. 415–453). Lake Zurich, IL: Vocational Consultants Press.

Reno, V. P., Mashaw, J. L., & Gradison, B. (Eds.). (1997). *Disability: Challenges for social insurance, health care financing, and labor market policy*. Washington, DC: National Academy of Social Insurance.

Research Triangle Institute. (1998). *A longitudinal study of the Vocational Rehabilitation service program.* Washington, DC: Rehabilitation Services Administration.

Research Triangle Institute. (2002). *Longitudinal study of the Vocational Rehabilitation services program. Second final report: VR services and outcomes*. Washington, DC: Rehabilitation Services Administration.

Rest, J. R. (1984). Research on moral development: Implications for training psychologists. *The Counseling Psychologist, 12*(3), 19–29.

Rich, P. (1993). The form, function, and content of clinical supervision: An integrated model. *The Clinical Supervisor, 11*, 137–178.

Ridley, C. R. (1995). *Overcoming unintentional racism in counseling and therapy.* Thousand Oaks, CA: Sage.

Ridley, C. R., & Kleiner, A. J. (in press). Multicultural counseling competence: History, themes, and issues. In D. B. Pope-Davis, H. L. K. Coleman, W. M. Liu, & R. L. Toporek (Eds.), *The handbook of multicultural competencies.* Thousand Oaks: Sage.

Rigazio-DiGilio, S. A., & Ivey, A. E. (1993). Systemic cognitive-developmental therapy: An integrative framework. *Family Journal: Counseling and Therapy for Couples and Families, 1,* 208–219.

Riggar, T. F., & Hansen, G. R. (1986). Problem-solving, performance-based continuing education: A new RCEP paradigm. *Journal of Applied Rehabilitation Counseling, 17*(2), 47–50.

Riggar, T. F., & Matkin, R. E. (1984). Rehabilitation counselors working as administrators: A pilot investigation. *Journal of Applied Rehabilitation Counseling, 15*(1), 9–13.

Riggar, T. F., & Patrick, D. (1984). Case management and administration. *Journal of Applied Rehabilitation Counseling, 15*(3), 29–33.

Riggar, T. F., Crimando, W., & Bordieri, J. E. (1991). Human resource needs: The staffing function in rehabilitation—Part II. *Journal of Rehabilitation Administration, 15*, 135–140.

Riggar, T. F., Crimando, W., Bordieri, J., & Phillips, J. S. (1988). Rehabilitation administration preservice education: Preparing the professional rehabilitation administrator, manager and supervisor. *Journal of Rehabilitation Administration, 12*(4), 93–102.

Riggar, T. F., Flowers, C. R., & Crimando, W. (2002). Emerging workforce issues: Empowering change. *Journal of Rehabilitation Administration, 26,* 143–156.

Riggar, T. F., Hansen, G., & Crimando, W. (1987). Rehabilitation employee organizational withdrawal behavior. *Rehabilitation Psychology, 32,* 121–124.

Riggar, T. F., Crimando, W., & Pusch, B. D. (1993). Human resource development: Learning never ends. *Journal of Rehabilitation Administration, 17,* 38–49.

Rimmerman, A., Botuck, S., & Levy, J. M. (1995). Job placement for individuals with psychiatric disabilities and supported employment. *Psychiatric Rehabilitation Journal, 19,* 38–43.

Rinas, J., & Clyne-Jackson, S. (1988). *Professional conduct and legal concerns in mental health practice.* Norwalk, CT: Appleton & Lange.

Robinson, T. L., & Howard-Hamilton, M. F. (2000). *The convergence of race, ethnicity, and gender: Multiple identities in counseling.* Upper Saddle River, NJ: Prentice-Hall.

Roessler, R. (1990). A quality of life perspective on rehabilitation counseling. *Rehabilitation Counseling Bulletin, 34*(2), 82–90.

Roessler, R. T. (2002). TWWIIA initiatives and work incentives: Return-to-work implications. *Journal of Rehabilitation, 68*(3), 11–16.

Roessler, R. T., & Rubin, S. E. (1992). *Case management and rehabilitation counseling: Procedures and techniques* (2nd ed.). Austin: Pro-Ed.

Roessler, R. T., & Schriner, K. F. (1991). The implications of selected employment concerns for disability policy and rehabilitation practice. *Rehabilitation Counseling Bulletin, 35*(1), 52–67.

Rogers, E. S., Martin, R., Anthony, W. A., Massaro, J., Crean, T., & Penk, W. (2001). Assessing readiness for change among persons with severe mental illness. *Community Mental Health Journal, 37,* 97–112.

Rollnick, S., Heather, N., & Bell, A. (1992). Negotiating behavior change in medical settings: The development of brief motivational interviewing. *Journal of Mental Health, 1,* 25–27.

Rosenberg, M. J. (2001). *e-learning: Strategies for delivering knowledge in the digital age.* New York: McGraw-Hill.

Rosenthal, D. A., & Berven, N. L. (1999). Effects of client race on clinical judgment. *Rehabilitation Counseling Bulletin, 42,* 243–264.

Ross, C. K. (1979). Supervision theory: A prescription for practice. *Journal of Rehabilitation Administration, 3,* 14–19.

Roth, W. (1985). The politics of disability: Future trends as shaped by current realities. In L. Perlman & G. Austin (Eds.), *Social influences in rehabilitation planning: Blueprint for the 21st century* (pp. 41–48). Alexandria, VA: National Rehabilitation Association.

Rothman, R. A. (1987). *Working: Sociological perspectives.* Englewood Cliffs, NJ: Prentice-Hall.

Rothstein, M. A. (1991). The law-medicine interface in assessing vocational capacity. In S. J. Sdheer (Ed.), *Medical perspectives in vocational assessment of impaired workers* (pp. 407–422). Gaithersburg, MD: Aspen.

Rotter, J. B. (1966). Generalized expectancies for internal versus external control of reinforcement. *Psychological Monographs, 80*(1), 1–28.

Rotter, J. B. (1975). Some problems and misconceptions related to the construct of internal versus external control of reinforcement. *Journal of Consulting and Clinical Psychology, 43,* 56–57.

Rubin, S. E., & Rice, J. M. (1986). Quality and relevance of rehabilitation research: A critique and recommendations. *Rehabilitation Counseling Bulletin, 30,* 33–42.

Rubin, S. E., Chan, F., Bishop, M., & Miller, S. M. (in press). Psychometric validation of the Sense of Well-Being Inventory for program evaluation in rehabilitation. *Professional Rehabilitation.*

Rubin, S. E., & Roessler, R. T. (1978). *Foundations of the vocational rehabilitation process.* Baltimore: University Park Press.

Rubin, S. E., & Roessler, R. T. (1987). *Foundations of the vocational rehabilitation process* (3rd ed.). Austin, TX: Pro-Ed.

Rubin, S. E., & Roessler, R. T. (1995). *Foundations of the vocational rehabilitation process* (4th Ed.). Austin, TX: Pro-Ed.

Rubin, S. E., & Roessler, R. T. (2001). *Foundations of the vocational rehabilitation process* (5th ed.). Austin, TX: Pro-Ed.

Rubin, S. E., Chan, F., & Thomas, D. (in press). Assessing changes in life skills and quality of life resulting from rehabilitation services. *Journal of Rehabilitation.*

Rubin, S. E., Matkin, R. E., Ashley, J., Beardsley, M. M., May, V. R., Onstott, K., et al. (1984). Roles and functions of certified rehabilitation counselors. *Rehabilitation Counseling Bulletin, 27*, 199–224.

Rumrill, P. D., & Scheff, C. M. (1996). Enhance productivity and reduce turnover with worksite safety and disability management. *Journal of Long-Term Care Administration, 24*, 32–35.

Rusalem, H. (1976). A personalized recent history of vocational rehabilitation in America. In H. Rusalem & D. Malikin (Eds.), *Contemporary vocational rehabilitation* (pp. 29–45). New York: New York University Press.

Rusch, N., & Corrigan, P. W. (2002). Motivational interviewing to improve insight and treatment adherence in schizophrenia. *Psychiatric Rehabilitation Journal, 26*(1), 23–32.

Rusk, H. A. (1977a). *Rehabilitation medicine* (4th ed.). St. Louis: Mosby.

Rusk, H. A. (1977b). *A world to care for: The autobiography of Howard A. Rusk, M.D.* New York: Random House.

Sales, A. (2002). History of rehabilitation movement: Paternalism to empowerment. In J. Andrews & C. Faubion (Eds.), *Rehabilitation services: An introduction for the human services professional* (pp. 1–42). Osage Beach, MO: Aspen Professional Services.

Salzman, M. B. (2001). Cultural trauma and recovery: Perspectives from terror management theory. *Trauma, Violence, & Abuse*, *2*, 172–191.

Sarno, J., & O'Brien, J. (2002). Surf's up! Consumer use of the Internet. In D. Dew, M. McGuire-Kuletz, & G. Alan (Eds.), *Using the Internet as a resource to the work of the state VR counselor* (pp. 65–90). Washington, DC: The George Washington University Press.

Sartain, A., & Baker, A. (1978). *The supervisor and the job* (3rd ed.). New York: McGraw-Hill.

Savin-Williams, R. C. (1990). *Gay and lesbian youths: Expressions of identity.* New York: Hemisphere.

Savin-Williams, R. C., & Cohen, K. M. (Eds.). (1996). *The lives of lesbians, gays, and bisexuals: Children to adults.* Fort Worth, TX: Harcourt.

Sawisch, L. P. (1989). Workers compensation: Strategies for lowering cost and reducing worker suffering. In E. M. Welsh (Ed.), *Creating a context for disability management.* Fort Washington, PA: LRP Publications.

Sax, C. (2002a). Assistive technology online instruction: Expanding the dimensions of learning communities. In M. J. Scherer (Ed.), *Assistive technology: Matching device and consumer for successful rehabilitation* (pp. 213–227). Washington, DC: APA Books.

Sax, C. (2002b). Assistive technology education: An online model for rehabilitation professionals. *Disability and Rehabilitation, 24*(1–3), 144–151.

Sax, C., & Duke, S. (2002). Integration of AT education by rehabilitation professionals. In R. Simpson (Ed.), *Proceedings of the RESNA 25th International Conference,*

Technology & Disability: Research, Design, Practice, and Policy (pp. 189–191). Arlington, VA: RESNA Press.

Scassa, T. (2001). Text and context: Making sense of Canada's new personal information protection legislation. *Ottawa Law Review, 32,* 1–34.

Schelat, R. K. (2001). The predictive capacity of the working alliance in vocational rehabilitation outcomes. *Dissertation Abstract, 61*(7-B), 3553.

Scherer, M. J. (1998). *Matching person & technology process and accompanying assessment instruments*, revised edition. Webster, NY: Institute for Matching Person & Technology. [http://members.aol.com/IMPT97/MPT.html].

Scherer, M. J. (2000). *Living in the state of stuck: How assistive technology impacts the lives of people with disabilities* (3rd. ed.). Cambridge, MA: Brookline Books.

Scherer, M. J. (Ed.). (2002). *Assistive technology: Matching device and consumer for successful rehabilitation.* Washington, DC: APA Books.

Scherer, M. J., & Galvin, J. C. (1996). An outcomes perspective of quality pathways to the most appropriate technology. In J. C. Galvin & M. J. Scherer (Eds.), *Evaluating, selecting and using appropriate assistive technology* (pp. 1–26). Gaithersburg, MD: Aspen.

Scheurich, J. J. (1993). Toward a discourse on white racism. *Educational Researcher, 22,* 5–10.

Schmidt, M. J., Riggar, T. F., Crimando, W., & Bordieri, J. E. (1992). *Staffing for success: A guide for health and human service professionals.* Newbury Park, CA: Sage.

Schoemaker, P. J. H. (1995). Scenario planning: A tool for strategic thinking. *Sloan Management Review, 36*(2), 25–40.

Schriner, K. F. (1990). Why study disability policy? *Journal of Disability Policy Studies, 1*(1), 1–7.

Schultz, J. C., Copple, B. A., & Ososkie, J. N. (1999). An integrative model for supervision in rehabilitation counseling. *Rehabilitation Education, 13,* 323–334.

Schultz, J. C., Ososkie, J. N., Fried, J. H., Nelson, R. E., & Bardos, A. N. (2002). Clinical supervision in public rehabilitation counseling settings. *Rehabilitation Counseling Bulletin, 45*, 213–222.

Schur, E. M. (1971). *Labeling deviant behavior: Its sociological implications*. New York: Harper and Row.

Scofield, M., Pape, D., McCracken, N., & Maki, D. (1980). An ecological model for promoting acceptance of disability. *Journal of Applied Rehabilitation Counseling, 11*(4), 183–187.

Scotch, R. K. (2000). Disability policy. *Journal of Disability Policy Studies, 11*(1), 6–11.

Scotch, R. K., & Berkowitz, E. D. (1990). One comprehensive system? A historical perspective on federal disability policy. *Journal of Disability Policy Studies, 1*(3), 1–19.

Seidenfeld, M. (1998). The art of supervision. *Supervision, 59,* 14–16.

Seitel, F. (1984). *The practice of public relations.* Columbus, OH: Charles E. Merrill.

Selman, R. (1980). *The growth of interpersonal understanding: Developmental and clinical analysis*. New York: Academic Press.

Sforza, N. (1997). Is fear a good motivator? *Incentive, 171*(10), 47.

Shaffer, D. R. (1993). *Developmental psychology: Childhood and adolescence* (3rd ed.). Pacific Grove, CA: Brooks/Cole.

Shapson, P. R., Wright, G. N., & Leahy, M. J. (1987). Education and the attainment of rehabilitation competencies. *Rehabilitation Counseling Bulletin, 31*, 131–145.

Shaw, L. R. (1995). Forensic rehabilitation: Historical and future perspective. In W. H. Burke (Ed.), *The handbook of forensic rehabilitation* (pp. 1–16). Houston: HDI Publishers.

Shaw, L. R., Leahy, M. J., & Chan, F. (1999). Case management: Past, present, and future. *Health care and disability management* (pp. 39–60). Lake Zurich, IL: Vocational Consultants Press.

Shaw, L. R., McMahon, B. T., Chan, F., & Hannold, E. (2002). *Enhancement of the working alliance: Achieving expectation convergence by implementation of a training protocol.* Manuscript submitted for publication.

Sheppard, C., Bunton, J., Menifee, S., & Rocha, G. (1995). Rehabilitation service providers: A minority perspective. *Journal of Applied Rehabilitation Counseling, 26*(2), 36–40.

Sherman, S., & Robinson, N. (Eds.). (1982). *Ability testing of handicapped people: Dilemma for government, science, and the public.* Washington, DC: National Academy Press.

Shilts, R. (2000). *And the band played on: Politics, people, and the AIDS epidemic* (1st Stonewall Inn ed.). New York: St. Martin's Press.

Shrey, D. (1979). The rehabilitation counselor in industry: A new frontier. *Journal of Applied Rehabilitation Counseling, 9*, 168–172.

Shrey, D. (1995). Worksite disability management and industrial rehabilitation. In D. Shrey & M. Lacerte (Eds.), *Principles and practices of disability management in industry* (pp. 3–53). Winter Park, FL: GR Press.

Shrey, D., & Lacerte, M. (Eds.). (1995). *Principles and practices of disability management in industry.* Boca Raton, FL: St. Lucie Press.

Silva, F. (1993). *Psychometric foundations and behavioral assessment.* Newbury Park, CA: Sage.

Sink, J., & Porter, T. (1978). Convergence and divergence in rehabilitation counseling and vocational evaluation. *Rehabilitation Counseling Bulletin, 9,* 5–20.

Sleister, S. (2000). Separating the wheat from the chaff: The role of the vocational expert in forensic vocational rehabilitation. *Journal of Vocational Rehabilitation, 14*, 119–129.

Smart, D.W., & Smart, J. F. (1997). DSM-IV and culturally sensitive diagnosis: Some observations for counselors. *Journal of Counseling and Development, 75,* 392–398.

Smart, J. (1999). Issues in rehabilitation distance education. *Rehabilitation Education, 13*, 187–206.

Smart, J. F. (2001). *Disability, society, and the individual.* Austin, TX: Pro-Ed.

Smith, D. A. (2002). Validity and values: Monetary and otherwise. *American Psychologist, 57,* 136–137.

Smith, D. C., & Growick, B. (1999). The vocational consultant as an expert in divorce litigation. *The Rehabilitation Professional, 7*, 30–34.

Sobsey, D. (1994). *Violence and abuse in the lives of people with disabilities: The end of silent acceptance.* Baltimore: Brookes.

Social Security Administration. (2002). *Social Security regulations: Rules for determining disability and blindness.* Washington, DC: U.S. Government Printing Office.

Sosin, M., & Caulum, S. (1983). Advocacy: A conceptualization for social work practice. *Social Work, 28*(1), 12–17.

Spooner, S. E., & Stone, S. C. (1977). Maintenance of specific counseling skills over time. *Journal of Counseling Psychology, 24*, 66–71.

Sprinthall, N. A., Peace, S. D., & Kennington, P. A. D. (2001). Cognitive-developmental stage theories for counseling. In D. C. Locke, J. E. Myers, & E. L. Herr (Eds.), *The handbook of counseling* (pp. 109–130). Thousand Oaks, CA: Sage.

Starr, P. (1982). *The social transformation of American medicine.* New York: Vintage.

Statistics Canada. (1993). *1991 Health and Activity Limitation Survey.* Ottawa: Author.

Stebnicki, M. A. (1998). Clinical supervision in rehabilitation counseling. *Rehabilitation Education, 12*, 137–159.

Stebnicki, M. A., Allen, H. A., & Janikowski, T. P. (1997). Development of an instrument to assess perceived helpfulness of clinical supervisory behaviors. *Rehabilitation Education, 11*, 307–322.

Steeves, L., & Smithies, R. (1998). Disability management in Canada: Rights and responsibilities. *Employee Benefits Journal, 23,* 37–39.

Steinburg, R. M., & Carter, G. W. (1983). *Case management and the elderly.* Lexington, MA: Brooks.

Stensrud, R. (2001). What employers want from us: Interviews with employers. *Journal of Job Placement and Development, 16,* 36–38.

Stensrud, R., & Ashworth, D. (2002). Information technology and organizational change. In D. Dew, M. McGuire-Kuletz, & G. Alan (Eds.), *Using the Internet as a resource to the work of the state VR counselor* (pp. 91–101). Washington, DC: The George Washington University Press.

Stensrud, R., & Gilbride, D. (1994). Revitalizing employer development: Placement in the ADA era. *Journal of Job Placement, 9,* 12–15.

Stoltenberg, C., & Delworth, U. (1987). *Supervising counselors and therapists.* San Francisco: Jossey-Bass.

Stone, D. A. (1984). *The disabled state.* Philadelphia: Temple University Press.

Stone, G. L. (1997). Multiculturalism as a context for supervision: Perspectives, limitations, and implications. In D. B. Pope-Davis & H. L. K. Coleman (Eds.), *Multicultural counseling competencies: Assessment, education and training, and supervision* (pp. 263–289). Thousand Oaks, CA: Sage.

Stout, J. K. (1984). Supervisors' structuring and consideration behaviors and workers' job satisfaction, stress, and health problems. *Rehabilitation Counseling Bulletin, 28,* 133–138.

Strauser, D., Keim, J., & Ketz, K. (2002). The relationship between self-efficacy, locus of control and work personality. *Journal of Rehabilitation, 68*(1), 20–26.

Strickland, T. (1996). The HIAA Study: Rehabilitation/case management programs yield substantial cost savings. *The Case Manager, 7,* 67–69.

Strohmer, D. C., & Leierer, S. J. (2000). Modeling rehabilitation counselor judgment. *Rehabilitation Counseling Bulletin, 44,* 3–9, 38.

Strohmer, D. C., Shivy, V. A., & Chiodo, A. L. (1990). Information processing strategies in counselor hypothesis testing: The role of selective memory and expectancy. *Journal of Counseling Psychology, 37,* 465–472.

Sue, D. W., & Sue, D. (1999). *Counseling the culturally different: Theory and practice* (3rd ed.). New York: John Wiley & Sons.

Sue, D. W., Arredondo, P., & McDavis, R. J. (1992). Multicultural counseling competencies and standards: A call to the profession. *Journal of Counseling and Development, 70,* 477–486.

Sue, D. W., Ivey, A. E., & Pedersen, P. B. (Eds.). (1996). *A theory of multicultural counseling and therapy.* Pacific Grove, CA: Brooks/Cole.

Sundberg, N. D. (1977). *Assessment of persons.* Englewood Cliffs, NJ: Prentice-Hall.

Sundberg, N. D., & Tyler, L. E. (1962). *Clinical psychology.* New York: Appleton-Century-Crofts.

Surgeon General Report. (2001). *Mental health: Culture, race, and ethnicity.* Department of Health and Human Services. Washington, DC: U.S. Government Printing Office.

Sutton, R. G., & Kessler, M. (1986). National study of the effects of socioeconomic status on clinical psychologists' professional judgment. *Journal of Consulting and Clinical Psychology, 54,* 275–276.

Swan, W. (1989). *Swan's how to pick the right people program.* New York: Wiley & Sons.

Szufnarowski, J. (1972). Case development: An organized system of steps and functions for the rehabilitation counselor. In T. J. Ruscio & J. P. Atsaides (Eds.), *Case development in rehabilitation what, why, how?* (pp. 19–27). Springfield, MA: Rehabilitation Services Department of Springfield College.

Szymanski, E. M. (1985). Rehabilitation counseling: A profession with a vision, an identity, and a future. *Rehabilitation Counseling Bulletin, 29*(1), 2–5.

Szymanski, E. M. (1991). The relationship of the level of rehabilitation counselor education to rehabilitation client outcome in the Wisconsin Division of Vocational Rehabilitation. *Rehabilitation Counseling Bulletin, 35,* 23–37.

Szymanski, E. M., & Danek, M. M. (1992). The relationship of rehabilitation counselor education to rehabilitation client outcome: A replication and extension. *Journal of Rehabilitation, 58,* 49–56.

Szymanski, E. M., & Parker, R. M. (1989). Relationship of rehabilitation client outcome to level of rehabilitation counselor education. *Journal of Rehabilitation, 55,* 32–36.

Szymanski, E. M., Leahy, M. J., & Linkowski, D. C. (1993). Reported preparedness of certified counselors in rehabilitation counseling knowledge areas. *Rehabilitation Counseling Bulletin, 37,* 146–162.

Szymanski, E. M., Herbert, J. T., Parker, R. M., & Danek, M. M. (1992). State vocational rehabilitation agency counselor education and performance in Pennsylvania, Maryland, and Wisconsin. *Journal of Rehabilitation Administration, 16,* 109–113.

Szymanski, E., Linkowski, D., Leahy, M., Diamond, E., & Thoreson, R. (1993a). Human resource development: An examination of perceived training needs of Certified Rehabilitation Counselors. *Rehabilitation Counseling Bulletin, 37,* 163–181.

Szymanski, E. M., Linkowski, D. C., Leahy, M. J., Diamond, E. E., & Thoreson, R. W. (1993b). Validation of rehabilitation counseling accreditation and certification knowledge areas: Methodology and initial results. *Rehabilitation Counseling Bulletin, 37,* 109–122.

Tannebaum, S. J. (1986). *Engineering disability: Public policy and compensatory technology.* Philadelphia: Temple University Press.

Tarvydas, V. M. (1987). Decision making models in ethics: Models for increased clarity and wisdom. *Journal of Applied Rehabilitation Counseling, 18*(4), 50–52.

Tarvydas, V. M. (1995). Ethics and the practice of rehabilitation counselor supervision. *Rehabilitation Counseling Bulletin, 38*, 294–306.

Tarvydas, V. M., & Cottone, R. R. (1991). Ethical responses to legislative, organizational and economic dynamics: A four level model of ethical practice. *Journal of Applied Rehabilitation Counseling, 22*(4), 11–18.

Tarvydas, V. M., & Cottone, R. R. (2000). The code of ethics for rehabilitation counselors: What we have and what we need. *Rehabilitation Counseling Bulletin, 43*, 188–196.

Tarvydas, V., & Leahy, M. J. (1993). Licensure in rehabilitation counseling: A critical incident in professionalization. *Rehabilitation Counseling Bulletin, 37,* 92–108.

Tarvydas, V. M., O'Rourke, B. J., & Malaski, C. (2003). Ethical climate. In R. R. Cottone & V. M. Tarvydas (Eds.), *Ethical and professional issues in counseling* (pp. 110–126). Upper Saddle River, NJ: Merrill/Prentice-Hall.

Tenth Institute on Rehabilitation Issues. (1983). *Functional assessment.* Dunbar: West Virginia University, West Virginia Research and Training Center.

Tepper, B. J. (2000). Consequences of abusive supervision. *Academy of Management Journal.* Abstract in: *Journal of Personal Selling & Sales Management.* (2001). *21*(1), 80–81.

Texas Workers' Compensation Commission (n.d.). *History of workers' compensation.* Retrieved October 19, 2002, from http://www.twcc. state.tx.us/information/historyofwc.html.

Thessellund, T. A., & Cox, R. (1996). Vocational case managers in early return-to work agreements. *The Journal of Care Management, 2*, 34–36, 40, 78.

Thielsen, V. A., & Leahy, M. J. (2001). Essential knowledge and skills for effective clinical supervision in rehabilitation counseling. *Rehabilitation Counseling Bulletin, 44*, 196–208.

Thomas, K. R. (1991). *Rehabilitation counseling: A profession in transition.* Athens, GA: Elliott & Fitzpatrick.

Thomason, T., Burton, J. F., Jr., & Hyatt, D. E. (Eds.). (1998). *New approaches to disability in the work place*. Madison: University of Wisconsin.

Thompson, A. (1990). *Guide to ethical practice in psychotherapy.* New York: John Wiley & Sons.

Thompson, N. (1992). Staff supervision. *Nursing Homes Long Term Care Management, 41*(5), 15–18.

Tinsley, H. E. A., Bowman, S. L., & Ray, S. B. (1998). Manipulation of expectancies about counseling and psychotherapy: Review and analysis of expectancy manipulation strategies and results. *Journal of Counseling Psychology, 35,* 99–108.

Tinsley, H. E. A., De St. Aubin, T. M., & Brown, M. T. (1982). College students' help seeking preferences. *Journal of Counseling Psychology, 29,* 52–533.

Titchkosky, T. (2001). Disability: A rose by any other name? "People-first" language in Canadian society. *The Canadian Review of Sociology and Anthropology, 38*(2), 125–140.

Tombazian, C. M. (1994). Looking to your future: Managing change through strategic planning. *Managers Magazine, 69*(9), 16–21.

Tooman, M. (1986). The job placement division. *Journal of Rehabilitation, 52,* 35–38.

Toporek, R. L., & Liu, W. M. (2001). Advocacy in counseling: Addressing race, class, and gender oppression. In D. B. Pope-Davis & H. L. K. Coleman (Eds.), *The intersection of race, class, and gender in multicultural counseling* (pp. 385–416). Thousand Oaks: Sage.

Toporek, R. L., & Reza, J. V. (2000). Context as a critical dimension of multicultural counseling: Articulating personal, professional, and institutional competence. *Journal of Multicultural Counseling and Development, 29*(1), 13–30.

Torjman, S. (2001). Canada's federal regime and persons with disabilities. In D. Cameron & F. Valentine (Eds.), *Disability and federalism: Comparing different approaches to full participation* (pp. 150–196). Kingston, ON: McGill-Queen's University Press.

Tucker, C. M., McNeil, P., Abrams, J. M., & Brown, J. G. (1988). Characteristics important to a rehabilitation supervisor: Perceptions of vocational rehabilitation staff. *Journal of Rehabilitation Administration, 12,* 40–43.

Turk, D. C., & Salovey, P. (1985). Cognitive structures, cognitive processes, and cognitive-behavior modification: II. Judgments and inferences of the clinician. *Cognitive Therapy and Research, 9,* 19–33.

Tversky, A., & Kahneman, D. (1974). Judgment under uncertainty: Heuristics and biases. *Science, 185,* 1124–1131.

28th Institute on Rehabilitation Issues. (2002). *Distance education: Opportunities and issues for public vocational rehabilitation programs.* Washington, DC: Rehabilitation Services Administration, U.S. Department of Education.

U.S. Bureau of the Census. (1990). *Geographic tools (Fact finder for the nation).* Washington, DC: U.S. Government Printing Office.

U.S. Department of Labor. (n.d.). *The Federal Employees' Compensation Act.* Retrieved October 19, 2002, from http://www. dol.gov/esa/regs/compliance/owcp/fecafact.htm

Vandergoot, D. (1987). Review of placement research literature: Implications for research and practice. *Rehabilitation Counseling Bulletin, 31,* 243–272.

Vandergoot, D. (1992). The marketing responsibilities of placement professionals. *Journal of Job Placement, 8,* 6–9.

Vandergoot, D. (2002). Marketing: Revisited, again. *Journal of Job Placement and Development, 16,* 16–20.

VanHoose, W. H., & Kottler, J. A. (1985). *Ethical and legal issues in counseling and psychotherapy.* San Francisco: Jossey-Bass.

Vasquez, M. J. T. (1996). Will virtue ethics improve ethical conduct in multicultural settings and interactions? *The Counseling Psychologist, 24*(1), 98–104.

Viranyi, S., Crimando, W., Riggar, T. F., & Schmidt, M. J. (1992). Promoting mentoring relationships in rehabilitation. *Journal of Rehabilitation Administration, 16,* 56–61.

Vocational Evaluation and Work Adjustment Association. (1975). Vocational evaluation project final report. *Vocational Evaluation and Work Adjustment Bulletin, 8* [Special Issue].

Waddell, J. R., & Waddell, A. (1997). Are your employees afraid of you? *Supervision, 58*(10), 3–4.

Wainer, H. (2000). *Computerized adaptive testing: A primer* (2nd ed.). Mahwah, NJ: Erlbaum.

Walker, K., Johnson, G., Sanders, J., & Nikias, V. (1998). Rehabilitation service delivery systems in Canada: Transition and innovation. *Journal of Visual Impairment and Blindness, 92,* 113–116.

Wampold, B. (2001). *The Great Psychotherapy Debate.* Mahwah, NJ: Lawrence Erlbaum Associates.

Washburn, W. (1992). *Worker compensation disability and rehabilitation: An alert to claimants.* Arlington, VA: CEDI.

Watkins, C. E. (1997). The ineffective psychotherapy supervisor: Some reflections about bad behaviors, poor process, and offensive outcomes. *The Clinical Supervisor, 6,* 163–180.

Webber, R. A. (1975). *Management: Basic elements of managing organizations.* Homewood, IL: Richard D. Irwin.

Weed, R. O., & Riddick, S. N. (1992). Life care plans as a case management tool. *The Case Manager,* Jan/Feb/Mar, 26–35.

Weed, R. O., & Field, T. F. (1994). *Rehabilitation consultant's handbook* (revised ed.). Athens, GA: Elliot & Fitzpatrick.

Weed, R. O., & Field, T. F. (2001). *Rehabilitation consultant's handbook, revised.* Athens, GA: Elliot & Fitzpatrick.

Weed, R. O., & Hill, J. A. (2001). *CRC exam: Guide to success* (7th ed.). Athens, GA: E & F Vocational Services.

Weinrach, S. G., & Thomas, K. R. (1998). Diversity-sensitive counseling today: A postmodern clash of values. *Journal of Counseling and Development, 76,* 115–122.

Weiss, D. J. (1985). Adaptive testing by computer. *Journal of Consulting and Clinical Psychology, 53,* 774–789.

Weiss, D. J., & Vale, C. D. (1987). Adaptive testing. *Applied Psychology: An International Review, 36,* 249–262.

Weiss, W. H. (1998). Communications: Key to successful supervision. *Supervision, 59*(9), 12–14.

Welfel, E. R. (2002). *Ethics in counseling and psychotherapy: Standards, research, and emerging issues* (2nd ed.). Pacific Grove, CA: Brooks/Cole.

Wendover, R. (1989). *Smart hiring.* Englewood Cliffs, NJ: Prentice-Hall.

WHOQOL Group. (1995). The World Health Organization Quality of Life Assessment (WHOQOL): Position paper from the World Health Organization. *Social Science & Medicine, 41*(10), 1403–1409.

Wiley, M. L., & Ray, P. B. (1986). Counseling supervision by developmental level. *Journal of Counseling Psychology, 33,* 439–445.

Willey, D. A. (1978). Caseload management for the vocational rehabilitation counselor in a state agency. *Journal of Applied Rehabilitation Counseling, 9*(4), 156–158.

Willingham, W. W., Ragosta, M., Bennett, R. E., Braun, H., Rock, D. A., & Powers, D. E. (1988). *Testing handicapped people.* Boston: Allyn & Bacon.

Wilson, K. B. (2002). Exploration of VR acceptance and ethnicity: A national investigation, *Rehabilitation Counseling Bulletin, 45*(#), 168–169.

Wolfensburger, W. (1972). *The principle of normalization in human services.* Toronto: National Institute on Mental Retardation.

World Health Organization. (1980). *International classification of impairments, disabilities, and handicaps: A manual of classification relating to the consequences of disease.* Geneva, Switzerland: Author.

World Health Organization. (2001). *International classification of functioning, disability, and health: ICF.* Geneva: Author.

Wright, B. A. (1983). *Physical disability—A psychosocial approach.* New York: Harper & Row.

Wright, B. A. (1991). Labeling: The need for person-environment individuation. In C. R. Snyder & D. R. Forsyth (Eds.), *Handbook of social and clinical psychology: The health perspective* (pp. 469–487). New York: Pergamon.

Wright, G., Leahy, M., & Sharpson, P. (1987). Rehabilitation skills inventory: Importance of counselor competencies. *Rehabilitation Counseling Bulletin, 31,* 107–118.

Wright, G. N. (1980). *Total rehabilitation.* Boston: Little, Brown.

Wright, G. N., & Fraser, R. T. (1975). *Task analysis for the evaluation, preparation, classification, and utilization of rehabilitation counselor track personnel.* Wisconsin Studies in Vocational Rehabilitation Monograph No. 22, Series 3. Madison: University of Wisconsin.

Wulf, J., & Nelson, M. L. (2000). Experienced psychologists' recollections of predoctoral internship supervision and its contributions to their development. *The Clinical Supervisor, 19*, 123–145.

Wulff, J. J. (1994). Case management practices. In B. T. McMahon & W. R. Evans (Eds.), *The shortest distance: The pursuit of independence for persons with acquired brain injury* (pp. 131–142). Winter Park, FL: PMD Publishers Group.

Yate, M. (1987). *Hiring the best.* Boston: Bob Adams.

Yelin, E. H. (1992). *Disability and the displaced worker.* New Brunswick, NJ: Rutgers University Press.

Yelin, E. H. (1997). The employment of people with and without disabilities in an age of insecurity. *The Annals of the American Academy of Political and Social Science, 549*, 117–128.

Yoon, J., & Thye, S. (2000). Supervisor support in the work place: Legitimacy and positive affectivity. *Journal of Social Psychology, 140,* 295+. Retrieved November 28, 2002, from EBSCO database.

Young, M. E. (1998). *Learning the art of helping: Building blocks and techniques.* Columbus, OH: Merrill.

Young-Eisendrath, P. (1988). Making use of human development theories in counseling. In R. Hayes & R. Aubrey (Eds.), *New directions for counseling and human development* (pp. 66–84). Denver, CO: Love Publishing.

Yuen, R. K. W., & Tinsley, H. E. A. (1981). International and American students' expectancies about counseling. *Journal of Counseling Psychology, 28,* 66–69.

Yuker, H. E. (Ed.). (1988). *Attitudes toward persons with disabilities.* New York: Springer.

Zadney, J., & James, L. (1977). Time spent on placement. *Rehabilitation Counseling Bulletin, 21,* 31–38.

Zautra, A., Beier, E., & Cappel, L. (1977). The dimensions of life quality in a community. *American Journal of Community Psychology, 5*(1), 85–97.

Zhan, L. (1992). Quality of life: Conceptual and measurement issues. *Journal of Advanced Nursing, 17*, 795–800.

Zola, I. K. (1989a). Aging and disability: Toward a unified agenda. *Journal of Rehabilitation, 55*(4), 6–8.

Zola, I. K. (1989b). Toward a necessary universalizing of a disability policy. *Milbank Quarterly, 67,* 401–428.

Zola, I. K. (1993). Disability statistics, what we count and what it tells us. *Journal of Disability Policy Studies*, *4,* 9–39.

Zuckerman, M. (1990). Some dubious premises in research and theory on racial differences: Scientific, social, and ethical issues. *American Psychologist*, *45,* 1297–1303.

Index